The World Encyclopedia of
BOMBERS

BOMBERS

AN ILLUSTRATED HISTORY OF BOMBER AIRCRAFT, THEIR ORIGINS AND EVOLUTION

FRANCIS CROSBY

OF THE IMPERIAL WAR MUSEUM DUXFORD

HERMES HOUSE

For Vanessa and Gemma.
Special thanks are due to Derek and Marjorie Brammer
for their considerable help with research and administration.

This edition is published by Hermes House

Hermes House is an imprint of
Anness Publishing Ltd
Hermes House
88–89 Blackfriars Road
London SE1 8HA
tel. 020 7401 2077
fax 020 7633 9499
info@anness.com

© Anness Publishing Ltd 2004

A CIP catalogue record for this book
is available from the British Library.

Publisher: Joanna Lorenz
Editorial Director: Judith Simons
Project Editor: Felicity Forster
Copy Editors: Judy Cox and Jeremy Nichols
Designer: Ian Sandom
Indexer: Tim Ellerby
Editorial Reader: Rosanna Fairhead
Production Controller: Steve Lang

10 9 8 7 6 5 4 3 2 1

PAGE 1: **Boeing B-17 Flying Fortress.**
PAGES 2–3: **Sepecat Jaguar.**

Contents

6 Introduction

The History of Bombers
10 Birth of the bomber
12 Early bombing raids
14 Bomber aircraft technology
up to 1945
16 Bombers of the Spanish Civil War
18 The Blitz
20 The Dambusters
22 The Mighty Eighth Air Force
24 The Doolittle raid
26 The atomic bomb raids
28 Bomber aircraft development
since World War II
30 Cold War bombers
32 Strategic Air Command
34 Bomber aircraft defences
from 1945
36 V-bombers
38 The Falklands Black Buck raids
40 Operation El Dorado Canyon
42 Gulf War bombers

**A–Z of World War
Bombers: 1914–45**
46 Aichi D3A
46 Amiot 143
47 Arado Ar 234 Blitz
48 Armstrong Whitworth Whitley
50 Avro Anson
51 Avro Manchester
52 Avro Lancaster
54 Boeing B-17 Flying Fortress
56 Boeing B-29 Superfortress
58 Breguet Bre.14
58 Breguet Bre.19
59 Breguet 691/693
60 Bristol Blenheim
62 Bristol Beaufighter
64 Bristol Beaufort
64 Bristol Brigand
65 Caproni Ca.133

65 Caproni Ca.135
66 Consolidated B-24 Liberator
68 Consolidated PBY-5A Catalina
70 Consolidated Vultee PB4Y-2/
P4Y-2 Privateer
71 CRDA/CANT Z.1007 Alcione
71 Curtiss B-2 Condor
72 Curtiss SB2C Helldiver
73 de Havilland/Airco DH4
73 de Havilland/Airco DH9A
74 de Havilland/Airco DH10 Amiens
76 de Havilland Mosquito
78 Dornier Do17
79 Dornier Do217
80 Douglas B-18 Bolo
81 Douglas SBD-5 Dauntless
82 Douglas A-20 Boston/Havoc
84 Douglas A-26/B-26 Invader
86 Fairey III family
86 Fairey Fox
87 Fairey Hendon
88 Fairey Swordfish
90 Fairey Battle
92 Fairey Barracuda
94 Farman F.220 series
94 Farman M.F.11 Shorthorn
95 Fiat B.R.20 Cicogna
96 Focke-Wulf Fw200
98 Gotha bombers
100 Grumman Avenger
102 Handley Page Halifax
104 Handley Page Hampden
105 Handley Page Heyford
106 Handley Page O/400
107 Hawker Typhoon
108 Heinkel He111
110 Heinkel He177
112 Ilyushin Il-2 Shturmovik
114 Ilyushin Il-4
116 Junkers Ju 52/3m
118 Junkers Ju 87 Stuka
120 Junkers Ju 88
122 Kawanishi H8K

124 Lockheed Hudson
126 Martin bomber series
127 Martin Maryland
127 Martin Baltimore
128 Martin Mariner
130 Martin B-26 Marauder
132 Mitsubishi G4M
134 North American B-25
Mitchell
136 Short Stirling
138 Short Sunderland
140 Tupolev SB
141 Tupolev TB-3
141 Tupolev Tu-2
142 Vickers Vimy
144 Vickers Virginia
145 Vickers Wellesley
146 Vickers Wellington
148 Vultee Vengeance
149 Yokosuka D4Y Suisei
149 Yokosuka P1Y1

**A–Z of Modern Bombers:
1945 to the Present Day**
152 Aermacchi MB-339
153 AMX International AMX
154 Avro Lincoln
156 Avro Shackleton
158 Avro Vulcan
160 BAC/BAE Strikemaster
162 British Aircraft Corporation TSR.2
164 BAE Systems Harrier
166 Blackburn Buccaneer
168 Boeing B-47 Stratojet
170 Boeing B-52 Stratofortress
172 Boeing/McDonnell Douglas/
Northrop F/A-18 Hornet
174 Breguet Alize
175 Breguet/Dassault Atlantic
176 Convair B-36 Peacemaker
178 Convair B-58 Hustler
180 Dassault Mystère/Super Mystère
182 Dassault Etendard and
Super Etendard

184 Dassault Mirage III family
186 Dassault Mirage IV
188 de Havilland Venom
189 Douglas A-3 Skywarrior
190 Douglas Skyraider
192 English Electric/BAC/Martin B-57
Canberra
194 Fairchild Republic A-10
Thunderbolt II
196 Fairey Gannet
198 General Dynamics F-111
200 Grumman A-6 Intruder/EA-6 Prowler
202 Handley Page Victor
204 Hawker Siddeley/British Aerospace
Nimrod
206 Ilyushin Il-28
208 Lockheed P2V Neptune
210 Lockheed P-3 Orion
212 Lockheed S-3 Viking
214 Lockheed Martin F-117A
Nighthawk
216 McDonnell Douglas A-4 Skyhawk
218 McDonnell Douglas F-4 Phantom II
220 McDonnell Douglas/Boeing F-15
222 Mikoyan-Gurevich MiG-27
224 Myasishchev M-4
226 North American A3J/A-5 Vigilante
228 North American F-100
Super Sabre
230 Northrop Grumman B-2 Spirit
232 Panavia Tornado IDS
234 Republic F-105 Thunderchief
236 Rockwell B-1 Lancer
238 Sepecat Jaguar
240 Sukhoi Su-25
242 Tupolev Tu-22/Tu-22M
244 Tupolev Tu-95
246 Tupolev Tu-160
248 Vickers Valiant

250 Glossary
251 Key to flags
252 Acknowledgements
254 Index

Introduction

The earliest days of using aircraft as bombers saw pilots tossing small improvised bombs over the side of their aircraft on to a rather surprised enemy below. Hitting the target was more luck than judgement. This is a far cry indeed from the bomber aircraft of today that can fly around the world at several hundred miles an hour and arrive undetected in enemy airspace to drop precision-guided bombs down the chimney of a target and destroy it with no damage to surrounding buildings.

Once it was appreciated that the combination of aircraft and bombs was more than a novelty, military strategists were soon calling for more and bigger bombs to be carried. This required larger aircraft with more than one engine to carry the greater payload. Range then became an issue as the bombers had to be able to reach targets far beyond the front line. Engine technology and performance, as well as a greater understanding of aerodynamics, became considerations as the bombers had to be able to climb to heights away from enemy guns and fighters, or have sufficient speed to outrun the latter. Once the enemy started to try to knock the new bombers out of the sky, they had to defend themselves by carrying machine-guns and cannon. Technological advances saw the monoplane emerge, then largely replace the biplane in bomber fleets by

TOP: **The crew of an RAF Coastal Command B-17 Flying Fortress being briefed in 1943.** ABOVE: **Smoke pours from the remains of a bridge in France destroyed by Allied bombers around D-Day, 1944.**

World War II. Advances in construction techniques brought the use of more metal, specifically lightweight but strong alloys, and less wood and canvas.

The dawn of the jet engine opened up many opportunities for designers, but the long-range piston-engine bombers designed for use in World War II remained the mainstay of post-war bomber forces. Then, as atomic weapons appeared, bomber aircraft no longer had to carry many tons of bombs at a time when one massively destructive bomb would do the same job.

During the Cold War, as the United States and the Soviet Union faced each other across thousands of miles of sea or polar ice caps, the priority was the development of aircraft that could fly as quickly as possible across the world to bomb the enemy. The Cold War has fuelled bomber development since World War II, and most of the bomber aircraft in service around the world today were conceived during the Cold War. Large swept-wing jet bombers such as the Boeing B-47, Tupolev Tu-16, Boeing B-52 and Myasishchev M-4 were the principal bomber aircraft in the opposite inventories. All were good aircraft, but designers sought improvements in performance. The US B-58 Hustler was a Mach 2 nuclear bomber, but it proved to have insufficient range for the job required of it. Both Soviet and US engineers produced the brilliantly innovative variable-geometry designs with "swing wings" – the Tu-22M, F-111 and the B-1B. These aircraft, with wings spread, could cruise to their targets and then, with wings swept, could carry out high-speed, low-level attacks of which their larger fixed-sweep counterparts were simply not capable.

While bomber aircraft have evolved hugely since World War I, so have the weapons they can carry. "Dumb" free-fall conventional bombs are now complemented by "smart" munitions, which can be guided very precisely to a target. Bomber aircraft can also carry air-to-surface missiles, which were used in World War II, allowing them to attack a range of

TOP: **The ruins of Hiroshima in 1945 bear testimony to the massive destructive power of a single atomic bomb.** ABOVE: **A "smart" bomb being loaded on to an F-117A Nighthawk for Operation Desert Storm of the Gulf War, 1991.**

targets from a safe distance, such as troop concentrations, buildings, shipping or radar installations. Nuclear weapons remain an option for a number of nations around the world, but no weapon of this kind has been used in anger since the two raids on Japan in 1945.

The "stealth" aircraft currently in service with the US Air Force (F-117 and B-2) are remarkable examples of aviation technology, and were both produced as a result of the Cold War. Bomber aircraft became so sophisticated that people needed technological aids – radar – to find them. The designers of "stealth" aircraft have used technology to make the planes invisible again, creating the same surprise amongst the enemy that the manual bombing raids did in the early days of air warfare.

The performance figures quoted in this book should be seen as a broad indicator of an aircraft's capabilities. Aircraft performance and capability can vary considerably even within the same marks of an aircraft type. If bombs are carried, for example, maximum speed can be reduced. Also, the maximum speeds quoted are top speeds achieved at the optimum altitude for that particular aircraft type, and should not be seen as the definitive top speed for the aircraft at all altitudes.

ABOVE: **The futuristic-looking and adventurous delta-winged Avro Vulcan of the Royal Air Force, nicknamed the "tin triangle", first went to war in the Falkland Islands in 1982. It was extremely popular at air shows all over the world.**

The History of Bombers

From the early improvised bombers of World War I to the atomic bombers that ended World War II, and their successors which arguably kept peace during the Cold War, bomber aircraft have been a potent weapon at military leaders' disposal. Bombers evolved from slow short-range machines carrying light bomb loads through to the mighty B-52 Stratofortress which can fly around the world unrefuelled while carrying an enormous amount of weaponry, including "smart" bombs and cruise missiles. The latest generation of bomber aircraft are the "stealth aircraft" which can pass undetected through the most complex air defence systems.

While high speed and high altitude were once the aim of bomber designers, making maximum use of technology is now their goal. Total obliteration of the enemy is no longer the sole aim of bomber aircraft. We live in a very different world to that of almost a century ago when the first bombers lumbered into the air. Television beams live pictures of bombing raids into our homes and every mission can unleash a political storm. "Smart" precision weapons are therefore widely used to minimize avoidable loss of life and collateral damage.

LEFT: **Lockheed P2V Neptune.**

Birth of the bomber

Although the US Army was the first to drop a bomb from an aeroplane in 1910, it was the Italians who first dropped them in anger against the Turks in 1911. Few of the early bombs were purpose-made, and modified artillery shells fitted with fins were common, sometimes tossed over the side of the aircraft or suspended alongside or beneath the aircraft and dropped at the right time (again trial and error played a large part in this) by the removal of a pin or even a piece of string. While nations debated the morals of bombing and the most effective technique, the Italians simply got on with learning the hard way – at war. It is worth considering that aircraft were operating as bombers some years before the evolution of the scouts that became fighters.

TOP: **The Russian plane Ilya Mourometz, designed by Igor Sikorsky, was the world's first four-engined aircraft, and could fly over great distances for the time.** ABOVE: **An Italian-operated example of the pioneering Voisin bomber. This version was powered by a 190hp Isotta-Franschini V.4B engine.**

> "Another popular fallacy is to suppose that flying machines could be used to drop dynamite on an enemy in time of war."
> William H. Pickering,
> *Aeronautics*, 1908

Before the start of World War I, the Austro-Hungarians, French, Germans and Russians were all developing specialized bomber aircraft to carry ordnance to and then drop it on a target. Britain had experimented with dropping bombs from aircraft pre-war, but did not build dedicated bombing aircraft until after war had broken out. Many different types of aircraft were used for bombing early in the war, some having the ability to carry an observer or bombs in place of the observer. However, the key to making bombing a potential war-winning military tool was to develop an aircraft that could defend itself while carrying a large cargo of bombs to the heart of the enemy's location.

The first true bomber aircraft used in combat was the French-designed Voisin. Of steel frame construction, the Voisin had a crew of two plus up to 60kg/132lb of bombs. Power was provided by a 70hp engine that drove a pusher propeller. The Voisin earned its spurs when attacking Zeppelin hangars

at Metz-Frascaty on August 14, 1914. The pioneering aircraft remained in production throughout World War I and was improved constantly, with engine power increasing from 70hp to 155hp. Most impressive was the increase in bomb load up to 300kg/660lb by the end of hostilities.

The French Aviation Militaire began to organize its Voisins into bomber squadrons in September 1914, and eventually had a bomber force of over 600 aircraft which conducted a sustained bombing campaign on the Western Front from May 1915.

On the Eastern Front, the Imperial Russian Air Service soon followed the French lead, and were equipped with the world's first four-engine aircraft, the Ilya Mourometz, designed by Igor Sikorsky. This large aircraft, very advanced for the time, had its first flight in May 1913 and was developed to carry up to 999kg/2200lb of bombs. The most advanced version could remain airborne for five hours at altitudes of around 2743m/9000ft at speeds of 85mph. The type carried out the first of over 400 bombing missions on the Eastern Front in February 1915.

The nations that fought in World War I all had differing views on bombing strategies. Britain's Royal Naval Air Service, Royal Flying Corps and then the Royal Air Force focused on the tactical use of bombing in support of ground troops – the British would also carry out revenge attacks if they felt that the enemy had overstepped the mark.

French planners did not have aircraft in their inventory that would reach Germany, and were in the difficult position of not wanting to bomb areas of France occupied by Germany. In addition, they feared revenge bombing of unoccupied French towns within reach of German aircraft. Meanwhile, Germany was developing aircraft that could cross France and strike at London itself.

TOP: **A classic photograph of a World War II RAF bomber over its target during a bombing raid.** ABOVE: **A detailed photograph of a German Gotha bomber's bomb load.** BELOW LEFT: **British Avro 504s of the Royal Naval Air Service made an early bombing raid on the Zeppelin factory at Freidrichshafen in November 1914.** BELOW: **An early propaganda photograph showing a manual bomber delivering a personalized bomb by hand.**

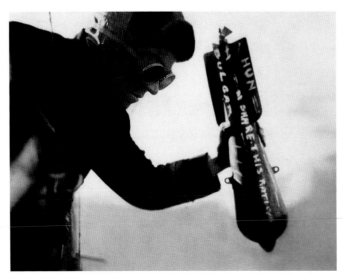

Eighth's bombers were vulnerable to attacks by German Luftwaffe fighters. During the spring, summer and autumn of 1943, Eighth Air Force losses of aircraft and aircrew sometimes reached 12 per cent for a day's raid and at one point it became statistically impossible for a bomber crewman to survive a 25-mission tour of duty. The effect that this had on morale was considerable.

When the Eighth Air Force fighters became able to escort the bombers all the way to their targets and back, the losses slowly began to drop back to what were considered to be acceptable levels, although they remained high.

The Eighth also participated in the preparation for the invasion of occupied Europe in June 1944 by bombing German missile sites and defences, and by flying special operations to support French resistance fighters and Allied ground troops. Later in the war, the Eighth also flew humanitarian missions dropping food and supplies to civilians liberated from Nazi rule.

The Mighty Eighth compiled an impressive record during World War II. Seventeen Congressional Medals of Honor went to Eighth Air Force personnel, and by the end of World War II they had been awarded a number of other medals, including 220 Distinguished Service Crosses and 442,000 Air Medals. Many more awards made to Eighth Air Force veterans after the war remain uncounted. There were 261 fighter aces (with five confirmed kills or more) in the Eighth Air Force in World War II. Thirty-one of these aces had 15 or more aircraft kills each. Another 305 enlisted gunners were also acknowledged as aces.

By the end of the war in Europe, the Eighth had fired over 100 million rounds of ammunition and dropped 703,550 tonnes/ 692,470 tons of bombs at a cost of 4162 heavy bombers and 2222 fighter aircraft lost.

The actions of the Mighty Eighth played a major role in disrupting Germany's war economy and transportation system and, ultimately, in the destruction of Nazi Germany.

ABOVE LEFT: **The G-model of the Flying Fortress, equipped with a chin turret, was able to defend itself against head-on attack – a weak spot on earlier models. Flying in box formations, the bombers would provide cover for each other against enemy fighters.** ABOVE: **B-17s raining down bombs on enemy targets.** LEFT: **The B-24 Liberator is often over- shadowed by the B-17, but it was deployed in greater numbers than the Boeing bomber. This photograph taken in the summer of 1944 shows a B-24 sheathed in flames over Austria – it crashed within minutes.**

The Doolittle raid

The April 1942 air attack on Japan, launched from the aircraft carrier USS *Hornet* and led by Lieutenant Colonel James H. Doolittle, was at that point the most daring operation undertaken by the United States in the Pacific War. Though conceived as a diversion that would also boost American and Allied morale, the raid generated strategic benefits that far outweighed its limited goals.

The raid had its roots in a chance remark that it might be possible to launch twin-engined bombers from the deck of an aircraft carrier, making feasible an early air attack on Japan. On hearing of the idea in January 1942, US Fleet commander Admiral Ernest J. King and Air Forces leader General Henry H. "Hap" Arnold responded enthusiastically. Arnold assigned Doolittle to assemble and lead a suitable air group. The well-tested and proven B-25 Mitchell medium

RIGHT: **Doolittle (left) and Captain Mitscher on board the USS *Hornet* just before the historic bombing of Tokyo in April 1942.** BELOW: **The North American B-25 Mitchell was a rugged bomber that made its combat debut by sinking a Japanese submarine on December 24, 1941. The type went on to become one of the most widely used aircraft of World War II, serving with many Allied air forces.**

bomber was selected, and tests showed that it could indeed fly off a carrier while carrying bombs and enough fuel to reach and attack Japan, and then continue to friendly China.

Recruiting volunteer aircrews for the top-secret mission, Doolittle began special training for his men and modifications to their aircraft. The new carrier *Hornet* was sent to the Pacific to carry out the Navy's part of the mission, which was so secret that her Commanding Officer, Captain Mitscher, had no idea of his ship's part in the operation until just before 16 B-25s were loaded on to his flight deck. *Hornet* sailed on April 2, 1942, and headed west to be joined in mid-ocean on April 13 by USS *Enterprise*, which would provide limited air cover.

The plan called for an afternoon launch on April 18, around 643km/400 miles from Japan, but enemy vessels were met before dawn on April 18. The small enemy boats were believed to have radioed Japan with details of the American carriers heading their way, so Doolittle's Raiders had to take off immediately while still more than 965km/600 miles from their target.

Most of the 16 B-25s, each with a crew of five, attacked the Tokyo area, while some bombed Nagoya. Damage to Japanese military targets was slight, and none of the aircraft reached China, although virtually all the crews survived.

Japan's military leaders were nevertheless horrified and embarrassed by the audacious raid. The Americans had attacked the home islands once and could do it again, and so the Japanese were forced to keep more ships and aircraft in the home islands in case of further US attacks. These

significant military resources could have been used against American forces as they attacked island after island while making their way closer to Japan.

Combined Fleet Commander Admiral Isoroku Yamamoto proposed that the Japanese removed the risk of any similar American raids by destroying America's aircraft carriers in the theatre. This move led the Japanese to disaster at the Battle of Midway a month and a half later.

Perhaps the most significant result of the Doolittle mission was the hard-to-quantify but very real effect that it had on American morale. The United States was finally hitting back after Pearl Harbor, and the brave men who were the Doolittle Raiders raised the confidence and morale of all Americans, civilians and military alike.

ABOVE: **The start of the Pacific War – the Japanese attack on Pearl Harbor, on December 7, 1941.** ABOVE RIGHT: **The Doolittle Raiders en route to their mission aboard the *Hornet*.** RIGHT: **An historic photograph of a B-25 leaving the deck of the *Hornet* at the start of the bombing mission over Tokyo. The raid's effects went far beyond the material damage caused by the bombs dropped that day.**

The atomic bomb raids

"Sixteen hours ago, an American airplane dropped one bomb on Hiroshima, Japan, and destroyed its usefulness to the enemy. That bomb had more power than 20,000 tons of TNT. It had more than two thousand times the blast power of the British Grand Slam, which is the largest bomb ever yet used in the history of warfare... It is an atomic bomb. It is a harnessing of the basic power of the universe." US President Harry Truman, August 6, 1945.

In late 1944, the United States began full-scale air raids on Japan, and by late spring 1945, the US 20th Air Force had destroyed or disabled many of Japan's major cities with fire-bombing raids. However, Japanese ground forces in the Pacific continued to fight, and the US military believed the death toll among US personnel would rise dramatically as the Allies moved closer to the Japanese home islands. Meanwhile, two billion US dollars had been spent and 200,000 people were working on the Manhattan Project to produce a super-weapon – the atomic bomb. After a successful test on July 16, 1945, it was decided that one instant devastating blow to a Japanese city might persuade the Japanese to surrender and save perhaps hundreds of thousands of lives on all sides.

In late 1943, Manhattan Project scientists were confident enough to tell the Army Air Forces (AAF) to begin

ABOVE: **The B-29 was the world's most advanced bomber and the only aircraft in the US inventory really capable of carrying out the demanding mission. This B-29, preserved in the USA, is the only flying example of the Superfortress.**
BELOW: **Col. Paul Tibbets (centre, with pipe), commander of the historic mission, pictured with the ground crew of the *Enola Gay* and the aircraft on Tinian. Tibbets was a highly experienced combat pilot who had taken part in early Eighth Air Force raids from Britain. The *Enola Gay* is preserved in the USA.**

preparing for the atomic bomb's use. The B-29, the world's most advanced bomber, was the obvious choice for the delivery vehicle and, under the leadership of Colonel Paul Tibbets, a hand-picked unit trained hard for one job – dropping atomic bombs.

Fifteen specially modified Boeing B-29 Superfortresses were prepared for "special weapons" delivery. The 509th Composite Group was the first USAAF bombardment group to be organized, equipped and trained for atomic warfare, needless to say under complete secrecy. Tibbets emphasized high-altitude flying, long-range navigation and the use of radar in training to prepare the crews for a high-altitude release of the bomb many miles from their base. They also worked on an escape manoeuvre that would avoid the shock wave that could damage or destroy the aircraft.

As part of the training, a 4540kg/10,000lb bomb was dropped, designed to simulate the actual "Fat Man" atomic bomb later dropped at Nagasaki. Loaded with high explosive, these were named "pumpkin" bombs because of their shape and colour. From November 1944 to June 1945, the 509th trained continually for the first atomic bomb drop. In April 1945, the group had moved to a new base on Tinian in the Mariana Islands, only 2333km/1450 miles from Tokyo.

Hiroshima was chosen as the first target, with Kokura and Nagasaki as second and third targets. The attack would occur as soon after August 2 as the weather allowed.

At 08:15 hours on August 6, B-29 *Enola Gay*, piloted by Tibbets, dropped the 4406kg/9700lb atom bomb codenamed "Little Boy" over Hiroshima.

> "My God, what have we done?"
> Robert Lewis, co-pilot of the *Enola Gay*, the B-29 that dropped the first atomic bomb, August 6, 1945

The devastation caused by the bomb brought no response to the demand for unconditional surrender, and conventional bombing raids continued. On August 9, B-29 *Bockscar* dropped the second and only remaining complete atom bomb in the US arsenal, codenamed "Fat Man", over Nagasaki. The primary target had been the city of Kokura, but clouds had obscured it. With fuel running low due to a fuel transfer problem, the pilot Chuck Sweeney proceeded to the secondary target, Nagasaki, a leading industrial centre. When the bomb detonated, it felt as though *Bockscar* was "being beaten with a telephone pole", said a member of the crew.

Japan surrendered unconditionally on August 14, and on August 28, US aircraft began landing the first occupation forces at Tokyo. B-29s were now dropping food, medicine and other supplies to US Allied prisoners. World War II was finally over, but the Atomic Age had dawned.

TOP: **Hiroshima photographed in March 1946, still showing the utter devastation caused by the explosion of the "Little Boy" atomic bomb on August 6, 1945. The bomb exploded 610m/2000ft above the centre of Hiroshima, and 6.5km²/4sq miles of the city were wiped out instantly. Anything beneath was turned to ashes, and only a few concrete buildings survived the blast – but in ruins.** ABOVE: *Enola Gay* **returns to its base on Tinian following the first atomic bombing mission. Tibbets said of the raid, "...we had seen the city when we went in and there was nothing to see when we came back."** LEFT: **The mushroom cloud over Nagasaki following the detonation of the "Fat Man" atomic bomb on August 9, 1945. Japan surrendered unconditionally five days later.**

Bomber aircraft development since World War II

The effectiveness of heavy bomber campaigns during World War II and the use of the ultimate weapon, the atomic bomb, meant that from the end of the war until the end of the 1950s, the heavy bomber was central to the military planning of the world's most powerful nations. The protagonists on the world stage were desperate to get a technological edge in case the Cold War ever heated up. Massive retaliation and mutually assured destruction awaited the players in a World War III unless new technology could provide one side with the upper hand and a means of total defeat of the enemy. The period was typified by major investment in experimental programmes, from flying wings to flying saucers. After the war, swept-wing jet bomber aircraft gradually replaced straight-wing piston-powered types, although turboprop bombers remain in front-line Russian service today in the form of the Tupolev Tu-95/142 "Bear" bomber/anti-submarine aircraft.

Greater knowledge of "area rule" (the design approach that produces a fuselage contour with the lowest possible transonic wave drag) came in the 1950s and helped engineers and aircraft designers beat the so-called "sound barrier" and produce aircraft capable of supersonic speeds in level flight. The quest for high speed was typified by the B-58 Hustler.

Jet engine technology progressed rapidly after the war. The Canberra B.2 was powered by the 2952kg/6500lb thrust Avon 101, while the B-47 had 3266kg/7200lb thrust J47-GE-25 turbojets. These bestowed a performance vastly better than the bombers in service just a few years previously. Compare that to the 13,980kg/30,780lb afterburning thrust of the B-1B Lancer's F-101 GE-102 turbofans. Afterburning or reheat capability was developed in the late 1940s to give jet-powered aircraft an emergency boost of energy when required.

The 1957 Soviet launch of the Sputnik satellite sent shockwaves through the Western world as everyone was quick to realize that if a satellite could be launched into space, an atomic device could also be launched using the same missile at London or Washington. There followed in the USA a crash programme in missile development, which culminated in a vast and potent missile arsenal in the USA. One result of this was that funding for the development of the manned bomber, which many thought was becoming a dinosaur, was a fraction

BELOW: **This photograph taken at Boeing's plant in Wichita, Kansas, shows B-47 Stratojets in final assembly. Development of this aircraft began before World War II ended. Stratojets entered USAF service in 1952, and were the USA's best nuclear deterrent in the period before ICBM missiles.**

LEFT: The Panavia Tornado is one of the few variable-geometry or "swing-wing" aircraft to have entered front-line service. The Tornado has been the backbone of the Royal Air Force's bomber capability since the mid-1980s. This Tornado was pictured during the Gulf War, where the type specialized in daring and risky low-level attacks. BELOW: The Rockwell B-1 Lancer was designed to meet a mid-1960s requirement and, having survived cancellation, finally entered service in 1986. This was one of the last long-range strategic bombers to be built, and its impressive low-level high performance allows it to penetrate sophisticated air defences. While no true stealth technology was built into the B-1, it was designed with a small radar profile for such a large and capable aircraft.

ABOVE: The B-2 Spirit is a long-range strategic heavy bomber designed from the outset as a stealthy combat aircraft. It combines reduced infrared, acoustic, electromagnetic, visual and radar signatures, making the aircraft very hard to detect or track. RIGHT: A Lockheed F-117A Nighthawk "stealth fighter" under construction. This aircraft was the world's first to exploit low-observable stealth technology – its surfaces and edge profiles reflect hostile radar into narrow beam signals away from enemy radar detectors.

of that spent on missile forces. Despite the presence of nuclear weapons in the world, which some people saw as a stabilizing factor, large and bloody wars continued to erupt around the world, and strategic bombers were not necessarily the best aircraft to have in the inventory.

The philosophy of massive retaliation seemed inflexible when what was needed was a flexible response, particularly for smaller conventional operations. This was a period of uncertainty in bomber history, and no bomber programmes were initiated and completed in the decade from 1960 to 1970.

Early jet bombers continued to use the materials and construction techniques of piston-powered aircraft. High-speed flight put extreme stresses on airframes,

so engineers looked beyond aluminium and magnesium alloys, and introduced titanium alloys and special steels. Carbon fibre composites are now widely used and are three times as strong while weighing half as much as aluminium alloys.

A truly innovative development of the post-war period was the swing or variable-geometry wing, in which the wings can move automatically from the swept to the spread position to maximize the aircraft's aerodynamic performance as required.

On take-off, the spread position generates more lift and gets the aircraft off the ground sooner. Once in the air, the wings sweep back for high-speed flight. Only a handful of swing-wing bombers, such as the F-111 and the Tornado, have seen service.

Cold War bombers

Cold War rivalry and tensions between the United States/NATO and the Soviet Union/Warsaw Pact fuelled the development on both sides of more efficient and destructive bomber aircraft at almost any cost. Research, design and development were accelerated to a pitch that would have been unlikely had it not been for the Cold War.

In the immediate post-war period the Soviet Union's main bomber programme was the Tu-4, copied from US B-29s acquired during World War II. The Soviets reportedly spent two years carefully dismantling the US aircraft and studying the finest details of both structure and systems. The Tu-4 programme effectively kick-started Soviet post-war bomber development, the helping hand unwittingly given to them by their ideological enemies of the next four decades. The Soviet B-29 copies were produced from 1945 until 1953.

The years of the Cold War saw each side making a technological leap and the other mirroring or trying to improve the aircraft available should World War III have erupted. It was equally important to devise ways of countering new bombers through developing higher-performance fighters, early-warning and anti-aircraft technology,

> "It is an ironic, but accurate fact, that the two strongest powers are the two in the most danger of devastation."
> John F. Kennedy, June 10, 1963

ABOVE: **Royal Air Force Meteor fighters formating on and refuelling from a USAF Boeing KB-29 tanker converted from a standard B-29. Inflight refuelling was a vital means of extending the reach of Cold War combat aircraft – both fighters and bombers. Co-operation of this kind between the USAF and the RAF was common throughout the Cold War, and continues to this day.**

and specifically surface-to-air missiles. The USA usually took the lead, but there were some notable exceptions.

The priority for the USA was to develop a bomber that could strike around the world without the need for forward bases. They wanted the ability to fight the Soviet Union even if Europe fell and they had to launch strikes from the continental USA. The Soviet aim was also to reach its enemy from the other side of the world. One bomber that almost met this requirement, needing only one mid-air refuelling, was the English Electric Canberra-derived Martin B-57. However, the aircraft could not carry the large weapon load required over such vast distances.

Range was not enough: the aircraft also had to be able to avoid the unwelcome attentions of defending fighters by flying either higher or faster, or both. The B-36 had a top speed of 661kph/411mph, which was slower than many fighters of the World War II era. The answer for the USA came in the form of the B-47 Stratojet, Boeing's swept-wing, six-jet-engined design. The Tu-16, which used technology derived directly from the B-29, was the Soviet equivalent of the B-47 Stratojet, both of them first-generation swept-wing jet bombers.

Moscow's 1954 May Day parade fly-past saw the public debut of the Myasishchev M-4 long-range strategic bomber, which gave the Soviets the reach to hit the USA. The mighty Boeing B-52 Stratofortress had had its maiden flight a year earlier and in it the USAF finally got a high-performance bomber with intercontinental range. By the 1960s there were many experts who considered the bomber to be obsolete because new, highly accurate and destructive long-range missiles became available on both sides of the Iron Curtain. Despite this, bomber development continued, not just in the USA and the Soviet Union. Britain's V-bomber force included the highly advanced and complex Vulcan and Victor jet bombers which, although not having intercontinental range, could, with air-refuelling, have reached targets very far away from the UK. Similarly, France's Force de Dissuasion, equipped with high-speed Mirage IV bombers, was created as a potent deterrent against would-be aggressors.

ABOVE: **A picture considered impossible during the Cold War – a USAF B-52 Stratofortress parked near a Tupolev Tu-95 "Bear". These two very different bomber types faced each other across an ideological divide that lasted decades.**

BELOW: **Two classic British bomber types: a Handley Page Victor converted for tanker duties refuels two Blackburn Buccaneers. The Victor was in RAF service as a bomber from 1958 until the late 1970s. The Buccaneer, technically the last-ever all-British bomber, served in the Royal Navy and Royal Air Force from 1960 into the early 1990s.** BOTTOM: **The French were keen to develop their own nuclear deterrent and created the French Strategic Air Command's Force de Dissuasion. Equipped with the potent and high-performance Mirage IV, the force was ready for action around the clock from 1964 to 1996. Here, a Mirage IV refuels from a dedicated KC-135FR tanker.**

In the Tupolev Tu-22M, the Soviet Union created the first swing-wing strategic bomber, a major development. The American equivalent, the Rockwell B-1 project, was cancelled because of fears of rising costs. The Rockwell design was resurrected, and entered service as the highly capable B-1B Lancer. The development in bombers which really did take design into a new age was the unveiling of the Northrop B-2 Spirit, the "stealth bomber", believed to be the most expensive aircraft ever. Inspired by the Northrop Flying Wings of the 1940s, the B-2 was conceived during the Cold War as a long-range heavy bomber that could penetrate the world's most sophisticated air defences undetected and then drop up to 16 nuclear bombs. Aircraft such as the B-2 and the B-52 will be flying for many years to come. In the case of the B-52, the aircraft is expected to remain in service until 2045, a century after the start of the "war" for which it was designed to fight.

BELOW: **The Rockwell B-1 was conceived at the height of the Cold War, but is expected to stay in the front line for many years to come. The type saw extensive action during the 2003 war in Iraq.**

Strategic Air Command

Strategic Air Command (SAC) was established in the USA on March 21, 1946, and in October that year its mission was defined: SAC was to attain an immediate state of combat readiness and to stand by for immediate operations, either alone or jointly with other forces, against enemies of the USA. In addition, SAC was required to develop, test and improve strategic bombardment tactics. Together with Tactical Air Command, SAC formed the offensive element of the USAF that existed for more than four decades.

On October 19, 1948, Lt. General Curtis E. Le May took command of SAC and went on to build it into the most powerful military force ever. Survivability was key to SAC's deterrence capability, so Le May moved the SAC Headquarters to the remote Offutt Air Force Base, Nebraska. SAC personnel were in no doubt as to the importance of their mission when Le May told them, "We are at war now!" Le May's aim was to build SAC into a force that could unleash such firepower and destruction on an enemy that they would no longer have the will or ability to wage war.

After slow development, the advent of the Korean War brought more funds to the USAF, enabling SAC to expand rapidly. Another driving factor in the development of SAC was the growing threat of Soviet military development, principally in the development of the Soviet hydrogen bomb, which was first tested on August 12, 1953.

To reduce the risk to its aircraft from enemy attack, SAC began to disperse them to bases across the USA, and did not have too many concentrated at a single location. In addition, SAC began acquiring bases around the world (in England, Greenland and Spain, among other locations) to improve its aircraft's ability to reach enemies anywhere.

BELOW: **The B-52, one of the greatest combat aircraft ever built, was the aircraft Le May was waiting for. Its entry into service in 1955 gave SAC the ability to fly around the world, strike at targets and fly home again. Although it was designed as a nuclear bomber, the Vietnam War showed the B-52's capabilities as a conventional bomber.**

LEFT: **This fine comparison shows the relative size of two of SAC's earliest bombers, the B-29 Superfortress (left) and the B-36 Peacemaker. The B-36 was the largest bomber ever to serve with the USAF, and for a decade in the late 1940s and early '50s, the Peacemaker provided SAC with a long-range strategic bomber deterrent.**
BELOW: **Taken in October 1955, this photograph shows two RB-47s, the reconnaissance variant of SAC's Stratojet bomber.**

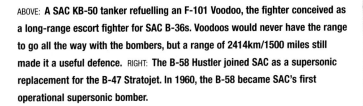

ABOVE: **A SAC KB-50 tanker refuelling an F-101 Voodoo, the fighter conceived as a long-range escort fighter for SAC B-36s. Voodoos would never have the range to go all the way with the bombers, but a range of 2414km/1500 miles still made it a useful defence.** RIGHT: **The B-58 Hustler joined SAC as a supersonic replacement for the B-47 Stratojet. In 1960, the B-58 became SAC's first operational supersonic bomber.**

Initially equipped with tired World War II aircraft types, by the mid-1950s SAC was operating its first all-jet bomber, the B-47 Stratojet. By 1955, SAC was being equipped with the mighty B-52 (still the backbone of the USAF bomber force around half a century later), the B-58 Hustler and, equally importantly, the KC-135 jet tanker, which gave SAC a truly global reach. SAC demonstrated its ability to strike anywhere around the world when three B-52s made a non-stop round-the-world flight. By the late 1950s, SAC was complementing its airborne nuclear forces with ballistic nuclear missiles.

By 1960, a third of SAC's bombers and tankers were on 15-minute ground alert, combat-ready and armed for nuclear war. By July 1961, half of SAC's bombers and tankers were on ground alert while a number of nuclear-armed bombers were constantly airborne. From February 1961, SAC kept an

Airborne Command Post in the air at all times, ready to take control of SAC forces in the event of an attack on the SAC HQ at Offut. From 1964 to 1973, SAC bombers flew thousands of bombing missions in South-east Asia, and the Linebacker II campaign in December 1972 is thought to have brought the North Vietnamese back to the peace table.

The collapse of the Soviet Union at the end of the Cold War brought an end to the threat of Soviet aggression. Following the Gulf War in 1991, a restructuring of the United States Air Force brought the stand-down of Strategic Air Command. On June 1, 1992, Strategic Air Command passed into the history books, hailed by many as winners of the Cold War.

Bomber aircraft defences from 1945

Most of the bombers in service in the post-war period had some type of defensive gun armament. B-29s, like their B-17 predecessors, bristled with guns in tail, waist and ventral positions. In the late 1940s and early '50s it was felt that, provided a bomber could fly higher and faster than defending fighters and anti-aircraft fire, it would get to its target unscathed. This was the philosophy behind the wartime de Havilland Mosquito and the jet-powered English Electric Canberra which first flew in 1949 – in bomber configuration, neither type carried defensive armament.

Guns continued to be installed in bombers, although guns in nose positions were omitted as bomber aircraft began to fly higher and faster. The Avro Shackleton may well have been the last front-line bomber in service with this form of

armament. The B-52, however, did retain a group of remotely controlled cannon in the tail, which was only deleted in later versions. Even the high-speed Tupolev Tu-22M had two radar-controlled cannon in its tail. Today the backbone of Britain's bomber force, the Panavia Tornado GR4, has a 27mm/1.05in cannon in the nose.

World War II proved the value of fighter escort for large fleets of bombers, and this no doubt prompted the decision to trial a very unusual defensive installation in the B-36 Peacemaker. The B-36 was so large that its forward bomb

RIGHT: **Few aircraft have had the capability to carry another aircraft for defence, but Strategic Air Command's B-36 Peacemaker could. Trials with an F-85 Goblin were followed by more using an F-86 Thunderstreak.**
BELOW: **The structure of "stealth" aircraft, such as the Lockheed F-117 Nighthawk pictured, and the materials from which they are made, are central to their defence and survivability.**

bay had room to carry a McDonnell F-85 Goblin jet fighter that could protect the bomber from enemy fighters and then return to the aircraft.

However, the unarmed Mosquito approach held good until anti-aircraft missile technology produced missiles that could down a jet aircraft at 18,300m/60,000ft. Most anti-aircraft missiles were fired at targets tracked on radar, which then directed the missile to the vicinity of the target. The missile would switch to its own homing facility and look for a heat source, normally the aircraft's engine jet pipe. The same technique was used by most air-to-air fighter-launched missiles. A hit from a missile was usually enough to bring down any aircraft – warheads varied from high explosive to "shrapnel" types, and some were even nuclear-tipped. Bombers began to employ various means of confusing would-be attackers. Radar-controlled missiles would only function if the radar could find and lock on to its target. Bombers carry electronic jamming devices which will find and jam the appropriate enemy fire control radars of anti-aircraft guns and missiles. On some missions, for example the Libya raids carried out

by the USAF, dedicated jamming aircraft (EF-111s) went in ahead of the main attack force. During the RAF's Black Buck bombing raids on the Falklands, specialized Shrike anti-radar missiles were fired by Vulcan bombers.

Most bombers now carry special rear warning radar to alert crews to unwelcome attention from the rear. On-board equipment detects missile locks from fighter aircraft or missiles. The bomber can then take evasive action and deploy bundles of chaff (strips of metal foil) to create a confusing radar image, and also flares which fire 20 to 30 times around the aircraft, presenting a plethora of brilliantly hot, burning objects that hopefully draw the heat-seeking missile away.

"Stealth" aircraft revolutionized bomber operations because potential enemies at the time relied on defence radars to pick up incoming bombers. Most radars cannot pick up the stealth aircraft and, if they did, heat-seeking missiles would be thwarted thanks to the ingenious cooling and dissipation of hot exhaust gases from the aircraft's engines, which reduced the aircraft's infrared signature. All future bomber aircraft will be made using stealth technology.

FAR LEFT: **In contrast to the hi-tech tail defences of the B-52, the Tu-95 Bear retains two 23mm/ 0.9in cannon in the tail which can be fired manually. The tail turret is clearly inspired by that of the Tu-4 B-29 copy produced in the Soviet Union in the years following World War II.** LEFT: **The tail of the B-52 has changed considerably during its time in service. It was initially armed with four remotely controlled 12.7mm/0.5in machine-guns. In the H-model pictured, the tail defence is the 20mm/0.78in "minigun", part of the AN/ASG-21 Defensive Fire Control system. Note also the tail warning and search radomes above the gun.**
BELOW LEFT: **Even the Mach 2-capable Panavia Tornado carries cannon armament in the nose.**
BELOW: **Avro Shackleton. The "Shack" was probably the last front-line bomber with nose guns.**

V-bombers

Britain's V-bombers – the Vulcan, Victor and Valiant – were the last of the Royal Air Force's long-range heavy bombers, and they were Britain's airborne nuclear deterrent from 1955 until 1968.

The concept of the force, not seen as one of mixed aircraft types at first, had its origins in a 1946 Air Ministry Operational Requirement calling for a bomber able to carry a 4542kg/ 10,000lb atomic bomb to a target 2775km/1725 miles away, from a base anywhere in the world. The aircraft was required to deliver its bomb deep into enemy territory and avoid destruction by enemy aircraft or anti-aircraft defences.

Four very different jet-powered designs from four different companies made it from the drawing board in response to the requirement. Avro and Handley Page both proposed futuristic, aerodynamically adventurous designs judged to be sufficiently risky that Vickers and Shorts were invited to develop their rather simpler and thus less risky designs as something of an insurance policy for the RAF. The Air Staff asked for the Vickers design, ultimately named Valiant, to be produced over the Short Sperrin as the interim aircraft, while the advanced Avro and Handley Page aircraft were developed into the Vulcan and Victor respectively. These aircraft represented a massive technological leap for an air force equipped with Lancasters, Lincolns and latterly old B-29s loaned by the

TOP: **XA901 was a Vulcan B.1 and was one of the earlier Vulcans to be produced. The total number of B.1s built was 45, the last delivered to the RAF in April 1959. The all-white, anti-flash paint scheme was intended to offer some protection against the effects of the flash following a nuclear detonation.**
ABOVE: **Elements of the V-force were rotated overseas to Akrotiri in Cyprus, the location photographed here in 1970. From Cyprus, the bombers would have been able to reach targets beyond the range of UK-based aircraft. Beneath this Vulcan's nose is a tanker version of the Victor bomber.**

Americans. Looking back, it took surprisingly little time – only nine years – for the jet-powered nuclear bombers to reach squadron service.

The V-bombers were effectively designed around Britain's own atomic bomb, which was developed in parallel with the aircraft. Britain's first operational atomic bomb, "Blue Danube", a free-fall plutonium bomb, was available in November 1953, but it was not until 1955 that Britain's first atomic bomber unit, No.138 Squadron, was operational with its Valiants at RAF Wittering. Although the jet-powered Canberra had been in Bomber Command service since 1951, its bomb bay was too small to take the British A-bomb that became available.

It was January 1957 before the first Vulcans entered service with the RAF's 230 OCU (Operational Conversion Unit) at Waddington, and the type was entering squadron service by the summer. November 1957 saw the Victor deliveries beginning and the Handley Page bomber was in squadron use from April 1958. Ten RAF airfields were updated to become V-bomber bases, while a further 26 were earmarked as V-bomber dispersal bases in times of international tension.

The V-force possessed massive destructive capability, and its credibility as an effective deterrent against would-be aggressors – specifically the Soviet Union – rested on its ability to get airborne and get to the target if required. The V-force perfected the QRA (quick reaction alert), whereby a number of aircraft were fuelled, armed and ready to be airborne in just four minutes, the amount of time it would take for a detected Soviet ballistic missile to impact on UK bases. The credibility of the V-force was in question once Soviet anti-aircraft technology developed to the point that a U-2 spyplane was shot down over the USSR from an altitude of 19,810m/65,000ft in May 1960. The answer was to bring the V-force down to low level, operating below the effective height of most enemy radars, only climbing to an altitude of 3660m/12,000ft to drop the deadly cargo. By now the force was carrying the Yellow Sun hydrogen bomb, which was replaced by the WE177 weapon in the mid-1960s. Later-mark Victors and Vulcans were armed with the Blue Steel stand-off

TOP: **The enormous Blue Danube atomic bomb, around which the V-bombers were designed. This all-British weapon was a free-fall plutonium bomb.** ABOVE: **The Vickers Valiant was the most conventional of the three V-bomber designs, and was ordered as insurance should the more advanced Victor and Vulcan be problematic.** BELOW: **The Victor first flew in prototype form just seven years after the end of World War II, yet this aircraft served in the RAF until 1993 when the last tanker versions were retired. The Victor could carry the greatest bomb load of the V-bombers, an impressive 15,890kg/35,000lb.**

missile with a range of 161km/100miles. This enabled the V-bombers to improve the launch aircraft's survivability over heavily defended targets.

When the strategic deterrent role passed from the V-force to the Royal Navy's Polaris submarines in 1969, these aircraft remained in front-line service (although the Valiant had been withdrawn by then) and were still very potent weapon platforms with the ability to carry many tons of bombs, including nuclear payloads, if required.

The Falklands Black Buck raids

When Argentina invaded the Falklands in 1982, Britain's campaign to regain the islands was made more difficult because of the sheer distances involved. Once Britain's Task Force was ready to re-take the islands, Argentine air defences on the Falklands had to be disabled. Firstly, the runway at Port Stanley had to be made unusable for Argentine aircraft, as it was assumed that, given time, the Argentine air force would base Mirage and Skyhawk fighters there, which could have made things very difficult for the Task Force. Without a Falklands base, these combat aircraft operating from the Argentine mainland were near the limits of their operating radius. Secondly, Argentine radar sites had to be neutralized so that the British Harriers of the Task Force could not be attacked or detected. The missions had to take place in total secrecy from friendly territory which led the military planners to one choice: Ascension Island, a small British dependency in the Atlantic almost 6436km/4000 miles from the Falklands. There was only one aircraft in the RAF inventory that could carry a heavy bomb load over the considerable distances involved – the Vulcan.

TOP: **The Vulcan finally saw action after almost three decades of service when the type was used to carry out the longest bombing raids ever contemplated.**
ABOVE: **The raid was only possible with a complex series of inflight refuellings from Victor tankers which themselves had to be refuelled to get back to base.**

The missions to the Falklands were codenamed "Operation Black Buck", and five were ultimately flown. Three were directed against the runway at Stanley, while a further two attacked radar sites on the islands. The logistics of these missions are staggering, and with the distance from Ascension to the Falklands a 16-hour round trip of over 12,389km/7700 miles, they were at that point the longest bombing missions in history.

LEFT AND BELOW: **A key aim of the Black Buck missions was to put the Port Stanley runway out of action. This was essential to prevent its use by Argentine Mirage (left) and Skyhawk (below) aircraft which posed a significant threat to the British Task Force. Both were near the end of their range operating from the Argentine mainland, and they could be contained by the British Harriers.**

Each Black Buck Vulcan had to be refuelled numerous times by RAF Victor tankers also operating from Ascension, and some of the tankers themselves had to be refuelled to get home. Although many RAF Vulcans had refuelling probes, they had not been used for some time. There followed a period where serviceable refuelling probes were sought, one apparently coming from a Vulcan in a museum. Because of the great distances involved over the ocean, the Vulcans needed improved navigation aids, which came in the form of equipment allegedly acquired from a British Airways store. In addition, the Vulcan's throttle controls were modified to allow pilots unlimited power from the Olympus engines.

The first Black Buck mission took place from April 30 to May 1, 1982. Loaded with 21 x 454kg/1000lb bombs, two Vulcans took off from Ascension for the eight-hour trip to their target, escorted by no fewer than 11 Victor tankers which had to refuel the bombers or each other to reach the Falklands and return.

One of the Vulcans developed a technical problem and had to return to base, leaving a lone Vulcan – XM607 – to carry out the mission. Dwindling numbers of tankers flew on with the Vulcan while the empty tankers returned to Ascension, many with barely enough fuel to land. The last Victor transferred so much fuel to the Vulcan that it only had enough left to get within 644km/400 miles of Ascension, and another Victor had to launch to refuel the incoming "dry" tanker.

About 482km/300 miles from Stanley, the Vulcan descended to 92m/300ft above the sea to avoid detection, and about 64km/40 miles out the aircraft climbed to 3050m/10,000ft to begin the bombing run. Then, 16km/10 miles from the target, an anti-aircraft gun radar was detected, but was jammed by equipment on the Vulcan supplied by the Americans. Twenty-one 454kg/1000lb bombs were dropped in a diagonal line across the runway, one hitting the runway dead-centre.

The effect of this and subsequent Black Buck raids was more on Argentine morale than the Argentine military machine. If Vulcans could reach the Falklands, they could reach the Argentine mainland and, as a result, many Argentine fighters were kept back to defend against a possible raid on Argentina. The raids had been a success.

LEFT: **XM607 was one of the Vulcan B.2s that carried out the Black Buck raids. Armed with 21 x 454kg/1000lb bombs, the Vulcan dropped the bombs obliquely across the runway. Argentina then feared that an attack on the mainland might also have been feasible.**

Operation El Dorado Canyon

In 1986, following a number of terrorist attacks on US citizens and interests, US intelligence cited "incontrovertible" evidence that the incidents were sponsored by Libya. On April 14, 1986, the United States launched Operation El Dorado Canyon against Libya. Part of the operation called for UK-based USAF F-111 crews to fly one of the longest combat missions in history.

US President Ronald Reagan wanted to mount a strike against the regime of Libyan leader Colonel Gadaffi, but first sought cooperation from the Western Allies. The USAF's 48th Tactical Fighter Wing in England had been working on plans for a strike, which assumed that the F-111s could fly through French airspace to strike at Libya. Western media speculation about the strike caused the plan to be changed to include support aircraft (EF-111 and US Navy A-7 and EA-6B) to carry out the suppression of enemy defences. The US Navy role in the operation grew, as the raid had to hit Gadaffi hard.

RIGHT: **The map used by Secretary of Defense Weinberger at the White House briefing which told the world of Operation El Dorado Canyon.** BELOW: **An F-111 leaves the runway at RAF Lakenheath in Suffolk, England, to take part in what was then the longest bombing mission in history. The F-111 is a very fast and accurate low-level bomber, but the aircraft was not designed for gruelling 13-hour missions like the Libya raids.**

Plans were further complicated when France, Germany, Italy and Spain all refused to cooperate in a strike. Only Britain cooperated by allowing the use of its soil to launch the attack. A radically different plan was drawn up. The F-111s would now navigate over the ocean around France and Spain, pass east over the Strait of Gibraltar and then over the Mediterranean to line up for their bombing run on Libya.

It would be a gruelling round trip of 10,298km/6400 miles, taking 13 hours and needing from eight to twelve inflight refuellings for each of the bombers. The F-111 crews, trained for missions against the Soviet Union, were familiar with 2-hour NATO sorties, so El Dorado Canyon placed a tremendous strain on the crews and the aircraft's complex systems.

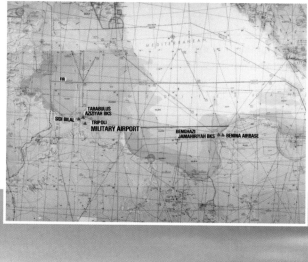

US planners tabled a joint USAF/USN attack against five major Libyan targets. Two were in Benghazi: a terrorist training camp and a military airfield. The other three targets were in Tripoli: a terrorist naval training base; the former Wheelus AFB; and the Azziziyah Barracks compound, which housed the HQ of Libyan intelligence and also contained one of five residences that Gadaffi was known to have used. Eighteen F-111s were to strike the Tripoli targets, while US Navy aircraft were to hit the two Benghazi sites.

At 17:36 GMT on April 14, 24 F-111s left Lakenheath, six of them spare aircraft set to return after the first refuelling. Five EF-111 electronic warfare aircraft also launched. This was the start of the first US bomber mission from British soil since the end of World War II. The US Navy attack aircraft came from carriers of the Sixth Fleet operating in the Mediterranean. Coral Sea provided eight A-6E medium bombers and six F/A-18C Hornets for strike support. America launched six A-6Es, plus six A-7Es and an EA-6B for strike support. They faced a hazardous flight because Libya's air defence system was virtually on a par with that of the Soviet Union. Timing was critical, and the USAF and USN attacks had to be simultaneous to maximize the element of surprise so that the strike aircraft could get in and out as quickly as possible.

Of the 18 F-111s that headed for Libya, five had aborted en route, so at around midnight GMT, 13 F-111s reached Tripoli. The first three elements hit the Azziziyah Barracks. One element struck the Sidi Balal terrorist training camp while the two remaining elements, armed with parachute-retarded 225kg/500lb bombs, struck Tripoli airport, destroying a number of aircraft in the process. The F-111s carried out their attack at speeds around 740kph/460mph and heights of 60m/200ft.

EF-111As and Navy A-7s, A-6Es, and an EA-6B armed with HARM and Shrike anti-radar missiles flew in defence suppression roles for the F-111s. Across the Gulf of Sidra, Navy A-6E aircraft attacked the Al Jumahiriya Barracks at Benghazi, and to the east the Benina airfield.

News of the attack was being broadcast in the USA while it was underway. One F-111 aircraft was lost over Tripoli, possibly hit by a SAM, and its crew were killed. The F-111s spent only 11 minutes in the area of the targets, then faced a long flight home with yet more inflight refuellings.

The operation was never intended to be a means of toppling Gadaffi, but he is known to have been very shaken when bombs exploded near him. When he next appeared on state television, he was certainly subdued. Most importantly, the raids demonstrated that even in those pre-"stealth" days, the USA had the capability to send its high-speed bombers over great distances to carry out precision attacks. The raid was considered a success, but the situation between the USA and Gadaffi remained unresolved until an uneasy peace was agreed 17 years later.

BELOW: **This photograph, taken on February 12, 1986, shows the deck of the USS *Saratoga* (CV-60) as flight-deck crews prepare EA-6B Prowlers, F-14 Tomcats and A-7 Corsairs for operations in the southern Mediterranean. Tension was high between the USA and Libya, and on March 24, 1986, the US Navy destroyed a SAM site after USN aircraft were targeted unsuccessfully by Libyan missiles.**

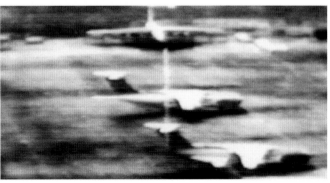

ABOVE: **A still from film taken by a USAF F-111 as the US attack on the military side of Tripoli airport begins. 225kg/500lb bombs were dropped on these Soviet-made Il-76 transports, which the USA believed transported military and subversive materials around the world. The film was shot at night using the F-111's Pave Tack laser-guided delivery system.** LEFT: **Photographs taken by US Navy aircraft on April 15, 1986 show the damage caused at Benina airfield by the previous day's attack carried out by USN aircraft.**

Gulf War bombers

The air campaign against Iraq was launched on January 16, 1991, the day after the United Nations' deadline for Iraqi withdrawal from Kuwait expired. Operation Desert Shield had become Desert Storm. The scale and strength of the Allied air attacks on one night were staggering, and the initial air attack removed much of Iraq's ability to defend itself against further air assaults. The air campaign was conducted by the USA, Saudi, British, French, Italian and Free Kuwaiti, as well as various Arab air forces.

Lockheed F-117 "stealth fighters" flew to the Iraqi capital of Baghdad and destroyed command and control centres. As Baghdad's anti-aircraft defences (seven times greater than that of Hanoi later in the Vietnam War) blazed away at targets it could not see, the F-117s were delivering 907kg/2000lb laser-guided bombs down ventilation shafts and through doorways to destroy underground bunkered facilities. Meanwhile, cruise missiles were also taking out targets with pinpoint accuracy. Seven USAF B-52Gs had taken off from Barksdale Air Force Base, Louisiana, and headed towards the Persian Gulf. They flew a round trip of more than 22,526km/ 14,000 miles, remaining airborne for 35 hours, the longest combat mission in history at that time. The launch of their Boeing AGM-86C conventionally armed cruise missiles (first combat use for the weapon) was one of the opening salvoes

TOP: **Operating from RAF Fairford in Britain, eight USAF B-52s dropped a total of 1176 tonnes/1158 tons of bombs during 60 missions on mainly front-line Republican Guard targets.** ABOVE: **The Republic A-10 Thunderbolt proved to be a modern equivalent of the Hawker Typhoon, carrying out much the same job as the "Tiffie" after D-Day, attacking enemy armour and vehicles. However, the Typhoon was not armed with the A-10's deadly 30mm/1.18in cannon which fires 30 armour-piercing rounds per second.**

of the operation. Iraqi anti-aircraft defences then became targets themselves with scores of US defence suppression types such as the EF-111, F-4G Wild Weasels and EA-6 Prowlers launching anti-radiation missiles or using powerful jammers to cripple enemy electronic sensors.

LEFT: **The crew of RAF Victor K2 tanker XH671 head out to their aircraft for another mission in support of Desert Storm combat aircraft. These flying petrol stations were essential for aircraft such as Tornados and Buccaneers.**
BELOW: **An F-111 of the UK-based 48th Tactical Fighter Wing "in theatre" at Taif in Saudi Arabia during the Gulf War. In 2500 Gulf War F-111 missions, these fine aircraft destroyed 2203 targets, including artillery, 13 runways, 245 hardened aircraft shelters and 12 bridges.**

For a month, Coalition aircraft pounded away at any targets that might contribute to the Iraqi ground war effort. Precision bombs were used to minimize errors and casualties – a successful strike was one that hit within 3m/10ft of its mark.

In the first day of Desert Storm, 655 Coalition aircraft flew 1322 sorties against communication centres and airfields. Within 24 hours, the Coalition achieved air superiority and was then at liberty to destroy Iraq's command and control centres, and to cut communications between Kuwait and Baghdad.

Once defences were silenced, strike aircraft, including the Jaguar, F-16 and F/A-18, hit airfield complexes with conventional bombs. RAF Tornado bombers specialized in the use of the devastating JP233 runway denial weapon system against Iraqi runways. This weapon had to be used at low level, which led to relatively high losses among the RAF bomber crews. Hardened shelters were not able to protect Iraqi aircraft hidden within because the Coalition bombers were able to direct pinpoint attacks on the structures' doors.

Veteran Royal Air Force Buccaneers, normally deployed in the maritime attack role in the UK, were rushed to the Gulf for overland laser designation (target-marking) missions. Armed with Sidewinder AAMs for self defence, pairs of Buccaneers would operate with four Tornados, all carrying precision-guided bombs and the "Buccs" each carrying a laser pod – two were carried in case one became unserviceable, thus avoiding the entire mission

"We have carefully chosen our targets and we've bombed them with precision."
US Secretary of Defense
Dick Cheney, 1991

being scrubbed. The Buccaneer flew the first such mission on February 2 against the As Suwaira road bridge. These mixed Tornado/Buccaneer teams destroyed 20 road bridges over the Tigris and Euphrates rivers, very effectively breaking Iraqi supply lines to their invasion forces in Kuwait. Unknown to the Coalition, the Iraqis had run their fibre optic communications cables along the bridges, so every wrecked bridge added to communications chaos among the enemy.

Allied Air Forces then proceeded to pound the Iraqi land forces – specifically the divisions deployed in Kuwait and Southern Iraq. The USAF's veteran B-52 bombers, operating mainly from Diego Garcia in the Indian Ocean, decimated the morale of Iraq's Republican Guard. They delivered some 40 per cent of all the weapons dropped by Coalition forces and flew approximately 1620 combat sorties.

Coalition bombers continued to attack Iraqi targets until the invaders were driven from Kuwait, and on March 3, 1991, Iraq accepted the ceasefire.

LEFT: **A Royal Air Force Tornado GR1 at its base in Kuwait. The Tornado played a vital strike role during the war, initially tasked with hazardous low-level missions. In all, 1500 bombing raids were carried out by the swing-wing bombers.**

A–Z of World War Bombers

1914–45

There were no true bomber aircraft when World War I broke out, but military leaders were quick to realize the value of aircraft that could rain down destruction on their enemies from the air. While early bombing raids saw hand-held munitions tossed over the side of an aircraft, by the end of the Great War aircraft were being produced with the capacity to carry bomb loads of 800kg/1760lb over ranges in excess of 1000km/621 miles.

The specifications given to designers of new bomber aircraft in World War I were little changed by World War II, except in their magnitude. Some biplanes were still in front-line service. But by the end of World War II, bombers in service included the Boeing B-29, which had a range of 5229km/3250 miles and a top speed of 576kph/358mph. The weapons carried had changed in their destructive capacity. While the Handley Page bombers of World War I would have carried a number of 113kg/250lb bombs on a raid, the B-29 had to carry just one atomic bomb equivalent to 20,320 tonnes/20,000 tons of high explosives to destroy a city. The bomber had become a war-winning weapon.

LEFT: **Bristol Beaufort I.**

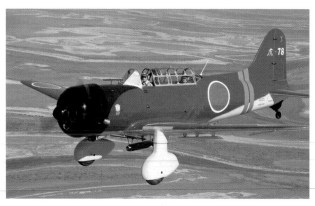

LEFT: **Although the D3A did not have a retractable undercarriage, large streamlined fairings over the fixed landing gear were used to make them more aerodynamic.**

Aichi D3A Val

First flight: January 1938
Power: One Mitsubishi 1,070hp Kinsei 44 radial piston engine
Armament: Two 7.7mm/0.303in machine-guns in upper forward fuselage plus one in rear cockpit; external bomb load of 370kg/816lb
Size: Wingspan – 14.37m/47ft 2in
Length – 10.20m/33ft 5in
Height – 3.80m/12ft 7in
Wing area – 34.9m²/375.67sq ft
Weights: Empty – 2408kg/5309lb
Maximum take-off – 3650kg/8047lb
Performance: Maximum speed – 385kph/239mph
Service ceiling – 9,300m/30,510ft
Range – 1470km/913 miles
Climb – 3000m/9845ft in 6 minutes

Aichi D3A

This two-seat low-wing monoplane dive-bomber, codenamed "Val" by the Allies, came to prominence on December 7, 1941, when a Japanese Naval Task force launched 183 aircraft, including 51 Aichi D3A-2s, from six aircraft carriers to attack Pearl Harbor's Battleship Row and other US Navy installations on the Hawaiian island of Oahu. One of the D3A-2's victims was the USS *Pennsylvania*.

The D3A first flew in January 1938, and between December 1939 and August 1945 the Aichi company built a total of 1495 aircraft in two main variants. The type D3A-1 entered service with the Imperial Japanese Navy in 1940 and was followed a year later by the D3A-2 which had the more powerful 1300hp Kinsei engine and increased fuel capacity. The D3A-2 was the main production version, with 1016 aircraft

being built by the time it became obsolete at the end of 1942. Over the following years, many were used as training aircraft, but as the war progressed and the Americans moved closer to the Japanese mainland, most of the remaining aircraft were used in kamikaze attacks against US naval ships at Leyte and Okinawa.

LEFT: **The Amiot 143 was probably the ugliest aircraft produced by a nation known for its appreciation of fine forms.**

Amiot 143

First flight: August 1934
Power: Two Gnome-Rhone 870hp Kirs 14-cylinder radial engines
Armament: Four 7.5mm/0.29in MAC 1934 machine-guns, one each in nose and dorsal turrets and fore and aft in ventral gondola; internal and external bomb load of up to 800kg/1761lb
Size: Wingspan – 24.53m/80ft 5in
Length – 18.26m/59ft 11in
Height – 5.68m/18ft 7in
Wing area – 100m²/1076.4sq ft
Weights: Empty – 6100kg/13,426lb
Maximum take-off – 9700kg/21,350lb
Performance: Maximum speed – 310kph/193mph
Service ceiling – 7900m/25,920ft
Range – 1200km/746 miles

Amiot 143

The lumbering Amiot 143 was a more powerful re-engined version of the Amiot 140 of 1931 vintage, and retained the fixed non-retractable undercarriage. This all-metal aircraft, with its distinctive two-deck fuselage, had a wing section so deep that the flight engineer could access the engines in flight. The large aerodynamic fairings that covered the wheels were 2.13m/7ft long.

Five French Groupes de Bombardement were equipped with this type in May 1940 when Germany invaded France and the Low Countries. After carrying out early raids dropping propaganda leaflets on Germany, they were restricted to night-bombing of the advancing German columns. In a rare daylight bombing raid against bridges on May 14, 1940, 12 out of 13 143s were shot down.

At the time of France's surrender, only 50 Amiot 143 aircraft remained, and these subsequently formed part of the French Vichy Air Force. By then obsolete, many were converted for use in the transport role.

LEFT: **The Blitz was the world's first operational jet bomber aircraft.** BELOW: **The development Ar 234s used a launch trolley with a steerable nosewheel and mainwheel brakes for taxiing. As this photograph shows, the trolley was released after take-off. Note the main landing skid beneath the fuselage and the smaller ones below the engine nacelles.** BOTTOM LEFT: **An early Blitz on its launch trolley.**

Arado Ar 234 Blitz

The origins of this type date back to a specification issued by the German Air Ministry in 1940 for a fast turbojet-powered single-seat reconnaissance aircraft. The design proposed by Arado, the Ar 234, went on to become the world's first jet-powered bomber.

The first prototype, the Ar 234V-1, first flew on June 15, 1943. and this was quickly followed by seven other prototypes, all using a launching trolley and landing skid arrangement since the aircraft's fuselage was so narrow that it could not take a conventional undercarriage. Once the aircraft reached 60m/197ft, the launch trolley was released and returned to earth on parachutes for re-use.

The third prototype, Ar 234V-3, was fitted with an ejection seat and had rocket-assisted take-off equipment

installed under the wings. During the prototype trials, the launch trolley arrangement had performed very well, but it was soon realized that the aircraft's immobility on landing would be a great disadvantage when it came to operational deployment. Turn-around times would be increased and the aircraft would be vulnerable to enemy air attack. It was therefore decided to abandon the trolley and skid, and all production aircraft had a conventional wheeled undercarriage fitted into the wider fuselage of the production B-series.

Despite being famed as the first jet bombers, early Ar 234s did serve as reconnaissance aircraft that readily avoided enemy interception. Some special examples also equipped an

Arado Ar 234B-2

First flight: June 15, 1943
Power: Two BMW 890kg/1962lb thrust 004B turbojets
Armament: External bomb load of 2000kg/4402lb
Size: Wingspan – 14.11m/46ft 3in
  Length – 12.64m/41ft 5in
  Height – 4.30m/14ft 1in
  Wing area – 26.4m²/284.18sq ft
Weights: Empty – 5200kg/11445lb
  Maximum take-off – 9850kg/21,608lb
Performance: Maximum speed – 742kph/461mph
  Service ceiling – 10,000m/32,808ft
  Range – 1630km/1013 miles
  Climb – 6000m/19,685ft in 17.5 minutes

experimental nightfighter unit. However, Germany's fortune and the Blitz's performance soon led to its development as a bomber that entered service with the Luftwaffe in October 1944. Operated by KG76, the aircraft's first operational missions were flown against targets during the Ardennes offensive in December 1944. This jet bomber unit was very active in the early weeks of 1945 by taking part in a ten-day series of attacks against the Ludendorff bridge at Remagen, which had been captured by the Americans. The Blitz was a pioneering aircraft which was closely studied by the Allies post-war.

Armstrong Whitworth Whitley

TOP: **Z9226 was a Whitley Mk V, pictured here during its service with No.10 Squadron, Bomber Command.** ABOVE: **A Bomber Command Whitley crew prepare for another mission. Note the unusual off-centre single machine-gun in the nose turret.**

The Whitley, designed in response to Air Ministry specification B.3/34, was an all-metal twin-engined monoplane bomber with retractable landing gear, and first flew on March 17, 1936. It entered service with the RAF in March 1937, was one of the first heavy night-bombers of the RAF and the first RAF aircraft with a stressed-skin fuselage. The high incidence of the aircraft's wing gave the Whitley a distinctive nose-down flying attitude. During the "phoney war" period, the RAF's Whitley squadrons bore the brunt of leaflet dropping raids over German cities, which resulted in many losses. On March 19, 1940, Whitleys dropped the first bombs on German territory during World War II when they attacked the Hornum seaplane base on the island of Sylt. The Whitley, together with the Wellington and Hampden – lightweights by the standards of later Bomber Command "heavies" – formed the backbone of the early British bomber offensive.

Heavy losses during the winter of 1940–1 and the introduction of four-engine aircraft meant that the Whitley's front-line activities were soon restricted to Coastal Command U-boat patrol duties over the approaches to their bases along the French Atlantic coast. Coastal Command's first success using air-to-surface-vessel (ASV) radar was by a Whitley VII of No.502 Squadron against U-Boat *U-206* in November 1941.

The Whitley I was delivered to the RAF off the drawing board while the Whitley IIs were completed with two-stage superchargers for the engines. The Mark III was part of the second production run. Though similar to the II, this version

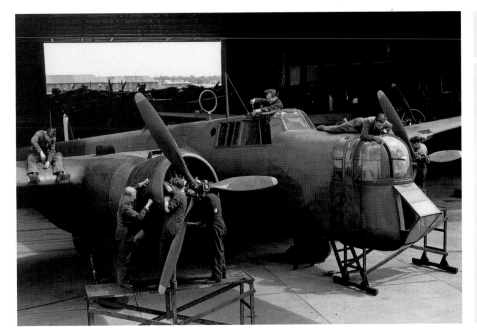

Armstrong Whitworth Whitley Mark V

First flight: March 17, 1936
Power: Two Rolls-Royce 1145hp Merlin X piston
　　engines
Armament: One 7.7mm/0.303in machine-gun in
　　nose turret; four in tail turret; up to 3178kg/
　　7000lb bomb load carried in bomb bay and
　　inner wings
Size: Wingspan – 25.6m/84 ft
　　Length – 21.5m/70ft 6in
　　Height – 4.57m/15ft
　　Wing area – 105.63m²/1137sq ft
Weights: Empty – 8785kg/19,350lb
　　Maximum take-off – 15,209kg/33,500lb
Performance: Maximum speed – 357kph/222mph
　　Service ceiling – 7930m/26,000ft
　　Range – 2654km/1650 miles
　　Climb – 244m/800ft per minute

ABOVE: **The famed Merlin engine did not power Whitleys until the introduction of the Mk IV. The aircraft shown here, undergoing intense but staged servicing, is a Mk III with Armstrong Siddeley Tiger engines.** RIGHT: **RAF Coastal Command operated Whitleys on maritime patrol duties. Initially standard bomber aircraft, such as that pictured, operated in the role. Later the Mk VII, specially equipped with ASV radar, could readily detect enemy vessels below.**

had a retractable ventral "dustbin" turret armed with two 7.7mm/0.303in machine-guns – this version could also carry larger bombs. The final 40 airframes of the second production run were completed as Whitley IVs with the famous Rolls-Royce Merlin engines and an increased fuel capacity.

The Mark V was similar to the Mark IV but replaced the manually operated turret with a Nash and Thompson-powered tail turret with four 7.7mm/0.303in machine-guns. As a result of combat experience, the rear fuselage of this version was also extended by 38cm/15in to improve the rear gunner's field of fire. Other changes included a revised fin shape, the addition of a leading de-icing facility and greater fuel capacity.

The Whitley VII was built specifically to serve with Coastal Command units on maritime reconnaissance duties. The VII was equipped with ASV Mk II radar and can be most readily identified from other versions by the four dorsal radar masts atop the rear fuselage, and numerous aerials carried. This model also differed by having a sixth crew member and extra fuel tankage in the bomb bay and fuselage. Compared to earlier versions with a range of 2011km/1250 miles, this version could reach distances of 3700km/2300 miles.

Earlier Bomber Command versions were phased out of front-line service from 1942, after which they were used as trainers and glider tugs – the aircraft was heavily used for training airborne troops for D-Day. During 1942–3, 15 Whitley Mk Vs were transferred to BOAC and given civil registrations to carry out Gibraltar-to-Malta supply flights. Some Whitleys served in the Fleet Air Arm until 1946 as flying classrooms to instruct on Merlin engine handling and fuel transfer.

ABOVE: **When phased out as bombers, early versions were switched to glider tug and paratroop training, thus playing a part in the success of D-Day.**

Avro Anson

The origins of the Anson lay in the Avro 652 light transport airliner that served with Imperial Airways from March 1935. The 652 had been built to meet an Imperial Airways requirement for an aircraft that could transport four passengers over a series of 676km/ 420 mile journeys at a cruising speed greater than 209kph/130mph. Roy Chadwick, who later worked on Avro's Lancaster and early stages of the Vulcan's design, led the design team to produce what was an innovative aircraft for the time.

The Avro 652 was swiftly adapted to meet a May 1934 Air Ministry requirement for a twin-engine coastal reconnaissance aircraft. The Anson differed from its civil predecessor by having different engines, rectangular, not round, windows and also in having "teeth" in the form of a hand-operated dorsal Armstrong Whitworth turret with a 7.7mm/0.303in Lewis machine-gun. In comparative trials, the Anson was pitted against a military version of the de Havilland Dragon Rapide designed to satisfy the same RAF requirement. The Avro design's greater range and endurance impressed the Air Ministry, and a large order was placed.

The Anson represented a major breakthrough for the Royal Air Force, being the first monoplane in RAF squadron service and also the first to employ the novel retractable undercarriage, even though it was hand-operated.

The prototype first flew in 1935, and Coastal Command's No.48 Squadron at Manston was the first operational Royal Air Force Anson unit. From 1936 until the start of World War II, Ansons served in front-line squadrons of RAF Coastal Command on general reconnaissance and search-and-rescue duties. By the outbreak of war in September 1939, the RAF had 760 Mk Is equipping 10 Coastal and 16 Bomber Command squadrons, where they served as an interim aircraft until other types, such as the Armstrong Whitworth Whitley, Lockheed Hudson and Handley Page Hampden, were available.

The Anson was right in the front line of Britain's defences at the time. On September 5, 1939, an Anson of No.500 Squadron made the first attack of the war on an enemy U-boat. In June 1940, three Ansons, attacked over the Channel by nine Luftwaffe Messerschmitt Bf109s, succeeded in shooting down two and damaging one of the German fighters. Having earned its spurs, the Anson, or "Faithful Annie" as it was nicknamed in RAF service, soon settled down to the more sedate career of a trainer and light transport aircraft, although some remained with Coastal Command in the air-sea rescue role during the war years. The Commonwealth Air Training Plan of 1939 saw almost all British and Commonwealth navigators, air gunners and wireless operators trained on Ansons. Purpose-built Anson trainers had dual controls and trailing edge flaps as well as a hydraulically operated undercarriage.

By the time production ceased in 1952, Avro had made over 8000 Ansons in Britain and a further 2882 in Canada. This was one of the longest production runs of any British aircraft. In addition to the RAF, the type had been operated by 12 other air forces around the world, including those of Australia, Belgium, Estonia, Finland, Egypt and the USA.

After the war, later versions of the Anson were largely used for transport purposes, and in March 1956 the Avro Anson completed 20 years' service with the RAF, rivalling the long service of its company predecessor, the Avro 504 biplane. The official retirement of the Anson from RAF service was on June 28, 1968, when the last six Ansons on the Southern Communications Squadron were withdrawn, setting a record at the time of 32 years in RAF service.

Avro Anson Mk I

First flight: March 24, 1935

Power: Two Armstrong Siddeley 335hp Cheetah IX radials

Armament: One fixed forward-firing 7.7mm/ 0.303in Lewis machine-gun, plus another in dorsal turret; 163kg/360lb bomb load

Size: Wingspan – 17.22m/56ft 6in
Length – 12.87m/42ft 3in
Height – 3.99m/13ft 1in
Wing area – 43.01m²/463sq ft

Weights: Empty – 2440kg/5375lb
Maximum take-off – 3632kg/8000lb

Performance: Maximum speed – 302kph/188mph
Ceiling – 5790m/19,000ft
Range – 1062km/660 miles
Climb – 293m/960ft per minute

Avro Manchester

The twin-engine prototype Manchester, the Avro 679, was flown from Ringway (now Manchester International Airport) with Avro chief test-pilot Sam Brown at the controls for the first time on July 25, 1939. The aircraft had been designed by Avro chief designer Roy Chadwick to Air Ministry Specification P.13/36, which called for a twin-engine bomber powered by the new Rolls-Royce Vulture engine. Handley Page had also entered the competition for this Air Ministry contract with its H.P.56 project, but owing to the slow development of the Vulture engine, the company decided to change its design to a four-engine aircraft using the Rolls-Royce Merlin V-12 engine. Their project was to become the very successful Halifax.

Even though the Vulture development programme had been constantly delayed by numerous problems, Chadwick still kept faith with the troublesome new engine. In January 1940 the Air Ministry placed an order for 1200 Manchester Mk 1s, and the aircraft entered service

with 5 Group Bomber Command in November 1940 as a replacement for the ageing Handley Page Hampden bomber.

The Manchester had an excellent airframe and should have been a good aircraft for Bomber Command, providing an increased bomb load capacity on existing bomber types, greater range and more defensive armament. Unfortunately, the Rolls-Royce Vulture engine was still very unreliable and also downrated on power from the original specification. As a result, the Manchester suffered a loss rate of 5.8 per cent on operational sorties, and many experienced bomber crews were also killed on training flights. This situation resulted in the Rolls-Royce Vulture engine development project being cancelled, and only 209 aircraft were delivered to the RAF bomber squadrons. Of these, 64 were lost on operations and a further 12 on training flights. The Manchester was withdrawn from service, and the last Bomber Command Manchester mission was a raid on Bremen on the night of June 25–6, 1942.

TOP: **The Manchester, a sound design, was plagued by engine problems, but the type was to metamorphose into one of the greatest bombers ever, the Lancaster.**

ABOVE: **The Manchester entered RAF service only 16 months after its maiden flight, such was the urgency to get bomber aircraft to combat units.**

Avro Manchester Mk 1

First flight: July 25, 1939

Power: Two Rolls-Royce 1760hp Vulture 24-cylinder piston engines

Armament: Eight 7.7mm/0.303in Browning machine-guns in power turrets in nose (2), mid-upper (2) and tail (4); internal bomb bay accommodating a maximum load of 4699kg/ 10,350lb

Size: Wingspan – 27.46m/90ft 1in
Length – 21.34m/70ft
Height – 5.94m/19ft 6in
Wing area – 105.63m²/1137sq ft

Weights: Empty – 13,362kg/29,432lb
Maximum take-off – 25,424kg/56,000lb

Performance: Maximum speed – 426kph/265mph
Ceiling – 5795m/19,000ft
Range – 2623km/1630 miles
Climb – Not available

Avro Lancaster

The Avro Lancaster became Great Britain's most famous four-engine bomber during World War II. It was developed from the ill-fated Manchester that suffered from unreliable Rolls-Royce Vulture engines. Even while the Manchester was being produced, the Avro design team, led by Chief Designer Roy Chadwick, investigated a possible four-engine replacement. The proposed four-engine Manchester Mk III, powered by Rolls Royce Merlin XX engines, was discussed with the Air Ministry on February 20, 1940. At first the proposal created little interest because most of the Merlin engine production was needed for Hurricane and Spitfire fighter aircraft. However in July 1940 the Air Ministry requested Avro to go ahead with their project and use as many Manchester components as possible in the new design.

Manchester airframe BT308 was designated project No.683 and fitted with four Rolls-Royce Merlin X engines on extended wings. This prototype model first flew on January 9, 1941 with the Manchester's triple tail fins but without ventral and dorsal turrets.

While the early handling trials were successful, a change in the tail configuration was recommended, and the original type of vertical tail surfaces were replaced by larger endplate surfaces on a wider-span tail-plane with the large central fin deleted. Exhaustive flying tests followed, and the now renamed Lancaster soon revealed its potential with excellent performances. The first production model prototype DG595 flew on May 13, 1941, and was later flown to Boscombe Down for service trials.

TOP: **The Lancaster first flew in combat on March 3, 1942, and was in the front line until the end of World War II. The Lancaster pictured is preserved in the UK by the RAF's Battle of Britain Memorial Flight.**
ABOVE: **This Mk I built by Metropolitan Vickers is being bombed-up prior to a mission.**

On June 6, 1941, Avro received a contract for 454 Lancaster Mk Is powered by four Merlin XX engines, plus two prototype Lancaster Mk IIs fitted with four Bristol Hercules VI engines.

On Christmas Eve, 1941, No.44 (Rhodesia) Squadron based at RAF Waddington in Lincolnshire received the first three production Lancaster Mk Is. The first operation with the Lancaster was carried out on March 3, 1942, when four aircraft of No.44 Squadron were detailed to lay mines in the Heligoland Bight. The Lancasters took off from Waddington at 18:15 hours and all returned safely five hours later.

The early-production Lancasters had a maximum gross take-off weight of 28,602kg/63,000lb and carried a variable bomb load up to a maximum of 6356kg/14,000lb. The bomb load mix depended upon the type of target to be attacked. For example, the bomb load for the demolition of industrial sites by blast and fire was codenamed "Cookie Plumduff" and this consisted of 1 x 1816kg/4000lb, 3 x 454kg/1000lb, plus up to six small bomb carriers loaded with 1.8kg/4lb or 13.62kg/30lb incendiaries. Later, heavier bomb loads would be carried, such as the 3632kg/8000lb Cookie, the 5448kg/12,000lb Tallboy and finally the 9988kg/22,000lb Grand Slam. The defensive armament consisted of a two-gun power turret fitted in the nose and mid-upper position plus a four-gun turret in the tail.

In February 1942 Air Chief Marshal Sir Arthur Harris became head of Bomber Command and prioritized the production of four-engine aircraft for his bomber force. Manufacturing capacity was increased by Avro but Rolls-Royce became concerned that they would not be able to satisfy the ever-increasing demand for the Merlin engines. This situation had been foreseen, and one alternative was to use a different engine – the Lancaster Mk II using the Bristol Hercules was already in the pipeline with an order for 300 placed with Armstrong Whitworth. The second solution was for the Packard Motor Corporation to manufacture the Merlin engine in the USA.

The first Lancaster Mk III powered by the Packard Merlin 28s came off the Avro production lines in August 1942. Although the Packard Merlin-powered Lancaster had almost identical performance to the Mk I, it was given the new designation because of different servicing requirements. The Packard Corporation also shipped Merlins over the Canadian border where the Victory Aircraft Company built 430 Lancaster Mk X aircraft.

With the deployment of the Mk III, a total of 7377 Lancasters were built between October 1941 and October 1945, equipping 57 RAF Bomber Command Squadrons by the end of World War II.

ABOVE: **The Lancaster was the only RAF aircraft able to carry Bomber Command's specialist ordnance such as Tallboy and Grand Slam bombs, as well as the famous "bouncing bomb".** BELOW: **The very large bomb bay of the Lancaster (the bomb bay doors are open in this photograph) enabled it to carry up to 6356kg/14,000lb of bombs. RAF Lancasters were not phased out until December 1953.**

ABOVE: **Post-war, the Lancaster was supplied to the French Navy who used the aircraft for maritime reconnaissance, as did the Royal Canadian Air Force who converted a number of Canadian-built "Lancs" for the same purpose.**

Avro Lancaster Mk I

First flight: January 9, 1941

Power: Four Rolls Royce or Packard 1460hp Merlin XX, 20 or 22s

Armament: Nose and dorsal turrets with two 7.7mm/0.303in Brownings, tail turret with four 7.7mm/0.303in Brownings; normal bomb load 6356kg/14,000lb or 9988kg/22,000lb single bomb with modifications to bomb bay

Size: Wingspan – 31.1m/102ft
Length – 21.1m/69ft 4in
Height – 5.97m/19ft 7in
Wing area – 120.45m²/1297sq ft

Weights: Empty – 16,344kg/36,000lb
Maximum take-off – 30,872kg/68,000lb

Performance: Maximum speed – 443kph/275mph at 4572m/15,000ft
Cruising speed – 322kph/200mph at 4572m/15,000ft
Service ceiling – 6706m/22,000ft
Range – 4072km/2530 miles
Climb – 6096m/20,000ft in 41 minutes, 36 seconds

Boeing B-17 Flying Fortress

In 1934 the United States Army issued a specification for a long-range, high-altitude daylight bomber for its Air Corps. The Boeing Aircraft Company responded with a prototype designated Model 299, powered by four 750hp Pratt & Whitney Hornet engines, which flew for the first time on July 28, 1935. Even though the prototype was destroyed in an accident, the project went ahead, and 13 Y1B-17s and one Y1B-17A were ordered for evaluation. After extensive trials these were designated B-17 and B-17A respectively. By the end of March 1940, the first production batch of 39 B-17Bs was delivered to the Army Air Corps, sporting a modified nose and enlarged rudder. Meanwhile, owing to the expansion of the Air Corps, a further order for 38 B-17Cs was placed. These aircraft were powered by four Wright 1200hp Cyclone engines and also featured other minor internal changes. In 1941, 20 of the B-17Cs were transferred to the RAF in England and designated Fortress Is for evaluation under combat conditions against the new generation of fast German day fighters. While the sleek four-engine all-metal Flying Fortress monoplane was unquestionably the most advanced heavy bomber in 1935, it failed with the RAF under high-altitude daylight bombing conditions by sustaining several losses, not only through enemy action but also because of mechanical and system failure.

Unfortunately for Boeing, by 1941 the B-17 had become outclassed in many respects by the new generation of medium and heavy bombers of Britain and Germany and, more importantly, that of another US aircraft company, Consolidated, whose four-engine B-24 Liberator had greater range, could carry a heavier bomb load and had better defensive armament. To retrieve the design from the verge of obsolescence, Boeing

ABOVE: **A fine air-to-air study of two B-17s preserved in flying condition in the USA. The B-17 first saw action in Europe with the Royal Air Force, who tested early models operationally. The trial was not successful because the once-advanced B-17 design had been overtaken by fighter developments.**

designed a new rear end for the aircraft. The fuselage was lengthened by 1.8m/6ft and deepened towards the rear to incorporate a tail gun position with two machine-guns projecting from the end of the fuselage. These were traversed manually and were aimed with a remote sight from the rear gunner's glazed cabin. A Sperry two-gun power turret sited in the upper fuselage aft of the pilot's cabin gave a field of fire from the horizontal plane to an all-round 75-degree elevation.

Also replacing the original under-gun emplacement just aft of the wing root came a semi-retractable rotating ball turret housing two machine-guns. In addition to the new defensive gun positions, both the hand-held guns firing through the waist openings were retained, plus the one in the radio operator's cabin. The nose armament, a single rifle-calibre machine-gun, remained unchanged, whereas all other weapons were of the larger 12.7mm/0.5in calibre, with greater range and hitting power. With this new ten-gun defensive system, the B-17E truly was a Flying Fortress.

The B-17E, with a crew of ten, was the first Flying Fortress type to see combat in the European Theatre of Operations with the US Army Air Corps. However, one defensive weakness still remained, and that was against head-on attack by high-performance German fighters armed with 20mm/0.78in cannon. A total of 512 B-17Es were built, and after further refinements the F-series entered production in April 1942.

RIGHT: **These preserved Flying Fortresses fly in formation reminiscent of the defensive boxes in which Eighth Air Force B-17s flew for their mutual protection during dangerous daylight missions.**

Over the next 18 months, 3400 B-17Fs were produced, including 61 long-range reconnaissance aircraft designated F-9s, plus another 19 delivered to RAF Coastal Command as the Fortress II.

The last production run of 86 B-17Fs were fitted with a chin-mounted power-operated Bendix turret, housing a pair of 12.7mm/0.5in machine-guns, which provided the extra fire power to help stave off the Luftwaffe frontal fighter attacks. The Bendix chin turret became a standard production item, and the type was designated B-17G. This variant started to enter service with the US Bombardment Groups in the autumn of 1943 and became the main production type, with 8680 aircraft built by the end of hostilities in Europe. Another 85 B-17Gs served with RAF Coastal Command as Fortress IIIs.

During World War II USAAF B17 Flying Fortresses flew 294,875 sorties to targets all over Europe, dropping 650,240 tonnes/640,000 tons of bombs at a cost of 4483 aircraft missing in action, plus other operational losses of 861.

RIGHT: **The B-17G model introduced the Bendix chin turret mounting two 12.7mm/0.5in machine-guns for defence against head-on attacks.**
BELOW: **Immortalized by the wartime propaganda film "Memphis Belle", many of the world's surviving B-17s – including the aircraft pictured here – came together for the filming of the 1990 blockbuster of the same name.**

Boeing B-17G Flying Fortress

First flight: July 28, 1935
Power: Four Wright 1200hp Cyclone R-1820-97 radial piston engines
Armament: Twin 12.7mm/0.5in machine-guns under nose, aft of cockpit, under centre fuselage and in tail, and single-gun mountings in side of nose, in radio operator's hatch and two waist positions; maximum bomb load 7990kg/ 17,600lb
Size: Wingspan – 31.62m/103ft 9in
Length – 22.78m/74ft 9in
Height – 5.82m/19ft 1in
Wing area – 131.92m²/1420sq ft
Weights: Empty – 13,488kg/29,710lb
Maximum take-off – 29,737kg/65,500lb
Performance: Maximum speed – 462kph/287mph
Ceiling – 10,920m/35,800ft
Range – 3220km/2000 miles
Climb – 427m/1400ft per minute

Boeing B-29 Superfortress

The B-29 Superfortress, the most advanced bomber produced during World War II, was the result of Boeing's reaction to specification XC-218, which called for a bomber with a range in excess of 8045km/5000 miles that could carry a bigger bomb load at a higher speed than the B-17B. Fortunately for Boeing, design work had been carried out on their next generation of heavy bombers over the preceding two years, and a full-scale mock-up of model 341 had been produced. This was remarkably close to specification XC-218, and so with a small amount of re-work, Boeing were able to submit their design. Three prototypes were ordered, and the first XB-29 flew on September 21, 1942. Meanwhile, a priority order for 1500 aircraft had been placed with Boeing following the Japanese attack on Pearl Harbor. The first YB-29 evaluation aircraft was delivered to the 58th Bombardment Wing in July 1943 and was followed three months later by the first batch of B-29-BW production aircraft. The Superfortress had many advanced features, including remotely controlled gun turrets and a partly pressurized fuselage.

RIGHT: **The B-29 was not used in Europe during World War II, instead being limited to the Pacific theatre.** BELOW: **The B-29 was a major technological leap forward for the USAAF, bringing huge increases in performance with it.**

At the end of 1943 the decision was made to use only the B-29 against the Japanese in the Pacific theatre. In the spring of 1944 the two fully equipped bombardment wings were deployed to bases in India and south-west China. The first bombing mission was flown on June 5 against Japanese targets in Thailand, and was followed a few days later by raids against the Japanese mainland. With the establishment of five air bases on the Mariana Islands in March 1944, the B-29 bombardment wings were able to mount a sustained bombing campaign against mainland Japan. It was from one of these bases in August 1945 that B-29 *Enola Gay* dropped the first atomic bomb on the city of Hiroshima, followed three days later by B-29 *Bockscar* dropping a second on Nagasaki. The Boeing bomber played a vital role in the defeat of Japan, who surrendered on August 14, five days after the Nagasaki raid.

Boeing B-29 Superfortress

First flight: September 21, 1942

Power: Four Wright 2200hp R-3350-57 radial engines

Armament: Four-gun turret over nose, two-gun turrets under nose, over and under rear fuselage, all with machine-guns of 12.7mm/0.5in calibre, plus one 20mm/0.78in and two 12.7mm/0.5in guns in tail; up to 9080kg/20,000lb bomb load

Size: Wingspan – 43.05m/141ft 3in
Length – 30.18m/99ft
Height – 9.01m/29ft 7in
Wing area – 161.27m²/1736sq ft

Weights: Empty – 31,843kg/70,140lb
Maximum take-off – 56,296kg/124,000lb

Performance: Maximum speed – 576kph/358mph
Ceiling – 9695m/31,800ft
Range – 5229km/3250 miles
Climb – 7625m/25,000ft in 43 minutes

ABOVE: **The B-29's performance and large bomb load made it the only choice for the delivery of the atomic bombs to Japan.** RIGHT: **The B-29 was used extensively during the Korean War, initially in support of ground troops but then more appropriately as a strategic bomber. Back in the USA, the Superfortress was the main aircraft of the fledgling Strategic Air Command.** BELOW: **The Soviet copy of the B-29, the Tu-4, influenced Soviet bomber design for years after they "acquired" it at the end of World War II.**

The B-29 may be famous or infamous for the atomic bomb raids, but the many conventional, largely incendiary, bombing raids carried out by the Superfortresses against Japan ultimately destroyed the centres of a number of large Japanese cities.

After the war, the B-29 became the mainstay of the newly formed USAF Strategic Air Command, and later saw continuous action during the three-year Korean War. Initially used in a tactical bomber role to halt the North Korean ground advance, the USAF B-29s were soon deployed in the role for which they were made – strategic bombing. Operating from bases in Japan, raids were carried out against industrial targets in North Korea.

The basic B-29 design underwent a number of modifications over the years. These variants included the SB-29 for air-sea rescue, the TB-29 trainer and the WB-29

tanker. The Royal Air Force operated the aircraft as the Washington, with 88 ex-USAF examples in service from 1950. Most were returned to the USA in 1954, but some remained in Bomber Command service until 1958.

The Soviet Union managed to produce a copy of the B-29, which was named the Tu-4 in Soviet service. These unlicensed copies were based on US aircraft which fell into Soviet hands at the end of World War II. In a programme unparalleled in ingenuity and audacity, the Soviet Union ultimately produced over 300 of their version. The Soviet Union's post-war atomic bomber fleet was therefore directly related to the three US B-29s which had originally made emergency landings on Soviet territory following bombing missions over Japan. America had given the Soviet Union the aircraft that could have been turned on the USA.

LEFT: **The Bre.14 replaced older types in front-line service from mid-1917. The type often attacked deep behind enemy lines.**

Breguet Bre.14

The prototype of this highly advanced two-seat light-bomber biplane made its first flight in November 1916, only six months after Breguet's chief engineer Louis Vuillierme began the design. The pilot was Louis Breguet, such was the significance and advanced nature of the aircraft. It was revolutionary for a French combat aircraft, having its engine and propeller at the front and, perhaps most impressively, it was made principally of lightweight Duralumin.

The Bre.14 A.2 production aircraft entered service with the Aeronautique Militaire in the spring of 1917 on the Western Front, and soon established a reputation among French aircrew for being robust and reliable. The principal bomber version used by France's strategic bomber force during World War I was the Bre.14 B.2.

By the end of World War I, orders for nearly 5500 Bre.14s had been placed with the Breguet aircraft manufacturing

company. The aircraft had been so successful after its introduction during the war that by the time the production line closed down in 1926, the total number of aircraft manufactured had reached 8000.

Post-war, it served in a number of roles such as light transport and air ambulance, and the type also pioneered mail routes in French equatorial Africa.

Breguet Bre.14

First flight: November 21, 1916
Power: One Renault 300hp 12F in-line engine
Armament: One fixed forward-firing 7.7mm/0.303in machine-gun, twin 7.7mm/0.303in Lewis machine-guns on mounting in rear cockpit; underwing racks for up to 40kg/88lb bomb load
Size: Wingspan – 14.36m/47ft 1in
　　　　Length – 8.87m/29ft 1in
　　　　Height – 3.3m/10ft 10in
　　　　Wing area – 47.5m²/511.3sq ft
Weights: Empty – 1030kg/2271lb
　　　　　Maximum take-off – 1565kg/3450lb
Performance: Maximum speed – 184kph/114mph
　　　　　　Ceiling – 6000m/18,290ft
　　　　　　Range – 700km/435 miles
　　　　　　Climb – 5000m/16,400ft in 39 minutes

LEFT: **The Bre.19 was well used by Spain in the 1920s and early '30s.**

Breguet Bre.19 A.2

First flight: May 1922
Power: One Lorraine 450hp 12Ed in-line piston engine
Armament: One fixed forward-firing 7.7mm/0.303in machine-gun and two more in rear cockpit; 700kg/1543lb bomb load under wings
Size: Wingspan – 14.83m/48ft 7.75in
　　　　Length – 9.61m/31ft 6.25in
　　　　Height – 3.69m/12ft 1.25in
　　　　Wing area – 50m²/538.31sq ft
Weights: Empty – 1387kg/3058lb
　　　　　Maximum take-off – 2500kg/5511lb
Performance: Maximum speed – 214kph/133mph
　　　　　　Ceiling – 7200m/23,620ft
　　　　　　Range – 800km/497 miles
　　　　　　Climb – 5000m/16,405ft in 29 minutes, 50 seconds

Breguet Bre.19

This aircraft, which had substantial amounts of aluminium alloy in its structure at an early stage in aircraft design, was built as a reconnaissance/bomber successor to Breguet's Bre.14 of World War I. It flew for the first time in March 1922 and, as a measure of progress, weighed the same as its Breguet predecessor but could carry a payload that was up to 80 per cent greater.

The Breguet company were excellent publicists and had the Bre.19 set countless world records to prove what an effective combat aircraft it was. As a result, in addition to use by the French, the aircraft was widely exported and was operated by nine other air forces. Licence-built versions were produced in Turkey, Belgium, Yugoslavia, Greece, Japan and Spain. Both sides of the

Spanish Civil War used the Bre.19 and the Chinese used the type against the Japanese in Manchuria. Greek Bre.19s were used against invading Italians in October 1940.

Breguet 691/693

The Breguet 690 series of military aircraft stemmed from a 1934 specification for a three-seat heavy fighter, which led to the Bre.690. The prototype twin-engine fighter's performance so impressed that, with war clouds gathering, the Bre.691 light attack variant (with Hispano-Suiza engines), which first flew in 1937, was swiftly put into production. This differed from the fighter version in having a bomb bay in which to carry 400kg/880lb of bombs. One hundred examples of the light bomber were ordered, but before they were all built, a new and improved version, the 693 powered by Gnome-Rhone engines, had appeared. The Bre.695 had American Pratt & Whitney Twin Wasp Junior engines. By the Fall of France, almost three hundred examples of all marks had made it to front-line units. Two French Air Force Groups GBA I/54 and II/54 were first to become fully equipped with the Bre.693. The type made its operational debut on May 12, 1940, attacking advancing German troop columns. Ten of the eleven 693s sent on the mission were destroyed. The crews battled on in spite of the overwhelming and more capable opposition, but

suffered heavy losses against the superior German single-engine fighters. By June 24, 1940, almost half of the Bre.693s in service were lost in the course of over 500 sorties in defence of their country.

The Vichy air force took over the remaining machines, and many of these were in turn seized by the Luftwaffe, who stripped the engines out to power some of their own aircraft. A number were passed on to Italy, who used the aircraft for operational training from 1942–3.

Breguet Bre.693 AB2

First flight: October 25, 1939
Power: Two 700hp Gnome-Rhone 14M Mars 14-cylinder radial engines
Armament: One 20mm/0.78in cannon and two 7.5mm/0.29in fixed forward-firing machine-guns, three 7.5mm/0.29in machine-guns fixed and obliquely rearward firing, plus one trainable; internal bomb load of 400kg/880lb
Size: Wingspan – 15.36m/50ft 5in
Length – 9.67m/31ft 8in
Height – 3.19m/10ft 5in
Wing area – 28.8m²/310sq ft
Weights: Empty – 3010kg/6625lb
Maximum take-off – 5500kg/12,105lb
Performance: Maximum speed – 475kph/295mph
Service ceiling – 8500m/27,885ft
Range – 1350km/839 miles
Climb – 4000m/13,120ft in 7 minutes, 12 seconds

ABOVE, LEFT AND BELOW: **The Bre.690 fighter from which the bomber variants were developed. The ground-attack version had different engines and a bomb bay. Breguet pilots fought bravely against invading German forces, but were swiftly overwhelmed.**

Bristol Blenheim

When the Bristol Blenheim bomber entered RAF service in 1937, it represented a huge leap forward for the service – the Mk I Blenheim was considerably faster than the 290kph/ 180mph Hind biplane it replaced and could outrun most contemporary fighters, many of which were biplanes. Initially developed as the Type 142, a fast eight-seat passenger plane, the aircraft that became the three-seat Bristol Blenheim bomber flew for the first time in April 1935. Britain First was the name given to the Type 142, which had been ordered by newspaper tycoon Lord Rothermere, who wanted a fast executive transport.

In August 1935 the Air Ministry issued Specification B28/35 covering the conversion of the aircraft to the bomber role, and this was designated Type 142M.

Major modifications followed, including raising the wing from a low to a mid-wing position to allow room for the internal bomb bay. The nose section was also redesigned to accommodate both pilot and observer/bomb-aimer. The third member of the crew was a mid-upper gunner, who was housed in a power-operated dorsal turret with a 7.7mm/ 0.303in Lewis machine-gun. The pilot could also fire a Browning 7.7mm/0.303in, which was installed in the port wing leading edge.

The Air Ministry placed an initial order for 150 Blenheim Mk Is in September 1935. This was followed with a second order in December 1936 for another 434 aircraft, after a series of successful trials. In March of the following year,

TOP: **Considered to be something of a forgotten bomber, the Blenheim gave the Royal Air Force a bomber aircraft with a performance that was superior to many fighters of the time.** ABOVE: **Over 1000 Blenheims were in service when war broke out, and it was a No.139 Squadron Blenheim that was first to fly over Germany on September 3, 1939.**

Wyton-based No.114 (Hong Kong) Squadron of 2 Group Bomber Command became the first RAF squadron to be equipped with the Blenheim Mk I. A total of 1134 Mk Is were built, with 1007 being on RAF charge by August 1939. This hot-rod bomber brought much interest from overseas customers, and export versions were supplied to Greece, Finland, Turkey, Romania, Lithuania and Yugoslavia.

By the start of World War II, the Mark I had been largely replaced by the Mark IV in UK-based RAF bomber units. The Blenheim Mk IV was basically a Mk I airframe with two Bristol Mercury XV radial engines fitted with de Havilland three-blade variable-pitch propellers. It also had a redesigned and enlarged nose and extra internal fuel tanks.

At the outbreak of war in September 1939, Royal Air Force bomber squadrons had 197 Blenheim Mk IVs on strength. On September 3, a Blenheim IV of Wyton-based No.139 Squadron became the first RAF aircraft of World War II to cross the German border, while flying a reconnaissance mission. On the next day, Blenheims of Nos.107 and 110 Squadrons took part in the RAF's first offensive operation of the war, when they unsuccessfully attacked German naval units in the Elbe Estuary. While at least three bombs struck the pocket Battleship *Admiral Scheer*, they failed to explode. No.107 Squadron lost four of its five aircraft on the raid, and these were Bomber Command's first casualties of World War II.

The defensive shortcomings of the Blenheim soon became apparent when the type suffered heavy losses while taking part in anti-shipping operations in the North Sea. The armament was subsequently increased to five machine-guns. In all, 1930 Mk IVs were built in the UK. Most of No.2 Group Blenheims were replaced in 1941 by the Douglas Boston and the de Havilland Mosquito.

The final British-built version of the Blenheim was the Mk V. Over 940 were built, the majority being the VD tropical variant. These were shipped out to North Africa to support the Eighth Army in the Western Desert but again, the Blenheims suffered appalling combat losses against the Messerschmitt Bf109s and were soon replaced by US-supplied Baltimores and Venturas.

In Canada, the Fairchild Aircraft Company built 676 Blenheims for the Royal Canadian Air Force, and these versions were designated the Bolingbroke Mk I to Mk IV. Finland operated the Blenheim until 1956.

RIGHT: **Blenheim IVs manned by Free French crews saw considerable action in North Africa.** BELOW: **The Blenheim was a versatile aircraft that achieved combat success in the day- and nightfighter as well as the bomber role. The aircraft pictured here is a Mark I nightfighter from RAF Squadron No.141.**

ABOVE: **This No.110 Squadron Blenheim IV sustained damage in air combat, and had to be patched before its next mission.**

Blenheim Mk I

First flight: June 25, 1936

Power: Two Bristol 920hp Mercury XV radial engines

Armament: One 7.7mm/0.303in Browning machine-gun in leading edge of port wing, one 7.7mm/0.303in Vickers machine-gun in dorsal turret; maximum internal bomb load of 454kg/1000lb

Size: Wingspan – 17.7m/58ft 1in
Length – 12.11m/39ft 9in
Height – 3m/9ft 10in
Wing area – 43.57m²/469sq ft

Weights: Empty – 3677kg/8100lb
Maximum take-off – 5675kg/12,500lb

Performance: Maximum speed – 428kph/266mph
Service ceiling – 8320m/27,280ft
Range – 1810km/1125 miles
Climb – 469m/1540ft per minute

Bristol Beaufighter

The Beaufighter came about when the Bristol company simply proposed a versatile, heavily armed aircraft that they thought the Royal Air Force needed. Using major elements of the Beaufort torpedo bomber already in production, the two-seat Beaufighter was produced quickly and joined front-line squadrons at the height of the Battle of Britain in 1940, only 13 months after the prototype first flew. Day fighter versions saw action in the Western Desert and Malta, while RAF Coastal Command also used the "Beau" to great effect, particularly over the Bay of Biscay against Junkers Ju 88s.

The development of combat aircraft relies entirely on the engines available to power the aeroplanes, and it was the improvements to the Bristol Hercules that led to the Beaufighter's development in a host of different roles. More power allowed designers to add more weight to the aircraft in the form of new weaponry, equipment, armour or fuel.

There were two significant Beaufighter developments in 1942 – a trial torpedo installation succeeded, and the type was experimentally and successfully armed with rocket projectiles.

By late 1942, Mk VICs were being completed with torpedo-carrying gear. The Beaufighter was now able to carry and launch a large torpedo (the British 45.7cm/18in or the US 57.2cm/22.5in) against shipping, and the first "Torbeau" unit

TOP: **The Beaufighter T.F. Mk X was a purpose-designed torpedo-carrying version that saw considerable RAF Coastal Command service.**

ABOVE: **T.F. Xs of No.404 Squadron RCAF, which formed part of the Banff Strike Wing in Scotland, carrying out sweeps against enemy shipping in the North Sea.**

was No.254 Squadron based at North Coates. Equipped with Mk VIC torpedo-fighters, the squadron first attacked enemy shipping with the new weapon on April 18, 1943. The Beaufort was soon phased out in favour of the new-found British torpedo-bomber.

The VIC was gradually replaced in Coastal Command service by a new purpose-designed torpedo-bomber version, the Beaufighter T.F. Mk X. This dedicated torpedo-bomber, powered by 1770hp Hercules XVII engines, was probably the best British anti-shipping aircraft in service in the later stages of World War II. The Hercules Mk XVII was developed to optimize the Beaufighter for low-level missions, and achieved peak power at just 152m/500ft. Dive brakes were also soon introduced as an aid in low-level attacks. The Mk X was the main production variant of the Beaufighter, with over 2200 produced. Normally flying with a crew of two, a third crew member could be carried to assist with torpedo-aiming. Using special equipment including a radio altimeter, the Beaufighter could make precision low-level, wave-top height attacks with torpedoes or rockets. Mk Xs ultimately carried the A.I. Mk VIII radar, adapted for use against surface targets, housed in the tell-tale "thimble-nose" radome. The Beaufighter X was an extremely effective anti-shipping aircraft, scouring the waters around Britain for German shipping. In March 1945, aircraft of Nos.236 and 254 Squadrons sank five German U-boats in just two days.

Beaufighters were also heavily used by Australian units on anti-shipping missions. Australia produced their own Beaufighter Xs, some 364 in total, which were known as T.F. Mk 21s. Powered by the Hercules XVIII, the T.F.21s entered service in 1944 and played a key role in the Royal Australian Air Force's support for the Allied advance into the East Indies. These Beaufighters' high-speed, low-level attacks caused the Japanese to nickname them "Whispering Death".

Post-war, a number of Beaufighters remained in RAF service, mainly in the Far East where they retired from front-line duties in 1950. Thirty-five RAF Beaufighters were converted for use as target tugs. Designated T.T.10, these aircraft served in the UK, Middle East and Far East until 1960.

ABOVE RIGHT: **The Beaufighter was originally conceived as a multi-role aircraft, and fighter versions, like the IIF pictured, appeared during the Battle of Britain.** RIGHT AND BELOW: **When the Beaufighter was equipped for carrying a torpedo later in the war, it became the best British anti-shipping aircraft of the time. Note the four cannon on the underside of the nose.**

Bristol Beaufighter T.F. Mk X

First flight: July 17, 1939
Power: Two Bristol 1770hp Hercules XVII 14-cylinder air-cooled radials
Armament: Four 20mm/0.78in cannon, six 7.7mm/ 0.303in machine-guns, one 7.7mm /0.303in machine-gun in dorsal position; one 726kg/ 1600lb or 965kg/2127lb torpedo, two 227kg/ 500lb bombs, eight 76.2mm/3in rocket projectiles
Size: Wingspan – 17.63m/57ft 10in
Length – 12.7m/41ft 8in
Height – 4.82m/15ft 10in
Wing area – 46.73m²/503sq ft
Weights: Empty – 7082kg/15,600lb
Maximum take-off – 11,440kg/25,200lb
Performance: Maximum speed – 512kph/318mph
Service ceiling – 4572m/15,000ft
Range – 2366km/1470 miles
Climb – 1524m/5000ft in 3 minutes, 30 seconds

LEFT: **A Beaufort I of No.217 Squadron RAF. With its raised "upper deck", the type is one of the easiest to identify.**

Bristol Beaufort

Bristol Beaufort I

First flight: October 15, 1938

Power: Two Bristol 1113hp Taurus VI 14-cylinder radial engines

Armament: Two 7.7mm/0.303in Vickers K guns in dorsal turret and one in port wing, plus one rearward-firing 7.7mm/0.303in Browning machine-gun under nose; up to 454kg/1000lb of bombs internally and 227kg/500lb externally, or one 728kg/1605lb torpedo semi-recessed

Size: Wingspan – 17.62m/57ft 10in

Length – 13.59m/44ft 7in

Height – 3.79m/12ft 5in

Wing area – 46.73m²/503sq ft

Weights: Empty – 5950kg/13,107lb

Maximum take-off – 9637kg/21,228lb

Performance: Maximum speed – 426kph/265mph

Ceiling – 5032m/16,500ft

Range – 2575km/1600 miles

Climb – 564m/1850ft per minute

Derived from the Bristol Blenheim, the Beaufort was the Royal Air Force's standard torpedo bomber from 1940–3. The Bristol Aeroplane Company started design work in 1935, and the twin Mercury engine prototype made its first flight in October 1938. However, because the Air Staff insisted on a four-man crew which increased the all-up weight, the aircraft's performance proved to be inadequate. After studying a number of engine options, it was decided to use the 1130hp Bristol Taurus engine. Extensive trials followed, and the Beaufort Mk I went into service with RAF Coastal Command in 1939. Nos.22 and 42 Squadrons became fully operational with the Mk I Beaufort in August 1940, carrying out mine-laying and attacks against shipping off the French and Dutch coast. On April 6, 1941, both these squadrons attacked and seriously damaged the German battlecruiser *Gneisenau* in Brest Harbour. For his actions during the raid, Flying Officer Kenneth Campbell of No.22 Squadron was posthumously awarded the VC.

In 1939, plans were made to manufacture the Beaufort in Australia to serve with the RAAF in the south-west Pacific. However, because of the difficulty of supplying the Taurus engine from Britain, locally made Pratt & Whitney Twin Wasp engines were fitted.

A total of 2080 Beauforts were built, including the 700 made in Australia.

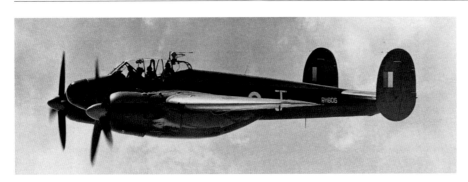

LEFT: **This Mark B.1 Brigand was converted to T.4 standard for training.**

Bristol Brigand

Bristol Brigand B.1

First flight: December 4, 1944

Power: Two Bristol 2810hp Centaurus 57 radial engines

Armament: Four 20mm/0.78in cannon; up to 907kg/2000lb of bombs, rockets or a torpedo

Size: Wingspan – 21.9m/71ft 10in

Length – 14.15m/46ft 5in

Height – 5.33m/17ft 6in

Wing area – 66.7m²/718sq ft

Weights: Empty – 11,622kg/25,600lb

Maximum take-off – 17,706kg/39,000lb

Performance: Maximum speed – 576kph/358mph

Service ceiling – 7930m/26,000ft

Range – 4506km/2800 miles

Climb – 456m/1500ft per minute

The robust Brigand, unpopular with some crews, was the last twin-piston-engine bomber to serve in the Royal Air Force. Originally designed as a long-range torpedo bomber to replace the Beaufighter, the Brigand had the wings and tail of Bristol's unsuccessful Buckingham bomber just as the Beaufighter had those of the Beaufort. In addition, it retained the Buckingham's twin Centaurus engines.

The aircraft first flew in December 1944, and although some were made as torpedo bombers, the type was mainly built as a light bomber for use in tropical climates to better suit the needs of the post-war RAF.

The Brigand light bomber first entered RAF service in early 1949 in Iraq, but the type is best known for its four years of bombing and rocket firing action against terrorists in Malaya from 1950–4.

However, Brigands were also used against the Mau Mau in Kenya. The RAF took delivery of 143 Brigands, a small number of which served in weather reconnaissance and radar training.

LEFT: **A Ca.133T transport version of the very useful type.**

Caproni Ca.133

Caproni Ca.133

First flight: 1935
Power: Three Piaggio 460hp Stella P VII C16 radial piston engines
Armament: Four 7.7mm/0.303in machine-guns in dorsal and ventral turrets and waist positions; up to 500kg/1100lb bomb load
Size: Wingspan – 21.24m/68ft 8in
Length – 15.36m/50ft 4.75in
Height – 4m/13ft 1in
Wing area – 65m²/699.65sq ft
Weights: Empty – 4194kg/9240lb
Maximum take-off – 6691kg/14,740lb
Performance: Maximum speed – 265kph/165mph
Service ceiling – 5500m/18,044ft
Range – 1350km/838 miles
Climb – 286m/940ft per minute

The three-engine Caproni Ca.133 was developed from the Ca.101 bomber/transport series of aircraft. Three engines, relatively low weight and a large wing meant the aircraft could operate from short and primitive airstrips. Over 500 aircraft were built, and the type was first used in action by the Italians in Ethiopia in 1936. During the Spanish Civil War the Nationalists operated ten of the bombers, while the Italians used the type as a paratroop aircraft for their 1939 invasion of Albania.

The Ca.133 was numerically an important aircraft for the Italians when that nation joined World War II in 1940. Fourteen bomber squadrons were equipped by the type, principally protecting Italy's African interests, but if caught by enemy fighters, these aircraft were easy prey. When the aircraft were obsolete as bombers, many served as ambulances as well as transports. The Ca.148 18-passenger transport was developed from the Ca.133, and served the Italian Air Force after the war.

This short take-off and landing aircraft was a workhorse. Even though the British RAF fighter squadrons in the Libyan western desert considered the Caproni Ca.133 to be easy prey, the aircraft continued to provide a valuable service to the Italian armed forces as a bomber, troop carrier and ambulance right up to the Italian surrender in 1943.

LEFT: **Photographed in November 1930, a Ca.135bis, the version that was exported to Hungary.**

Caproni Ca.135

First flight: April 1, 1935
Power: Two Piaggio 1,000hp P.XI RC40 14-cylinder radial piston engines
Armament: One 12.7mm/0.5in machine-gun in nose and dorsal turret and one in ventral position; bomb load of 1600kg/3527lb carried internally or beneath wings
Size: Wingspan – 18.80m/61ft 8in
Length – 14.40m/47ft 2in
Height – 3.40m/11ft 1in
Wing area – 60m²/645.84sq ft
Weights: Empty – 6106kg/13,450lb
Maximum take-off – 9556kg/21,050lb
Performance: Maximum speed – 440kph/273mph
Service ceiling – 7000m/22,965ft
Range – 2000km/1240 miles
Climb – 4000m/13,120ft in 13 minutes, 20 seconds

Caproni Ca.135

The Caproni Ca.135 was designed to meet a Regia Aeronautica fast medium-bomber specification, and flew in prototype form in 1935. This aircraft was a case of the old meeting the new as it was a monoplane but with wooden wings and a fuselage covered with metal at the front and fabric to the rear.

Ultimately, the type was never bought for the Italian Air Force and was only produced for export. Peru was an early customer and had 32 examples while Hungary purchased 180 Ca.135s for its Air Force in 1937, and used them against the Soviet Union. However, once the aircraft had entered service, it soon

became obvious that the Ca.135 was not a great aircraft, and the type was soon relegated to training and transport duties.

65

Consolidated B-24 Liberator

With the growing possibility of war erupting in Europe, in 1939 the US Army Air Corps expressed an interest in the Consolidated Aircraft Corporation's ideas for a new four-engine, long-range, high-flying heavy bomber. As a result, a contract for one prototype was placed with the Company in March 1939, and the aircraft was designated the XB-24. The flying surfaces that were the bases of the XB-24 design had been proven in the 1930s with Consolidated's PBY flying boat. The prototype construction advanced quickly over the next few months, and the aircraft took off on its maiden flight from Lindbergh Field, California, on December 29, 1939. It was powered by four 1200hp Pratt & Whitney R-1830-33 radial engines and could carry 3632kg/8000lb of bombs in its capacious fuselage. For defensive armament it had six hand-operated 7.7mm/0.303in Browning machine-guns. The B-24 was the first American heavy bomber with a tricycle undercarriage.

Seven pre-production YB-24 aircraft, ordered for US Army Air Corps evaluation, were soon coming off the San Diego assembly line in early 1941. These aircraft were re-designated XB-24Bs because they were fitted with Pratt & Whitney 1200hp R-1830-41 engines and General Electric B-2 turbo superchargers for high-altitude flight. Other modifications included an increase to the tail span of 0.6m/2ft. The first nine production B-24A Liberators were delivered to the USAAC in May 1941. These were quickly followed by a further development batch of nine aircraft designated B-24Cs, which differed from earlier versions by having three power turrets.

TOP: **Often overshadowed by the B-17, the B-24 was in fact produced in greater numbers than any other bomber ever.** ABOVE: **Liberator IIIs (B-24Ds) stationed at Aldergrove in Northern Ireland, April 1943. Note the aerials fixed to the port wing and nose.**

Further modifications followed before the first main production model, the B-24D, started to be delivered to the various Army Air Corps Bombardment Groups. This variant had a take-off weight increased to 25,424kg/56,000lb and was powered by Pratt & Whitney R-1830-43 engines, giving a top speed of 487kph/303mph at 7625m/25,000ft. Armament was now ten 12.7mm/0.50in machine-guns and a bomb load of 3995kg/8800lb. Range was also increased by 1046km/650 miles, giving a total range of 4586km/2850 miles.

Consolidated B-24D Liberator

First flight: December 29, 1939

Power: Four Pratt & Whitney 1200hp R-1830-65 radial engines

Armament: Two gun turrets in nose, tail, upper fuselage aft of cockpit and under centre fuselage, and single manual guns in waist (beam) positions, totalling 10 12.7mm/0.5in machine-guns; normal bomb load of 3995kg/8800lb

Size: Wingspan – 33.35m/110ft
Length – 20.47m/67ft 2in
Height – 5.49m/18ft
Wing area – 97.36m²/1048sq ft

Weights: Empty – 15,436kg/34,000lb
Maximum take-off – 29,510kg/65,000lb

Performance: Maximum speed – 467kph/290mph
Service ceiling – 8540m/28,000ft
Range – 3220km/2000 miles
Climb – 6100m/20,000ft in 22 minutes

In September 1942, the 93rd Bombardment Group became the first B-24D bombardment group to join the Eighth Air Force in England. A month later, the 44th BG arrived in the UK, also equipped with B-24s. By the end of the war in Europe, 3800 Liberators had been accepted by the Eighth Air Force. Of these, almost a third were lost in action over enemy territory.

In all, five production plants produced 19,256 Liberators between May 1941 and the end of hostilities in 1945. The Ford Motor Company, using mass-production techniques perfected for the automobile industry, built 6792 at its Willow Run plant alone.

Although the B-24 was more technologically advanced than the B-17, it is often eclipsed in history by the Boeing bomber. The facts are however quite clear – the B-24 was produced in greater numbers than any bomber in aviation history.

In August 1943, B-24s carried out one of the most famous USAAF bombing raids of World War II. Fifty-six out of

TOP: **Post-war, the B-24 was used by other nations. This is a Royal Canadian Air Force B-24.** ABOVE LEFT: **This B-24, Diamond Lil is preserved in the USA by the Commemorative (formerly Confederate) Air Force as a tribute to the aircrew who made the ultimate sacrifice in defence of freedom.** ABOVE: **In RAF service, the B-24G was designated Liberator G.R.V.**

179 bombers were lost during the mission, a daring low-level attack on the Romanian oil fields, which supplied one-third of the Third Reich's high-octane fuel. Only the Liberator could reach these targets from the nearest friendly airfields in North Africa.

France had ordered 120 Liberators, but fell to the Germans in 1940 before the aircraft were delivered. Royal Air Force Coastal Command was quick to appreciate the long range of the B-24, and took over the French order. The first RAF Liberator took to the air in January 1941. The Liberator played a key role in the RAF's war against German U-boats in the Battle of the Atlantic.

Consolidated PBY-5A Catalina

The Consolidated Aircraft Corporation received a contract for a prototype flying boat from the US Navy in February 1928. The aircraft was designated XPY-1, and was designed for alternative installations of either two or three engines. However, it was the initial configuration that ultimately evolved into the most outstanding monoplane flying boat of the 1930s, the PBY Catalina.

The contract for the construction of the PBY prototype was issued to Consolidated in October 1933, and the aircraft flew for the first time in March 1935. Aircraft were delivered to the US Navy's Patrol Squadrons from October 1936. As part of a training exercise and also to demonstrate the aircraft's long-range endurance capabilities, Patrol Squadron VP-3 flew a non-stop round-trip mission from San Diego, California, to the Panama Canal Zone in 27 hours, 58 minutes, covering a distance of 5297km/3292 miles.

The PB1s were powered by 850hp Pratt & Whitney R-1830-64 engines, but in 1937 the engines were upgraded to 1000hp, and 50 aircraft were ordered, designated PB-2s. The third variant, the PB-3, was delivered to the Soviet Union in 1938 along with a manufacturing licence. The Soviet PB-3 was powered by two Russian-built 950hp M87 engines, and designated GST. The PB-4 variant also appeared in 1938 with large mid-fuselage blister observation and gun positions.

In April 1939, the US Navy ordered a prototype amphibious version that could land on water or land (with a retractable undercarriage), designated XPBY-5A. After service evaluation

TOP AND ABOVE: **The Royal Air Force made extensive use of the Catalina during World War II, having first evaluated the type in July 1939. The aircraft shown at the top of the page is in fact a Canso, the amphibious version which could operate from land or sea thanks to a retractable undercarriage.**

tests, orders were placed by the US Navy. The Royal Air Force had already shown interest in the type, aware of the gathering war clouds in Europe and the need to patrol British waters far from land. One aircraft was flown over from the USA for RAF evaluation, and as soon as war was declared 30 examples of the amphibious version were ordered. These were delivered to the RAF in early 1941 and were in service almost immediately, named the Catalina by the British. The US Navy also adopted the name Catalina in 1942. During a patrol on May 26, 1941,

LEFT: **The PBY was the most numerous and the most successful flying boat of World War II. It entered US Navy service in 1936 and equipped 21 patrol squadrons by the start of the war.** BELOW: **The Catalina's ingenious retractable floats became the aircraft's wingtips when retracted.**

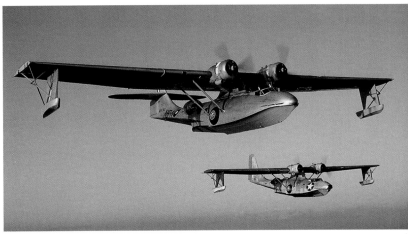

ABOVE: **US Navy Catalina amphibians (PBY-5As) tied down at their Aleutian bases, World War II.** RIGHT: **RAF Catalinas operated in the Atlantic, Mediterranean and the Indian Ocean, and took part in the protection of Arctic convoys while based in Russia.**

a Catalina of No.209 Squadron operating from Castle Archdale in Northern Ireland spotted the German battleship *Bismarck* once Royal Navy ships had lost the enemy ship.

The RAF had 650 Catalinas, and many served in the Atlantic. Two Royal Air Force Catalina pilots who operated in the Atlantic were awarded the Victoria Cross for gallant attacks on German submarines in the open sea. British "Cats" also operated in Ceylon and Madagascar patrolling the Indian Ocean, while aircraft operating from Gibraltar were on station for the 1942 Allied landings in North Africa. The last U-boat sunk by RAF Coastal Command was destroyed by a No.210 Squadron Catalina on May 7, 1945.

The PBY-5A variant was used widely during World War II by a number of countries. Canadian-built versions of the flying boat were also produced, and were known as "Cansos" by the Royal Canadian Air Force. Further development of the Catalina led to the fitting of more powerful 1200hp engines, revised armament and search radar equipment. By the end of production in 1945, over 4000 Catalinas had been made, making it the most-produced flying boat in history.

Catalinas were operated by many air arms around the world, including Australia, Brazil, France, the Netherlands, New Zealand, South Africa and the Soviet Union. A number remain in civilian use today, and are popular attractions at air shows.

Consolidated PBY-5 Catalina

First flight: March 1935
Power: Two Pratt & Whitney 1200hp R-1830-92 Twin Wasp 14-cylinder radial engines
Armament: Two 12.7mm/0.5in machine-guns in bow turret and one in each beam blister, one 7.62mm/0.3in machine-gun in ventral tunnel; war load of up to 1816kg/4000lb of bombs, mines or depth charges, or two torpedoes
Size: Wingspan – 31.7m/104ft
  Length – 19.45m/63ft 10in
  Height – 6.15m/20ft 2in
  Wing area – 130m²/1400sq ft
Weights: Empty – 9493kg/20,910lb
  Maximum take-off – 16,080kg/35,420lb
Performance: Maximum speed – 288kph/2135mph
  Ceiling – 4480m/14,700ft
  Range – 4095km/2545 miles
  Climb – 189m/620ft per minute

Consolidated Vultee PB4Y-2/P4Y-2 Privateer

Consolidated PB4Y-2 Privateer

First flight: September 1943

Power: Four 1350hp Pratt & Whitney R-1830-94 Twin Wasp 14-cylinder radials

Armament: Twelve 12.5mm/0.50in machine-guns; up to 2725kg/6000lb of bombs

Size: Wingspan – 33.53m/110ft
Length – 22.73m/74ft 7in
Height – 9.17m/30ft 1in
Wing area – 97.4m²/1048sq ft

Weights: Empty – 17,018kg/37,485lb
Maximum take-off – 29,510kg/65,000lb

Performance: Maximum speed – 381kph/237mph
Service ceiling – 6309m/20,700ft
Range – 4505m/2800 miles
Climb – 332m/1090ft per minute

After seeing the threat that German U-boats posed to Britain, the importance of effective and hard-hitting long-range maritime reconnaissance/anti-submarine aircraft was appreciated early in World War II. The US Navy wanted a purpose-designed aircraft for the job rather than a converted bomber, having already operated a maritime version of the hugely successful B-24 Liberator designated the PB4Y-1.

Three B-24Ds were taken from the San Diego B-24 production line and rebuilt with a fuselage dramatically extended by 2.1m/7ft. The whole interior of the aircraft was changed substantially, and armament was changed to better suit the intended role. Engine cowlings were changed and turbochargers were deleted from the engines because the Privateers were to operate at relatively low altitude. The other obvious modification was the very large single tail fin in place of the B-24's distinctive twin-fin arrangement.

The prototype XPB4Y-2 Privateer flew in September 1943, and an order was placed for 1370 aircraft. Deliveries began in July 1944, and the aircraft were used exclusively in the Pacific theatre, where they patrolled in support of amphibious operations. At war's end, 736 had been

delivered, when the rest of the order was cancelled.

Post-war, six US Navy squadrons continued to fly Privateers, and the aircraft flew numerous missions during the Korean War, at which time it was redesignated the P4Y-2. It was used increasingly as a Cold War electronic intelligence-gathering platform.

Eleven served with the US Coast Guard (designated P4Y-2G) to deal with the USCG's developing search-and-rescue mission, then retired from the military in the early 1960s. A number fly on in the USA as fire-bombers because their capacious fuselage can carry huge amounts of water and fire-inhibitors.

TOP, ABOVE AND BELOW: **The Privateer was essentially a single-finned, lengthened B-24 Liberator developed specifically during World War II for the US Navy. The type was only used in the Pacific, and one unit was equipped with pioneering anti-shipping glide-bombs – a primitive "smart" weapon.**

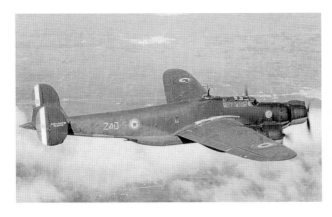

LEFT: **The Alcione (kingfisher) was used on both sides – pro-Allies and Axis – in Italy. The model pictured is the Z.1007bis, which was the major production version.**

CRDA/CANT Z.1007 Alcione

CRDA/CANT Z.1007bis Alcione

First flight: May 1937
Power: Three Piaggio 1000hp P.Xlbis RC 40 14-cylinder two-row radial engines
Armament: One 12.7mm/0.5in Breda-SAFAT machine-gun in both dorsal and ventral position, one 7.7mm/0.303in machine-gun in each beam hatch position; 2000kg/4410lb bomb load or two 454kg/1000lb torpedoes
Size: Wingspan – 24.8m/81ft 4in
Length – 18.4m/60ft 4in
Height – 5.22m/17ft 1.5in
Wing area – 70m²/753.47sq ft
Weights: Empty – 8626kg/19,000lb
Maximum take-off – 13,633kg/30,029lb
Performance: Maximum speed – 450kph/280mph
Service ceiling – 8082m/26,500ft
Range – 1795km/1115 miles
Climb – 472m/1550ft per minute

Cantieri Riuniti dell'Adriatico (CRDA), also known as CANT, specialized in flying boats, one of which was the three-engine Z.506B Airone twin-float seaplane. A landplane version was an obvious development to investigate, and this flew for the first time in May 1937. Following successful testing, the aircraft was put into widespread production, and was built totally of wood. The Z.1007 became one of the most important

bombers in the Italian Air Force inventory. The Z.1007bis and Z.1007ter were the main production versions, with 526 built – while the ter version had the more powerful 1175hp Piaggio P.XII engines, it carried a lighter 1000kg/2205lb bomb load. There were also subvariants of the bis, with Serie I–III having a single fin and Serie IV–IX being twin-fin aircraft. Like so many medium bombers designed in the mid-1930s,

the Alcione fared very badly against modern fighters. In spite of this, the aircraft were well-used in the Italians' Greek and Balkan campaigns, throughout the Mediterranean and even over the Russian front.

Curtiss B-2 Condor

LEFT: **A Condor of the 11th Bombardment Squadron from March Field, California, pictured in July 1932.**

Curtiss B-2 Condor

First flight: July 1927
Power: Two Curtiss 600hp GV-1570 in-line piston engines
Armament: Six 7.62mm/0.3in machine-guns; up to 1138kg/2508lb bomb load
Size: Wingspan – 27.43m/90ft
Length – 14.43m/47ft 4.5in
Height – 4.95m/16ft 3in
Wing area – 138.97m²/1496sq ft
Weights: Empty – 4222kg/9300lb
Maximum take-off – 7078kg/15,591lb
Performance: Maximum speed – 212kph/132mph
Ceiling – 5215m/17,100ft
Range – 1296km/805 miles
Climb – 259.3m/850ft per minute

The Curtiss XB-2 was a direct development of the Martin MB-2 (NBS-1) built by Curtiss, and used steel tubing instead of wood for the construction of the fuselage. The XB-2 prototype was ordered by the US Army in 1926 and the first flight took place in July 1927. The aircraft's engines had distinctive tall radiators which jutted up above the engine nacelles. The aircraft also

featured unusual defences in that each nacelle had a gunner's position at the rear, which it was hoped would offer a better field of fire than fuselage positions.

The B-2 had twin rudders and twin horizontal stabilizers, which even by 1927 standards were somewhat outmoded. Twelve aircraft were finally ordered at a unit cost of 76,373 US dollars – this was a great deal of money,

and had initially caused the Army to favour other designs, as had the size of the B-2, which made it too big for hangars of the time. Nevertheless, from 1929 these B-2s equipped the 11th Bombardment Squadron and constituted the US's only heavy bomber capability for a time. Canvas-covered biplanes like the B-2 soon became obsolete.

Curtiss SB2C Helldiver

The Curtiss SB2C was the second Curtiss US naval aircraft to be called Helldiver, but shared little but a name with the earlier aircraft. The Helldiver is another aircraft whose contribution to the final Allied victory is often underestimated. Said to be a handful at low speeds, the two-man Helldiver first flew in December 1940 but did not see action until November 1943 when it took part in a carrier strike against Rabaul. The Helldiver became the most successful Allied dive-bomber of World War II, and certainly made a major contribution to the successful outcome of the war in the Pacific. The aircraft had good range, making it a very useful weapon for action in the great expanse of the Pacific. The aircraft packed a significant punch and could carry 454kg/1000lb of bombs under its wings, while a torpedo or further 454kg/1000lb could be carried in the internal bomb bay.

Later improvements to this already more than capable combat aircraft included an uprated Wright Cyclone engine and hardpoints for carrying rocket-projectiles.

The Helldiver saw considerable action in the battles of the Philippine Sea and Leyte Gulf, and played a significant part in the destruction of the Japanese battleships *Yamato* and *Musashi*. As the Allies moved towards the Japanese home islands, Helldivers were active in the Inland Sea and helped deal the deathblow to the Japanese Navy.

Post-war, Helldivers were the only bombers in the US Navy, and continued to equip USN units until 1948, when the Douglas Skyraider was introduced.

Other post-war operators of the Helldiver included the Italian, Greek and Portuguese navies. Helldivers fought on with the French Navy and were used by them in Indo-China. Thailand took delivery of six Helldivers in 1951, and retired the aircraft in 1955.

TOP AND ABOVE: **After an unimpressive service debut, the Helldiver became the standard US Navy "scout-bomber" for the remainder of World War II.**

Curtiss SB2C-4 Helldiver

First flight: December 18, 1940

Power: One Wright 1900hp Wright R-2600-20 Cyclone radial engine

Armament: Two 20mm/0.78in cannon in wings, two 7.62mm/0.3in machine-guns in rear cockpit; 454kg/1000lb of bombs or a torpedo carried internally, plus an additional 454kg/1000lb of bombs and rocket projectiles carried under wings

Size: Wingspan – 15.16m/44ft 9in
Length – 11.17m/36ft 8in
Height – 4.01m/13ft 2in
Wing area – 39.2m²/422sq ft

Weights: Empty – 4788kg/10,547lb
Maximum take-off – 7543kg/16,616lb

Performance: Maximum speed – 434kph/270mph
Service ceiling – 8875m/29,100ft
Range – 1987km/1235 miles
Climb – 549m/1800ft per minute

LEFT: **DH4s stationed in France during World War I.**

de Havilland/Airco DH4

de Havillland/Airco DH4

First flight: August 1916

Power: Various, but typically one Rolls-Royce 250hp Eagle VIII in-line piston engine

Armament: Two fixed forward-firing 7.7mm/0.303in Vickers machine-guns and two in rear cockpit; provision for 209kg/460lb of bombs

Size: Wingspan – 12.92m/42ft 4in
Length – 9.35m/30ft 8in
Height – 3.35m/11ft
Wing area – 40.32m²/434sq ft

Weights: Empty – 1083kg/2387lb
Maximum take-off – 1575kg/3472lb

Performance: Maximum speed – 230kph/143mph
Ceiling – 6710m/22,000ft
Endurance – 3 hours, 45 minutes
Climb – 1830m/6000ft in 4 minutes, 50 seconds

The DH4 was arguably the most successful light bomber to see action during World War I. The biplane was designed by Geoffrey de Havilland in response to a 1914 War Office requirement for a two-seat day bomber for service with the Royal Flying Corp (RFC) and Royal Navy Air Service (RNAS). Some have compared the aircraft's versatility in World War I to that of its de Havilland successor, the twin-engine Mosquito, whose many applications in World War II are well documented.

The DH4 was originally designed around the 200hp Beardmore-Halford-Pullinger engine. However, there were many development problems with the new engine, so no fewer than seven different engine types were fitted to production aircraft. Various sub-contractors to de Havilland built

1449 aircraft in the UK and in the USA a further 4846 were produced by three US companies. These US models were powered mainly by the 400hp Packard Liberty engine. The DH4 entered front-line service in 1917.

LEFT: **This DH9A, E8673, was built by the Aircraft Manufacturing Co. Ltd.**

de Havilland/Airco DH9A

First flight: July 1917 (DH9)

Power: One Packard 420hp Liberty 12 V-type piston engine

Armament: One fixed forward-firing 7.7mm/0.303in Vickers machine-gun and one or two 7.62mm/0.3in Lewis machine-guns in rear cockpit; provision for 299kg/660lb of bombs on external pylons

Size: Wingspan –14.01m/45ft 11in
Length – 9.22m/30ft 3in
Height – 3.45m/11ft 4in
Wing area – 45.22m²/486.7sq ft

Weights: Empty – 1270kg/2800lb
Maximum take-off – 2108kg/4645lb

Performance: Maximum speed – 198kph/123mph
Ceiling – 5105m/16,750ft
Endurance – 5 hours, 15 minutes
Climb – 1980m/6500ft in 8 minutes, 55 seconds

de Havilland/Airco DH9A

The DH9 was derived from the successful DH4, and first entered Royal Flying Corps service with No.103 Squadron in December 1917. The following March, it went into action on the Western Front with No.6 Squadron, but the engine was found to be underpowered. With a full bomb load of 299kg/660lb mounted on external pylons, it could only climb to around 4575m/15,000ft, which was 2135m/7000ft lower than the DH4 it replaced. There was also a very high rate of engine failure during bombing operations.

The disappointing performance was found to be entirely due to the problematic BHP engine, which only developed 230hp instead of the anticipated 300hp. In order to overcome the problem, the BHP engine was replaced by the 420hp Packard Liberty engine. These models, designated DH9A, went on to be some of the finest bomber aircraft of World War I.

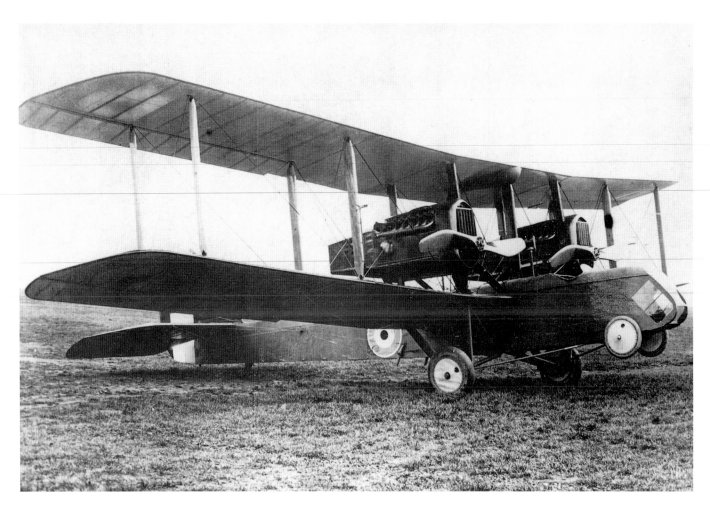

de Havilland/Airco DH10 Amiens

The DH3 produced in 1916 was a large twin-engined pusher configuration biplane heavy bomber. The design was not put into production, and both prototypes were scrapped within a year. The Royal Flying Corps still needed heavy bombers with the range to hit strategic German targets well beyond the front line, and the situation was made more pressing when Germany began its Gotha bomber raids in daylight over London in 1917. Geoffrey de Havilland, realizing that there was not time to start to design a new aircraft from scratch, revisited the DH3 design and used it as the basis for the new bomber aircraft.

The DH10 was similar in layout to the DH3, but was bigger overall and much more robust. The design was swiftly translated into a real aircraft, powered by two BHP 230hp in-line engines in pusher arrangement. The prototype Amiens I (serial C8658) had its maiden flight on March 4, 1918. The trailing edges of the wing had the tell-tale cut-out to allow clearance for the pusher propeller blades. Two other prototypes had the engines installed in the tractor configuration, with the propellers facing forwards. The tractor prototypes were powered by the 360hp Rolls-Royce Eagle VIII (Amiens II, serial C8659, first flight April 20) and the 400hp Liberty 12 (Mk III). In both tractor and pusher configuration, the power plants were positioned between the wings mounted on struts. The fourth prototype had the Liberty engines mounted right on the lower wing, and the performance improved – this version was designated Amiens IIIA or DH10A. Test-flights proved the worth of the design, and the aircraft could fly faster while carrying twice the bomb load of the DH9.

TOP: **The second Amiens prototype. Developed from the earlier DH3, the DH10 arrived just too late to see action during World War I.** ABOVE: **The Amiens IIIA, also known as the DH10A.**

This very capable aircraft was delivered too late for service in World War I, and only eight had been delivered to No.104 Squadron of the then Royal Air Force by the time of the Armistice. Had the war progressed, the aircraft would have been sure to prove its worth in combat.

The original wartime order had been for 1291 aircraft to be built by seven different companies and most were cancelled at the war's end. Some 220 were built, half being the IIIA version engined with either Liberty or Eagle power plants.

Post-war, the Amiens equipped No.216 Squadron in Egypt until it was succeeded by the Vimy in 1923. In Europe the type was well known for its airmail activity, which began in 1919 with No.120 Squadron flying between Hawkinge and Cologne, significantly improving communications with the British Army of the Rhine. In May 1919 an Amiens became the first aircraft to haul mail at night. In June 1921, DH10s pioneered the mail service between Cairo and Baghdad, reportedly using tracks in the desert to assist with navigation.

No.60 Squadron (originally No.97), based at Risalpur on the North West Frontier of India, was the only Royal Air Force unit to use the Amiens bomber in anger. In November 1920 and January 1922 the type was used to carry out bombing raids against rebels in India. The type was replaced there by the DH9A in 1923.

LEFT: The gentleman peering into the cockpit gives a good idea of the DH10's size.
BELOW: Around 220 DH10s were built for Royal Flying Corps/Royal Air Force use, and they served until the early 1920s. BOTTOM: A DH10 fitted with tropical radiators, believed to be of No.216 Squadron, based in Egypt.

de Havilland/Airco DH10 Amiens Mk III

First flight: March 4, 1918
Power: Two 400hp Liberty 12 in-line piston engines
Armament: Two 7.7mm/0.303in machine-guns in nose and rear cockpit; up to 408kg/900lb bomb load
Size: Wingspan – 19.96m/65ft 6in
Length – 12.08m/39ft 7.5in
Height – 4.42m/14ft 6in
Wing area – 77.79m²/837.4sq ft
Weights: Empty – 2535kg/5585lb
Maximum take-off – 4086kg/9000lb
Performance: Maximum speed – 180kph/112mph
Ceiling – 5030m/16,500ft
Endurance – 6 hours
Climb – 4575m/15,000ft in 34 minutes, 30 seconds

de Havilland Mosquito

TOP AND ABOVE: **The Mosquito, the "Wooden Wonder", was one of the first true multi-role aircraft, equally at home in bomber, fighter, nightfighter and photo-reconnaissance roles. The aircraft pictured at the top of the page is a B.Mk V, serial DK338.**

Dubbed the "Wooden Wonder", the Mosquito became the most versatile aircraft to see action during World War II. The Mosquito was a true multi-role combat aircraft which started life in late 1938 as a private venture outline design for a bomber/reconnaissance aircraft that could fly so fast and so high that no defensive armament would be needed.

The wooden construction was chosen because it was very strong when laminated and also kept down the weight, thus providing an excellent high-performance airframe. Another advantage of using wood was that furniture manufacturers could be subcontracted to make the fuselage, wings and tail-plane without disrupting Britain's already overstretched aircraft industry. Wood construction also avoided the use of strategic materials.

Even so, it was only after the start of World War II that Britain's Air Ministry seriously considered the proposal – and then with some caution – but in November 1940 the Mosquito first flew and convinced the sceptics that it was indeed a remarkable aircraft. Priority production was ordered for the bomber version, and meanwhile the photo-reconnaissance and fighter prototypes were prepared.

The first Mosquito prototype was in the Bomber configuration and with its clean airframe and powerful Merlin engines, the aircraft soon proved that it had exceptional performance and handling characteristics. The Mosquito remained the fastest combat aircraft in the world until 1944. Successful service trials quickly followed and the original March 1940 order for 50 aircraft was subdivided into ten Photo-Reconnaissance Mark Is, ten Bomber Mark VIs and 30 Nightfighters Mark II.

The first Mosquitoes to enter service with the RAF were the Photo-Reconnaissance models in September 1941, and these were used for deep penetration missions over Germany and occupied Europe. During these operations the Mosquito crews found that they were able to outpace all the latest German fighter aircraft.

On November 15, 1941, No.105 Squadron, which was based at RAF Swanton Morley in Norfolk, received its first Mosquito B.IV bomber. However, production of the new aircraft was slow, and it was not until May 1942 that the Squadron flew its first operational sorties to Cologne.

In mid-1943, the B.IX was introduced with increased bomb capacity and the "Oboe" navigational aid for Pathfinder duties. These specialist bombers would lead RAF Bomber Command's Pathfinder Force over enemy territory and lay down target markers. This greatly improved the accuracy of Bomber Command raids and made a significant contribution to the RAF's strategic night-time bomber offensive against the Third Reich.

Fighter-bomber versions were also developed, and the FB.Mk VI became the most widely used of all Mosquito fighters. This version was a day or night intruder, able ultimately to carry up to two 227kg/500lb bombs as well as the usual fighter armament. RAF Coastal Command was quick to see the potential of the type and soon began to use the VI, armed with underwing rockets, as a maritime strike aircraft.

Mosquito crews soon acquired a reputation for the ability to deliver their bomb loads with pinpoint accuracy over both short and long distances. This was ably demonstrated on

February 18, 1944, when 19 Mosquitoes blasted open a German jail at Amiens, which held French resistance fighters. Later, in October 1944, the Gestapo HQ at Aarhus University, Jutland, was bombed with such precision that Danish Resistance leaders were able to escape.

In all, 7781 Mosquitoes were built in some 50 variants before production ceased in 1950. The B35 was the ultimate bomber variant of the "Mossie", and it remained in service with RAF Pathfinder units until being replaced by the jet-powered Canberra in 1953. Versions of the Mosquito remained in front-line service with the RAF until December 15, 1955. The Mosquito was a truly magnificent British aircraft.

ABOVE: **The Mosquito had a bomb-carrying capability that staggered crews of heavy bombers. Here, an aircraft of No.692 Squadron based at Gravely in the UK is being loaded with a 1817kg/4000lb bomb for a wartime mission.**
LEFT: **A Mosquito B.Mk IX.** BELOW: **The DZ313 was a B.Mk IV Mosquito powered by Merlin 21 engines.**

de Havilland Mosquito B.IV

First flight: November 25, 1940
Power: Two Rolls Royce 1230hp Merlin 21 12-cylinder liquid-cooled in-line piston engines
Armament: 908kg/2000lb bombs
Size: Wingspan – 16.51m/54ft 2in
Length – 12.47m/40ft 10in
Height – 4.66m/15ft 3in
Wing area – 42.18m²/454sq ft
Weights: Empty – 5947kg/13,100lb
Maximum take-off – 10,160kg/22,380lb
Performance: Maximum speed – 612kpg/380mph
Service ceiling – 9455m/31,000ft
Range – 1963km/1220 miles
Climb – 878m/2880ft per minute

Dornier Do17

In 1932 the German Ordnance Department issued development guidelines to a number of leading German aircraft companies for the design and construction of a twin-engine medium bomber with a retractable undercarriage. Dornier designated the project Do17, and covered up the military aspects of the development by describing the aircraft as a fast mail-plane for Deutsche Lufthansa and also a freight carrier for the German State Railways.

On May 17, 1933, the go-ahead was given for the construction of two prototypes, one a high-speed commercial aircraft and the other for "freight" with special equipment – in other words, a bomber. The Do17 bomber prototype first flew in November 1934, and its superior performance caused much concern outside Germany.

At the International Air Show at Dübendorf, Switzerland in 1937, the Do17 MV1 proved to be the leader in its class. It even outpaced a number of European countries' front-line day fighters, including those of France and Czechoslovakia.

The first military examples, the Do17E high-speed bomber and the Do17F long-range reconnaissance aircraft, entered service with the Luftwaffe and saw action during the Spanish Civil War. Both variants were powered by two BMW VI 12-cylinder V-type engines, the Do17F having extra fuel tanks and two bomb bay cameras.

Further development of the Do17 E- and F-types led to the Do17M medium bomber and the Do17P reconnaissance model powered by Bramo 323 radial engines. The definitive variant was the Do17Z, with an extensively glazed cockpit, "beetle" eye, glazed nose and uprated Bramo 323 A-1 engines.

Nicknamed the "Flying Pencil", over 500 Do17Z models were built. Although this aircraft could outpace most contemporary fighters when it entered service with the Luftwaffe in 1938, it soon became obsolete after suffering heavy losses during the Battle of Britain. Nevertheless early in the war, as the Nazis swept through Poland, Norway, the Low Countries and France, the Do17 medium bomber was a key weapon in the German arsenal.

TOP: **The Do17 "Flying Pencil", combat-tested during the Civil War in Spain, was one of the Luftwaffe's most important bomber types.**

ABOVE: **The Do17Z was the main production version, and entered Luftwaffe service in 1938.**

Dornier Do17Z-2

First flight: November 23, 1934 (prototype)
Power: Two BMW Bramo 1000hp 322P Fafnir 9-cylinder radial engines
Armament: One or two 7.92mm/0.31in machine-guns in the windscreen, nose, dorsal and ventral positions; internal bomb load of 1000kg/2205lb
Size: Wingspan – 18m/59ft
Length – 15.8m/51ft 10in
Height – 4.60m/15ft 1in
Wing area – 55m²/592sq ft
Weights: Empty – 5210kg/11,467lb
Maximum take-off – 8590kg/18,906lb
Performance: Maximum speed – 410kph/255mph
Ceiling – 8200m/26,905ft
Range – 1500km/932 miles
Climb – 3000m/9843ft in 8 minutes, 40 seconds

Dornier Do217

TOP AND ABOVE: **The Do217, although mainly inspired by the earlier Do215, was a larger aircraft and differed considerably in many ways. The Do217 could carry the greatest bomb load of all the Luftwaffe bombers of the period.**

At the beginning of 1938 manufacturing specification No.1323 was issued to Dornier for a fast, flexible aircraft that could be used as a medium bomber, long-range reconnaissance or smoke-laying aircraft.

The Do217 was derived from the highly successful Do17/215 series of bombers but was very different to the earlier aircraft. In order to get a quick flying prototype, Dornier modified a Do17-M by adding the Do17Z all-round vision cockpit and increasing the size of the fuselage to enlarge the bomb bay capacity.

The Do217 V-1 prototype first flew in October 1938 but crashed seven days later during single-engine flying tests. The second prototype, Do217 V-2, carried on with the flying-test schedule over the following three months. On February 25, 1939, the third prototype took to the air powered by two Jumo 211-A engines in place of the in-line DB 601s. The Jumo engines were now regarded as essential if the desired performance was to be achieved, and they were fitted to the next two prototypes. However, many other power plants were tried before a final decision was made to use two BMW 801 radials on production models.

The 217 was initially developed as a bomber that carried a greater load than any German bomber of the time. The first production run started at the end of 1940 with the Do217 E-1 medium bomber variant. It was followed by the E-2 and E-3 versions, which differed from the E-1s in their defensive armament and were intended for dive-bombing operations. The Do217 E-4 was identical to the E-2 version apart from a heavy machine-gun in the nose. Other sub-variants included the E-2/R-4 torpedo bomber, the E-2/10 maritime patrol and the E-5, which was capable of carrying radio-controlled air-to-surface missiles.

Dornier Do217 E-2

First flight: October 4, 1938
Power: Two BMW 1580hp 801ML 14-cylinder radial piston engines
Armament: One 20mm/0.78in cannon in lower port side of nose, one 13mm/0.5in machine-gun in dorsal turret and one in ventral step position, one 7.92mm/0.31in machine-gun in nose and one in each side of cockpit; 4000kg/8804lb bomb load
Size: Wingspan – 19m/62ft 4in
Length – 18.20m/ 59ft 8in
Height – 5.03m/16ft 6in
Wing area – 57m²/613.5sq ft
Weights: Empty – 8855kg/19,490lb
Maximum take-off – 16,465kg/36,239lb
Performance: Maximum speed – 515kph/320mph
Ceiling – 9000m/29,530ft
Range – 2800km/1740 miles
Climb – 210m/690ft per minute

Other variants followed, including the three-seat 217J fighter-bomber and nightfighter versions. Both differed from the 217 bomber by having a solid nose in place of the bomber version's "greenhouse" nose for a bomb-aimer.

The J-1 was a fighter-bomber, operational from February 1942, armed with four nose-mounted 7.92mm/0.31in machine-guns and four 20mm/0.78in cannon in addition to dorsal and ventral gun positions, each mounting a pair of 13mm/0.51in guns.

Douglas B-18 Bolo

The twin-engine B-18 Bolo was the first Douglas medium bomber, and was derived from the successful twin-engined DC-2 commercial transport. The B-18 was intended to replace the Martin B-10 in USAAC service. During Air Corps bomber trials at Wright Field in 1935, the B-18 prototype competed with the Martin 146 (an improved B-10) and the four-engine Boeing 299, forerunner of the B-17 Flying Fortress. Surprisingly, only 13 YB-17s were ordered at first as the Army General Staff chose the less costly Bolo and, in January 1936, ordered 133 of the Douglas bombers. Later, 217 more were built as B-18As with a "shark" nose in which the bomb aimer's position was extended forward over the nose gunner's position.

In addition to 133 B-18s, 217 improved B-18As were built, 20 of which were transferred to the Royal Canadian Air Force and designated Digby 1s. During the winter of 1939–40, over 100 B-18As were upgraded to the B-18B standard by installing specialist radio equipment for maritime patrol operations in American and Caribbean waters. These aircraft were used to seek and report the position of German U-boats operating off the US east coast.

The B-18 Bolos were the most numerous US bombers deployed outside the country as the United States entered World War II.

Many B-18s were destroyed by the Japanese at Pearl Harbor on December 7, 1941, and by early 1942 improved aircraft replaced the Bolo as a front-line bomber. Many B-18s were then used as transports or for paratroop training, or modified as B-18Bs for going on anti-submarine duty.

TOP : **The distinctive Douglas tail points to the Bolo's DC-2 origins.**
ABOVE: **This often overlooked bomber was the main type in US use pre-war.** BELOW LEFT: **The bomb aimer's position was over the nose gunner's position, giving the Bolo the so-called "sharknose" look.**

Douglas B-18A Bolo

First flight: April 1935
Power: Two Wright 1000hp R-1820-53 Cyclone
9-cylinder radial engines
Armament: One 7.62mm/0.30in machine-gun
in nose, dorsal and ventral positions; up to
2951kg/6500lb of bombs
Size: Wingspan – 27.28m/89ft 6in
Length – 17.63m/57ft 10in
Height – 4.62m/15ft 2in
Wing area – 89.65m²/965sq ft
Weights: Empty – 7409kg/16,321lb
Maximum take-off – 12,563kg/27,673lb
Performance: Maximum speed – 346kph/215mph
Service ceiling – 7,285m/23,900ft
Range – 1931km/1200 miles
Climb – 3048m/10,000ft in 9 minutes, 54 seconds

Douglas SBD-5 Dauntless

Douglas SBD-5 Dauntless

First flight: July 1935

Power: One Wright 1200hp R-1820-60 Cyclone 9-cylinder radial engine

Armament: Two 12.7mm/0.5in fixed forward-firing machine-guns in upper part of the forward fuselage, two trainable 7.62mm/0.3in machine-guns in rear cockpit; external bomb or depth charge load of 1021kg/2250lb

Size: Wingspan – 12.66m/41ft 6in
Length – 10.09m/33ft 1in
Height – 4.14m/13ft 7in
Wing area – 30.19m²/325sq ft

Weights: Empty – 2963kg/6521lb
Maximum take-off – 4858kg/10,700lb

Performance: Maximum speed – 410kph/255mph
Ceiling – 7786m/25,530ft
Range – 2519km/1565 miles
Climb – 457m/1500ft per minute

The most successful American dive-bomber of World War II had its origins in a 1934 Northrop proposal for a new US Navy dive-bomber based on the Northrop A-17 light attack bomber.

A prototype was ordered and first flew in July 1935, designated XBT-1. After a series of service trials, an order was placed for 54 BT-1 models. The first production batch was fitted with the 825hp Wright R-1535-94 engine. However, the last one off the production line was fitted with a 1000hp R-11820-32 engine and designated XBT-2. Further modifications followed, and after the Northrop Corporation became a division of Douglas in August 1937, the aircraft was redesignated XSBD-1.

It was June 1940 before the US Marine Corps started to receive a batch of 57 Dauntless SBD-1s with their distinctive, large perforated flaps. A few weeks later, the US Navy ordered 82 SBD-2 aircraft with increased fuel capacity, protective cockpit armour and autopilot. After further modifications, the Navy received over 400 SBD-3s during the summer of 1941. By the end of the year, the Dauntless formed the attack element of the US Navy's carrier-based air group in the Pacific. After the Japanese strike on Pearl Harbor, the SBDs operated from the US aircraft carriers *Lexington* and *Yorktown* during the early months of 1942. They carried out numerous offensive operations against enemy shipping and island shore installations in the build-up to the battle of the Coral Sea. During this battle, the SBDs were joined by the Douglas TBD Devastator torpedo aircraft, and together they attacked and sank the Japanese light carrier *Shoho* and damaged the fleet carrier *Shokaku*. This was followed in June 1942 by the Battle of Midway, where SBDs from the carriers *Enterprise*, *Hornet* and *Yorktown* had a major success by sinking the Japanese carriers *Akagi*, *Kaga* and *Soryu*, and damaging the *Hiryu* so badly that it had to be scuttled. By the end of the battle, Japan had lost most of its capital ships in the Pacific.

In October 1942 the SBD-4 made its appearance fitted with radar and radio navigation equipment. This was followed in large quantities by the SBD-5, which had a more powerful 1200hp engine. One SBD-5 was fitted with a 1350hp R-1820-66 engine and used as a prototype for the SBD-6. This was the last Dauntless variant to be produced, and it appeared in early 1944.

ABOVE: **The Dauntless inflicted massive damage on enemy ships in the Pacific war, serving the US Navy and Marine Corps throughout World War II.**
BELOW: **This photograph shows the SBD's trademark perforated flaps.**

Douglas A-20 Boston/Havoc

The story of the Douglas DB-7 family of combat aircraft is complicated by the variety of names by which the numerous bomber, nightfighter and intruder versions were known. The complex DB-7/A-20/Havoc/Boston story began with Douglas submitting their DB-7 to meet a 1938 US Army

TOP: **The solid-nosed A-20G was the most numerous and main operational variant of the series serving in Europe, the Mediterranean and the Pacific, mainly in the low-level attack role.** ABOVE: **An RAF Boston III – note the forward gun blister fairing housing just above the nosewheel, containing the 7.7mm/0.303in machine-guns.**

specification for an attack aircraft. The result was an advanced and complex design which incorporated the novel nosewheel undercarriage arrangement for better pilot visibility on the ground. The aircraft also featured a highly unusual emergency second control column for the rear gunner's use in the event of the pilot being incapacitated.

France placed an order for 100 DB-7 models in February 1940, and some of these aircraft did see service with the French Armée de l'Air. Some of these aircraft flew to Britain to fight on against the Nazis, while some remained to be used by the Vichy Air Force. However, the principal early user of the Douglas design in Europe was the Royal Air Force, with whom the Havoc nightfighter/intruder version entered service in April 1941. A three-seat intruder version carried a 908kg/2000lb bomb load for use against targets in France, and was certainly a nuisance to the enemy under cover of darkness.

The first of the DB-7 series to serve as an RAF bomber was the Boston III variant (USAAF A-20C). This daylight bombing role was the one for which the aircraft was first designed. The first IIIs arrived in the UK from the USA in the summer of 1941 and soon replaced the Blenheims of No.2 Group, carrying out anti-shipping missions as well as bombing raids. A total of 781 Boston IIIs were delivered to the RAF, and the first to enter service did so with No.88 Squadron at Swanton Morley in October 1941. They saw action for the first time on February 12, 1942, and went on to fly many missions against targets in France, Belgium and the Netherlands, frequently flying perilously low to avoid enemy defences. They also took part in attacks on the German warships *Scharnhorst*, *Prinz Eugen* and *Gneisenau*, when they took part in the famous channel dash. The IIIs also served with the RAF in Italy, Tunisia and Algeria. On July 4, 1942, RAF Bostons attacked airfields in Holland – this raid was unusual because six of the aircraft involved were flown by crews of the US Eighth Air Force, giving the Mighty Eighth its first taste of battle in Europe. As more heavy bombers entered RAF service, the Bostons were restricted to tactical operations.

As part of the D-Day operations, British-based Bostons of the Second Tactical Air Force generated smoke screens over the invasion beaches. 1944 also saw the introduction of the Boston IV (the A-20G in USAAF service) and the Boston V (USAAF A-20H) distinguished from earlier versions by its power-operated gun turret. This version served with the RAF in the Second Tactical Air Force until the end of war in Europe in close co-operation with advancing ground troops. In USAAF service, the A-20G served with the Ninth Air Force in Europe, the Twelfth in the Mediterranean and in the Pacific with the Fifth Air Force. Around half of all the A-20G models produced were supplied to the Soviet Union. Total production of all versions was 7478 aircraft.

ABOVE: **USAAF Havocs first saw action when they came under attack during the Japanese strike at Pearl Harbor in December 1941.**

RIGHT: **An early A-20A Havoc.** BELOW: **BD121 was built as a Boston I, then converted to Havoc intruder standard. Note the flame damper exhausts and matt black paint for maximum concealment at night.**

Douglas Boston IV/A-20G

First flight: October 26, 1938 (Douglas 7B prototype)

Power: Two Wright 1700hp R-2600-23 14-cylinder radial engines

Armament: Six 12.7/0.50in machine-guns in the nose, two in dorsal position and one in ventral position; bomb load of 1816kg/4000lb

Size: Wingspan – 18.69m/61ft 4in
Length – 14.63m/47ft 11in
Height – 5.36m/17ft 7in
Wing area – 43.11m²/464sq ft

Weights: Empty – 7256kg/15,984lb
Maximum take-off – 12,348kg/27,200lb

Performance: Maximum speed – 546kph/339mph
Service ceiling – 7869m/25,800ft
Range – 3380km/2100 miles
Climb – 3048m/10,000ft in 7 minutes, 6 seconds

Douglas A-26/B-26 Invader

There are some combat aircraft that have served in two major wars, but few have served in three conflicts spread over more than two decades. The Invader did just that in World War II, Korea and Vietnam.

In 1940, before it could get detailed information on combat experiences in Europe, the USAAF issued a requirement for an attack aircraft to be built in three different prototype forms – attack, nightfighter and bomber. After the prototypes had flown (the XA-26 bomber version was first to fly, on July 10, 1942) it was the attack version that was selected first for production under the designation A-26B. Armed with six machine-guns in the solid nose and up to 14 more in remotely controlled turrets or underwing gunpacks, the heavily-armed Invader could also carry up to 1816kg/4000lb of bombs. This was a formidable and fast ground-attack aircraft – it was in fact the fastest American bomber of World War II.

The A-26B made its debut in the European theatre with the US Ninth Air Force in November 1944. The destructive power of the aircraft was used to maximum effect by bombing, ground strafing and launching rocket attacks in advance of the Allied ground forces as they fought their way through Europe. The aircraft was also used for dropping allied agents into enemy territory. Invaders had entered service in the Pacific at the same time.

1945 saw the entry of the A-26C into front-line service, and this version differed by having only two guns in a glazed nose and room for a bomb-aimer's position. This version saw little

TOP: **The A-26 was the fastest bomber the USA had in its World War II inventory.**
ABOVE: **The Invader served in three major conflicts of the 20th century, and had three designations in its service life.**

use before the end of the war, by which time 1091 examples had been built compared to 1355 B-models.

In the immediate post-war period, some Invaders were converted for use as target tugs for the US Navy, designated JD-1 (later the UB-26J). In 1948, USAF A-26 aircraft were redesignated B-26, not to be confused with the unrelated Martin B-26 Marauder withdrawn from USAF service in 1948.

LEFT: *My Baby*, B-26B, pictured in Korea in 1950. Note the nose, bristling with guns. BELOW: **Equally potent armament can be seen in the nose of this French Air Force Invader pictured in Indo-China, March 1951.**

In 1950, USAF Invaders took part in the first (and three years later the last) combat mission of the Korean War, where over 450 Invaders – both B-26B and B-26C models saw extensive USAF service, principally as night-intruders. Meanwhile, France also used them in Indo-China against the Viet Minh.

As tensions grew in Vietnam, Invaders were deployed to South Vietnam in 1962 and although they were painted in South Vietnamese markings, the aircraft flew into combat with US crews on board. After an aircraft disintegrated in mid-air due to wing stress problems, the B-26 was withdrawn from Vietnam. However, the USAF was keen to not lose the capability of the B-26 and invited On Mark Engineering, a company who had already carried out civilian conversions of the B-26, to produce a very heavily armed, dedicated counter-insurgency (COIN) version for use in South-east Asia. Low-hour airframes were extensively converted, essentially producing 40 brand new aircraft, the B-26K. These rebuilt aircraft saw extensive use in Vietnam in the ground-attack and interdiction roles until 1970, often flown by men younger than the aircraft itself.

The Invader's identity crisis was further complicated in 1966, when the B-26K was redesignated the A-26A for political reasons. The USAF wanted to base B-26K Invaders in Thailand, but the Thai government did not want bombers operating from their country. The B-26K was simply redesignated the A-26A, an attack aircraft, which was acceptable to the Thai government.

Some air forces still had Invaders as front-line aircraft into the late 1970s. When the fast Invader was declared surplus, many were well-used for civilian purposes, from executive transports to firebombers and crop-sprayers.

ABOVE: **The A/B-26 Invader family of aircraft served extensively around the world, with some still on active duty into the 1970s.**

Douglas B-26B Invader

First flight: July 10, 1942
Power: Two Pratt & Whitney 2000hp R-2800-27 18-cylinder radial piston engines
Armament: Ten 12.7mm/0.50in machine-guns mounted in nose, dorsal and ventral turrets; bomb load of 1816kg/4,000lb
Size: Wingspan – 21.34m/70ft
Length – 15.42m/50ft
Height – 5.64m/18ft 6in
Wing area – 50.17m²/540sq ft
Weights: Empty – 10,373kg/22,850lb
Maximum take-off – 15,890kg/35,000lb
Performance: Maximum speed – 571kph/355mph
Service ceiling – 6740m/22,100ft
Range – 2253km/1400 miles
Climb – 610m/2000ft per minute

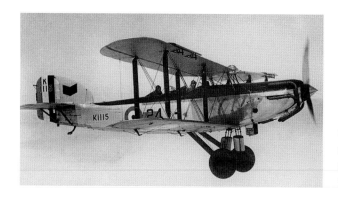

LEFT: **Operating from land and sea, the Fairey III served the RAF and Royal Navy into the 1930s.**

Fairey III family

Originally a World War I twin-float seaplane, this general-purpose biplane aircraft was converted by Fairey into a landplane, the Fairey IIIA. This entered Royal Navy service as a two-seat carrier-borne bomber. The IIIB was a floatplane version, while the IIIC had a much more powerful engine. The Fairey IIID was the second most numerous variant produced, and appeared in RAF landplane but mainly Royal Navy floatplane versions. In the spring of 1926, four RAF Fairey IIIDs carried out a 22,366km/13,900-mile long-distance formation flight from Northolt (near London) to Cape Town and back through Greece, Italy and France. IIIDs were exported to Australia, Portugal, Sweden and the Netherlands.

The Fairey IIIF, a much-improved development of the IIID, was the most numerous variant, with 597 aircraft produced. This aircraft, again in landplane and floatplane versions, gave sterling service in the RAF and Fleet Air Arm in Britain and overseas from 1927 until the mid-1930s. The obvious successor to the excellent IIIF was another IIIF which

is what the RAF's Fairey Gordon and Royal Navy Seals were. The two-man Gordon was a IIIF fitted with a different engine and other minor changes, while the Seal was a three-seat naval version with a float conversion option and an arrestor hook. Members of this family of aircraft served from World War I through to the early days of World War II – quite an achievement.

Fairey IIIF Mk IV

First flight: March 19, 1926
Power: One Napier 570hp Lion XIA 12-cylinder V-type engine
Armament: One 7.7mm/0.303in Vickers machine-gun in front fuselage and one 7.7mm/0.303in Lewis gun in rear cockpit; provision for 227kg/500lb bomb load under lower wing
Size: Wingspan – 13.94m/45ft 9in
Length – 11.19m/36ft 8.6in
Height – 4.26m/14ft
Wing area – 40.74m²/438.5sq ft
Weights: Empty – 1762kg/3880lb
Maximum take-off – 2743kg/6041lb
Performance: Maximum speed – 193kph/120mph
Service ceiling – 6710m/22,000ft
Range – 644km/400 miles
Climb – 305m/1000ft per minute

LEFT: **A visit to the USA by Richard Fairey brought the D-12 engine to Britain.**

Fairey Fox

The Fairey Fox was designed around a licence-built copy of the compact but powerful American Curtiss D-12 engine. The powerplant's comparatively small cross-section permitted almost unprecedented streamlining of the aircraft's nose, which reduced drag and in turn allowed higher speed. The prototype Fairey Fox light bomber biplane first flew on January 3, 1925, and was soon shown to be 81kph/50mph faster than existing

Royal Air Force bombers. Perhaps more alarmingly, the wood and fabric Fox could outpace contemporary fighters too.

In August 1926, No.12 Bomber Squadron, based at RAF Northholt, became the only RAF squadron, due to peacetime military economies, to be fully equipped with the Fox. It was replaced with Hawker Harts in RAF service in 1931. However, Avions Fairey in Belgium undertook production and built a further

178 aircraft. Nine Belgian Air Force squadrons were equipped with Foxes at the time of the German invasion in May 1940, and the crews of these aircraft fought bravely against a bigger enemy.

Fairey Fox I

First flight: January 3, 1925
Power: One Fairey 480hp Felix (licence-built Curtiss D-12) piston engine
Armament: One fixed forward-firing 7.7mm/0.303in Vickers machine-gun and one on flexible mount in rear cockpit; up to 227kg/500lb bomb load
Size: Wingspan – 11.58m/38ft
Length – 9.50m/31ft 2in
Height – 3.25m/10ft 8in
Wing area – 30.1m²/324.5sq ft
Weights: Empty – 1184kg/2609lb
Maximum take-off – 1869kg/4117lb
Performance: Maximum speed – 251kph/156mph
Service ceiling – 5185m/17,000ft
Range – 1046km/650 miles
Climb – 5795m/19,000ft in 39 minutes, 45 seconds

Fairey Hendon

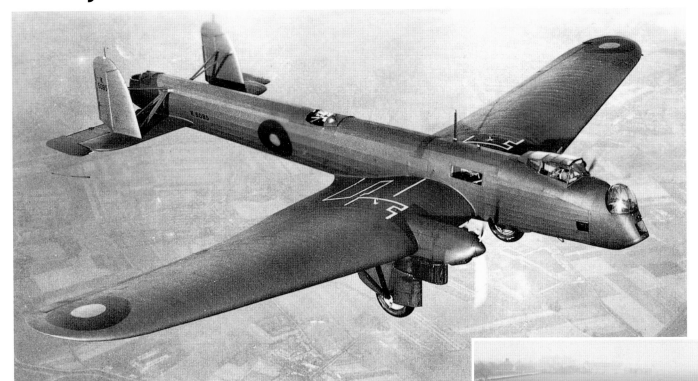

The Fairey Hendon is often overlooked by historians due to the small numbers of the type that ultimately entered Royal Air Force service. Built to meet a 1927 Air Ministry specification for a heavy night-bomber, the Hendon (known as the Fairey Night Bomber until three years later) first flew in November 1931. Unusually for the time, it was a monoplane and carried its bombs internally. The twin-fin arrangement allowed room for a defensive tail position from which a gunner could provide effective rear defence. Production aircraft also featured enclosed cockpits, which were far from standard, while the engines appeared in streamlined nacelles which, along with a fixed but streamlined undercarriage, minimized drag.

The prototype, powered by Bristol Jupiter engines, crashed during tests which led to some delays in its development. The aircraft was repaired and re-engined with more powerful Rolls-Royce Kestrel engines, but the biggest delay was official dithering over what was an advanced design for the period. The decision to produce the

ABOVE: **K5085 was built by Fairey at their Stockport plant as a Hendon II with enclosed cockpit and nose turret.** RIGHT: **An early Hendon with Fairey Gordons in the background.**

aircraft was delayed, incredibly, for four years, by which time the design was verging on obsolescence.

Production Hendons (Mark II) were finally built between September 1936 and March 1937, but only 14 aircraft were built as a further order for 60 was cancelled. Power was provided by Kestrel VI engines, and the Mark II also had a turret for the nose gunner.

When the type eventually made it into service, the 14 aircraft were allocated to No.38 Squadron (based at Mildenhall and later Marham) and later to No.115 Squadron, which formed from the nucleus of a No.38 flight. The Hendon, with its all-metal fabric-covered structure, was the first monoplane in RAF squadron service.

The Fairey Hendon night-bomber quickly became obsolete and was replaced by the Vickers Wellington just before the start of World War II.

Fairey Hendon II

First flight: November 1931

Power: Two Rolls-Royce 600hp Kestrel VI in-line piston engines

Armament: Three 7.7mm/0.303in Lewis guns in nose, dorsal and tail positions; up to 753kg/1660lb of bombs carried internally, or alternatively 15–20 troops

Size: Wingspan – 31.03m/101ft 9in
Length – 18.53m/60ft 9in
Height – 5.72m/18ft9in
Wing area – 134.43m²/1447sq ft

Weights: Empty – 5799kg/12,773lb
Maximum take-off – 9080kg/20,000lb

Performance: Maximum speed – 251kph/156mph
Service ceiling – 6557m/21,500ft
Range – 2188km/1360miles
Climb – 286m/940ft per minute

Fairey Swordfish

The Swordfish holds a special place in aviation history because it is one of the few combat aircraft to be operational at both the start and end of World War II. This remarkable aircraft was also the last British military biplane in front-line service, and had the distinction of serving longer than the aircraft intended to replace it in Fleet Air Arm service. The "Stringbag" was developed from an earlier failed Fairey design and first flew in April 1934, designated TSR (torpedo spotter reconnaissance).

After successful service trials, a contract to supply 86 Swordfish Mk Is to the Royal Navy's Fleet Air Arm was signed. The Swordfish entered service with No.825 Squadron in July 1936, and over the next three years a further 600 aircraft were delivered, equipping 13 Fleet Air Arm squadrons. During World War II another 12 squadrons were formed.

The wartime exploits of this deceptively frail-looking aircraft are legendary. Its first major action was against the Italian naval base at Taranto on November 11, 1940. HMS *Illustrious* launched 21 Swordfish of Nos.815 and 819 Squadrons to make a night attack on the Italian fleet. During the raid the Swordfish destroyed three battleships, two destroyers, a cruiser and other smaller ships for the loss of only two of the attacking aircraft. The attack crippled the Italian fleet and eliminated the opportunity for Italian warships to bolster German naval strength in the Mediterranean.

Other notable actions include the crippling of the German battleship *Bismarck* in May 1941. Swordfish from the Royal Navy carriers HMS *Victorious* and HMS *Ark Royal* were involved in the search for the German battleship. The first Swordfish attack, led by Lieutenant Commander Esmonde,

LEFT: Each of these D-Day period Swordfish bears stripes on both sets of wings and the fuselage, giving the aircraft a zebra-like appearance. There were few Allied biplanes in the front line at the time of D-Day.

BELOW: The "Stringbag" was involved in many notable World War II actions, the most famous of which is probably the Swordfish attack on the Italian fleet at Taranto.

was launched from *Victorious* but none of the torpedoes from the nine aircraft caused serious damage. During the second attack, delivered by 20 Swordfish from the *Ark Royal*, a torpedo severely damaged *Bismarck's* rudder, greatly limiting the ship's manoeuverability. The pursuing British task force was then able to catch and finally sink *Bismarck* with naval gunfire.

Then in February 1942, crews of No.825 Squadron carried out a gallant attack against the *Scharnhorst*, *Gneisenau* and *Prinz Eugen*, during which all six aircraft were shot down. Only five of the 18 crew members survived. For his bravery and leadership under fire, Lieutenant Commander Esmonde, veteran of the *Bismarck* mission and leader of the attack, was posthumously awarded the Victoria Cross.

While the Mk I was an all-metal, fabric-covered aircraft, the Mk II Swordfish which entered service in 1943 had metal-clad lower wings to enable the aircraft to fire rocket projectiles.

Later the same year, ASV (air-to-surface-vessel) radar was installed between the aircraft's fixed undercarriage legs on Mk IIIs, while the Mk IV had an enclosed cockpit.

During the desperate Battle of the Atlantic, there were simply not enough aircraft carriers to escort Allied convoys across the ocean. As a stopgap measure to provide some protection for the convoys, Britain converted grain ships and oil tankers to become MAC ships (Merchant Aircraft Carriers). Grain ships, fitted with a 122m/400ft flight deck, a below-deck hangar and lift, operated four Swordfish. The tankers had a 140m/460ft flight deck but no hangar in which to accommodate their three Swordfish – the MAC Swordfish suffered considerable wear and tear.

From 1940 all development and production of the Swordfish passed from Fairey to the Blackburn Aircraft Company, which built 1699 of the 2391 aircraft produced. The last RN Swordfish squadron disbanded in May 1945.

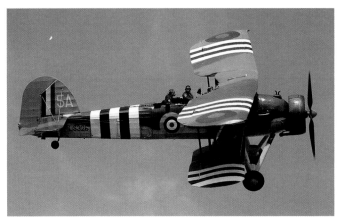

ABOVE: **The Swordfish outlasted the aircraft intended to replace it in Fleet Air Arm service, the Albacore.** LEFT: **An excellent air-to-air study of Swordfish, complete with 45cm/18in torpedo. Note the bomb shackles beneath the wing.** BELOW: **Thirteen Fleet Air Arm squadrons were equipped with the "Stringbag" when war broke out.**

Fairey Swordfish Mk I

First flight: April 17, 1934
Power: One Bristol 690hp Pegasus IIIM3 9-cylinder
  air-cooled radial engine
Armament: One fixed 7.7mm/0.303in Browning
  machine-gun in the nose and one flexible
  7.7mm/0.303in Vickers or Lewis machine gun in
  the rear cockpit; one 45cm/18in 731kg/1610lb
  torpedo or one 681kg/1500lb mine or bombs
Size: Wingspan – 13.87m/45ft 6in
  Length – 10.87m/35ft 8in
  Height – 3.76m/12ft 4in
  Wing area – 56.39m²/607sq ft
Weights: Empty – 2134kg/4700lb
  Maximum take-off – 3409kg/7510lb
Performance: Maximum speed – 222kph/138mph
  Service ceiling – 5029m/16,500ft
  Range – 1658km/1030 miles unloaded
  Climb – 3050m/10,000ft in 15 minutes, 2 seconds

Fairey Battle

The Fairey Battle which first flew on March 10, 1936 was initially known as the Fairey Day Bomber. It had its origins in a 1932 Air Ministry specification, and was a single-engine light bomber with a crew of three, designed to replace the Hind and Hart biplanes in Royal Air Force service. This low-wing stressed-skin monoplane was the epitome of modern aircraft design in the mid-1930s, replacing fabric-covered biplanes and boasting a retractable undercarriage, variable-pitch propellers and a cockpit canopy. Impressively, it could carry twice the bomb load over the twice the distance of the aircraft it was to replace. Nevertheless when it went to war, it was an aircraft out of time and proved to be under-powered and inadequately armed for modern air combat.

The famous Merlin engine is forever linked to the Battle of Britain duo, the Spitfire and Hurricane, but the Fairey Battle was the first aircraft to be fitted with the new high-performance Rolls-Royce engine. The five main marks of the Battle (I–V) were designated thus depending which version of the Merlin engine, I to V, was used for power.

Battles entered RAF service in May 1937 and ultimately equipped 15 RAF bomber squadrons. By the time Britain entered World War II in September 1939, over 1000 aircraft were in service with the RAF.

TOP: **Three Stockport-built Fairey Battle Is of No.218 Squadron, Royal Air Force. The Battle could carry a much greater bomb load than those aircraft that it replaced, but it was underpowered.** ABOVE: **K4303, the Battle prototype, pictured over a Fairey airfield. Note that this aircraft has a propeller spinner fitted, but service aircraft did not have this refinement.**

When Britain sent the Advanced Air Striking Force to France in September 1939, ten squadrons of Battles were the main offensive component. On September 20, 1939, a Battle of No.88 Squadron claimed the first German aircraft downed on the "western front". However, the Battle was no match for nimble monoplane fighters, and was simply no longer suited to unescorted daylight missions. On September 30, 1939, when four out of five Battles of No.150 Squadron were shot down by Bf109s, unescorted missions ceased.

Fairey Battle Mk I

First flight: March 10, 1936

Power: One Rolls-Royce 1030hp Merlin 12-cylinder piston engine

Armament: One 7.7mm/0.303in machine-gun in leading edge of starboard wing and one in rear cockpit; bomb load of 454kg/1000lb

Size: Wingspan – 16.45m/54ft
Length – 12.90m/42ft 4in
Height – 4.57m/15ft
Wing area – 39.2m²/422sq ft

Weights: Empty – 3018kg/6647lb
Maximum take-off – 4899kg/10,792lb

Performance: Maximum speed – 414kph/257mph
Service ceiling – 7930m/26,000ft
Range – 1609km/1000 miles
Climb – 280m/920ft per minute

TOP: **Over 1000 Battles were in RAF service when war broke out, and the type was sent into action early in the conflict. All was well until the Battle faced the best Luftwaffe fighters on the day and suffered heavy losses. By 1941 most were being used for training.** ABOVE: **On one operation in May 1940, 40 out of 71 aircraft were lost on a daylight raid against enemy targets.** RIGHT: **The Fairey P4/34, inspired by the Battle and resembling a scaled-down version of it, began as a light bomber prototype. The aircraft was developed into a two-seat fighter for the Royal Navy, the Fulmar.**

When the Blitzkrieg reached France in May 1940, these Battles were thrown into the thick of the fighting in desperation, doing battle with the most modern German fighters, and they suffered terrible losses. On May 10, operating at heights of around 76m/250ft, the Battles attacked German ground forces with delayed-fuse bombs and suffered high losses from ground fire – 13 of 32 aircraft were lost. On May 14, a force of 71 Battles was sent to bomb German bridges at Sedan and only 31 aircraft returned to their bases.

By the end of June 1940, all Battles were recalled to Britain but the type continued to be used for attacks against enemy-held Channel ports as well as the crucial raids against the German invasion barges in the Channel ports in September 1940.

Once removed from front-line duties, Battles were used as training aircraft, target-tugs and for teaching air gunnery. A dedicated two-cockpit Battle Trainer, a truly strange-looking aircraft, helped many British and Commonwealth pilots earn their wings.

Eight hundred were shipped to Canada and 400 to Australia for these purposes under the Empire Air Training Scheme (EATS). Battles remained in Royal Australian Air Force use until 1949.

Battles were also exported to Turkey (29), South Africa (190 plus) who used them in action in East Africa, and Belgium where 18 were built under licence by Avions Fairey. These Belgian Battles suffered the same fate at their RAF counterparts as they bravely fought against much more modern aircraft.

Fairey Barracuda

The Fairey Aviation Company's response to Specification
S.24/37 for a Fairey Albacore replacement was the three-
seat Barracuda, which had its maiden flight on December 7,
1940. Testing highlighted some shortcomings that were
resolved in the second prototype, but this did not fly until
June 1941. Britain's aviation industry was focusing on the
production of fighters and bombers at the time, and the new
torpedo bomber just had to wait. Service trials were therefore
not complete until February 1942, after which the more
powerful Merlin 32 was fitted. The new engine was required
to cope with the increasing weight of the Barracuda due to
a beefing-up of the structure and additional equipment to be
carried. The re-engined Barracuda became the Mark II, the
main production variant of the type. The Mark IIs began to
enter service in early 1943, the first 12 Mark IIs going to
No.827 Squadron, then re-forming at Stretton. By May 1943,
many squadrons of the Fleet Air Arm became fully equipped
with Barracuda Mk IIs and then joined carriers of the home
and Far Eastern fleets. The Barracuda has a number of claims
to fame – it was the first British carrier-based monoplane of
all-metal construction to enter service with the Fleet Air Arm,
as well as being the first monoplane torpedo bomber. A total
of 1688 Barracuda Mk IIs were built by Fairey, as well as
Westland, Blackburn and Boulton Paul.

The Barracuda Mark III (912 examples built by Fairey and
Boulton Paul) was developed to carry air-to-surface-vessel
radar in a radome blister under the rear fuselage, and first flew

TOP: **A fine air-to-air study of a Fairey (Heaton Chapel-built) Barracuda
Mk I.** ABOVE: **A great visual explanation of the below-deck space saving
that can be achieved by having naval aircraft with folding wings.**

in 1943. The radar enabled the Barracuda to track its prey
much more effectively. In European waters, Mark IIIs equipped
with ASV radar flew anti-submarine patrols from small escort
carriers, using rocket-assisted take-off to get clear of the
short decks.

In April 1944, the carriers *Victorious* and *Furious* sent 42
Barracudas to carry out a dive-bombing attack on the German
pocket battleship *Tirpitz*, then at anchor in Kaa Fjord, Norway.

The Barracudas were part of Operation Tungsten, the aim of which was the destruction of the enemy ship. The Barracudas had practised long and hard for the operation, and attacked in a steep dive despite heavy defensive flak. They scored 15 direct hits with armour-piercing bombs for the loss of only two aircraft. *Tirpitz* was so damaged in the raid that it was out of action for three months, and the Navy was able to channel its resources elsewhere, at least for a time.

Nos.810 and 847 Squadrons, Fleet Air Arm, which were embarked on HMS *Illustrious*, introduced the Barracuda to the Pacific theatre of operations in April 1944, when they supported the US Navy in a dive-bombing attack on the Japanese installations on Sumatra.

In all, 17 operational Fleet Air Arm squadrons were equipped with Barracudas during World War II. Wartime production of the Fairey Barracuda totalled 2541 aircraft. In 1945, production started on the more powerful Mk V, later designated the TF.5, but only 30 models of this variant were built and were used as trainers during the post-war period.

No fewer than 2572 Barracudas of all marks were delivered to the FAA. Barracudas were also operated by the French and Dutch Fleet Air Arms.

ABOVE RIGHT: **The Barracuda was instrumental in severely damaging the *Tirpitz* during April 1944.** RIGHT: **The ultimate Barracuda, the Mk V appeared too late for war use, and was destined for post-war training instead.** BELOW: **With the carrier deck crew watching intently, a Fleet Air Arm Barracuda prepares to catch the arrestor wire with its hook.**

Fairey Barracuda Mk II

First flight: December 7, 1940
Power: One Rolls-Royce 1640hp Merlin 32 V-12 piston engine
Armament: Two 7.7mm/0.303in Browning machine-guns in rear cockpit; one 735kg/1620lb torpedo or one 454kg/1000lb bomb beneath fuselage, or four 204kg/450lb or six 113kg/250lb bombs, depth charges or mines under wings
Size: Wingspan – 14.99m/49ft 2in
Length – 12.12m/39ft 9in
Height – 4.60m/15ft 1in
Wing area – 34.09m²/367sq ft
Weights: Empty – 4245kg/9350lb
Maximum take-off – 6401kg/14,100lb
Performance: Maximum speed – 367kph/228mph
Ceiling – 5060m/16,600ft
Range – 1851km/1150 miles
Climb – 1524m/5000ft in 6 minutes

LEFT: **The Farman can only be described as an amazing looking contraption, but it did carry out a daring night raid on Berlin.**

Farman F.220 series

Farman F.222.2

First flight: October 1937
Power: Four Gnome-Rhone 920hp 14N 14-cylinder
    radial piston engines
Armament: One 7.5mm/0.29in machine-gun
    in nose, dorsal and ventral turrets; up to
    3900kg/8584lb bomb load
Size: Wingspan – 36m/118ft 1.25in
    Length – 21.45m/70ft 4.5in
    Height – 5.2m/17ft 0.3in
    Wing area – 186m²/2002sq ft
Weights: Empty – 10,800kg/23,770lb
    Maximum take-off – 18,700kg/41,159lb
Performance: Maximum speed – 360kph/224mph
    Ceiling – 8000m/26245ft
    Range – 2200km/1367 miles
    Climb – 3000m/9840ft in 9 minutes, 40 seconds

The unmistakable Farman F.220 series of heavy bombers might have been one of the older designs in Armée de l'Air service, but it was still the only four-engined bomber in the Allied inventory of 1940.

The series had its origins in the F.210 of 1930, which began the distinctive box cross-section fuselage retained by descendent bombers for the next decade. The aircraft had a very high wing, and four radial engines arranged in back-to-back pairs so that each engine nacelle had both a pusher and puller propeller. Despite its ungainly appearance, its performance was good for the time. When war broke out, the F.221 and the F.222 versions carried out leaflet raids over Germany, and during the fight for France the aircraft carried out 63 bombing missions over Germany and occupied France. The series reached its technological peak with the F.223 (renamed NC.223 when the Farman company merged), one of which carried out an epic and courageous night-bombing attack on Berlin on the night of June 7–8, 1940.

LEFT: **The M.F.11 was the first military trainer in Australia, and this example is preserved in that country.**

Farman M.F.11 Shorthorn

First flight: 1914
Power: One Renault 70hp 8-cylinder piston engine
Armament: One machine-gun for the observer; up
    to eighteen 7.3kg/16lb bombs on underwing racks
Size: Wingspan – 16.15m/53ft
    Length – 9.5m/31ft 2in
    Height – 3.9m/12ft 9.5in
    Wing area – 57m²/613.56sq ft
Weights: Empty – 550kg/1210lb
    Maximum take-off – 840kg/1849lb
Performance: Maximum speed – 100kph/62mph
    Ceiling – 3800m/12,470ft
    Endurance – 3 hours, 45 minutes
    Climb – 90m/295ft per minute

Farman M.F.11 Shorthorn

The Maurice Farman M.F.11 (S.11 in British service) was developed from the earlier M.F.7 known as the Longhorn due to the long structural "horns" that supported the forward elevator. The M.F.11 was therefore inevitably known as the Shorthorn as it lacked the forward elevator. This was replaced by a hinged elevator attached to the tail.

The aircraft first flew in 1914 and was of pusher configuration, so lent itself to reconnaissance and bombing. Adopted by most of the Allied air arms, the Shorthorn was often equipped with dual controls and was used as a trainer throughout the war. The M.F.11 was available with floats for operation from calm water.

Britain's Royal Naval Air Service took delivery of around 90 examples. One aircraft piloted by the daring Commander Samson made a lone night attack against enemy targets at Ostend. He dropped 18 7.3kg/16lb bombs, having used the flare from a Very pistol to illuminate his targets below.

Fiat B.R.20 Cicogna

This aircraft was one of a long line of Italian combat aircraft designed by Rosatelli from 1919, all designated with the prefix B.R. for Bombardamento Rosatelli. The B.R.20 was designed and entered production remarkably quickly, and the prototype had its maiden flight in February 1936. Incredibly, the Cicogna (stork) equipped combat units by the end of that year. The B.R.20 was an advanced all-metal aircraft for the time, and Italy's Aviazione Legionaria took the type into action in support of the Nationalists during the Spanish Civil War. It flew alongside German Heinkel 111s, proved to be very effective, and could hold its own when faced with the fighters of the day. Spain purchased 25 of their own and also negotiated a manufacturing licence which was never taken up.

The aircraft was successfully exported to Venezuela and also to Japan, which operated 85 examples in China under the designation Type 1 Model 100. By the time Italy entered World War II in 1940, the B.R.20 was effectively obsolete.

The improved and streamlined B.R.20M (M for modificato) accounted for around half of the 602 B.R.20s built, and featured heavier defensive armament and protective armour.

Well known for its use in the Balkan and Western Desert campaigns, this Italian bomber was actually deployed against the British mainland for a brief spell, a fact that is often overlooked. Keen to promote joint military operations with the Germans and possibly believing German propaganda that the RAF would

ABOVE: **The B.R.20 was the subject of an unusual trade agreement with Japan – 85 of the bombers were supplied in exchange for large deliveries of soya beans.** BELOW LEFT: **This once-advanced bomber was obsolete by 1940.**

be a pushover, Mussolini sent a fleet of B.R.20 bombers escorted by Italian fighters to the Channel coast for operations against England.

On November 1, 1940, a formation of around ten B.R.20s, escorted by 40 CR42 fighters, set course to attack the docks at Harwich. Eight of the bombers were claimed as destroyed by the RAF and the Italians withdrew within weeks.

Fiat B.R.20 Cicogna

First flight: February 10, 1936
Power: Two 1000hp Fiat A.80 engines
Armament: One 12.7mm/0.5in machine-gun in nose, dorsal and ventral turret; internal bomb load of 1600kg/3522lb
Size: Wingspan – 21.56m/70ft 8in
Length – 16.68m/54ft 8in
Height – 4.75m/15ft 7in
Wing area – 74m²/796.5sq ft
Weights: Empty – 6500kg/14,306lb
Maximum take-off – 10,340kg/22,758lb
Performance: Maximum speed – 440kph/273mph
Ceiling – 8000m/26,250ft
Range – 2750km/1709 miles
Climb – 6000m/19,685ft in 25 minutes

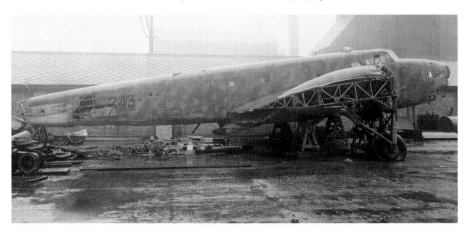

Focke-Wulf Fw200

The Fw200 Condor maritime reconnaissance bomber aircraft had its origins in a Deutsche Lufthansa airliner. The Fw200 was a low-wing, all-metal, four-engine monoplane with fully retractable undercarriage which could carry 26 passengers. The aircraft was a headline-grabber in 1937, and set numerous records pre-war for non-stop flights from Germany to New York and Tokyo. Finland, Denmark and Brazil ordered the airliner but the military capabilities of the large aircraft were not lost on the Japanese who were the first to ask for a military long-range maritime-reconnaissance version. This development prototype, known as the Fw200V-10, had a large below-floor cabin grafted on to the underside of the fuselage, which carried the aircraft's bomb load as well as defensive machine-guns. The aircraft's obvious applications came to the attention of the Luftwaffe, who then requested a prototype of their own, the Fw200C, for evaluation. As World War II broke out and the Luftwaffe needed a long-range maritime-patrol and attack aircraft, their prototype version was pressed into production.

TOP AND ABOVE: **The military potential of the Fw200 was apparently first considered by the Japanese. Had Germany developed the Condor into a heavy bomber early in the war and produced large numbers, this could have been a major threat to Britain. However, the Luftwaffe were more concerned with tactical aircraft than "heavies".**

The first Luftwaffe unit to receive the Condor (and its main operator for the war) was Kampfgeschwader (KG) 40 in April 1940. With a crew of five (pilot, co-pilot and three gunners), the Condor flew its first mission against British shipping on April 8, 1940, while operating from Denmark. Two months later, the unit was transferred to France, from where it operated until

Focke-Wulf
Fw200C-3 Condor

First flight: July 27, 1937 (civil model)

Power: Four BMW-Bramo 1200hp 323R-2 Fafnir 9-cylinder radial engines

Armament: One 7.92mm/0.31in gun in forward dorsal turret, one 13mm/0.5in gun in rear dorsal position, two 13mm/0.5in guns in beak positions, one 20mm/0.78in gun in forward position of ventral gondola and one 7.92mm/ 0.31in gun in aft ventral position; maximum bomb load of 2100kg/4622lb

Size: Wingspan – 32.85m/107ft 9in
Length – 23.45m/76ft 11in
Height – 6.30m/20ft 8in
Wing area – 119.85m²/1290sq ft

Weights: Empty – 17,005kg/37,428lb
Maximum take-off – 24,520kg/53,968lb

Performance: Maximum speed – 360kph/224mph
Service ceiling – 6000m/19,685ft
Range – 3560km/2212 miles
Climb – 200m/656ft per minute

ABOVE: **Operating from France, and not in huge numbers, the Fw200s caused great losses to British shipping.** BELOW RIGHT: **The Condor could also act as an airborne command post, directing U-boats towards allied shipping.**

late 1944. By the end of September 1940, the Condors had sunk 91,440 tonnes/90,000 tons of Allied shipping, and Churchill soon referred to these aircraft as "the scourge of the Atlantic".

By December 1940, 36 aircraft were operational, and during 1941, 58 Mk C-2s were built, fitted with bomb racks in the outboard engine nacelle and beneath the wing. Structural problems with the Condor's rear fuselage manifested themselves early in the aircraft's career, with a number simply breaking their backs on landing. An improved, strengthened version with much more powerful engines, the Fw200C-3, was being built by mid-1941.

As the Condor became more numerous and crews learned the art of maritime surveillance and attack, the aircraft became a major threat to Allied shipping – 328,185 tonnes/ 323,016 tons (116 ships) were sunk during April 1941 alone. The radius of operation could be extended even further as long-range fuel tanks would increase endurance from the normal 9 hours, 45 minutes to 18 hours.

The final version of the Condor to see service was the Fw200C-6 armed with a Henschel Hs293B air-to-surface missile beneath each wing. The total wartime Fw200 production was 252 aircraft.

Despite the relatively small numbers, the Condor fleet proved to be a major concern for the Allies – not only could the Condor attack a ship on its own, it could also direct U-boats towards convoys. The Condor's reign ended in late 1944 as the Allies overran Luftwaffe bases in France. Surviving Fw200s earned their keep as transports. The chief of the Gestapo, Heinrich Himmler, had a Condor as his personal transport. Well armoured, the VIP transport boasted a large leather chair, as well as a personal escape hatch for the occupant.

ABOVE: **The "scourge of the Atlantic", as Churchill once described the Condor fleet, was only stopped when the Allies seized their French bases after D-Day.**

Gotha bombers

As a result of unexpected and seemingly unstoppable bombing raids by German bombers over London in 1917–18, for some civilians the word "Gotha" became synonymous with terror. Development of the series of bombers began in 1915 with the Gotha G.II, which entered service on the Eastern Front in the autumn of 1916. Repeated engine failures led to its withdrawal and the appearance of the G.III with two machine-guns and the more reliable Mercedes D IVa engine. By December 1916, 14 were in front-line service, each able to carry a 400kg/880lb bomb load.

The Germans had been keen to carry out sustained bombing raids over London, and were able to do this with their Zeppelin airships until British defences got the measure of their hydrogen-filled adversaries. A heavier-than-air alternative was needed, and so the Gotha G.IV was conceived. Some sources claim the aircraft's development was greatly helped by the capture of a brand new Handley Page O/400 in early 1917.

The G.IV was made of wood and steel, and covered with plywood and fabric. An unusual feature was the "firing tunnel" tested on some G.IIIs, which enabled the gunner to fire down "through" the floor to defend the aircraft's rear most effectively by eliminating the blind-spot favoured by stalking fighter aircraft. Power was provided by two Mercedes D.IVa in-line piston engines mounted between the wings and driving pusher

TOP AND ABOVE: **The Gotha was one of the first bombers able to take the war far beyond the front line and right to the heart of the enemy's homeland. Gotha raids on London in 1917–18 caused panic and damage to morale.**

propellers. To give clearance to the spinning wooden prop blades behind the wings, the trailing edge of the upper wing had a large section removed. When testing proved the soundness of the aircraft's design, production began by Gotha, LVG and Siemens-Schuckert.

When formations of Gothas headed to hostile territory they were able to cover each other with defensive fire from their two 7.92mm/0.31in Parabellum machine-guns, something lone Zeppelin raiders lacked on their 51 bombing raids over Britain in World War I. The G.IV was able to carry up to 500kg/1100lb of bombs in cradles beneath the wing, and two primitive rectangular bomb bays between the pilot and the rear crewman contained up to six bombs, each stacked one on the other so that as the lowest bomb was released, all of the rest followed.

The first large Gotha raid on Britain took place on May 25, 1917, when 21 Gothas bombed Folkestone in Kent, killing almost 100 civilians. Within three weeks, the first daylight raid on London was carried out by a formation of 14 Gothas. The raids continued each day, with the Gothas flying at heights of 3050–4880m/10,000–16,000ft up the Thames Estuary, too high for the defenders to reach them. However, to achieve these altitudes the Gothas had to reduce their bomb load, which was at its maximum on night raids when lower altitudes were safer. The raids against southern England were launched mainly from the German bases St Denis Westrem and Gontrode in Belgium. These airfields were frequently attacked by British bombers trying to remove the threat to the homeland at source. The Gotha raids were costly in lives but were also damaging financially and psychologically for the civilians who experienced the raids. By early 1918, the raiders were suffering heavy losses to the guns of the fast-climbing British S.E.5a and Sopwith Camel defending fighters, even at night.

August 1917 had seen the introduction of the G.V, an improved version of the IV which featured more aerodynamic engine nacelles to reduce drag. The final versions in service were the G.Va, with a biplane tail assembly and a shorter nose, and the G.Vb which had a nose wheel for improved landing safety on night operations.

The 22 Gotha raids on Britain had seen these early bombers drop a remarkable total of 84.3 tonnes/83 tons of bombs on the country.

TOP RIGHT: **A Gotha V, featuring more streamlined engine nacelles.**
RIGHT: **The Gotha G.VII was produced as a long-range reconnaissance aircraft, with the nosegun position deleted and the engines repositioned closer to the fuselage and in a puller configuration.** BELOW: **Formations of Gothas were early users of the box formation best associated with the Eighth Air Force bombers of World War II. The Gothas positioned themselves to provide mutual cover against enemy aircraft.**

Gotha G.V

First flight: Early 1917
Power: Two Mercedes 260hp D IVa in-line piston engines
Armament: Two 7.92mm/0.31in machine-guns on mounts in nose and dorsal positions; up to 500kg/1100lb bomb load
Size: Wingspan – 23.7m/77ft 9in
Length – 11.86m/38ft 11in
Height – 4.3m/14ft 1.25in
Wing area – 89.5m²/963.4sq ft
Weights: Empty – 2740kg/6030lb
Maximum take-off – 3975kg/8748lb
Performance: Maximum speed – 140kph/87mph
Ceiling – 6500m/21,325ft
Range – 500km/311 miles
Climb – 3000m/9840ft in 28 minutes

Grumman Avenger

TOP AND ABOVE: **The Grumman Avenger and Tarpon, one and the same. The Royal Navy quickly dropped the Tarpon name and standardized on the original US one. The excellent Avenger was designed in just five weeks.**

Grumman's large single-engine torpedo bomber certainly lived up to the name "Avenger" given to it on the day that Japan attacked Pearl Harbor. Procured in great quantities, the type saw action with Allied air arms in virtually all theatres of operation in World War II. Of the 9836 aircraft produced, 2290 were built by Grumman (and designated TBF) while the remaining TBM models were manufactured by the General Motors Eastern Division.

The Avenger was designed in just five weeks, and was first flown on August 1, 1941. With a three-man crew, the aircraft featured an internal weapons bay, gun turret and a rear defensive gun position. A door on the right-side rear of the wing allowed access into the rear fuselage, which was packed with equipment, flares, parachutes and ammunition. At the lower level, the bombardier was provided with a folding seat from which he could either man the lower rear machine-gun, or face forward and aim the aircraft for medium-altitude level bombing. The pilot sat in a roomy and comfortable cockpit above the leading edge, and enjoyed an excellent view.

Only one aircraft returned from the six that made the Avenger's combat debut at the Battle of Midway in June 1942. Despite this poor start, the Avenger went on to become one of the great naval combat aircraft of World War II, being involved in the destruction of more than 60 Japanese warships. It was the first US single-engined aircraft able to

carry the hard-hitting 560mm/22in torpedo (as well as depth charges, rockets and bombs) and was also the first to boast a power-operated gun turret. Torpedoes launched by US Navy Avengers were largely responsible for the sinking of the large Japanese battleships *Yamato* and *Musashi*.

The Royal Navy received 402 Avengers (TBF-1Bs) under the Anglo-American Lend-Lease arrangement with the first squadron, No.832 Squadron (on board HMS *Victorious*), being equipped in early 1943. Although originally designated Tarpon Mk I for British service, they were later redesignated Avenger Mk I. Around 330 TBM-1s were also supplied to the Royal Navy, and designated Avenger Mk II.

Delivery of the TBM-3 began in April 1944, with the Royal Navy receiving the 222 TBM-3 aircraft designated Avenger Mk III by the British. Torpedo bomber versions remained in

ABOVE AND RIGHT: **Although the Avenger had a shaky combat debut during the Battle of Midway, it was soon shown to be among the best naval fighting aircraft ever produced. Avengers lived up to their name and were solely or partly responsible for the destruction of over 60 Japanese naval targets.**

RN service until 1947 and then, in 1953, the Royal Navy began acquiring anti-submarine versions designated the Avenger AS Mk IV or AS Mk V. The Avenger finally retired from the Royal Navy in 1962.

In 1951, the Royal Canadian Navy anti-submarine units were re-equipped with wartime Avengers which had been overhauled and updated. In 1955, a further eight Avengers entered Canadian service in the Airborne Early Warning role, carrying large and powerful equipment. New Zealand acquired two squadrons of Grumman Avengers, which were used as

dive-bombers by Nos.30 and 31 Squadrons. Secondary roles undertaken by the Kiwi Avengers included the spraying of Japanese gardens with diesel oil and target drogue towing.

Post-war, the type was also adapted to a wide variety of civilian uses, including crop-spraying and water-bombing. During 1947 an Avenger was used for trials of aerial seed-sowing and fertilizing in New Zealand. With an additional auxiliary fuel tank converted into a hopper installed in the bomb bay, it could carry 1017kg/2240lb of fertilizer.

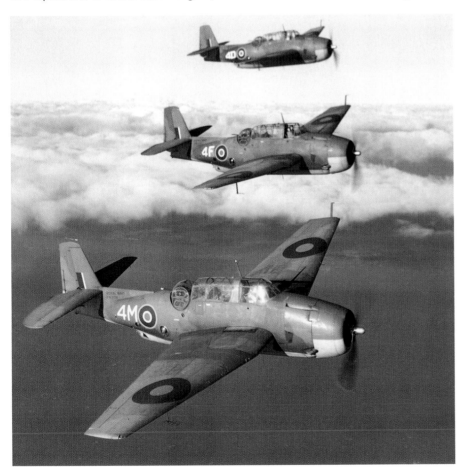

Grumman TBM-3 Avenger

First flight: August 1, 1941
Power: One Wright 1900hp R-2600-20 radial engine
Armament: Two 12.7mm/0.5in fixed forward-firing machine-guns in the upper part of the forward fuselage, two trainable 7.62mm/0.3in machine-guns in rear cockpit; external bomb or depth charge load of 1021kg/2250lb
Size: Wingspan – 16.51m/54ft 2in
Length – 12.48m/40ft 11in
Height – 5m/16ft 5in
Wing area – 45.52m²/490sq ft
Weights: Empty – 4787kg/10,545lb
Maximum take-off – 8124kg/17,895lb
Performance: Maximum speed – 444kph/ 276 mph
Ceiling – 7625km/25,000ft
Range – 1609km/1000 miles
Climb – 328m/1075ft per minute

LEFT: **Three Avengers of No.846 Squadron, Fleet Air Arm, pictured in December 1943. Torpedo-armed British Avengers served until 1947, but anti-submarine versions flew on in Fleet Air Arm service until 1962.**

101

Handley Page Halifax

RAF Fighter Command's Hurricane was always overshadowed by the Spitfire, and in Bomber Command the Halifax was regularly eclipsed by the Lancaster, despite the Handley Page bomber's significant contribution to the Allied victory in World War II. The Halifax preceded the Lancaster into Bomber Command service and was the first four-engine RAF "heavy" to drop bombs on Germany in World War II.

TOP: **A Halifax II of No.35 Squadron (note the TL code on the aircraft), a unit of the Bomber Command Pathfinder Force (PFF). This aircraft, W7676, was lost on a raid on Nuremberg on the night of August 28–9, 1942.** ABOVE: **A clear illustration of the destruction caused by large, heavy bomber raids.**

Originally designed as a twin-engine monoplane to Specification P.13/36 using the ill-fated Rolls Royce Vulture engine, the Halifax underwent a radical redesign in 1937. The aircraft was uprated with four 1280hp Merlin X engines and defensive armament for the seven-man crew, which was comprised of two 7.7mm/0.303in Browning machine-guns in the nose turret, two in beam positions and four in the rear turret. The prototype first flew in October 1939, the first production aircraft entering service with RAF Bomber Command a year later with No.35 Squadron of No.4 Group. The Halifax's first bombing operation saw six aircraft of No.35 attack enemy targets in Le Havre, France, on the night of March 11–12, 1941.

The Halifax Mk I was built in three groups, Series I, II and III, the difference being the permitted take-off weight of each. The Series III also had an increased fuel capacity. The Mk II was again made in three series. The Series I was powered by four 1390hp Merlin XX engines and had increased fuel capacity. The two hand-held machine-guns in the aircraft's waist positions were deleted and replaced by a Boulton Paul twin-gun turret in the dorsal position. Flame-damping exhaust muffs were removed to improve performance, and the little-used nose turret was also eliminated. The Halifax II Series IA was powered by 1460hp Merlin 22 engines housed in low-drag cowlings. For forward defence, a single machine-gun was mounted through a redesigned Perspex nose cone and a four-gun low-drag dorsal turret was also fitted. Later production Series IA aircraft also introduced the rectangular vertical tail

RIGHT: **Life went on as normally as possible around RAF bomber bases. Here, a serviceman lends a hand with a pitchfork. In the background is DT807, a Halifax II built by the English Electric Company.**

surfaces that became synonymous with the Halifax. These modifications raised the aircraft's speed by 32kph/20mph compared with the Mk I.

The next major development was the Mk III model, which was powered by four 1615hp Bristol Hercules XVI radial engines. The first example flew in July 1943. Other modifications included a retractable tail wheel and an H2S radar scanner in a blister beneath the lower rear fuselage or a ventral gun as standard. On later production examples, extended wingtips were introduced, thereby raising the span to 31.76m/104ft 2in. This new wing was used on all subsequent Halifax variants. The Halifax Mk IV was a project only and by the time the ultimate Mk VI and VII bomber versions were produced in 1944, the Halifax was showing its age and very few were produced. In 1944 some Mk IIIs, Vs and VIIs were converted for paratroop-dropping and glider-towing in preparation for the D-Day offensive.

A total of 6176 aircraft were built and, although overshadowed by the Avro Lancaster, the Handley Page Halifax proved to be a far more versatile aircraft in that it could be adapted to many different roles. The Halifax squadrons of the RAF flew 82,773 operational sorties for the loss of 1884 aircraft (2.2 per cent) during World War II. The last Halifaxes were phased out of Royal Air Force and French Armée de l'Air service in 1952.

RIGHT: **A Halifax Mk I of No.76 Squadron.** BELOW: **An aircraft of No.10 Squadron. Although in the shadow of the "Lanc", the Halifax was produced in great numbers and played a key role in the ultimate Allied victory.**

Handley Page Halifax Mk III

First flight: October 25, 1939
Power: Four Bristol 1615hp Hercules VI or XVI 14-cylinder two-row radial engines
Armament: One 7.7mm/0.303in machine-gun in nose position, four 7.7mm/0.303in machine-guns each in dorsal and tail turrets; internal bomb load of 6,583kg/14,500lb
Size: Wingspan – 31.75m/104ft 2in
Length – 21.82m/71ft 7in
Height – 6.32m/20ft 9in
Wing area – 118.45m²/1275sq ft
Weights: Empty – 17,706kg/39,000lb
Maximum take-off – 30,872kg/68,000lb
Performance: Maximum speed – 454kph/282mph
Ceiling – 7320m/24,000ft
Range – 3194km/1985 miles
Climb – 229m/750ft per minute

LEFT: **The squadron code "KM" identifies these Hampden Mk Is as aircraft of No.44 Squadron.**
BELOW: **Men of a No.83 Squadron Hampden leaving their aircraft after a flight early in World War II.**

Handley Page Hampden

The Handley Page Hampden prototype H.P.52 first flew in June 1936, and after Royal Air Force trials and various modifications, the type entered service with No.5 Group, RAF, during the summer of 1938. This five-seat medium bomber was so fast and manoeuvrable that Handley Page initially presented it to the RAF as a fighter-bomber. The pilot had a fixed forward-firing gun in addition to the aircraft's three manually operated Lewis guns for all-round defence. This defensive system gave the Hampden the edge over its British rivals because it didn't suffer from the drag and weight penalties of heavy gun turrets. In fact, the Hampden bomb load was almost equal to that carried by the bigger Whitley and Wellington, and it was almost as fast as the Blenheim medium bomber.

By the start of World War II, eight RAF squadrons were fully operational and took part in the early raids against German naval shore installations and shipping in the North Sea. However, daylight raid formations over enemy territory soon encountered opposition from fast German single-engine fighters, and the Hampden squadrons suffered heavy losses. In fact, casualties were so high that the Hampdens were taken off operations until they could be equipped with much better armament and armour. By then the decision had been taken that RAF Bomber Command would become mainly a night-raiding force, which no doubt saved many Hampden crews' lives.

Nicknamed the "Flying Suitcase" because of the cramped crew positions in a very narrow fuselage, the Hampden had a successful career with No.5 Group during the summer of 1940, bombing Germany itself, mine-laying and bombing invasion barges in continental ports along the English Channel. It had a separate and successful career as a long-range torpedo bomber with RAF Coastal Command until late 1943.

A total of 1430 Hampden medium bombers were built before the type was replaced in RAF squadron service by the Avro Manchester from 1941.

Handley Page Hampden Mk II

First flight: June 21, 1936

Power: Two Bristol 1000hp Pegasus XVIII 9-cylinder radial engines

Armament: One 7.7mm/0.303in machine-gun in port side of forward fuselage, one in nose position, two in dorsal and two in ventral positions; bomb load of 1816kg/4000lb

Size: Wingspan – 21.08m/69ft 2in
Length – 16.33m/53ft 7in
Height – 4.55m/14ft 11in
Wing area – 62.06m²/668sq ft

Weights: Empty – 5348kg/11,780lb
Maximum take-off – 8515kg/18,756lb

Performance: Maximum speed – 409kph/254mph
Ceiling – 5795m/19,000ft
Range – 3034km/1885 miles
Climb – 300m/980ft per minute

LEFT: **Daylight raids early in the war showed that the Hampden had defensive deficiencies.**

Handley Page Heyford

The Heyford was the last biplane bomber in RAF service and even looked dated when new, its fixed spatted landing gear doing nothing to improve its appearance. The Heyford's wings were of metal frame with fabric covering, while the fuselage was half metal (forward) and half fabric-covered. Despite this, the Heyford was the most important British bomber of the mid-1930s.

Three prototypes were ordered for evaluation in 1927, the first having its maiden flight in June 1930. Successful testing led to the type being ordered, and when production ended in July 1936, 15 Heyford Mk I, 21 Heyford Mk IA, 16 Heyford Mk II and 70 Heyford Mk III aircraft had been delivered. The marks differed little except in the type of engines installed, all Rolls-Royce Kestrels.

Perhaps the most striking visual feature of the bomber was that its fuselage was mounted on the upper wing. This gave the pilot and defensive gunners an excellent field of vision. To protect the aircraft's blind spot below and to the rear, a retractable ventral "dustbin" turret could be lowered from beneath the rear fuselage.

The centre section of the lower wing was thick enough to contain cells for the carriage of bombs. It is a matter of opinion if the proximity of the bomb cells to the ground made for speedy re-arming since armourers had to lie on the ground beneath the aircraft to secure the bombs in place.

The first unit to be equipped with the type in November 1933 was No.99 Squadron based at Upper Heyford. Nos.7, 9, 10, 38, 78, 97, 102, 148, 149 and 166 Squadrons followed.

As Whitleys and Wellesleys appeared from 1937, the Heyford was gradually phased out, the last being replaced by Wellingtons in 1939. The type continued to be used for training purposes until being finally retired in July 1941.

TOP: **K3500, Heyford I of 99 Squadron. The aircraft was lost after an engine failure at night in May 1937. Note the bomb shackles under the wing.**
ABOVE: **A Heyford crew of No.10 Squadron poses for the camera. The gunner's exposed position cannot have been a popular one.**

Handley Page Heyford Mk IA

First flight: June 1930 (prototype)
Power: Two Rolls-Royce 575hp Kestrel IIIS 12-cylinder piston engines
Armament: Three 7.7mm/0.303in machine-guns in nose, dorsal and ventral "dustbin" positions; up to 1589kg/3500lb bomb load
Size: Wingspan – 22.86m/75ft
    Length – 17.68m/58ft
    Height – 5.33m/17ft 6in
    Wing area – 136.56m²/1470sq ft
Weights: Empty – 4177kg/9200lb
    Maximum take-off – 7672kg/16,900lb
Performance: Maximum speed – 229kmh/142mph
    Ceiling – 6405m/21,000ft
    Range – 1481km/920 miles with reduced bomb load
    Climb – 213m/700ft per minute

Handley Page O/400

Given that powered flight was so new, Handley Page's World War I series of large night-bombers was a remarkable achievement. The Handley Page O/400 was a refinement of the earlier O/100, which was designed to an Admiralty specification for a dedicated bomber aircraft – at the time (1914) this was a revolutionary idea. O/100s were operational in France in 1916, and revision of the design (increased fuel capacity and better engines) led to the hugely successful O/400 bomber. Five hundred and fifty were built in Britain and a further 100 were produced in the USA. The O/400 was a very large aircraft, and in daylight would have been easy prey for capable German fighters. It was therefore used as a night-bomber and could carry ordnance up to the size of the 749kg/1650lb bomb, the heaviest used by the British during World War I.

Charged with attacking enemy industrial targets, the O/400s would fly in fleets of up to 40 a night. These raids were the first true strategic bombing raids in history, and the large Handley Page bombers were seen by some military leaders as the future of waging war. More than 400 O/400s operated with the Royal Air Force before the Armistice of November 1918, equipping Nos. 58, 97, 115, 207, 214, 215 and 216 Squadrons of the RAF. In August 1918 an O/400 was attached to No.1 Squadron of the Australian Flying Corps serving in the Middle East. No.1 worked with T.E. Lawrence, whose Arab associates, impressed by the sheer size of the aircraft, reportedly called it "The Father of all aeroplanes".

The type served in the RAF until late 1919, when it was replaced by the Vickers Vimy. Post-war, ten O/400s were converted from military to civil configuration and used in the UK by Handley Page Transport Ltd.

ABOVE AND BELOW: **The O/400 was a large aircraft, and the ability to fold back the wings on the ground made for easier stowage. The lone proud airman (below) gives a good idea of the aircraft's sheer size.**

Handley Page O/400

First flight: December 17, 1915

Power: Two Rolls-Royce 360hp Eagle VIII Jupiter VIII piston engines

Armament: Various bomb loads, sixteen 50.8kg/112lb bombs or one 749kg/1650lb bomb, two 7.7mm/0.303 Lewis Guns in nose, two Lewis guns in mid-upper position, and single Lewis firing through lower rear trapdoor

Size: Wingspan – 30.48m/100ft
Length – 19.17m/62ft 10.75in
Height – 6.72m/22ft 0.75in
Wing area – 153.1m²/1648sq ft

Weights: Empty – 3859kg/8502lb
Maximum take-off – 6065kg/13,360lb

Performance: Maximum speed – 157kph/98mph
Service ceiling – 2590m/8500ft
Range – 1046km/650 miles
Climb – 3048m/10,000ft in 40 minutes

Hawker Typhoon

The Typhoon was designed around the new Rolls-Royce and Napier 24-cylinder 2000hp engine then under development, and flew for the first time in February 1940. Development and production problems delayed the Typhoon's delivery to the RAF until August 1941, when it became the RAF's first 643kph/400mph fighter. However, the extent of engine and structural problems in its early days was such that the large Hawker fighter was almost withdrawn from service. Instead, the problems were resolved and a use was found for the Typhoon's high low-level speed. Luftwaffe Focke-Wulf 190s had been carrying out hit-and-run raids along Britain's south coast, and the Typhoon, with its top speed of 663kph/412mph, was the only British fighter that could catch them. Typhoons destroyed four raiders within days of being deployed.

Following the success of night raids over occupied France in November 1942, the fighter was employed increasingly for offensive duties, strafing enemy airfields, shipping, roads, railways and bridges. From 1943, "Tiffies" went on the offensive, attacking targets in

France and the Low Countries, and when carrying rocket projectiles, they proved to be truly devastating aircraft.

Just prior to D-Day (June 6, 1944), Typhoons attacked German radar installations. These high-risk daylight attacks against heavily defended targets robbed the enemy of their radar "eyes" when they needed them most.

Relentless day and night attacks by RAF Typhoons on German communications targets greatly aided the D-Day operations. The aircraft that was once almost scrapped from RAF service eventually equipped no fewer than 26 squadrons of the 2nd Tactical Air Force. The Typhoon's original bomb load of 227kg/500lb gradually increased to 908kg/2000lb, the heaviest payload of any fighter-bomber. With eight 27.2kg/60lb rocket projectiles beneath the wing in which were buried four 20mm/0.78in cannon each firing 600 rounds per minute, at low level the "Tiffie" was a monster that harried German ground forces throughout Normandy. Later Typhoons had the bubble cockpit canopy in place of the earlier "glasshouse" framed cockpit, which improved visibility.

TOP AND ABOVE: **Although designed as a pure fighter, it will be as a ground-attack type that the Typhoon will perhaps be best remembered. The "Tiffie" inflicted massive damage on German forces before, during and after the D-Day landings. Note the rockets beneath the wing of the aircraft pictured immediately above.**

Hawker Typhoon IB

First flight: May 27, 1941 (Production IA)

Power: Napier 2180hp Sabre IIA 24-cylinder sleeve-valve liquid cooled piston engine

Armament: Four 20mm/0.78in cannon in outer wings and racks for eight rockets or two 227kg/500lb bombs

Size: Wingspan – 12.67m/41ft 7in
   Length – 9.73m/31ft 11in
   Height – 4.67m/15ft 4in
   Wing area – 25.92m²/279sq ft

Weights: Empty – 3995kg/8800lb
   Maximum take-off – 6015kg/13,250lb

Performance: Maximum speed – 663kph/412mph
   Ceiling – 10,736m/35,200ft
   Range – 821km/510 miles (with bombs)
   Climb – 914m/3000ft per minute

Heinkel He111

The prototype of the Heinkel He111 first flew in February 1935 and owed many of its design features to the earlier single-engine He70 which set eight world speed records in 1933. Designed in 1934 as a twin-engine high-speed transport and revealed to the world as a civil airliner in 1935, the He111 was in fact secretly developed as the world's most advanced medium bomber. Six He111 C-series airliners went into service with Lufthansa in 1936 but even the airliner versions served a military purpose, as two He111s in Lufthansa markings flew secret photographic reconnaissance missions over the Soviet Union, France and Britain.

It took the installation of 1000hp Daimler-Benz DB 600A engines and the improved all-round performance they bestowed to make the He111 a viable military aircraft. The first mass-produced bomber versions, the He111 E and He111 F, were desperately effective in the testing-ground that was the Spanish Civil War, where, as part of the Condor Legion, they flew in support of the Fascists. The effectiveness of Blitzkrieg tactics was due in no small part to the Heinkel bomber – the bombing of Guernica sent a clear message around the world about the military might of the Luftwaffe. The speed of the He111 enabled it to outpace many of the fighter aircraft pitted against it in Spain, but this led the Germans to assume incorrectly that their bombers would reign supreme in the European war that was to come.

ABOVE AND BELOW: **A German bomber, built in Spain post-war, powered by British engines. These aircraft were Spanish licence-built CASA 2.111s, and served the Spanish Air Force into the 1960s. These were the "Heinkels" that appeared in the film "Battle of Britain".**

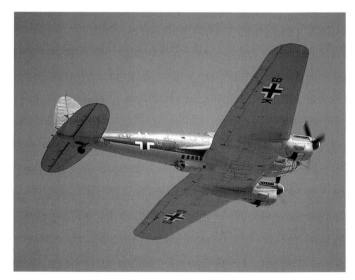

However, the Heinkel's shortcomings were exposed when it came up against the more modern fighters of the Royal Air Force – the Spitfire and the Hurricane. Although by sheer weight of numbers, the He111s did inflict much destruction on Britain during the early stages of World War II, losses mounted and the Heinkel was soon restricted to night operations and other specialized missions.

Under cover of darkness during the Blitz of 1940–1, the He111 continued to perform as an effective bomber, inflicting serious blows against its British enemies, including the devastating raids on Coventry.

Due to a German decision to focus on mass production of existing weapons rather than invest in development of newer ones, the He111 laboured on long after it should have been retired. He111s were developed for use as torpedo bombers, glider tugs and troop transports, and in the last year of the war they served as air launch platforms for V1 flying bombs targeted against British cities. Perhaps the strangest development of the He111 was the joining of two aircraft at the wing, with an additional section of wing containing a fifth engine. Twelve examples of this truly strange-looking aircraft were produced as tow aircraft for the large Messerschmitt Me321 transport gliders. By the end of World War II, however, the He111 was used mainly as a transport aircraft.

By the end of 1944, over 7300 He111s had been built for the Luftwaffe, while a further 236 were licence-built by the Spanish manufacturer CASA. The Spanish machines (designated CASA 2.111) were identical to the He111 H-6 produced in Germany and half were powered by Junkers engines supplied from Germany. The rest of the Spanish aircraft, built post-war, had Rolls-Royce Merlin engines. Spain continued to operate the Heinkel bombers until 1965.

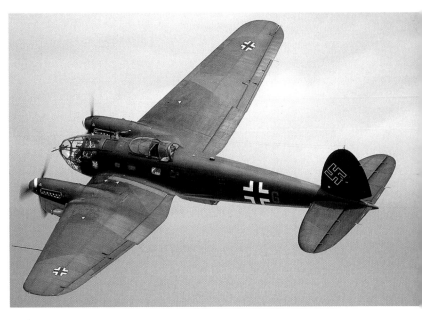

ABOVE RIGHT: **The Spanish machines were the same as the He111 H-6.** RIGHT: **The real thing – a formation of Luftwaffe He111s.** BELOW: **Groundcrew attending to a Luftwaffe He111 early in World War II.**

Heinkel He111 H-16

First flight: February 24, 1935 (prototype)
Power: Two Junkers 1350hp Jumo 211F piston engines
Armament: One 20mm/0.78in MG FF cannon in nose, one 13mm/0.51in MG131 gun in dorsal position, two 7.92mm/0.31in MG15 guns in rear of ventral gondola and two 7.92mm/0.31in MG81 guns in each of two beam positions; up to 2500kg/5503lb of bombs carried internally and externally
Size: Wingspan – 22.60m/74ft 1in
Length – 16.40m/53ft 9in
Height – 4m/13ft1in
Wing area – 86.50m²/931.07sq ft
Weights: Empty – 8680kg/19,105lb
Maximum take-off – 14,000kg/30,814lb
Performance: Maximum speed – 436kph/271mph
Service ceiling – 8390m/27,500ft
Range – 1950km/1212 miles
Climb – 4500m/14,765ft in 30 minutes

Heinkel He177

Had the Nazis produced an atomic bomb, as the Luftwaffe's only heavy bomber it was the He177 Greif (griffon) that would have carried it. At the end of World War II a sole aircraft undergoing modification for the role was discovered in Czechoslovakia. Given the number of these aircraft that had to turn back from missions due to engine problems, the bomb might have posed more of a threat to Germany than anywhere else. Of all the aircraft in the Luftwaffe's World War II inventory, the He177 had the greatest military potential and caused the greatest amount of trouble to its air and ground crews.

In many ways, it is surprising that the aircraft made it to production at all because it was proposed to meet a baffling 1938 requirement for a large, long-range heavy bomber and anti-shipping aircraft that could deliver a sizeable 2000kg/4402lb bomb load in medium-angle dive-bombing attacks. It has to be borne in mind that while the Allies embraced the concept of strategic air power as a means of waging war, the Luftwaffe was always a tactical air power adjunct to German land forces. That different philosophy explained the lack of large, heavy bombers in the wartime Luftwaffe.

RIGHT AND BELOW: **Having emerged from an ill-considered specification, the He177 proved to be the only German four-engined "heavy" of World War II. In mid-1944, there were raids on the Eastern Front of up to 90 of these troublesome aircraft.**

At a glance, the six-seat He177 has two engines, but on closer inspection each Daimler-Benz DB-610 engine is in fact a pair of coupled DB605 engines driving a single propeller shaft. The designers decided that was a good way to reduce drag, but any benefits were far outweighed by the innumerable problems caused by these troublesome engines which regularly caught fire in the air, even at cruising speeds. Six out of the eight prototypes crashed and out of the first 35 pre-production A-0 models, built mainly by Arado, many were written off through take-off accidents or fires in flight. A further 130 A-1 versions were built by Arado, while Heinkel were responsible for the production of the A-3 and A-5 versions, of which 170 and 826 respectively were constructed.

The aircraft itself was essentially a good design, and the slim tubular fuselage and long wings gave a range of 5500km/3417 miles – far beyond anything else in the Luftwaffe inventory. The engine was the design's Achilles

heel, and plagued its service record. The type in A-1 form was first used in action by KG (*Kampfgeschwader*) 40 for maritime strike and reconnaissance missions from bases in France. The aircraft could carry an impressive range of anti-shipping ordnance, including the Henschel Hs 293 missile, which was guided after launch to its target by the bombardier's joystick in the gondola beneath the nose. The missile "pilot" followed the missile's course thanks to flares at the rear of the missile. Torpedoes and sea mines could also be deployed.

During January to March 1944 the Luftwaffe's KG40 and KG100 carried out what were known as the Steinbock raids. These revenge raids were in response to the Allies' escalating attacks against German cities and were aimed at London. The planners knew the single most effective way that the aircraft could attack and hope to evade interception by the Royal Air Force's increasingly efficient nightfighter force. The aircraft climbed to around 9000m/29,527ft over the coast of Europe and then, at full power, began a shallow dive towards Britain. By the time the aircraft were over England they were at speeds of around 700kph/435mph, which made the aircraft hard to catch but did little for bombing accuracy. The raids were ineffective and although of the 35 aircraft that took part in the numerous raids only four were destroyed by British defences, many had to turn back repeatedly with engine fires and other malfunctions.

Following the D-Day landings, He177 anti-shipping missions from France ceased, but the type was still in use as a missile launch platform against the Allies in early 1945.

On the Eastern Front, KG4 and KG50 were first to use the He117 in the pure bomber role, and some aircraft were also fitted with huge 50mm/2in or even 75mm/2.93in anti-tank guns.

ABOVE: **An He117 A-5/R2 carrying a Henschel Hs 293A anti-shipping missile. The weapon could be carried on a special pylon fitted beneath the forward bomb bay or beneath the wing.** RIGHT AND BELOW: **The RAF evaluated certain captured enemy aircraft. Note that in both these photographs the Luftwaffe markings have been overpainted with RAF roundels, and broad D-Day invasion-type stripes have been applied to the wings and rear fuselage to deter friendly would-be attackers. The aircraft pictured on the right has had "Prise de Guerre" painted on its side.**

Heinkel He177 A-5

First flight: November 19, 1939
Power: Two Daimler-Benz 2950hp DB 610A piston engines
Armament: Three 7.92mm/0.31in machine-guns, three 13mm/0.51in machine-guns and two 20mm/0.78in cannon in nose, tail, dorsal and ventral gondola positions; up to 1000kg/2201lb of bombs and two anti-shipping missiles
Size: Wingspan – 31.44m/103ft 1.75in
  Length – 20.4m/66ft 11.25in
  Height – 6.39m/20ft 11.75in
  Wing area – 102m²/1097.95sq ft
Weights: Empty – 16,800kg/36,976lb
  Maximum take-off – 31,000kg/68,231lb
Performance: Maximum speed – 490kph/304mph
  Ceiling – 8000m/26,245ft
  Range – 5500km/3417 miles
  Climb – 260m/853ft per minute

Ilyushin Il-2 Shturmovik

During the 1930s, the Soviet government was very interested in developing a dedicated purpose-designed anti-tank aircraft. Various projects came to nothing, then in 1938, as war seemed inevitable, a team under Sergei V. Ilyushin at the Soviet Central Design Bureau (TsKB) produced a new design, a two-seat aircraft designated the TsKB-55 which first flew in December 1939. The Ilyushin design was then redesignated BSh-2, for Bronirovanni Shturmovik or Armoured Assault Aircraft. Although some of the aircraft, now designated Il-2, did reach front-line units by the time of the June 1941 German invasion, the new and unfamiliar aircraft had little impact. By now the Soviets were concerned that many of

ABOVE AND BELOW LEFT: **More Il-2s were built than any other aircraft in history. When told of production problems with the type, Stalin said the tough, hard-hitting aircraft were "needed by the Red Army like it needs air or bread". The large hollow above the engine directed air to the engine's radiator intake.**

their aircraft factories might be overrun by the Germans, so development and production of the Il-2 ceased while the factories were relocated beyond the Urals. This was a massive undertaking, and all the more remarkable because Il-2s were coming off the new refined production lines only two months after the relocation of the production facilities.

This heavily-armoured ground-attack monoplane was the backbone of the Soviet ground-attack units during World War II and was one of the most formidable aircraft used in the conflict. Perhaps the key to the aircraft's success was its survivability due to the extraordinary amounts of protective armour which was not installed but was part of the aircraft's structure itself, guarding the pilot, engine, fuel tank, cooling system and bomb bays.

The aircraft first flew in single-seat form on October 12, 1940, and went on to be the most produced aircraft in history, with more than 36,000 built. The heavily armoured Il-2 reached front-line units in May 1941. Though devastating against ground targets, the aircraft was no match for modern fighter aircraft when Soviet fighter cover was not available, and it

suffered heavy losses from the Luftwaffe. The solution was proposed in February 1942 – the two-seat Il-2m3, which was in fact the original configuration proposed by Ilyushin. The second crewman manned a 12.7mm/0.5in machine-gun for rear protection but he was not as protected by armour as the pilot and was seven times more likely to be killed in action. The forward-firing armament of two 20mm/0.78in cannon was also replaced by two high-velocity 23mm/0.9in cannon.

On November 19, 1942, the Red Army launched a counterattack against the German offensive in Stalingrad, and their white Shturmoviks were the masters of the air. Over the following four days the Il-2s carried out around 1000 sorties attacking German armour, artillery and troops. The Ilyushin aircraft was a key part of the Soviet counterattack which led to the German surrender at Stalingrad on February 2, 1943.

The Il-2m3 had four small bomb bays that could carry up to 192 2.5kg/5.5lb PTAB anti-tank bomblets which the aircraft would scatter over enemy columns. It was also equipped with the DAG-10 grenade launcher which would eject small aerial mines on parachutes in the path of pursuing aircraft.

By mid-1943, Shturmovik pilots had perfected their tactics. Flying in groups of eight to twelve aircraft in open country, they would attack soft targets such as personnel or soft-skinned vehicles by simply skimming in as low as 5m/16ft. Against armoured columns, they would attack straight down the column or weave across it repeatedly, scattering the PTAB anti-tank bombs from as low as 100m/320ft. Bunkers or emplacements were attacked using dive-bombing techniques. To tackle armour formations on a battlefield, the Il-2s would form their "circle of death" above and around the enemy below. Aircraft would peel off it, turn and attack the tanks below almost at their leisure, knowing that a large part of the sky above was protected by the encircling Il-2s. Ground fire less than 20mm/0.78in calibre held no fear for the well-armoured Shturmoviks. The attacks would continue until the aircraft expended fuel and ammunition.

The Il-2's contribution to the pivotal Soviet victory at Kursk was considerable. The aircraft destroyed 70 tanks of the 9th Panzer Division in just 20 minutes, killed 2000 men and destroyed 270 tanks of the 3rd Panzer Division in just two hours, and virtually wiped out the 17th Panzer Division.

TOP AND ABOVE: **The rear gunner of Il-2m3 frequently had the aft cockpit canopy removed to improve his or her field of fire. The aircraft in the foreground immediately above bears the legend "Avenger".** BELOW LEFT: **The Il-10 replaced the Il-2 in production in 1944. With fighter-like handling, the Il-10 was a major redevelopment of the Il-2, which remained in service in the Eastern Bloc into the late 1950s.**

Ilyushin Il-2m3 Shturmovik

First flight: March 1941 (production Il-2)
Power: One Mikulin 1720hp Am-38F piston engine
Armament: Two 23mm/0.9in wing-mounted machine-guns and one 12.7mm/0.5in machine-gun for gunner; up to six 100kg/220lb bombs or two 250kg/551lb bombs plus eight rocket projectiles under outer wing
Size: Wingspan – 14.6m/47ft 10.75in
Length – 11.65m/38ft 2.5in
Height – 4.17m/13ft 8in
Wing area – 38.5m²/414.42sq ft
Weights: Empty – 4525kg/9959lb
Maximum take-off – 6360kg/13,998lb
Performance: Maximum speed – 410kph/255mph
Service ceiling – 6000m/19,690ft
Range – 765km/475 miles
Climb – 5000m/16,405ft in 12 minutes

Ilyushin Il-4

Always overshadowed by its Western counterparts, the Il-4 was produced in great quantities, and was one of the best bomber aircraft of World War II. It was derived from the Ilyushin DB-3, a record-breaking long-range bomber that first flew in prototype form in 1935. The second prototype, the TsKB-30, amazed the world when it flew from Moscow to Canada, a distance of 8000km/4971 miles. The DB-3 served in great numbers with the Long Range Aviation and Naval Aviation elements of the Soviet Air Force, and carried out early bombing raids on Germany in World War II. The 7.62mm/0.3in rifle-calibre armament of the DB-3 proved inadequate against Finnish fighters in the 1939–40 Winter War, but was never significantly improved.

An improved version, the DB-3F, was developed in 1938, one of the requirements being that assembly was to be very straightforward for mass production. The new version bore little resemblance to its predecessor, having a streamlined and extensively glazed nose. It was also more heavily armoured than its predecessor, more so when it saw action because the gunners proved to be a popular target for enemy fighter pilots.

Test-flights were concluded by June 1939 and the type, redesignated Il-4 in 1940, was ordered into production. After the German invasion, production had been disrupted by moving the lines to the safety of Siberia. During the production run in 1942, wood was introduced in place of some metal components made of scarce light alloys. Metal was reintroduced as soon as it became available. Manufacture of the Il-4 continued until 1944, by which time 5256 had been built.

TOP AND ABOVE: **The Ilyushin DB-3 bomber was a record-breaker, and its defensive armament (7.62mm/0.3in) was one of the aircraft's few shortcomings.**

A fourth crew member, the "hatch" gunner, was added to improve defence, and two external fuel tanks were also added, which resulted in an 18 per cent increase in the fuel and an additional 600km/373 mile range. The outer wing was redesigned with leading-edge sweepback, thus improving stability and control. New, more efficient propellers and bigger split-flaps were installed to improve short-field operations.

The Il-4 was used for long-range bombing missions, but was equally efficient hauling its maximum bomb load of 2500kg/5502lb over short distances to attack tactical targets. The first Soviet bombing raid on Berlin was carried out by naval Il-4s on the night of August 8–9, 1941.

LEFT: **The upper gun turret of the DB-3F was fitted with a 12.7mm/0.5in machine-gun.** BELOW: **These aircraft were the backbone of Soviet long-range bomber capability.**

ABOVE: **The Il-4 proved itself to be among the best bomber aircraft produced by the Soviet Union in World War II. Note the very thick flying suits worn by the crew in this photograph, and also the machine-gun in the centre of the aircraft's nose.**

Il-4 crewman Lieutenant I.M. Chisov was thrown clear of his exploding aircraft following a German fighter attack in January 1942. Without a parachute, he fell 6710m/22,000ft into a snow-filled ravine and, though badly injured, lived to tell the tale.

The Il-4 was also developed as a mining and torpedo bomber equipped with a 940kg/2069lb torpedo for attacks against German shipping in the Baltic. Some pilots were happy to carry two of these heavy weapons at the same time. These naval Il-4s were also equipped with six RS-82 rocket projectiles beneath the wing for suppression of flak ships and other defences.

The type remained in Soviet military use after the end of World War II into the 1950s, and was given the NATO codename "Bob". An improved version, the Il-6, was designed for high-altitude operations powered by two 1500hp diesel engines, but was never flown.

Ilyushin Il-4

First flight: 1939
Power: Two 1100hp M-88B radial piston engines
Armament: One 12.7mm/0.5in and two 7.62mm/ 0.3in machine-guns on mounts in nose and dorsal positions; up to 2500kg/5502lb bomb load
Size: Wingspan – 21.44m/70ft 4.25in
 Length – 14.8m/48ft 6.75in
 Height – 4.1m/13ft 5.5in
 Wing area – 66.7m²/717.98sq ft
Weights: Empty – 5800kg/12,766lb
 Maximum take-off – 11,300kg/24,871lb
Performance: Maximum speed – 430kph/267mph
 Ceiling – 9700m/31825ft
 Range – 3800km/2361 miles
 Climb – 270m/886ft per minute

Junkers Ju 52/3m

The Junkers Ju 52/3m is one of the greatest aircraft ever built. Though simple and unwieldy by modern standards, with a fixed undercarriage and corrugated construction, the robust Junkers was built in great numbers and served in a variety of roles from bomber to ski-equipped airliner. It equipped no fewer than 30 airlines pre-war and remained in service with a Swiss airline half a century after the type first flew.

The 3m (for three engines or *Motoren*) was developed from a single-engine version of the same aircraft, the Ju 52. The 3m version first flew in April 1932 and quickly became the standard aircraft of Lufthansa, accounting for three-quarters of its fleet. The military applications of this rugged and capable aircraft were clear to the German militarists, who encouraged the development of a military bomber-transport version. The Ju 52/3mg3e, powered by three BMW 525hp 132A-3 engines, could carry six 100kg/220lb bombs. It had a faired gun position on top of the fuselage rear of the wing and a primitive "dustbin" turret, each mounting a 7.92mm/0.31in machine-gun. As a transport, it could carry 18 troops or 12 stretchers.

This version became the first type to equip the first bomber group of the fledgling and secretly developing Luftwaffe, and it debuted as a bomber in 1936 during the Spanish Civil War with Germany's Condor Legion. Initially the Junkers ferried more than 10,000 Moroccan troops to Spain in support of the

TOP: **The "Tante Ju" (Auntie) Junkers, developed throughout its service, was the aerial workhorse of Nazi Germany.** ABOVE: **The Ju 52/3m was the standard airliner of Lufthansa, making up most of its fleet in the mid-1930s. The aircraft pictured here is still operated by the German airline and appears at air shows around Europe.**

Fascists, but then began bombing Republican targets and supporting ground troops battling for control of Madrid.

In March 1937 the Ju 52s, which were then considered to be slow, were tasked with night-time bombing of Republican-held territory. For the rest of the war the Ju 52 was used for moving large numbers of troops and supplies. That said, by the end of the war the Junkers bombers had dropped 6096 tonnes/6000 tons of bombs – the Ju 52 had played an important part in Franco's victory.

By the outbreak of World War II, the Ju 52 was obsolete as a bomber but was used on a vast scale as a transport aircraft. Over 1000 Ju 52s were in service with the Luftwaffe

LEFT: **The Ju 52 had a fixed undercarriage – one of its recognition features, together with the type's corrugated metal skin.**

at the start of World War II, but at peak, around 5000 examples of the rugged workhorse were used by the Third Reich. Hitler himself used a Ju 52 as his private transport for a time. Ju 52s transported the attacking army and their supplies during the German invasions of Norway, Denmark, France and the Low Countries in 1940.

In May 1941, around 500 Ju 52s took part in the huge airborne assault by the Germans on the island of Crete. Numerous versions appeared during the war with improved radio equipment, auto pilot and different self-defence armament. Minesweeper and glider tug versions also saw service. The Ju 52 was used on all fronts on which the Third Reich fought, and was a vital part of the Nazi war machine.

However, production of the aircraft was not limited to Germany. In post-war France, 400 examples of a version designated the AAC 1 Toucan were built, a number of them serving in the French Air Force and Navy. These French machines saw active service in the Algerian and Indo-China conflicts. Meanwhile in Spain CASA, who also produced a version of the Heinkel He111, built 170 aircraft designated C-352-L. An often forgotten Ju 52 fact is that ten reconditioned examples captured from the Luftwaffe flew with British European Airways in the immediate post-war years.

ABOVE LEFT: **Each aircraft in this formation of Ju 52s has its ventral "dustbin" gun turret deployed – another unpopular gunner position.** ABOVE: **The type was improved constantly (the aircraft shown here has streamlined housings over the wheels), and appeared in a multitude of versions.**

Junkers Ju 52/3mg3e

First flight: October 13, 1930 (Ju 52 single-engine version)
Power: Three BMW 725hp 132A-3 radial piston engines
Armament: One 7.92mm/0.31in machine-gun each in dorsal position and retractable ventral "dustbin" turret; 500kg/1100lb bomb load
Size: Wingspan – 29.24m/95ft 11.5in
   Length – 18.9m/62ft
   Height – 5.55m/18ft 2.5in
   Wing area – 110.5m²/1189sq ft
Weights: Empty – 5720kg/12,589lb
   Maximum take-off – 10,500kg/23,110lb
Performance: Maximum speed – 265kph/165mph
   Service ceiling – 5900m/19,360ft
   Range – 1000km/620 miles
   Climb – 3000m/9840ft in 17 minutes, 30 seconds

Junkers Ju 87 Stuka

The Stuka (short for *Sturzkampfflugzeug* or dive-bomber) is one of the best-known wartime Luftwaffe-combat types and certainly the easiest to recognize with its inverted gull wings and fixed undercarriage. Like many Luftwaffe aircraft, the Ju 87 was designed to provide tactical support to the army in land actions.

Although dive-bombing was used as an attack technique in World War I, no aircraft in that conflict was specifically designed for the role. Junkers developed the first dedicated dive-bomber, the K47, in the 1920s and test-flew the aircraft in 1928. Most of these aircraft were exported to China amidst great secrecy because Germany was still bound by the post-World War I agreement that it should not be producing weapons of war.

German strategists saw the potential of the dive-bomber as an effective weapon when used in close support of ground forces, reducing the enemy's resistance before ground forces advanced. Still amidst great secrecy, Germany decided to manufacture dedicated dive-bomber aircraft, and in 1933 Henschel developed the Hs123 while Junkers continued to work on their K47. The Henschel design was a biplane, but the Ju 87 (derived from the K47) was a single-engine monoplane which broke with the Junkers tradition of corrugated skin construction. The prototype was powered, ironically as later events proved, by a Rolls-Royce Kestrel engine, and had its

TOP: **Shortly before World War II began, the new Ju 87B had re-equipped all Luftwaffe Stukageschwaden.** ABOVE: **Evaluated under combat conditions in Spain, the Stuka became a key aircraft in the Blitz strategy.**

maiden flight in May 1935. The Luftwaffe were very impressed by the potent new dive-bomber and, with testing complete, the Stuka began to enter service in 1937. These early Stukas were sent to Spain and the Civil War for operational evaluation with the German Condor Legion.

In the first production version, the Ju 87A-1, a single fin replaced the two of the prototype, dive brakes were fitted to the outer wings, and the British engine was replaced by a Junkers Jumo 210Ca 640hp engine. The A-2 model can be identified by the larger undercarriage fairings and was powered by the supercharged 680hp Jumo 210Da.

By early 1939, all the A-series aircraft were relegated to training duties, and all dive-bomber units began equipping with the more powerful Ju 87B series, powered by the 1200hp

Jumo 211Da direct-injection engine. More streamlined spats over the landing gear appeared, and the latest Stukas were now equipped with an automatic dive control. The B-2 was improved further and could carry up to 1000kg/2200lb of bombs. The D-series fitted with the 1410hp Jumo 211J-1 engine introduced more armour to protect the crew. Various sub-types saw action, including night ground-attack versions armed with cannon. From 1942, the Ju 87G-1 dedicated anti-tank version was in action on the Eastern Front.

The Stuka's automatic dive control enabled the pilot to pre-set a pull-out height should he black out in the course of a steep dive-bombing attack. On commencing the dive attack, the pilot adjusted the dive angle manually by referring to red indicator lines painted on the canopy showing 60, 75 and 80 degrees from horizontal. The pilot would visually aim the aircraft at his target until a signal light on the altimeter illuminated, telling the pilot to press the bomb-release button on the top of the control column. The automatic pull-out would commence as the bombs left their cradles. The bombs would

follow the same course to the target as the aircraft had during its dive, while the pilot would experience around 6g as the aircraft automatically levelled out to begin its climb skywards.

The rear gunner operated a machine-gun which might keep defending fighters at a safe distance, but a Stuka was easy prey for fast modern fighters. With air superiority achieved and against obsolete fighters in Poland and the Low Countries the Stuka was able to hold its own, but when it came up against the Hurricanes and Spitfires of the RAF large numbers were destroyed on cross-Channel missions. The Ju 87 had a slow top speed and could not climb away quickly. Accordingly, it was withdrawn from operations against the UK, but the type continued to serve in Greece, Crete, North Africa, Malta and on the Eastern Front.

The Stuka was more than a dive-bomber – it was also a psychological weapon. The wheel covers were fitted with sirens that would wind up as the aircraft went into their dive – this created terror among the enemy below. Whistles were also known to be fitted on to the fins of the bombs to ensure a similar effect as the ordnance fell. The total number of Stukas produced was around 5700 aircraft.

ABOVE: **A D-series Stuka, complete with extra armour for crew protection.**

RIGHT: **A Ju 87B, the version which introduced automatic dive control.**

BELOW: **Unmistakable with its inverted gull wings – the Stuka.**

Junkers Ju 87D-1

First flight: 1940

Power: One Junkers 1410hp Jumo 12-cylinder piston engine

Armament: Two 7.92mm/0.3in machine-guns in wings and two in rear cockpit; up to 1800kg/3962lb bomb load

Size: Wingspan – 13.8m/45ft 3.5in
Length – 11.5mm/37ft 8.75in
Height – 3.9m/12ft 9.5in
Wing area – 31.9m²/343.38sq ft

Weights: Empty – 3900kg/8584lb
Maximum take-off – 6600kg/14,526lb

Performance: Maximum speed – 410kph/255mph
Ceiling – 7290m/23,915ft
Range – 1535km/954 miles
Climb – 5000m/16,405ft in 19 minutes, 48 seconds

Junkers Ju 88

Said by many to be the most important German bomber of World War II, the Ju 88 was in front-line service from the start to the end of the war. The Ju 88 is widely described as the "German Mosquito", because like the de Havilland aircraft, the Ju 88 was an extremely versatile design and was developed from a bomber for use in the dive-bomber, torpedo-bomber, close support, reconnaissance, heavy fighter and nightfighter roles.

In January 1936, the ReichsLuftMinisterium (RLM, the German Air Ministry) released specifications for a new fast bomber that could carry a bomb load of over 500kg/1100lb. The Junkers Flugzeug und Motorenwerke company responded with the Junkers Ju 88, designed largely by two American nationals employed for their expertise in stressed-skin construction. Construction of the prototype began in May 1936 with the first flight of the Ju 88-V1 taking place on December 21, 1936. A total of five prototypes were built, and one, the Ju 88-V5, made several record-breaking speed flights. In 1937, the specification was modified to include dive-bombing capabilities as well as an increased payload and range. The Ju 88-V6 was the first prototype built to meet the new specification, and it flew on June 18, 1938. In the autumn of 1938, the RLM chose the Ju 88 to become the latest bomber to join the Luftwaffe, and the Ju 88A production version began to reach front-line units in 1939. When war did eventually break out in September 1939, it was the Ju88A-1

TOP: **The Ju 88 was without doubt the most versatile aircraft operated by the Luftwaffe in World War II, and was in production throughout the conflict.**
ABOVE: **The fastest of the principal German bombers, the Ju 88 was found to have poor defensive armament.**

that entered service, although the first recorded mission was not flown until later in that month. The arrival of the Ju 88 was a significant boost to Germany's bomber forces, and although it was heavier than both the Dornier Do17 and the Heinkel He111, even when it carried a substantial bomb load, it was still the fastest of the three. Unlike other Luftwaffe bomber types such as the Heinkel He111, the Ju 88 was not battle-tested in the Spanish Civil War.

The strong and manoeuvrable Ju 88 was a key Luftwaffe aircraft in the 1940 Battle of Britain but in spite of its speed, it suffered at the guns of the faster British fighters. Although the Ju 88 had an extensive battery of machine-guns for defence, all forward machine-guns except that operated by the pilot had to be operated by the flight engineer who had to leap from one gun to another as British fighters assaulted the aircraft. As a result of combat experiences, the bomber was modified to carry extra defensive guns as well as more armour to protect the crew.

The A-series was the standard bomber version of the Ju 88. About 20 Ju 88As were sold to Finland in 1939, and mass production of the Ju 88 started in 1940 with the A4. Large numbers of the Ju 88A-4 were built with longer wings to carry heavier bomb loads of up to 2500 or 3000kg/5502 or 6603lb. Despite this, the 88 continued to operate successfully from rough fields. By the end of the war, 17 different subtypes of the Ju 88A had been designed. One of the most bizarre came from a 1944 RLM request to Junkers to develop a composite aircraft consisting of a fighter aircraft mounted on top of an unmanned heavy bomber aircraft. This Mistel combination aircraft was then flown to the target, where the fighter's pilot released the bomber, which was filled with explosives and plummeted to earth while the fighter returned to base. These Mistel weapons used old Ju 88s coupled to Messerschmitt Bf109s or Focke-Wulf Fw190s. About 85 Mistel combinations were built by the end of the war but only a few missions were flown.

RIGHT: **A Ju 88A-4 pictured over the Eastern Front in 1943.**
BELOW: **The large "glasshouse" nose of the Ju 88 gave the crew excellent forward vision.**

ABOVE: **The aircraft pictured here is a Ju 88A-5. Bombing, dive-bombing, nightfighting and reconnaissance were all roles carried out by the great varieties of Ju 88s produced during the war.**

Junkers Ju 88A-4

First flight: December 21, 1936 (Ju 88 prototype)
Power: Two Junkers Jumo 1340hp 211J-1 piston engines
Armament: One 7.9mm/0.308in machine-gun in front cockpit, one 13mm/0.51in or two 7.9mm/0.308in machine-guns in front nose, two rearward-firing 7.9mm/0.308in machine-guns in rear cockpit and one 13mm/0.51in or two 7.9mm/0.308in machine-guns at rear of gondola beneath nose; up to 3600kg/7923lb carried internally and externally
Size: Wingspan – 20m/65ft 7in
Length – 14.4m/47ft 2.6in
Height – 4.85m/15ft 11in
Wing area – 54.5m²/586.6sq ft
Weights: Empty – 9860kg/21,041lb
Maximum take-off – 14,000kg/30,814lb
Performance: Maximum speed – 433kph/269mph
Ceiling – 8200m/26,900ft
Range – 2730km/1696 miles
Climb – 400m/1312ft per minute

Kawanishi H8K

When Japan first went to war with the Allies, its standard maritime patrol flying boat was the Kawanishi H6K. The type performed well in the early stages of the war in the reconnaissance and bombing roles until it came up against Allied fighters, when it suffered severe maulings. It had entered service in 1938 and, thinking ahead, the Japanese Navy immediately issued a specification for a replacement with a 30 per cent higher speed and 50 per cent greater range.

The requirement called for a long-range aircraft with better performance than Britain's Short Sunderland or the American Sikorsky XPBS-1. The designers produced one of the finest military flying boats ever built, and certainly the best of World War II.

To give the aircraft the required range, it carried eight small unprotected fuel tanks in the wings and a further six large tanks in the fuselage or, more correctly, hull. The hull tanks were partially self-sealing and also boasted a carbon dioxide fire extinguisher system. Ingeniously, the tanks were placed so that if any leaked, the fuel would collect in a fuel

TOP: **The H8K entered Imperial Japanese Navy service in late 1941 and first flew into action in March the following year.** ABOVE: **Fitted with beaching gear, this H8K, codenamed "Emily" by the Allies, is undergoing engine runs.**

"bilge" and then be pumped to an undamaged tank. The aircraft was a flying fuel tank, with 15,816 litres/3479 gallons being a typical fuel load and accounting for some 29 per cent of the take-off weight. The aircraft positively bristled with defensive armament – 20mm/0.78in cannons were carried in powered nose, dorsal and tail turrets, with two more in opposite beam blisters. A further three 7.7mm/0.303in machine-guns were in port and starboard beam hatches and in the ventral position. The crew positions were well armoured.

ABOVE: **The H8K was the fastest flying boat of World War II.** ABOVE RIGHT: **The Japanese boat was larger overall than the famed Sunderland used by the RAF.** RIGHT: **Well armed and with excellent overall performance, the H8K was a formidable opponent for Allied fighter aircraft.**

The Navy was appropriately impressed with the aircraft, but flight-testing of the H8K in late 1940 was far from uneventful, and numerous features of the aircraft had to be revised. The heavy aircraft's narrow hull, for example, caused uncontrollable porpoising in the water – when the nose lifted from the water's surface, the whole aircraft became unstable. The design team revised the hull, and production of the H8K1 (Navy Type 2 Flying Boat Model 11) began in mid-1941. Total production was a mere 175 aircraft produced in the H8K1, H8K2 (improved engines, heavier armament and radar) and 3H8K2-L (transport) versions.

The H8K was powered by four 1530hp Kasei 11s or 12s. The latter bestowed better high-altitude performance and powered late-production H8K1s. The aircraft's offensive load, carried under the inner wing, was either two 801kg/1763lb torpedoes, eight 250kg/550lb bombs, or 16 60kg/132lb bombs or depth charges.

The H8K made its combat debut on the night of March 4–5, 1942. The night-bombing raid on the island of Oahu, Hawaii, was over so great a distance that even the long-range H8K had to put down to refuel from a submarine en route. Although bad weather meant that the target was not bombed, the raid showed that the H8K was a formidable weapon of war. It was the fastest and most heavily defended flying boat of World War II, and one which Allied fighter pilots found hard to down in aerial combat.

The H8K's deep hull lent itself to the development of a transport version, the H8K2-L, with two passenger decks. The lower deck reached from the nose to some two-thirds of the fuselage, while the upper deck extended from the wing to the back of the hull. Seats or benches could accommodate from 29 passengers or 64 troops in differing levels of comfort. Armament was reduced, as was fuel-carrying capability with the removal of the hull tanks.

Kawanishi H8K2

First flight: Late 1940
Power: Four Mitsubishi 1850hp Kasei radial
  engines
Armament: 20mm/0.78in cannon in bow, dorsal
  and tail turrets and in beam blisters, plus four
  7.7mm/0.303in machine-guns in cockpit, ventral
  and side hatches
Size: Wingspan – 38m/124ft 8in
  Length – 28.13m/92ft 4in
  Height – 9.15m/30ft
  Wing area – 160m²/1722sq ft
Weights: Empty – 18,380kg/40,454lb
  Maximum take-off – 32,500kg/71,532lb
Performance: Maximum speed – 467kph/
  290mph
  Ceiling – 8760m/28,740ft
  Range – 7180km/4460 miles
  Climb – 480m/1575ft per minute

Lockheed Hudson

The Lockheed Hudson, the first American-built aircraft to be used operationally by the RAF during World War II, was designed to meet an urgent 1938 British requirement for a long-range maritime patrol bomber and navigation trainer. Lockheed's response, after five days and nights of frenzied work, was a militarized version of the proven Lockheed 14 Super Electra. The original Lockheed Model 10 Electra was a ten-seat civil airliner which first flew in February 1934. The larger and more powerfully engined Super Electra carried 12 passengers and first flew in July 1937. Howard Hughes made a high-profile round-the-world trip in a Super Electra, and it was this type of aircraft that took Prime Minister Chamberlain to meet Hitler in September 1938. In June 1938 the British Purchasing Commission placed an order for the Lockheed aircraft, stipulating that 200 aircraft had to be delivered by the end of December 1939. A further 50 aircraft would be bought if they could be delivered by the same date.

The Hudson was an all-metal mid-wing monoplane with an eliptical cross-section fuselage and a transparent nose for bomb-aiming. Fowler flaps were fitted to improve short-field performance. The crew normally consisted of a pilot, navigator, bomb-aimer, radio operator and gunner. Armament consisted of a bomb load of up to 454kg/1000lb (in later models) and up to seven machine-guns in nose, dorsal turret, beam and ventral hatch positions.

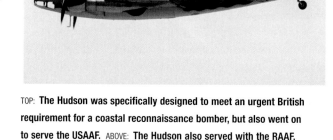

TOP: **The Hudson was specifically designed to meet an urgent British requirement for a coastal reconnaissance bomber, but also went on to serve the USAAF.** ABOVE: **The Hudson also served with the RAAF, RNZAF and RCAF.**

The first flight of a Hudson I (as a modified existing aircraft there was no need or time for a prototype) was on December 10, 1938, and the first of the RAF's aircraft arrived at Liverpool docks within two months. It may be hard to believe now, but the Hudson was considered something of a hot-rod compared to the Anson it replaced in RAF service. It climbed at 366m/1200ft per minute compared to the 220m/720ft per minute of the Anson, and had a top speed around 30 per cent greater than that of the "Annie". The Hudson Mk I began squadron service with RAF Coastal Command's No.224 Squadron in the summer of 1939, and by September No.233 Squadron was also equipped, soon followed by No.220. Shortly after war broke out, Hudsons also equipped

LEFT: **The first American-built aircraft used in action by the RAF during World War II.**
BELOW LEFT: **A Hudson of No.85 Squadron RAF.**
BELOW: **Hudsons and A-29s saw action in the Mediterranean, Pacific, Indian Ocean, Carribbean and Atlantic.**

Nos.206 and 269 Squadrons. All these aircraft flew vital maritime patrol and anti-shipping missions in defence of the UK. At peak strength, the RAF's Hudson force amounted to 17 squadrons.

The Hudson earned its spurs on October 8, 1939, when a No.224 Squadron Hudson Mk I shot down a Dornier Do18D flying boat off Jutland, the first German aircraft to be claimed by the RAF during the war. In early 1940, Hudsons began to be equipped with air-to-surface-vessel radar. Based at Aldergrove in Northern Ireland, Hudsons carried out dedicated anti-submarine patrols from August 1940. The Hudson's first victory against a U-boat occurred on August 27, 1941, when an aircraft operating out of Iceland bombed and damaged *U-570* which, following strafing attacks, surrendered. A total of 25 U-boats were put out of the war by RAF Hudsons.

Hudsons also took part in more conventional operations, with 35 participating in the RAF's second "thousand bomber" raid. The Hudsons of No.161 Squadron took part in top-secret operations delivering (and retrieving) agents, arms and other supplies into enemy territory under cover of darkness.

Total production amounted to 2584, and Hudsons were also operated by the RCAF, RAAF and RNZAF fighting in the Mediterranean, South Pacific, Indian Ocean, North Atlantic and Caribbean. China, Portugal and Brazil also purchased the Lockheed bomber. The USAAF had 490 (as the A-29), the US Navy 20 (as the PBO-1), and a further 300 were military trainers (AT-18) in the USA. It was US Navy PBO-1s that sank the first two U-boats destroyed by US forces, and a Hudson that destroyed the first for the USAAF.

Lockheed Hudson Mk I

First flight: December 10, 1938
Power: Two Wright 1100hp GR-1820-G-102A radial piston engines
Armament: Two forward-firing 7.7mm/0.303in machine-guns, plus two others in dorsal turret; up to 635kg/1400lb bomb load
Size: Wingspan – 19.96m/65ft 6in
Length – 13.51m/44ft 4in
Height – 3.61m/11ft 10in
Wing area – 51.19m²/551sq ft
Weights: Empty – 5280kg/11630lb
Maximum take-off – 7945kg/17,500lb
Performance: Maximum speed – 396kph/246mph
Ceiling – 7625m/25,000ft
Range – 3154km/1960 miles
Climb – 3048m/10,000ft in 6 minutes, 18 seconds

Martin bomber series

The Martin Model 123 was designed and built as a private venture by the Glenn L. Martin Company of Baltimore, Maryland. The aircraft, which first flew in January 1932, was hugely influential because it broke with many design traditions and set new standards for US military combat types – it was the USAAC's first all-metal monoplane bomber.

The Model 123 was a mid-wing, all-metal monoplane, and the monocoque fuselage had corrugated top and bottom surfaces. The fuselage was sufficiently deep to allow the carriage of bombs in an internal bomb bay, as opposed to the external racks of many bombers in service at the time. The main landing gear retracted backwards to be semi-recessed into the rear of the engine nacelles. In this version, three of the crew of four sat in separate open cockpits atop the fuselage.

The US Army were interested in Martin's new "hot ship", and under the designation XB-907 the aircraft was extensively tested at Wright Field. Its speed of 317kph/197mph was ahead of all the fighters in USAAC service at the time.

The aircraft was returned to Martin for modifications, including the addition of a front gun turret in place of the far-from-popular open gun position in the nose.

However, the pilot's cockpit and the dorsal gunner positions remained open to the elements. The designation was changed to XB-907A when it was returned to the Army for more tests, then in January 1933 the Army ordered 48 production versions with enclosed cockpits, designated YB-10.

The type entered squadron service in June 1934. The major production version was the B-10B powered by 775hp Wright R-1820-33s, and production B-10B deliveries began in December 1935.

The B-12 was the same as the B-10 but was powered by Pratt & Whitney engines and had the ability to carry an auxiliary fuel tank in the bomb bay.

The B-10s and derivatives remained in service with US Army bombardment squadrons until aircraft like the B-17 were available in the late 1930s, by which time it was obsolete. No US Army B-10s participated in any combat during World War II, but export aircraft (Model 139) supplied to the Netherlands saw action against the Japanese in 1942. Other export customers were Argentina, China, the Soviet Union, Siam and Turkey. The sole remaining Martin B-10 is preserved by the United States Air Force Museum.

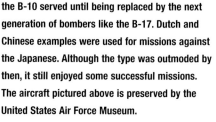

TOP AND ABOVE: **An advanced US bomber for the time, the B-10 served until being replaced by the next generation of bombers like the B-17. Dutch and Chinese examples were used for missions against the Japanese. Although the type was outmoded by then, it still enjoyed some successful missions. The aircraft pictured above is preserved by the United States Air Force Museum.**

Martin B-10B

First flight: January 1932 (Model 123)
Power: Two Wright 775hp R-1820-33 Cyclone radial piston engines
Armament: Three 7.62mm/0.3in machine-guns in nose and rear turrets and in ventral position; up to 1026kg/2260lb bomb load
Size: Wingspan – 21.49m/70ft 6in
Length – 13.64m/44ft 9in
Height – 4.7m/15ft 5in
Wing area – 62.99m²/678sq ft
Weights: Empty – 4395kg/9681lb
Maximum take-off – 7445kg/16,400lb
Performance: Maximum speed – 343kph/213mph
Ceiling – 7381m/24,200ft
Range – 1996km/1240 miles
Climb – 567m/1860ft per minute

LEFT: **Few Marylands remained in Britain, and the type became the first US-supplied bomber used by the RAF in North Africa.**

Martin Maryland

Martin Maryland Mk II

First flight: March 14, 1939
Power: Two Pratt & Whitney 1200hp R-1830-S3C4G Twin Wasp radial piston engines
Armament: Four 7.7mm/0.303in wing-mounted machine-guns, plus two more in dorsal and ventral positions; up to 908kg/2000lb bomb load
Size: Wingspan – 18.69m/61ft 4in
Length – 14.22m/46ft 8in
Height – 4.57m/14ft 11.75in
Wing area – 50.03m²/538.5sq ft
Weights: Empty – 5090kg/11,213lb
Maximum take-off – 7631kg/16,809lb
Performance: Maximum speed – 447kph/278mph
Ceiling – 7930m/26,000ft
Range – 1947km/1210 miles
Climb – 546m/1790ft per minute

The Martin 167 Maryland was built to a USAAC specification, but the type was only operated by France and Britain. It was designed for both reconnaissance and bombing, and four squadrons of the French Air Force were equipped with the type at the time of the German invasion in May 1940.

Britain ordered its own Marylands and took delivery of diverted French orders after France fell. This required all the considerable labelling in the aircraft to be changed from French to English. These early aircraft were designated Maryland Is in RAF service and were followed by the more powerfully engined Maryland IIs. A total of 225 aircraft served with the Royal Air Force and virtually all served in the Middle East.

Malta-based Marylands provided valuable reconnaissance cover in the region, and those of the Desert Air Force's Nos.39 and 223 Squadrons were effective light bombers. The type also equipped four South African Air Force squadrons active in the Western Desert.

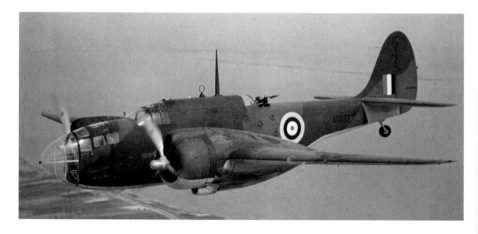

LEFT: **A Baltimore I in flight. Of the RAF's first batch of 400 aircraft, 41 were lost at sea in transit.**

Martin Baltimore Mk IV

First flight: June 14, 1941
Power: Two Wright 1660hp R-2600-19 Cyclone 14 radial piston engines
Armament: Four 7.7mm/0.303in wing-mounted machine-guns, two or four more in dorsal turret, two 7.63mm/0.3in in ventral position; up to 908kg/2000lb bomb load
Size: Wingspan – 18.69m/61ft 4in
Length – 14.8m/48ft 5.75in
Height – 5.41m/17ft 9in
Wing area – 50.03m²/538.5sq ft
Weights: Empty – 7018kg/15,460lb
Maximum take-off – 10,260kg/22,600lb
Performance: Maximum speed – 491kph/305mph
Ceiling – 7106m/23,300ft
Range – 1530km/950 miles
Climb – 4572m/15,000ft in 12 minutes

Martin Baltimore

Unlike the Maryland, the Baltimore was designed specifically to meet Royal Air Force requirements. Although it was developed from the Maryland and had the same wing, the Baltimore had more powerful engines and, most apparently, a deeper fuselage to allow better communication between the crew. Despite this, the narrow fuselage made movement around the aircraft in an emergency almost impossible. The RAF ordered 400 in May 1940 but 1575 were

ultimately produced for them. They were used solely in the Mediterranean, the first joining No.223 Squadron.

The crew of four consisted of a pilot, navigator/bomb-aimer, top gunner and a radio operator who also manned the ventral gun position. Baltimore Marks I to IV had 1600hp Wright GR-2600-A5B radial engines, while the V and VI had the upgraded 1700hp Wright engines.

Desert Air Force Baltimores flew day and night bombing missions in support

of ground troops in the North African campaign. Later, the type was used for intensive bombing ahead of invading Allied troops in Italy.

Martin Mariner

Martin had a history of producing flying boats, and in 1937 the company began work on a design to replace the Consolidated Catalina in US Navy service. Martin's Model 162, naval designation XPBM-1 (Experimental Patrol Bomber Martin 1), had a deep hull and shoulder-mounted gull wings, a flat twin-fin tail and inward-retracting wing floats. The gull wing design was used to produce the greatest possible distance between the engines and sea water. A less than half-scale single-seat version was produced to test the aerodynamics of the design, and its success led to the first flight of the full-scale prototype XPBM-1 in 1939.

The XPBM-1 prototype first flew in February 1939 and test-flights called for a redesign of the tail, which resulted in the dihedral configuration that matched the angle of the main wings. The aircraft had been ordered before the test-flight, so the first production model, the PBM-1, appeared quite quickly in October 1940 with service deliveries being complete by April 1941. By now the type was named Mariner. The PBM-1 had a crew of seven and was armed with five 12.7mm/0.5in Browning machine-guns. One gun was mounted in a flexible position in the tail, one was fitted in a flexible mount on each side of the rear fuselage, another was fitted in a rear dorsal turret and one was fitted in a nose turret. In addition, the PBM-1 could carry up to 908kg/2000lb of bombs or depth charges in bomb bays that were, unusually, fitted in the engine nacelles. The doors of the bomb bays looked like those of landing gear, but the Mariner was not amphibian at this stage.

In late 1940 the US Navy ordered 379 improved Model 162Bs or PBM-3s, although around twice that number were actually produced. This order alone required the

TOP: **A PBM-1 Mariner in flight, with power provided by two Wright R-2600-6 Double Cyclones.** ABOVE: **A Mariner being serviced in the Iwo Jima area, World War II. The PBMs were the eyes of the US fleet since landplanes based in the Marianas did not have the range for the required ocean patrol coverage.**

US government-aided construction of a new Martin plant in Maryland. The -3 differed from the -1 mainly by the use of uprated Pratt & Whitney 1700hp R-2600-12 engines, larger fixed wing floats and larger bomb bays housed in enlarged nacelles. Nose and dorsal turrets were powered on this version. Early PBM-3s had three-bladed propellers, but production soon included four-bladed propellers.

The PBM-3C, rolled out in late 1942, was the next major version, with 274 built. It had better armour protection for the crew, twin gun front and dorsal turrets, an improved tail turret still with a single gun, and air-to-surface-vessel radar. In addition, many PBM-3Cs were fitted with an underwing searchlight in the field.

US Navy Mariners saw extensive use in the Pacific, guarding the Atlantic western approaches and defending the Panama Canal. It was concluded that most Mariners were not likely to encounter fighter opposition, so much of the defensive armament was deleted – once the guns, turrets

LEFT: **A Mariner being prepared for hoisting by a US Navy seaplane tender, believed to be at the time of the Korean War.** BELOW: **US Navy Mariners flying over the Brazilian capital of Rio de Janeiro as they escorted an Allied convoy into port.**
BOTTOM LEFT: **The pilot of a US Navy PBM-3S starts his port engine as crewmen stand by in case of fire at a Caribbean naval air station, 1944. The large protuberance above the cockpit area is a powerful anti-submarine search radar.**

and ammunition were removed, the weight saving resulted in a 25 per cent increase in the range of the lighter PBM-3S anti-submarine version. However, the nose guns were retained for offensive fire against U-boats and other surface targets. Despite this development, a more heavily armed and armoured version, the PBM-3D, was produced by re-engining some 3Cs. Larger non-retractable floats and self-sealing fuel tanks were also a feature of this version.

Deliveries of the more powerfully engined PBM-5 began in August 1944, and 589 were delivered before production ceased at the end of the war. With the PBM-5A amphibian version (of which 40 were built), the Mariner finally acquired a tricycle landing gear. The Mariner continued to serve with the US Navy and US Coast Guard into the early 1950s, and over 500 were in service at the time of the Korean War. The USCG retired its last Mariner in 1958.

Martin PBM-3D Mariner

First flight: February 18, 1939 (XPBM-1)
Power: Two Wright 1900hp R-2600-22 Cyclone radial piston engines
Armament: Eight 12.7mm/0.5in machine-guns in nose, dorsal, waist and tail positions; up to 3632kg/8000lb of bombs or depth charges
Size: Wingspan – 35.97m/118ft
    Length – 24.33m/79ft 10in
    Height – 8.38m/27ft 6in
    Wing area – 130.8m²/1408sq ft
Weights: Empty – 15,061kg/33,175lb
    Maximum take-off – 26,332kg/58,000lb
Performance: Maximum speed – 340kph/211mph
    Ceiling – 6035m/19,800ft
    Range – 3605km/2240 miles
    Climb – 244m/800ft per minute

Martin B-26 Marauder

In 1939 the US Army Air Corps issued a demanding specification for a high-speed medium bomber, and Martin's Model 179 proposal was so impressive that the aircraft was ordered into production off the drawing board. The aircraft was a shoulder-wing monoplane with a spacious circular cross-section fuselage for a crew of five and a retractable tricycle landing gear for improved visibility on the ground.

The first aircraft flew on November 25, 1940, and the first B-26s went to the 22nd Bomb Group at Langley Field, Virginia. This was quite a transition because the B-26 weighed two and a half times as much as the B-18 it was replacing, and had a landing speed that was 50 per cent greater. Although the original specification was exceeded, the aircraft did exhibit difficult low-speed handling, which led to an early high accident rate. Modifications improved low-speed performance and revisions to training overcame the problem, and on December 8, 1941, the day after the Japanese attack on Pearl Harbor, the USA deployed B-26s to Australia.

The first B-26 mission flown was by the 22nd Bomb Group on April 5, 1942. Taking off from Garbutt Field, Australia, the aircraft first staged through an airfield near Port Moresby, New Guinea, before attacking the Japanese base at Rabaul in New Britain.

The A-model carried more fuel, heavier armament and could carry a torpedo for maritime attack. On June 4, 1942, during the Battle of Midway, four Marauders set off to carry out the type's first torpedo attack in action against Japanese

ABOVE: **In May 1943, the B-26 became the principal medium bomber of the US Ninth Air Force in Europe. The aircraft pictured here was restored to flying condition, and appears at US air shows.**

carriers. The torpedo runs began at 244m/800ft, the aircraft then dropping down to around 3m/10ft above the sea while under heavy attack from Japanese fighters. Two B-26s were lost in the attack, the other two were seriously damaged and none of the torpedoes found their mark. The conclusion drawn from this rare tragic chapter in B-26 history was that the type was simply unsuited to this form of attack.

By November 1942 the B-26Bs (with bigger engines, more armour and, in later aircraft, bigger wings) and B-26Cs (B-models produced in Nebraska) began to see action in North Africa with 12 units of the US 12th Air Force. These aircraft, operating in a tactical bomber role, supported Allied ground forces as they fought through Corsica, Italy, Sardinia, Sicily and then southern France.

B-26s of the US Ninth Air Force, initially based in Britain in support of the D-Day landings, ranged over northern Europe attacking airfields, roads, bridges, railroads and V-1 flying bomb facilities. Despite early safety issues, the Marauder went on to have the lowest attrition rate per sortie of any American aircraft operated by the US Air Forces in Europe.

Under Lend-Lease, the Royal Air Force ordered a total of 522 Marauders and deployed them all, like the Martin Maryland and Baltimore before them, only in the Mediterranean theatre

RIGHT: Because the B-26 was ordered straight from the drawing-board, there were no prototypes, but most of the first batch of 201 were retained for testing and training. The aircraft shown here is a JM-1, a US Navy/Marine Corps target tug/trainer version of the B-26B.

and with the South African Air Force. No.14 Squadron was the first RAF unit to be equipped in August 1942, and was operational within two months. RAF B-26s also supported Allied forces in Sicily, Sardinia and Italy, and by the end of March 1944 had dropped a total of 18,288 tonnes/18,000 tons of bombs. In March 1943 six squadrons of Free French Air Force Marauders became operational. Flying alongside other Allied B-26s, the French Marauders supported the Allied invasion of southern France in August 1944.

By the end of the war, the B-26 had flown 129,943 operational sorties in the European and Mediterranean theatres alone, dropping 172,092 tonnes/169,382 tons of bombs in the process and destroying 402 enemy aircraft.

ABOVE: Unit cost for the B-26 was 261,000 US dollars when it first entered service. This was reduced to 192,000 US dollars by 1944 owing to the numbers in production and refinement of the production lines. LEFT: Deliveries to the air force began in 1941, and the type was deployed to Australia the day after Pearl Harbor to combat any further Japanese aggression.

ABOVE: The Marauder I in RAF service was equivalent to the B-26A, and had a shorter wing than later models.

Martin B-26B Marauder 🇺🇸

First flight: November 25, 1940
Power: Two Pratt & Whitney 1920hp R-2800-43 radial piston engines
Armament: 12.7mm/0.5in machine-guns in nose, tail, top turret and fixed forward-firing on side of fuselage
Size: Wingspan – 21.64m/71ft
Length – 17.75m/58ft 3in
Height – 6.55m/21ft 6in
Wing area – 61.13m²/658sq ft
Weights: Empty – 10,896kg/24,000lb
Maximum take-off –16,798kg/37,000lb
Performance: Maximum speed – 454kph/282mph
Ceiling – 6405m/21,000ft
Range – 1851km/1150 miles
Climb – 4572m/15,000ft in 13 minutes

Mitsubishi G4M

The G4M, codenamed "Betty" by the Allies, was the Japanese Navy's principal heavy bomber of World War I. It was designed to an extremely exacting 1937 Imperial Japanese Navy specification for a land-based bomber capable of carrying a full bomb load over 3704km/2000 nautical miles. The performance was hard to achieve and came largely at the cost of protection of the crew (in terms of armour and defensive armament) and the aircraft's fuel tanks, which were contained in the aircraft wing but without armour or the ability to self-seal when damaged.

Nicknames such as "One-Shot Lighter" and the "Flying Cigar" were coined on both sides, reflecting the aircraft's tendency to explode in flames when hit in combat – the aircraft was not popular with its crews.

The prototype first flew in October 1939 and, being a basically sound design, the type progressed through flight-testing with production beginning in late 1940. The type, now designated Navy Type 1 Attack Bomber Model 11, began to reach front-line units in the summer of 1941. The next

RIGHT: **In service from mid-1943, the G4M2 was a refined version of the Japanese bomber but lacked the range of the earlier versions.**
BELOW: **G4M1s – the original version of Japan's numerically most important bomber, in service throughout the Pacific war.**

production version, the G4M1 Model 12, was powered by the Kasei 15 engine, which provided better performance at altitude. Late 1942 saw the appearance of the improved GM42 Model 22 with a new laminar-flow wing, larger tailplane and power provided by 1800hp Mitsubishi Kasei 21 engines.

Perhaps the type's most famous action took place on December 10, 1941, three days after the attack on Pearl Harbor. G4Ms and G3Ms of the 22nd Air Flotilla sank two British capital ships, the *Prince of Wales* and the *Repulse*, off the coast of Malaya. The two ships were the first capital ships ever to be sunk by air attack at sea while free to evade. In March 1942, G4Ms made the first bombing attacks on the port of Darwin in northern Australia.

A number of earlier models were designated G4M2e Model 24J when modified to carry the MXY-7 Okha piloted kamikaze missile. Due to the great weight increase, the G4M2e was very

Mitsubishi G4M3 Model 34

First flight: October 23, 1939

Power: Two Mitsubishi MK4T Kasei 25 radial engines

Armament: Four 20mm/0.78in cannon and two 7.7mm/0.303in machine-guns; up to 1000kg/2201lb of bombs or one 800kg/1761lb torpedo

Size: Wingspan – 25m/82ft 0.25in
Length – 19.5m/63ft 11.75in
Height – 6m/19ft 8.25in
Wing area – 78.13m²/840sq ft

Weights: Empty – 8350kg/18,378lb
Maximum take-off – 12,500kg/27,512lb

Performance: Maximum speed – 470kph/292mph
Ceiling – 9220m/30,250ft
Range – 4335km/2694 miles
Climb – 420m/1380ft per minute

ABOVE: **In the G4M3, the designers remedied the earlier versions' tendency to ignite so readily when hit in combat.** RIGHT: **The great range of the earlier G4Ms was only achieved at the expense of protective armour for the crew.** BELOW: **This "Betty", pictured near Singapore, was captured by the RAF in Malaya. In addition to RAF roundels, the aircraft bears the letters ATAIU SEA for Allied Technical Air Intelligence Unit, South-east Asia. The aircraft is being evaluated but flown by Japanese naval pilots under the close armed supervision of RAF officers.**

slow when carrying the weapon, and the combination had a disastrous combat debut on March 21, 1945, when most were shot down by carrier-based Allied fighter aircraft before they could launch their missiles.

Long range was not a prime concern once the Allies began to force their way towards Japan itself, and in the G4M3 Model 34, which first flew in early 1944, self-sealing fuel tanks and protective armour for the crew were introduced. Only 60 had been built by the end of the war.

In August 1942, Rabaul-based G4Ms flew the first counter-attacks against US forces invading Guadalcanal. Of 26 aircraft in the attack, at least 17 were shot down in a single raid. One aircraft damaged by ground fire made a suicide attack on the transport ship *George F. Elliott*. G4Ms operated throughout the six-month battle for Guadalcanal and suffered heavy losses.

By early 1943, the Japanese Navy had developed new techniques using "Betties" for night torpedo attack. On the night of January 29–30, 1943, during the Battle of Rennell Island, G4Ms successfully torpedoed and sank the heavy cruiser *Chicago*, and in February 1944 a Betty torpedoed the US carrier *Intrepid*. On August 19, 1945 it was two G4M1s that carried the Imperial Japanese delegation to discuss the final requirements for Japan's surrender with the Allies.

Mitsubishi built a total of 2416 G4Ms, including prototypes, in addition to 30 G6M1 escort fighter versions manned by crews of ten who had no fewer than 19 guns at their disposal.

North American B-25 Mitchell

TOP: **The B-25 made its combat debut in early 1942, and the type remained in the front line throughout World War II.** ABOVE: **FV914, an RAF Mitchell II (B-25D) looses its bomb load. The Mk II was the main version of around 800 examples operated by the RAF.**

In the late 1930s, the US Army was looking for an "Aircraft-Bombardment Type-Medium" to fill the gap in its inventory between its light and heavy bombers. North American's response was the NA-40, which developed into the B-25 Mitchell, one of the most widely used aircraft of World War II. The B-25 entered USAAF service in 1941 and was in action until the end of the war, but the type will forever be known as the aircraft that carried out the April 1942 Doolittle raid against Tokyo from the carrier USS *Hornet*. However, the first action of a B-25 was probably the sinking of a Japanese submarine on Christmas Eve 1941. The Mitchell was named after Colonel "Billy" Mitchell who was court-martialled in the 1920s for his far-sighted views on US air power and strategic bombing.

Early production versions were eclipsed by the much-redesigned B-25C/D, which was the same aircraft built at different locations – C-models were built by North American at Inglewood while Ds were produced at NA's Dallas plant. In total some 3909 examples of the C/D were built, and 533 were supplied to the Royal Air Force as Mitchell IIs. Under the Lend-Lease deal between Britain and the USA, the RAF acquired a total of over 800 examples of this robust and reliable bomber. The B-25 first entered RAF service with Nos.98 and 180 Squadrons in September 1942, and from August 1943 they operated as part of the Second Tactical Air Force, carrying out pre-D-Day attacks on targets in Northern France as well as on V-1 "doodlebug" sites in the Pas de Calais. A total of 870 C/Ds were also supplied to the Soviet Union.

The next production variant was the B-25G, which was developed from a C-model modified to carry a US Army 75mm/2.93in field gun in the nose. This seemingly far-fetched proposal resulted in the production of 405 examples which

North American B-25H Mitchell

First flight: August 19, 1940 (production B-25)
Power: Two Wright 1700hp R-2600-13 radial piston engines
Armament: One 75mm/2.93in cannon, fourteen 12.7mm/0.5in machine-guns; up to 1362kg/3000lb bomb load or one 908kg/2000lb torpedo, plus up to eight rocket projectiles
Size: Wingspan – 20.6m/67ft 7in
Length – 15.54m/51ft
Height – 4.8m/15ft 9in
Wing area – 56.67 m²/610sq ft
Weights: Empty – 9068kg/19,975lb
Maximum take-off – 16,365kg/36,047lb
Performance: Maximum speed – 442kph/275mph
Service ceiling – 7259m/23,800ft
Range – 4344km/2700 miles
Climb – 4572m/15,000ft in 19 minutes

ABOVE: **The Doolittle raid is the best-known B-25 mission, but the bomber carried out countless vital missions while serving with the USAAF, USN, USMC and RAF.** RIGHT: **The heavily armed B-25J was produced in greater numbers than any other version.**

carried 21 6.81kg/15lb shells for use against ground targets and shipping. The improved B-25H carried a lighter 75mm/2.93in gun but also had four 12.7mm/0.5in guns in the nose, a further four in blisters on the sides of the nose, two more in a dorsal turret and in the tail, two in the waist positions, as well as a bomb load of 1362kg/3000lb and up to eight rocket projectiles fired from beneath the wings. One thousand examples of this hard-hitting B-25 version were built, and they saw extensive service in the Pacific.

The most numerous version of all was the B-25J, with more than 4300 examples delivered before the end of the war. This example lost the 75mm/2.93in gun but retained the other armament of the H-model. This version saw action in the Pacific, the Mediterranean and in South-east Asia. In RAF service this version was known as the Mitchell III.

The B-25 was one of the most widely used aircraft of World War II, serving with the United States Army Air Forces, Navy and Marine Corps, and was supplied to the USSR, Britain, China, Australia, Canada, France and the Netherlands.

In January 1943, B-25s were ordered by the US Navy for the US Marine Corps. Their 706 B-25s (C,D, H and J-models) were designated PBJs, and supported marine landings during the island-hopping campaigns of the drive to the Japanese home islands.

Post-war, in addition to equipping smaller air forces, many B-25s were used as training and light transport aircraft. The last B-25 in US military service was a VIP transport retired on May 21, 1960. The aircraft's stability and ease of adaptation led a number to be used as camera ships for the film industry, and some fly on in this role today.

ABOVE: **The B-25 was widely operated post-war, and a number of B-25s are preserved by collectors and museums.**

TOP: **The Stirling III was the standard RAF bomber version from 1943.**

ABOVE: **The long undercarriage legs of the Stirling are clear in this photograph – the ground crew are dwarfed by the machine.**

Short Stirling

The Short S.29 Stirling was one of 11 designs proposed by numerous aircraft manufacturers to satisfy the Air Ministry Specification B12/36. This called for a four-engined heavy bomber that could carry a bomb load of 6356kg/ 14,000lb over a distance of 4827km/3000 miles. The wingspan of the new bomber was not to exceed 30.5m/100ft so that the aircraft could comfortably pass through the doors of most Royal Air Force hangars of the time. It was this limitation that really defined much of the Stirling's operating parameters. The wings did not have the lifting ability to carry a fully laden Stirling to the ideal higher altitudes, but at low altitude, the aircraft was the fastest of the RAF's heavies.

The Stirling was Short's first aircraft with a retractable undercarriage, as the company was more used to producing flying boats with hulls and floats. To test the soundness of their design Shorts first produced a half-scale prototype, which flew in September 1938. In testing, it was decided to increase the length of the undercarriage legs to increase the wing's angle of attack, which would in turn reduce take-off and landing runs. The solution was not without problems – the large and complex undercarriage led to a number of accidents in service. In addition, production Stirlings stood over 7m/nearly 23ft high as a result. It is worth noting that unlike the Lancaster (derived from the twin-engine Manchester) and the Halifax (originally to be powered by two Vulture engines), the Stirling was designed from the outset as a four-engined machine.

The Stirling was the first of the RAF's new four-engined bombers to fly, the full-size prototype first taking to the air in May 1939. At the end of the maiden flight, a brake locked on landing and the resulting crash wrote off the aircraft. The second prototype's first flight was almost as eventful when an engine failed on take-off. Despite these shaky beginnings, the Stirling reached front-line units in August 1940 when No.7 Squadron at RAF Leeming took delivery of the new heavy bomber. The type made its combat debut, again with No.7 then based at Oakington, on the night of February 10–11, 1941, when three aircraft dropped 56 227kg/500lb bombs on oil storage tanks near Rotterdam. RAF Stirlings attacked Berlin for the first time in April 1941 and the type participated in all the 1942 thousand-bomber raids.

Some shortcomings of the original design were addressed in the Mark III, powered by Hercules XVI engines, which became the standard Bomber Command version in 1943–4. However, by mid-1943 the Stirling was sustaining higher losses than other heavies, and one source states that within five months of being introduced, 67 out of 84 aircraft delivered were lost to enemy action or written off after crashes. During the year, the Stirlings were gradually phased out of the RAF's main bomber force and moved to attacks on less well-defended targets and less dangerous duties such as mine-laying. The Stirling's final Bomber Command operation was flown by No.149 Squadron against Le Havre on September 8, 1944.

However by mid-1944 the Stirlings had found a new lease of life as troop-carriers and glider-tugs, and they performed great service on D-Day. RAF Stirling units in action on D-Day were Fairford-based Nos.90 and 622, and from Keevil Nos.196 and 299 Squadrons.

As the Allies fought their way through Europe after D-Day, Stirlings were also used in support of the RAF's Second Tactical Air Force transporting 120 22.7 litre/5 gallon jerry cans full of petrol at a time. In addition to glider-tug duties, the Stirling was used to drop food supplies and ammunition to the French resistance, and also to drop airborne troops.

Post-war, a number of Stirling Vs (a dedicated transport version built for RAF Transport Command) were used as passenger aircraft between England and the continent for a brief time.

RIGHT: **Stirlings of No.7 Squadron, probably at Oakington in Cambridgeshire.**
BELOW: **Two Stirlings of No.7 Squadron fly across the flat open spaces of East Anglia.**

ABOVE: **The Stirling was a large aircraft but due to its construction, the largest bomb it could carry was 1816kg/4000lb. Here, an armourer prepares a "cookie" bomb prior to loading it aboard the waiting aircraft.**

Short Stirling Mk III

First flight: May 14, 1939 (full-size prototype)
Power: Bristol 1650hp Hercules XVI radial engines
Armament: Eight 7.7mm/0.303in machine-guns in nose, dorsal and tail turrets; up to 6356kg/14,000lb bomb load
Size: Wingspan – 30.2m/99ft 1in
　　　Length – 26.59m/87ft 3in
　　　Height – 6.93m/22ft 9in
　　　Wing area – 135.63m²/1460sq ft
Weights: Empty – 19,613kg/43,200lb
　　　Maximum take-off – 31,780kg/70,000lb
Performance: Maximum speed – 435kph/270mph
　　　Ceiling – 5185m/17,000ft
　　　Range – 950km/590 miles with full bomb load
　　　Climb – 244m/800ft per minute

Short Sunderland

The Sunderland is a rare type of military aeroplane – one that was derived from a civil aircraft. Based upon the Short C Class "Empire" flying boats operated by Imperial Airways in the 1930s, the Short "Sunderland" became one of the Royal Air Force's longest serving operational aircraft over the next two decades. One of the finest flying boats ever built, during World War II the Sunderland played a decisive role in the defeat of German U-boats in the Battle of the Atlantic.

Although the first flight of the prototype Sunderland took place in October 1937, the Air Ministry was already familiar with the aircraft's successful civilian counterpart, and had placed an order in March the preceding year.

In early June 1938 the first batch of production Sunderland Mk Is were delivered to No.230 Squadron based in Singapore. The Sunderland replaced the RAF's mixed fleet of biplane flying boats and represented a huge leap in capability.

By the outbreak of World War II in September 1939, three Coastal Command squadrons had become operational and were ready to seek out and destroy German U-boats. The Sunderland also became a very welcome sight to the many seamen from sunken vessels and airmen who had had to ditch their aircraft. When the British merchant ship *Kensington Court* was torpedoed 113km/70 miles off the Scillies on September 18, 1939, two patrolling Sunderlands had the entire crew of 34 back on dry land just an hour after the ship sank.

TOP: **This Sunderland was converted to "Sandringham" civilianized standard post-war, although some would say that life aboard a Sunderland was quite civilized. Few RAF combat aircraft have ever had a kitchen or, more correctly, a galley.** ABOVE: **A Mark II built by Shorts at Rochester, operated by No.10 Squadron. This Australian squadron became part of Coastal Command at the start of World War II, and operated in the Atlantic.**

The Sunderland, with its crew of ten, was heavily armed and became known to the Luftwaffe as the Flying Porcupine. Many times during the war a lone Sunderland fought off or defeated a number of attacking aircraft.

Although Sunderlands did engage in many a "shoot-out" with German vessels, sometimes the sight of the large aircraft was enough to have an enemy crew scuttle their boat – such was the case on January 31, 1940, when the arrival of an aircraft from No.228 Squadron prompted the crew of U-Boat *U-55* to do just that.

At the end of 1940 the Mk II was introduced, with four Pegasus XVIII engines with two-stage superchargers, a twin-gun dorsal turret, an improved rear turret and ASV (air-to-surface-vessel) Mk II radar. The most numerous version was the Mk III that first flew in December 1941. This variant had a modified hull for improved planing when taking off. This was

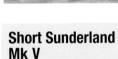

LEFT: **This Sunderland III, W3999, was the first production machine of the version, and had its maiden flight on December 15, 1941. The III had a dorsal gun turret as standard, as well as a refined hull.** BELOW LEFT: **A Sunderland V of No.230 Squadron. The Mk V entered RAF service in early 1945 and remained the standard RAF flying boat until 1959.** BELOW: **At home on water or in the air, the Sunderland's ability to find and destroy U-boats made it a key aircraft in the fight against Nazi Germany.**

followed by a larger and heavier version designated the Mk IV/ Seaford. After evaluation by the RAF, the project of the flying boat was abandoned.

The Sunderland Mk V was the final version, and made its appearance at the end of 1943. It was powered by four 1200hp Pratt & Whitney R-1830-90 Twin Wasp engines and carried ASV Mk VI radar. By the end of the final production run in 1945 a total of 739 Sunderlands had been built, and after World War II, many continued to serve with the British, French, Australian, South African and New Zealand air forces.

Post-war, RAF Sunderlands delivered nearly 5080 tonnes/ 5000 tons of supplies during the Berlin Airlift, and during the Korean War they were the only British aircraft to operate throughout the conflict. During the Malayan Emergency RAF Sunderlands carried out bombing raids on land against terrorists.

The Sunderland finally retired from the Royal Air Force on May 15, 1959, when No.205 Squadron flew the last sortie for the type from RAF Changi, Singapore, where the illustrious operational career of the Sunderland flying boat had begun 21 years earlier. However, the last air arm to retire the type from military service was the Royal New Zealand Air Force in March 1967. A total of 749 Sunderlands were built between 1937 and 1946.

Short Sunderland Mk V

First Flight: October 16, 1937 (prototype)
Power: Four Pratt & Whitney 1200hp R-1830 Twin Wasp 14-cylinder air-cooled radials
Armament: Eight 7.7mm/0.303in Browning machine-guns in turrets, four fixed 7.7mm/ 0.303in Browning machine-guns in nose, two manually operated 12.7mm/0.5in machine-guns in beam positions; 2252kg/4,960lb of depth charges or bombs
Size: Wingspan – 34.36m/112ft 9in
Length – 26m/85ft 3in
Height – 10.01m/32ft 11in
Wing area – 138.14m²/1487sq ft
Weights: Empty – 16,798kg/37,000lb
Maximum take-off – 27,240kg/60,000lb
Performance: Maximum speed – 343 kph/213mph
Ceiling – 5456m/17,900ft
Range – 4795 km/2980miles
Climb – 256m/840ft per minute

Tupolev SB

This aircraft is often incorrectly referred to as the SB-2, which is more a Western corruption of the designation SB-2-M100A meaning SB with 2xM100A engines. It was designed to a 1933 Soviet Air Force specification for a fast light bomber with a maximum level speed of 330kph/205mph, a ceiling of 8000m/26,250ft, range of 700km/ 434 miles and the ability to carry a 500kg/1100lb bomb load. The Tupolev ANT-40 SB (*skorostnoy bombardirovschik* or high-speed bomber) incorporated elements of earlier Tupolev designs and was of metal stressed-skin construction.

This fast, well-armed bomber first flew on April 25, 1934, with power provided by two US Wright Cyclone radials. After a landing accident it was rebuilt and re-engined with Soviet M-87 engines.

Production began in 1935, with early aircraft powered by 750hp M-100 engines and then 860hp 100As. The SB-2bis was the last production version, and first flew in October 1936 with power provided by two 960hp M-103s. Around 6650 SBs were built in total before production ended in late 1940.

SBs were supplied to the Republican forces during the Spanish Civil War. While some nations used Spain as a testing ground, providing aircraft and manpower free of charge, the Soviet Union required hard currency before allowing their aircraft to take part. SBs also saw action during the Nomonhan Incident, a border skirmish that became a small war against the Japanese in Mongolia during 1939. The type was also used against Finnish forces during the Winter War, but was beginning to show its age when faced with fast and agile fighters.

ABOVE: The SB was built in great numbers, and was the first stressed-skin aircraft built in the Soviet Union. The radial engines were later replaced with in-line powerplants, which bestowed better performance. BELOW LEFT: The SB was widely used, seeing action in the Spanish Civil War, and with the Chinese Air Force against Japan. Czech machines were seized by the Luftwaffe and used as target tugs.

At the start of Operation Barbarossa, the German invasion of the Soviet Union in June 1941, 71 out of 82 Bomber Air Regiments operated the type. Many were lost when attacked by Luftwaffe fighters when having no fighter protection of their own. The SB was one of the Soviet Air Force's primary bombers until its withdrawal began in 1943, by which time it was operating largely at night.

Czechoslovakia imported a number of SBs and then produced its own licensed version known as the B-71. Among a number of variants, Tupolev produced a civil transport, the PS-40, for Aeroflot.

Tupolev SB-2bis

First flight: April 25, 1934
Power: Two 960hp M-103 piston engines
Armament: Six 7.62mm/0.3in machine-guns; up to 600kg/1320lb bomb load
Size: Wingspan – 20.33m/66ft 8.5in
Length –12.57m/41ft 2.75in
Height – 3.25m/10ft 8in
Wing area – 56.7m²/610.33sq ft
Weights: Empty – 4768kg/10,494lb
Maximum take-off – 7880kg/17,344lb
Performance: Maximum speed – 450kph/280mph
Ceiling – 7800m/25,590ft
Range – 2300km/1429 miles
Climb – 400m/1310ft per minute

Tupolev TB-3

This large four-engined low-wing bomber was the most advanced bomber in the world for a time. It made its maiden flight on December 22, 1930, and production was underway within a year. The first service aircraft were delivered to the Soviet Air Force in early 1932.

Everything about this aircraft was big and it had a heavier maximum take-off weight than any other aircraft at the time. The TB-3s had a corrugated metal covering similar to that used by Junkers. The wings were so thick they contained "crawl-ways" giving access to the engines during flight. The pilot and co-pilot sat side by side in an open cockpit with separate windscreens.

Continually modified, over 500 of these bombers remained in service at the time of the German invasion in 1941, and some carried out night-bombing

LEFT: **Soviet TB-3s saw action against Finland, Japan and Poland, as well as invading German forces.**

Tupolev TB-3 M-17

First flight: December 22, 1930
Power: Four 715hp M-17F piston engines
Armament: Eight 7.7mm/0.303in machine-guns in nose and dorsal positions, and in two retractable underwing "dustbins"; up to 2000kg/4402lb bomb load
Size: Wingspan – 39.5m/129ft 7in
Length – 24.4m/80ft 0.75in
Height – 8.2m/26ft 9in
Wing area – 230m²/2475.8sq ft
Weights: Empty – 10,967kg/24,138lb
Maximum take-off – 17,200kg/37,857lb
Performance: Maximum speed – 197kph/122mph
Ceiling – 3800m/12,470ft
Range – 1350km/839 miles
Climb – Not known

attacks against the invaders. Paratroop conversions could carry up to 35 troops in the fuselage and wings.

Tupolev Tu-2

This potent medium bomber, initially known as the ANT-61, first entered Soviet Air Force service in 1942, and from the outset it proved to be a key weapon in the Soviet inventory. It was fast, very well armed, handled well and needed few upgrades or improvements during its service life. The Tu-2S, the second main production version, differed from earlier examples by having uprated engines, greater bomb load and heavier gun armament.

Unlike many of its contemporaries, the Tu-2 continued to serve after World War II and saw considerable use with North Korea during the Korean War. Wartime production was around 1100 but a further 1400 were built post-war.

LEFT: **Post-war, the Tu-2S served with the Polish and Chinese air forces.**

Tupolev Tu-2S

First flight: January 29, 1941 (prototype ANT-58)
Power: Two 1850hp Ash-82FNV radial piston engines
Armament: Two 20mm/0.78in cannon, three 12.7mm/0.5in machine-guns; up to 4000kg/8804lb bomb load
Size: Wingspan – 18.86m/61ft 10.5in
Length – 13.8m/45ft 3.5in
Height – 4.55m/14ft 11in
Wing area – 48.8m²/525.3sq ft
Weights: Empty – 7474kg/16,450lb
Maximum take-off – 11,360kg/25,003lb
Performance: Maximum speed – 550kph/342mph
Ceiling – 9500m/31,170ft
Range – 1400km/870 miles
Climb – 700m/2300ft per minute

Some Communist nations operated the type until 1961, which speaks volumes for the quality of the design of this bomber which had the NATO reporting name of "Bat".

Vickers Vimy

In 1917, the British were developing bombers capable of bombing the German heartland. Had World War I not come to an end in November 1918, these bombers, among them the Vickers Vimy, would have formed strategic bomber fleets attempting to pound Germany into submission. Although the war came to an end before the Vimy saw action, the type continued to serve in the RAF as a front-line bomber until the late 1920s.

The biplane Vimy was a large aircraft for its day with a wingspan of over 20m/68ft, and the prototype B9952 first flew on November 17, powered by two 207hp Hispano-Suiza engines. Of wooden construction and fabric-covered, the Vimy had a crew of three and could carry a bomb load in excess of a ton – this was a far cry from the hand-held bombs thrown overboard from the early World War I bombers.

Although many aircraft contracts were cancelled at the war's end, the Vimy continued to be supplied to the Royal Air Force. The main production version of the Vimy was the Mark IV powered by Rolls-Royce Eagle VIII engines, and some 240 were built – the first were delivered to the RAF in France in 1918 and the last batch were delivered to the RAF in 1925. The Vimy did not enter service fully until July 1919 when it joined No. 58 Squadron stationed in Egypt. In Britain, the first of the home squadrons to be equipped with the Vickers bomber was No.100 based at Spittlegate. No.7 Squadron was formed in June 1923 to operate Vimys, and was the Royal Air Force's UK-based heavy bomber until being augmented by the Vimys of Nos.9 and 58 Squadrons in 1924. By 1925 the Vimy

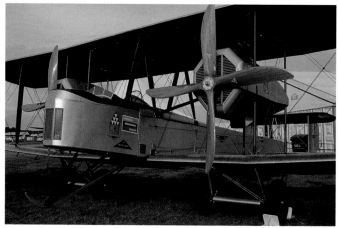

TOP: **A replica of Alcock and Brown's famous Atlantic-crossing Vimy. The Vimy's performance on that epic flight demonstrated the greatness of the design.**
ABOVE: **The Vimy was built for deep bombing missions into Germany, but some of these aircraft continued to fly in RAF service long after the end of the Great War.**

was being replaced by Vickers Virginias, but the aircraft of No.502 stationed in Northern Ireland remained in front-line service until 1929. The type was used increasingly for mail services, as a trainer and for parachute training. The Vimy design was also developed into the Vimy Commercial with an all-new large-diameter fuselage – a dedicated version was produced as the Vimy Ambulance for moving wounded personnel. The Vickers Vernon bomber-transport derivative became the first aircraft designed specifically for troop-carrying, and served mainly in Iraq in the mid- to late 1920s.

On June 14, 1919, the Vimy flew into the history books when a Vimy IV owned by the Vickers company and the thirteenth off the production line took off from Newfoundland

ABOVE AND LEFT: **Alcock and Brown's flight was an epic for its day. On their return to Britain, they became national heroes, having finally beaten the Atlantic.**

and headed eastward across the Atlantic. The two-man crew were Royal Air Force officers Captain John Alcock, who served as pilot, and Lieutenant Arthur Whitten-Brown, navigator. Also aboard the aircraft were around 3927 litres/865 gallons of highly flammable aviation fuel. For the transatlantic flight the Vimy was specially adapted – all military equipment was removed and the cockpit was widened so that the two fliers could sit side by side on a narrow wooden bench with a thin cushion for comfort. Once alterations had been made to Alcock and Brown's Vimy, the aircraft was dismantled, crated and transported to Newfoundland.

The epic, trailblazing flight, averaging 190km/118 miles per hour was far from uneventful – the pair faced snow, ice and fog, as well as extreme tiredness. Then at 08:40 hours the next morning, after a 16-hour flight, Alcock and Brown sighted Ireland, and within minutes prepared to land. The aircraft landed in a bog and nosed over, sustaining damage, but the pioneering airmen were unhurt. As well being knighted and feted throughout their country, Alcock and Brown won the Daily Mail newspaper's prize of 10,000 pounds offered in 1913 for the first successful crossing of the Atlantic.

ABOVE: **Vimys did not reach RAF units until the end of October 1918, and then only three machines were delivered.** ABOVE LEFT: **This Vimy was built by Vickers at Bexley, and was powered by Salmson engines.**

Vickers Vimy IV

First flight: November 30, 1917
Power: Two Rolls-Royce 360hp Eagle VIII in-line piston engines
Armament: Two Lewis guns, one each in nose and mid-upper positions; 1124kg/2476lb of bombs
Size: Wingspan – 20.7m/68ft
Length – 13.3m/44ft
Height – 4.7m/15ft
Wing area – 124m²/1330sq ft
Weights: Empty – 3225kg/7104lb
Maximum take-off – 5675kg/12,500lb
Performance: Maximum speed – 166kph/103mph
Service ceiling – 3660m/12,000ft
Range – 1448km/900 miles
Climb – 110m/360ft per minute

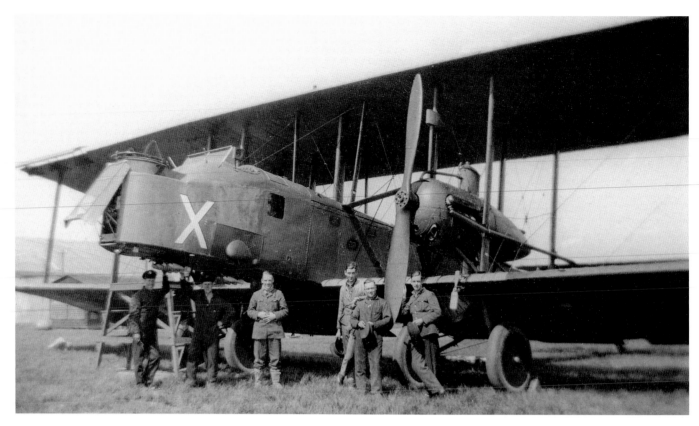

Vickers Virginia

The Virginia was the standard heavy night-bomber of the Royal Air Force from 1924 until 1937, a long service in those inter-war days. Structurally it differed little from the Vimy developed by Vickers in World War I, but its performance was slightly better than its predecessor and it could carry a greater bomb load. The type was designed to meet Air Ministry specification 1/21, and first flew at Brooklands in November 1922. RAF service deliveries began in late 1924, the first recipient units being Nos.7 and 58 followed by No.9. The

three squadrons took part in the famous Hendon Display in 1925, and the Virginias were popular participants at the annual show through to 1937.

The Virginia was modified considerably during its service career so that the final version in service, the X, was quite different to the early Marks. The prototype Virginia (J6856) had its Lion engines housed in rectangular nacelles, but production aircraft all featured smaller, oval-section nacelles. A total of 124 were built for the RAF in ten versions, and Marks I to V can be identified by the dihedral on the bottom wing only. The Mark VII introduced a lengthened and redesigned nose. The Mark X was the first version not to be of wooden construction, instead being all-metal with a fabric covering – this model accounted for 50 of the 124 aircraft built.

It was the Virginia that introduced the auto-pilot into RAF service, and when the type was replaced by newer bombers, it continued to serve as a parachute trainer, with jump-off platforms added to the rear of the engines. Some were still flying as engine test-beds in 1941.

TOP: **The Virginia was still a front-line bomber in 1937. Within seven years, the RAF was operating jet fighters.** ABOVE: **A Virginia taking part in early inflight refuelling experiments with a Westland Wapati.**

Vickers Virginia Mk X

First flight: November 24, 1922
Power: Two Napier 580hp Lion VBW-12 piston engines
Armament: One 7.7mm/0.303in machine-gun in nose and two more in the tail; up to 1362kg/3000lb bomb load
Size: Wingspan – 26.72m/87ft 8in
Length – 18.97m/62ft 3in
Height – 5.54m/18ft 2in
Wing area – 202.34m²/2178sq ft
Weights: Empty – 4381kg/9650lb
Maximum take-off – 7990kg/17,600lb
Performance: Maximum speed – 174kph/108mph
Ceiling – 4725m/15,500ft
Range – 1585km/985 miles
Climb – 152m/500ft per minute

ABOVE: **The roar of the Virginia's noisy Lion engines could be heard from miles away.**

Vickers Wellesley

The Vickers Wellesley was the first of the Vickers designs, and the first RAF aircraft to employ the unique geodetic construction developed by Barnes Wallis. Vickers had designed a biplane bomber to meet a 1931 general-purpose requirement G.4/31, and then as a private venture developed a monoplane derivative which became the Wellesley. The prototype flew on June 19, 1935, and sufficiently impressed the Air Ministry that in September an order was placed for 96 aircraft to specification 22/35, which was written around the Wellesley. As well as the unusual geodetic construction, the bomber carried innovative streamlined bomb panniers under the wings, thereby simplifying construction. In a 14-month production run which began in March 1937, a total of 176 examples were built.

The Wellesley entered RAF service in April 1937 with No.76 Squadron at Finningley, and ultimately equipped six UK-based Bomber Command squadrons. By the start of the war,

however, only four examples remained in service with Bomber Command in Britain, a hundred Wellesleys having been transferred to the Middle East. In an often overlooked episode of World War II, East Africa-based aircraft saw action against the Italians in 1940. The type also carried out maritime reconnaissance in the region until 1941.

The Wellesley is perhaps best known for its record-breaking flight undertaken in 1938 from Egypt to Australia. Three aircraft of the Long Range Development Flight set off on November 5, 1938, from Ismalia, Egypt. One had to abort en route but two Wellesleys, L2638 and L2680, flew non-stop to Darwin, Australia, covering 11,524km/7162 miles in a little over 48 hours and set a new world long-distance record. These aircraft only differed from service aircraft by having extra fuel tanks, accommodation for a third crew member and a Pegasus XXII in place of the usual XX. In service aircraft, the Mark II designation covered aircraft with a large continuous canopy over both cockpits.

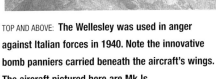
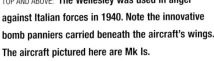

TOP AND ABOVE: **The Wellesley was used in anger against Italian forces in 1940. Note the innovative bomb panniers carried beneath the aircraft's wings. The aircraft pictured here are Mk Is.**

Vickers Wellesley

First flight: June 19, 1935
Power: One Bristol 925hp Pegasus XX
Armament: One forward-firing 7.7mm/0.303in machine-gun in right wing, plus one in rear cockpit; up to 908kg/2000lb bomb load carried in underwing panniers
Size: Wingspan – 22.73m/74ft 7in
  Length – 11.96m/39ft 3in
  Height – 3.75m/12ft 4in
  Wing area – 58.5m²/630sq ft
Weights: Empty – 2891kg/6369lb
  Maximum take-off – 5039kg/11,100lb
Performance: Maximum speed – 286kph/178mph
  Ceiling – 10,065m/33,000ft
  Range – 4168km/2590 miles
  Climb – 366m/1200ft per minute

145

Vickers Wellington

The Wellington was built using a unique and ingenious geodetic construction developed by the brilliant Barnes Wallis, who later developed the bouncing bomb. The aircraft's geodetic fuselage was built of a large criss-cross metal mesh which gave the aircraft incredible strength. This meant that fabric-covered Wellingtons came home with very large holes in them caused by flak or cannon fire when other aircraft would have broken up in mid-air. The "Wimpy", as the type was nicknamed (after J. Wellington Wimpy of the Popeye cartoons), first reached front-line service in October 1938 with No.99 Squadron at Mildenhall. The Wellington was the principal bomber of Bomber Command at the start of World War II with six squadrons on strength, and remained so until the four-engined heavies joined the force later in the war. On September 4, 1939, along with Blenheims, 14 Wellingtons of Nos.9 and 149 Squadrons flew the first offensive RAF bombing raid of the war against Germany.

The Wellington was Vickers' response to the British Air Ministry's 1932 specification B.9/32 for a twin-engined medium bomber. After its first flight in June 1936, the Wellington caused a stir when it made a public appearance at the annual Hendon air display later that year. The large streamlined monoplane bomber was a great advance on the biplanes that had been the norm.

The first production version to enter service was the I, which differed greatly from the prototype K4049. The fuselage shape was refined, and a retractable tailwheel was fitted together with gun turrets. The IA saw some armament changes

TOP: **This Wellington II served with No.104 Squadron RAF. The Mark II was a Mark IC, but powered by 1145hp Merlin X engines, and 400 examples were built.**

ABOVE: **The groundcrew of this Wellington had a novel means of recording the number of missions on the aircraft nose, taking inspiration from a popular beer advertisement of the period.**

but the Mark IC, of which 2685 were built, introduced beam guns instead of a ventral gun, and larger mainwheels were fitted. By mid-1941, more powerfully engined Wellington Mk IIs and Mk IIIs had entered service. As the Wellingtons flew on their daylight missions over enemy territory, the official belief was that when flying in formation the bombers would be able to defend themselves without fighter escort against marauding fighters. The reality was very different and Wellingtons, with their unsealed fuel tanks, proved to be very vulnerable. On December 18, 1939, Wellingtons of Nos.9, 37 and 149 Squadrons were sent to carry out a mission against the

LEFT: **Wellington ICs of No.311 Squadron. This photograph pre-dates the unit's transfer to Coastal Command in April 1942.** BELOW: **Wellingtons entered Coastal Command service in the spring of 1942. These Mk XIIIs had A.S.V. masts on the "spine" to search for submarines.**

ABOVE: **The end of the line – the Wellington X was the final bomber version, with over 3800 built. Post-war, many were converted to T.10 standard with a faired nose and the turret deleted.**

Schillig Roads and Wilhelmshaven. They were attacked by Luftwaffe fighters, and ten of the bombers were destroyed and three badly damaged. After this mission highlighted the aircraft's vulnerability, the Wellington was switched to night operations.

The Wellington proved to be a very successful night-bomber, and carried out bombing raids deep into Germany and Italy. The night of August 25–6, 1940 saw Wellingtons of Nos.99 and 149 Squadrons join Hampdens and Whitleys on Bomber Command's first attack on the heart of the Third Reich, Berlin. The Cologne raid of May 30, 1942 saw no fewer than 599 Wellingtons take part in the mission.

In September 1940, Wellingtons joined No.202 Group as the RAF's first long-range bombers in the Middle East. The type also saw use in the North African and Greek campaigns, and in 1942 India-based Wellingtons became the RAF's first long-range bombers operating in the Far East.

The Wellington fought on in Europe until it carried out its last offensive mission on the night of October 8–9, 1943 against Hanover. However, the "Wimpy" did continue to serve as a bomber elsewhere, and on March 13, 1945, aircraft of No.40 Squadron dropped 1816kg/4000lb "cookie" bombs on Trevisio in the Italian theatre.

Mention must also be made of the Coastal Command Wellingtons, fitted with 14.63m/48ft metal hoops that were used for exploding enemy mines in the sea below

by generating a strong magnetic field. Coastal Command Wellingtons also carried out anti-submarine duties, the first enemy vessel being sunk on July 6, 1942.

Post-war, many converted Wellingtons continued to serve as training aircraft into the mid-1950s. In all 11,461 Wellingtons were built, the last of which was rolled out on October 13, 1945.

Vickers Wellington IC

First flight: June 15, 1936
Power: Two Bristol 1000hp Pegasus XVIII radial engines
Armament: Two 7.7mm/0.303in machine-guns in nose and tail turrets, two in beam positions; up to 2043kg/4500lb bomb load
Size: Wingspan – 26.26m/86ft 2in
  Length – 19.68m/64ft 7in
  Height – 5.31m/17ft 5in
  Wing area – 78.04m²/840sq ft
Weights: Empty – 8424kg/18,556lb
  Maximum take-off – 12,939kg/28,500lb
Performance: Maximum speed – 378kph/235mph
  Cceiling – 5490m/18,000ft
  Range – 4104km/2550 miles
  Climb – 320m/1050ft per minute

Vultee Vengeance

The Vengeance was designed for the Royal Air Force, who considered that, following the combat successes of the Luftwaffe's Stuka during the Spanish Civil War and the Blitzkrieg, a dedicated purpose-designed dive-bomber should be in the RAF inventory. However, by the time the Vengeance was ready to enter service, the RAF had seen the vulnerability of the German dive-bomber through the gunsights of British fighters during the Battle of Britain. Accordingly, the RAF decided that the Vengeance was not suited to the European theatre but was appropriate for operations in the Far East and against challenging targets in Burma.

History has not been kind to the aircraft but in fact it was a very capable, stable and accurate bombing platform. In Burma, often operating out of range

of friendly fighter cover, Royal Air Force and Indian Air Force Vengeances played a key role in the battles against the Japanese for Imphal and Kohima, and carried out precision bombing raids against key bridges used for moving supplies to the Japanese.

The Royal Navy's Fleet Air Arm received a total of 113 Vengeances, 88 of which had been delivered by the end of August 1945, and the rest by early 1946. No FAA aircraft saw action; they were used mainly as target tugs.

The Royal Australian Air Force took delivery of great numbers of the Vengeance from 1942, some 342 in total. The RAAF operated the type in combat in New Guinea, and after withdrawal from front-line service, the Australian aircraft flew as target tugs and communications aircraft until they

ABOVE: **Vengeance Mk III of No.84 Squadron, Burma 1944.** BELOW LEFT: **RAAF Vengeance dive-bombers of No.24 Squadron returning from a raid on Alexishafen airstrip, February 27, 1944.**

were retired in 1946. Some of the Australian machines were modified for pesticide spraying in late 1945.

The Free French Air Force operated the Vengeance in North Africa, and the aircraft was also supplied to Brazil. The USAAF commandeered some of the aircraft intended for British use but these aircraft did not see combat. By the end of production in 1944, 1528 aircraft had been built in total.

Vultee A-35B Vengeance

First flight: July 1941 (first RAF aircraft)
Power: One Wright 1700hp Double Row Cyclone R-2600 radial piston engine
Armament: Six 7.7mm/0.303in machine-guns in wings and rear cockpit; bomb load of 908kg/ 2000lb
Size: Wingspan – 14.63m/48ft
Length – 12.12 m/39ft 9in
Height – 4.67 m/15ft 4in
Wing area – 30.84sq m/332sq ft
Weights: Empty – 4676kg/10,300lb
Maximum take-off – 7445kg/16,400lb
Performance: Maximum speed – 449kph/ 279mph
Service ceiling – 6800m/22,300ft
Range – 1931km/1200 miles
Climb – 366m/1200ft per minute

Yokosuka D4Y Suisei

LEFT: **The improved D4Y2 version of the unusually engined (for Japan) Suisei.**

LEFT: **The improved D4Y2 version of the unusually engined (for Japan) Suisei.**

Yokosuka D4Y2

First flight: November 1940
Power: One Aichi 1400hp Atsuta 32 piston engine
Armament: Two 7.7mm/0.303in forward-firing and one 7.92mm/0.31in rear-firing machine-gun; up to 800kg/1761lb bomb load
Size: Wingspan – 11.5m/37ft 8.75in
Length – 10.22m/33ft 6.25in
Height – 3.74m/12ft 3.25in
Wing area – 23.6m²/254sq ft
Weights: Empty – 2440kg/5370lb
Maximum take-off – 4250kg/9354lb
Performance: Maximum speed – 550kph/342mph
Ceiling – 10,700m/35,105ft
Range – 1465km/910 miles
Climb – 820m/2700ft per minute

Yokosuka was the location for the Imperial Japanese Navy's First Naval Air Technical Arsenal, which began to design a carrier-based single-engine dive-bomber in 1938. The resulting Suisei (comet), based on the Heinkel He118, was unusual as it was one of few Japanese combat types to be powered by a liquid-cooled engine, in this case a licence-built copy of the German DB 601.

In service from autumn 1942, the type served initially in the reconnaissance role (D4Y1-C), with the dedicated dive-bomber version (D4Y1) entering service in 1943. The type did not fare well against high-performance Allied fighters, and many fell to their guns due to poor protection for the crew and the lack of self-sealing fuel tanks. A total of 2038 were built, the D4Y2 having a more

powerful engine while the D4Y4 was a kamikaze suicide-bomber version which carried one 800kg/1761lb bomb. The Allied codename allocated to all versions was "Judy".

Yokosuka P1Y1

LEFT: **The fast and capable Ginga was like many other types used for suicide missions towards the end of the war.**

Yokosuka P1Y1 Ginga

First flight: Spring 1943
Power: Two Nakajima 1820hp Homare 11 radial piston engines
Armament: Two 20mm/0.78in cannon, one forward-firing, one rear-firing; up to 800kg/1760lb bomb load
Size: Wingspan – 20m/65ft 7.5in
Length –15m/49ft 2.5in
Height – 4.3m/14ft 1.25in
Wing area – 55m²/592sq ft
Weights: Empty – 7265kg/15,990lb
Maximum take-off – 13,500kg/29,713lb
Performance: Maximum speed – 547kph/340mph
Ceiling – 9400m/30,840ft
Range – 5370km/3337 miles
Climb – 650m/2133ft per minute

This aircraft was built to a 1940 Imperial Japanese Navy requirement for a fast, low-flying medium bomber with the ability to launch torpedo attacks. The prototype P1Y flew in August 1943 and showed great potential, but problems with development delayed its entry into service until early 1945 as the Navy Bomber Ginga (Milky Way) Model II.

Over 1000 were built but this potent combat aircraft was dogged by maintenance problems that stopped the bomber, which could outrun fighters at low level, being a thorn in the Allies' side. It was a complex machine and experienced, well-trained maintenance personnel were in short supply. The aircraft's range at over 5000km/

3105 miles was very impressive, but among other roles the Ginga was used as a suicide-bomber before the end of the war in the Pacific. The Allied codename for the bomber was "Frances".

A–Z of Modern Bombers

1945 to the Present Day

The devastating atom bomb raids on Japan that brought World War II to a close guaranteed, at least for a time, the future development of bombers in nations developing such weapons for themselves. Atomic weapons would only be effective if an efficient means of delivery was available. As the Cold War began, the immediate need on all sides was for bomber aircraft that could travel considerable distances, outperform enemy defences and then bomb effectively. Jet technology and greater understanding of aerodynamics led to bomber aircraft flying higher and faster, up to twice the speed of sound. The Cold War forced the development of new technology in many directions, perhaps most spectacularly in "stealth".

By the late 1950s and early '60s, anti-aircraft defence developments, notably SAM missiles and the development of intercontinental ballistic missiles, called the very need for bombers into question. However, ongoing conventional warfare the world over has proved the need for aircraft that can be operated flexibly. Very high speed is no longer a prerequisite for bombers, whereas survivability in today's highly sophisticated air warfare environment is vital.

LEFT: **Lockheed F-117 Nighthawk.**

Aermacchi MB-339

Aermacchi MB-339C

First flight: August 12, 1976

Power: One licence-built Rolls-Royce 1998kg/ 4400lb thrust Viper 680-43 turbojet

Armament: Up to 1816kg/4000lb of external weapons including bombs, rockets, cannon pods, anti-shipping missiles and air-to-air missiles

Size: Wingspan – 11.22m/36ft 10in
Length – 11.24m/36ft 11in
Height – 3.99m/13ft 1in
Wing area – 19.3m²/207.7sq ft

Weights: Empty – 3313kg/7297lb
Maximum take-off – 6356kg/14,000lb

Performance: Maximum speed – 902kph/560mph
Ceiling – 14243m/46,700ft
Range – 2035km/1263 miles
Climb – 9150m/30,000ft in 6 minutes, 40 seconds

The origins of the MB-339 advanced trainer/light attack aircraft date back to the mid-1950s when the hugely successful MB-326 trainer (and later light attack aircraft) was first designed. By the 1970s Aermacchi were considering a successor, and the MB-339 was born. The airframe shares a lot of its structure with the MB-326K light attack aircraft, with the forward fuselage redesigned to allow the tandem seating to be staggered vertically enabling the instructor to see over the pupil.

The resulting aircraft is stronger and has an uprated powerplant compared to the MB-326. Six hardpoints carrying up to 1816kg/4000lb give this nimble aircraft a powerful punch. The first prototype, I-NOVE, flew on August 12, 1976, and the first production MB-339A trainer was delivered to the Italian Air Force on August 9, 1979. Other customers included New Zealand, Argentina, Dubai, Ghana, Malaysia, Nigeria and Peru. Perhaps the most high-profile user of the MB-339 are the Italian Frecce Tricolori aerobatics display team.

The MB-339AM was a proposed maritime strike version, while the Viper 680-powered MB-339B is enhanced for the ground-attack role. The MB339-K (also known as the Veltro 2), was a single-seat attack version yet to be

produced. The next ground-attack version was the MB-339C. Also powered by the Viper 680-43, this version first flew on December 17, 1985, and can carry air-to-air and air-to-ground missiles as well as bombs. The first production customer for the C-model was the Royal New Zealand Air Force, who received their first three aircraft in April 1991.

The MB-339 FD is the latest and most advanced version of the MB-339 in service, and is equipped with self-defence systems for more realistic operational training and for increasing the aircraft survivability in combat.

TOP: **A Royal New Zealand Air Force MB-339. The advanced trainer was seen by many nations as a means of acquiring cost-effective ground-attack capability.** ABOVE: **MB-339Cs.** BELOW: **An Italian Air Force MB-339A.**

LEFT: **A Brazilian Air Force AMX performing a ground-attack demonstration. The aircraft is a fine example of technological and manufacturing co-operation between two nations thousands of miles apart.** BELOW: **The International AMX-T two-seat version.**

AMX International AMX

The AMX fighter-bomber originated from a requirement from the Italian Air Force for a ground-attack aircraft to replace its G91 and F-104s, and the Brazilians' need to replace their MB-326s.

A special consortium was set up to produce this very capable aircraft in both Italy and Brazil. Italian companies Alenia and Aermacchi produce around 70 per cent of the aircraft and Brazilian company Embraer is responsible for 30 per cent. Alenia manufactures the central section of the fuselage, radome, ailerons, spoilers and tail surfaces. Aermacchi is responsible for the forward fuselage, integration of the guns (one 20mm/0.78in cannon in Italian aircraft and two 30mm/1.18in cannon in Brazilian) and avionics, the canopy and the tail structure. Embraer is responsible for the air intakes, wings, leading edge slats, flaps, wing pylons and external fuel tanks. Elements are made in both countries and then shipped to the other as each has final assembly facilities. Power is provided by a non-afterburning

Rolls-Royce Spey 807 turbofan built under licence.

The prototype first flew in 1984 and the first AMX aircraft was delivered to the Italian Air Force in January 1989 and to the Brazilian Air Force in 1990. In total, 192 aircraft, 155 single-seaters and 37 AMX-T two-seaters have been delivered to Italy and Brazil. In December 2002, the Venezuelan Air Force signed a contract for 12 AMX-T aircraft.

Although the primary role of the AMX is ground attack, the aircraft is also highly effective in the air defence mission – in fact, so much so that in 1999, Italian Air Force AMXs were deployed as part of the NATO forces in Operation Allied Force against Serbia.

The AMX Advanced Trainer Attack (AMX-ATA) is a new AMX two-seater, multi-mission attack fighter for combat roles and advanced training. AMX-ATA incorporates new sensors, a forward-looking infrared, helmet-mounted display, a new multi-mode radar for anti-air and anti-ship capability, and new

AMX International AMX

First flight: May 15, 1984
Power: One licence-built Rolls-Royce 5008kg/ 11,030lb thrust Spey 807 turbofan
Armament: One 20mm/0.78in cannon (two 30mm/ 1.18in in Brazilian aircraft); weapons load of up to 3800kg/8364lb comprising bombs, rockets and air-to-air missiles
Size: Wingspan – 8.87m/29ft 2in
Length – 13.23m/43ft 5in
Height – 4.55m/14ft 11in
Wing area – 21m²/226.1sq ft
Weights: Empty – 6700kg/14,747lb
Maximum take-off – 13,000kg/28,613lb
Performance: Maximum speed – 915kph/568mph
Ceiling – 13,008m/42,650ft
Range – 1852km/1150 miles
Climb – 3126m/10,250ft per minute

weapon systems, including anti-ship missiles and medium-range missiles. The Venezuelan Air Force ordered eight AMX-ATAs in 1999 for the advanced trainer and attack aircraft role.

Avro Lincoln

The Lincoln, originally known as the Lancaster IV, was produced to meet a British Air Ministry requirement for a Lancaster replacement. In 1943, Air Ministry planners were turning their thoughts to developing a long-range bomber force (Tiger Force) for action in the Pacific. These new aircraft had to be able to cover the vast distances between likely take-off points and targets.

Elements of the Lancaster were indeed featured in the new design, and the family resemblance is clear, but the aircraft was a sufficiently different design to be named Lincoln instead. A larger fuselage was carried by a new wing and the aircraft was protected by heavier armament. The increased weight required a stronger undercarriage assembly. The prototype, with Captain Brown at the controls, took to the air for the first time at Ringway, Manchester, on June 9, 1944.

Lancaster production had to remain high, so Lincolns did not reach RAF squadrons until August 1945. World War II ended before the Lincoln made it to the Pacific theatre, but the aircraft equipped post-war Bomber Command in the difficult and tense period before the jet-powered V-Bombers were available.

Lincolns went on to equip around 20 squadrons of RAF Bomber Command but it was soon realized that the Lincoln was somewhat lacking in a world increasingly dominated by jets. This led to partial replacement in RAF service by hastily

TOP: **The Lancaster connection is clear, but there was much that was new about the Lincoln.** ABOVE: **The Lincoln I began to reach RAF units in August 1945.**

acquired ex-USAF B-29s. However, Lincolns did see action against communist terrorists in Malaya in 1950 and Mau-Mau dissidents in Kenya from 1953. Lincolns were finally replaced in the RAF by the V-Bombers from 1955. The last Lincolns in RAF service were used in radar development trials until May 1963.

Australia undertook construction of what was designated the Lincoln Mk 30 at the Government Aircraft Factory (GAF), and the first GAF Lincoln, A73-1, flew in March 1946. The first four were assembled mainly from British parts but the rest were manufactured locally. The GAF Lincolns were powered by both British and Australian engines. A number of special "heavy-lift" aircraft were known as Mk 30As. Twelve aircraft were completed as long-nosed Mk 31s, the nose housing three crew. The Lincoln GR.31 was a unique Australian version developed for anti-submarine work. Royal Australian Air Force Lincolns also took part in the Malayan Emergency.

In the latter stages of World War II, Canada had also ordered home production of the Lincoln to equip Canadian bomber units destined for the Pacific. When war ended, production was stopped after only six aircraft had been started. Post-war, the RCAF evaluated the Lincoln but chose not to produce or buy any more. The only export customer for British-built Lincolns was the Argentine Air Force, which acquired 30 Lincoln Mk IIs in 1947.

TOP: **The Lincoln II, or B.2 as it was known in service, differed from the Mk I in its engines, which were Merlin 66, 68A or 300s.** RIGHT: **For the tense years after World War II while the new jet bombers were developed, the Lincoln was Bomber Command's main weapon.** BELOW: **RAF Lincolns were used in combat in Malaya and Kenya.**

Avro Lincoln

First flight: June 9, 1944

Power: Four Rolls-Royce 1750hp Merlin 85 in-line piston engines

Armament: Two 12.7mm/0.5in machine-guns each in turrets in tail, nose and dorsal position; up to 6356kg/14,000lb of bombs

Size: Wingspan – 36.58m/120ft
Length – 23.86m/78ft 3.5in
Height – 5.27m/17ft 3.5in
Wing area – 132m²/1421sq ft

Weights: Empty – 19,522kg/43,000lb
Maximum take-off – 34,050kg/75,000lb

Performance: Maximum speed – 475kph/295mph
Service ceiling – 9302m/30,500ft
Range – 2366km/1470 miles
Climb – 245m/800ft per minute

Avro Shackleton

During World War II, Britain learned that enemy submarines could wreak havoc with seaborne supply routes in the Atlantic. While surface vessels can be effective against submarines, they can only patrol a relatively small area, and they themselves are at risk from submarines. In contrast, RAF Coastal Command's Lend-Lease Fortresses, Liberators and Catalinas were able to range over vast areas of ocean on a single patrol, and destroyed around 200 German submarines.

Realizing the strategic necessity for effective maritime reconnaissance aircraft in the RAF inventory, and mindful of the fact that Lend-Lease types would be returning to the USA, the Air Ministry issued a 1946 requirement for a British replacement. Avro's design, which became the Shackleton, was selected, possibly because the new aircraft was to employ some elements of the already familiar Avro Lincoln bomber. The Lincoln's wings and undercarriage were mated to a new design fuselage and the aircraft was powered by the higher-performance Griffon engines which turned six-blade contra-rotating propellers. Because of the very long duration of maritime patrol missions, crew comfort was taken seriously, as was soundproofing to protect the ten-man crew against the horrific noise levels generated by four snarling Griffons. Despite the best efforts of the designers, the main wing spar, which passed straight through the fuselage, continued to be a major obstacle when moving from the front to the rear of the aircraft, as had been the case on both the Lincoln and the Lancaster before it.

TOP: **The Shackleton protected Britain's interests on land, sea and in the air for over three decades.** ABOVE: **The Shackleton prototype, VW126, which had its maiden flight on March 9, 1949.**

The first of three Shackleton M.R.1 prototypes, VW126, took to the air on March 9, 1949. The M.R.I and M.R.IA (denoting differing powerplant detail) began to enter RAF service in February 1951. This first Shackleton version is easy to identify thanks to the large "chin" radome, which proved to be problematic as it failed to provide the ideal 360-degree cover and was susceptible to bird-strike. In the Mk 2 Shackleton, which entered RAF service in late 1952, the radar was moved back to the ventral position and was housed in a retractable radome. The nose of this version was also lengthened, and acquired a bomb-aimer's and a nose-gunner's position armed with two 20mm/0.78in Hispano cannons.

When the Shackleton M.R.3 entered service in late 1957, it introduced the tricycle undercarriage, much to the pilots' delight. Crews had voiced concerns over landing the tail-dragger versions because the Shackleton was a heavy aircraft to land with a tailwheel – several tons heavier than

Avro Shackleton M.R.2

First flight: June 17, 1952
Power: Four Rolls-Royce 2455hp Griffon 57A V-12 piston engines
Armament: Two pairs of 20mm/0.78in cannon; maximum weapons-bay load of 8172kg/ 18,000lb of bombs or depth charges
Size: Wingspan – 36.58m/120ft
  Length – 26.59m/87ft 3in
  Height – 5.1m/16ft 9in
  Wing area – 132m²/1421sq ft
Weights: Empty –25,379kg/55,900lb
  Maximum take-off – 39,044kg/86,000lb
Performance: Maximum speed – 500kph/311mph
  Ceiling – 6405m/21,000ft
  Range – 5440km/3380 miles
  Climb – 260m/850ft per minute

ABOVE: **Normally based at Lossiemouth in Scotland, this Shackleton AEW2 is pictured at Gibraltar.** LEFT: **The AEW2 Shackletons flew on long after their anticipated retirement, while a replacement was finalized.** BELOW: **The MR3 carried extra fuel for its long overwater flights in tip-tanks at the end of the wing.** BOTTOM: **The M.R.3 introduced the tricycle undercarriage, while the mid-upper turret of earlier versions was deleted.**

a Lancaster, for example. The tricycle gear also made taxiing rather less stressful for those on the flightdeck and probably for those on the ground too. More efficient braking, a greater fuel load, full sound insulation (needed on an 18-hour mission), a galley and rest area were all introduced in the Mark 3. It was this version that was exported to South Africa, whose No.35 Squadron operated them until 1984.

As more equipment was carried, the all-up weight rose sharply, so to assist with take-off from shorter runways, two Viper jet engines (similar to those used to power the BAC Strikemaster) were fitted to the outboard engine nacelles from 1966. The stresses caused by the use of this modification ultimately shortened the flying life of the Mk 3 aircraft.

The 1956 Suez crisis marked the Shackleton's "combat" debut, providing anti-submarine cover for the British and French ships below. "Shacks" were frequently involved in colonial policing and saw action in Oman, Kuwait and Borneo, but over the years the type also carried out humanitarian and relief missions in areas affected by natural disasters as far afield as Jamaica, Belize and Morocco. The Shackleton, with its long endurance and ability to carry a great deal of rescue equipment, made it an excellent search-and-rescue (SAR) platform.

However, the Shackleton's principal role was the tracking of potentially hostile vessels on and below the surface of the sea. For hunting submarines the aircraft carried a radar which could detect a submarine's snorkel as it broke the sea surface up to 56km/35 miles away.

From the late 1960s, Shackletons were gradually replaced by Nimrods in the maritime reconnaissance role, but the old Avro aircraft continued to fly into the 1980s, modified to serve in the airborne early warning (AEW) role, guarding mainly the northern approaches to Britain.

Avro Vulcan

The Vulcan, surely one of the most remarkable-looking aircraft ever built, seemed to owe more to the inhabitants of other planets than the German wartime research which influenced its design. The aircraft was Avro's futuristic and adventurous response to a 1946 Air Ministry Operational Requirement calling for a bomber able to carry a 4540kg/ 10,000lb atomic bomb to a target 2775km/1725 miles away.

The Avro Type 698 was conceived as a high-altitude atomic bomber, and was the first four-engine delta-wing aircraft. The unconventional wing shape was chosen because it combines good load-carrying capabilities and high subsonic speed at altitude. To help gain data for the radical new design, several "mini-Vulcans" research aircraft were built – the Avro Type 707s. Gradually the design was changed before the well-known Vulcan layout was finalized. What had been a flying wing with wingtip fins acquired a single central fin, the nose was extended and a distinct fuselage section evolved.

The prototype VX770 flew in August 1952, piloted by Wing Commander Roly Falk, and in 1953 the type 698 was officially named the Vulcan. Spectacular Farnborough appearances followed, the most amazing being a full roll at the 1955 show.

After a redesign of the wing and the addition of more powerful engines, the Vulcan B.1 entered RAF service in February 1957, and became operational with No.83 Squadron at Waddington in July of the same year. Britain's nuclear

TOP: **VX770, the Vulcan prototype, was powered by 2952kg/6500lb thrust Avon turbojets, a long way from the 9080kg/20,000lb thrust Olympus engines that powered the later B.2.** ABOVE: **Vulcan B.1, pictured with its fellow V-bomber, the Victor.**

deterrent force had to be effective and hard-hitting, and it became clear that the B.1 was increasingly vulnerable to the improved Soviet defences it would have to overcome if it were to strike deep into the Soviet Union. To increase the chances of the RAF crews reaching their objectives, the Vulcan B.2 was proposed, with more powerful engines, an electronic warfare (ECM) suite in an enlarged tailcone, and an inflight refuelling capability, along with an improved, larger wing. Some B.1s had a few B.2 improvements incorporated and were designated B.1As. With a longer range, the ability to carry a heavier bomb load (two nuclear weapons instead of one) and greatly improved self-defence capability, the B.2 ensured that the British nuclear strike force was a very real threat to the Soviet Union.

Even with the new and improved B.2, the delivery of free-fall nuclear weapons into the heart of the Soviet Union was probably still a one-way ticket for Vulcan crews. To improve their survivability, a stand-off nuclear missile – the Blue Steel – was developed, which could be launched 161km/100 miles away from the target. Blue Steels were carried partially recessed in the Vulcan's modified bomb bay.

Due to the improvements in Soviet air defence technology, the Vulcans became increasingly vulnerable at high level over enemy territory. The solution was to bring the Vulcan force down to low level, and the aircraft in service were upgraded to B.2A standard. More powerful Olympus engines were fitted, together with terrain-following radar in the nose and a warning radar atop the fin. The Vulcan's role changed when Royal Navy Polaris-equipped submarines took on responsibility for Britain's strategic nuclear deterrent, and they were switched to a tactical low-level penetration role.

However, it was with conventional weapons that the Vulcan first went to war in 1982, when it was used against Argentine positions on the Falkland Islands in what were then the longest bombing raids in history. Vulcans also served in strategic reconnaissance and air-refuelling tanker roles before being withdrawn from service in 1984 to be replaced by Tornadoes. Avro built 144 Vulcans in total, a small number considering the impact that the design had on the aerospace world, and the affection felt for the "tin triangle" by air-show fans the world over.

ABOVE RIGHT: **The Vulcan B.2 was able to carry two nuclear bombs and had increased survivability compared to earlier Vulcans.** RIGHT: **The Vulcan bomb bay carried extra fuel tanks in later versions, but was originally designed to carry the enormous Blue Danube bomb.** BELOW: **Compare the kinked leading edge wing of this B.2 to the pure delta of the prototype.**

Avro Vulcan B.2A

First flight: August 30, 1952 (Avro 698 prototype)
Power: Four Rolls-Royce 9080kg/20,000lb thrust Olympus 301 turbojets
Armament: Twenty-one 454kg/1000lb bombs, nuclear bombs or one Blue Steel stand-off missile
Size: Wingspan – 33.85m/111ft
Length – 30.5m/99ft 11in
Height – 8.26m/7ft 1in
Wing area – 368m²/3964sq ft
Weights: Empty – Approximately 37,682kg/83,000lb (Mk 1)
Maximum take-off – 113,500kg/250,000lb
Performance: Maximum speed – 1038kph/645mph
Ceiling – 16775m/55,000ft
Range – 5550km/3450 miles
Climb – Not published

BAC/BAE Strikemaster

The origins of the BAC 167 Strikemaster can be traced back to the piston-powered Hunting/Percival Provost basic trainer which first flew in 1950. Hunting swiftly proposed a jet-powered successor to the Provost – the Jet Provost – as a basic jet trainer for the Royal Air Force. Retaining the wings and tail of the original piston aircraft, the Jet Provost also introduced a tricycle undercarriage. From the mid-1950s, the "JP" was the RAF's standard basic jet trainer until it was finally retired in 1993, having being replaced by the Tucano.

The final production version of the Jet Provost was the Mk. 5 which introduced, among other refinements, a pressurized cabin. Following some exports of the Mk 5, it was this version that the manufacturers BAC (Hunting became part of the British Aircraft Corporation in 1961) developed as a private venture into a dedicated combat aircraft, the Strikemaster, which, as a two-seater, still retained a trainer capability.

The Strikemaster first flew in October 1967, and boasted side-by-side ejection seats and the ability to carry 1362kg/ 3000lb of ordnance on eight underwing hardpoints. Armament included free-fall or retarded bombs, gun packs or napalm. Alternatively, a reconnaissance pod, extra fuel tanks or a gun camera could be carried.

The aircraft's simplicity coupled with exceptionally good manoeuvrability and handling were features of the bomber, which attracted numerous overseas customers. Powered by a Rolls-Royce Viper turbojet, the aircraft was designed for operation from rough and short airstrips.

Customers for this very capable combat aircraft, which appeared in a variety of export versions, included Oman (Mk 82 and 82A), Singapore (Mk 84), Botswana, Ecuador (Mk 89), Kenya (Mk 87), Kuwait (Mk 83), New Zealand (Mk 88), Saudi Arabia (Mk 80 and 80A), Sudan (Mk 55) and South Yemen.

RIGHT: **This Strikemaster is painted in the colours of the Singapore Air Defence Command.** BELOW: **The Royal Saudi Air Force was a major customer for the Strikemaster.**

Apart from training, the Strikemaster was most commonly used for ground-attack and counter-insurgency operations. The aircraft of Ecuador, Oman and South Yemen are known to have seen combat – all 20 of the Sultan of Oman's Strikemasters have sustained battle damage.

Between 1968 and 1977, the Royal Saudi Air Force took delivery of a total of 47 Strikemasters in three separate batches. All the aircraft were used for training purposes at the King Faisal Air Academy in Riyadh until 1997, making the Strikemaster one of the longest serving aircraft in RSAF history.

Of the 16 Strikemasters acquired by the Royal New Zealand Air Force (where the aircraft was nicknamed "Blunty") in 1972, use of the aircraft was restricted after 1981 when cracks were discovered in the wing and tail structures of most RNZAF aircraft. The rigours of flying through low-level turbulence and

high usage were given as the likely causes. Replacing the wings of all their aircraft was considered too costly by the RNZAF, who retired them in 1992. Similar problems with the Strikemasters of Ecuador caused the grounding of their fleet for months at a time, while causes were identified and where possible remedied.

The final batch of new Strikemasters was delivered to Sudan in 1984. In all, 146 Strikemasters were sold around the world and many have now been refurbished for civilian use, surviving as "warbirds" in Britain, the USA and Australia.

BELOW LEFT: **In this view of an RNZAF Strikemaster, the side-by-side seats can be clearly seen.** BELOW: **The Strikemaster was one of the first small but capable and affordable trainer/ground-attack aircraft available to smaller nations. There was clearly a demand for this type, and the Strikemaster satisfied that for many nations.**

BAC Strikemaster

First flight: October 26, 1967

Power: One Rolls-Royce 1548kg/3410lb thrust Viper Mk 535 turbojet

Armament: Two 7.62mm/0.3in machine-guns; maximum bomb load of 1362kg/3000lb

Size: Wingspan – 11.23m/36ft 10in
Length – 10.27m/33ft 8.5in
Height – 3.34m/10ft 11.5in
Wing area – 19.85m²/213.7sq ft

Weights: Empty – 2812kg/6195lb
Maximum take-off – 5221kg/11,500lb

Performance: Maximum speed – 760kph/472mph
Ceiling – 12,200m/40,000ft
Range – 2224km/1382 miles
Climb – 1601m/5250ft per minute

ABOVE: **An Omani Strikemaster armed with bombs and rockets – the aircraft supplied to Oman saw considerable action.**

British Aircraft Corporation TSR.2

Few British aircraft have stirred as much controversy or strength of feeling as the TSR.2. The project's cancellation in 1965 was seen by many commentators as a political step that became the deathblow for Britain's troubled aviation industry.

The TSR.2 (Tactical Strike and Reconnaissance) was initially designed to meet a demanding 1957 Royal Air Force requirement for a Canberra tactical bomber replacement with terrain-following radar, advanced inertial navigation, supersonic speed at low level and Mach 2 at high altitude. In addition, the new aircraft would ideally have the capability to be operated from short, rough landing strips.

Despite the facts that the requirement become more demanding as development progressed, and that most of the TSR.2's systems were totally new to the British aviation industry, the aircraft began to take shape.

TSR.2's form was of course dictated by the missions it was designed to carry out, but by way of comparison it was longer than an Avro Lancaster but had a smaller wingspan than a Spitfire fighter. The short wingspan was essential for supersonic performance at very low altitude but would fail to generate sufficient lift for it to operate from short strips. The solution was to fit the aircraft with the most powerful blown flaps ever made, which used high-speed air blown over the flaps to make the wing produce massive amounts of lift at take-off and landing.

The TSR.2 carried equipment that is now commonplace but was extremely advanced for the time. A projected moving map, head-up display (HUD), one of the first terrain-following radars and a canopy coated with gold alloy to reflect nuclear

TOP: **XR219, the prototype TSR.2, during its test programme.** ABOVE: **The TSR.2 was equipped with pioneering terrain-following radar, which would have guided the aircraft at heights of 91m/200ft at the speed of sound.**

flash were all cutting-edge features of this remarkable aircraft. The avionics – purpose-designed for the aircraft – would have used forward- and side-looking radar and other systems to feed updated position and steering information to the pilot's HUD, the navigator, the weapon arming and release systems and the autopilot simultaneously. If the whole system had failed, the aircraft would have been automatically put in a climb. Among the materials used in the aircraft's construction were aluminium-copper alloys, aluminium-lithium alloys and ultra-high tensile steel.

The first flight of prototype XR219 took off from Boscombe Down on September 27, 1964, with Roland "Bee" Beamont at the controls and Don Bowen as navigator. The Olympus

BAC TSR.2

First flight: September 27, 1964
Power: Two Bristol Siddeley 14982kg/33,000lb thrust Olympus 22R turbojets
Armament: Up to 1816kg/4000lb of weapons on underwing pylons; proposed bomb load of up to 2724kg/6000lb
Size: Wingspan – 11.28m/37ft
  Length – 27.13m/89ft
  Height – 7.32m/24ft
  Wing area – 65.03m²/700sq ft
Weights Empty – 90,000kg/198,090lb
  Maximum take-off – 188,000kg/413,788lb
Performance: Maximum speed – 2390kph/1485mph
  Ceiling – 17,080m/56,000ft
  Range – 4827km/3000 miles
  Climb – 15,250m/50,000ft per minute
  (these figures may not have been achieved in testing but are in the aircraft's specification)

ABOVE LEFT: **XR222, the fourth TSR.2, is preserved at the Imperial War Museum Duxford in the UK.** LEFT: **XR222 prior to its "completion", at least for display purposes, at the Imperial War Museum Duxford.** BELOW LEFT: **During the 24 flights made by XR219, the aircraft's capabilities were clear to the crew.** BELOW: **A rare view of the "hotseat", the pilot's cockpit of TSR.2.**

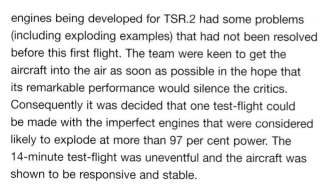

engines being developed for TSR.2 had some problems (including exploding examples) that had not been resolved before this first flight. The team were keen to get the aircraft into the air as soon as possible in the hope that its remarkable performance would silence the critics. Consequently it was decided that one test-flight could be made with the imperfect engines that were considered likely to explode at more than 97 per cent power. The 14-minute test-flight was uneventful and the aircraft was shown to be responsive and stable.

During further test-flights, the extremely complex aircraft showed that it had the potential to become one of the most formidable strike aircraft in the world. The aircraft made 24 flights and accumulated 13 hours and 9 minutes of flight time, including some at supersonic speeds, before the TSR.2 project was cancelled by the new Labour government on April 6, 1965. The government cited spiralling costs and the minimum 3-year delay in the TSR.2 reaching squadron service as reasons for the decision. The RAF never did receive an alternative to the TSR-2 as a supersonic strike successor to the Canberra.

BAE Systems Harrier

British innovation in aircraft design is perhaps best demonstrated by the Harrier. This truly remarkable aircraft, constantly improved and updated since its first uncertain hovering flight in October 1960, is still the only single-engined vertical or short take-off and landing (V/STOL) in service.

During the Cold War it was obvious that the West's military airfields would have been attacked very early in any offensive. Dispersal of aircraft and equipment was one option of response – the other was the Harrier, with its ability to operate from any small piece of flat ground. The fact that an aircraft can fly straight up with no need for forward movement still leaves spectators stunned over four decades after the prototype first flew.

The Harrier can take off and land vertically by the pilot selecting an 80-degree nozzle angle and applying full power. At 15–30m/50–100ft altitude, the nozzles are gradually directed rearwards until conventional wingborne flight is achieved. The key to the Harrier's vertical take-off lies with the vectored thrust from the Harrier's Pegasus engine, directed by four jet nozzles controlled by a selector lever next to the throttle in the cockpit. The nozzles swivel as one, directing thrust from directly to the rear to just forward of vertical. While hovering or flying at very low speeds, the aircraft is controlled in all lanes of movement by reaction control jets located in the nose, wing and tail. These jets are operated by the Harrier's conventional rudder pedals and control column.

The Harrier GR1 first entered squadron service with the RAF in October 1969, and many were subsequently upgraded to GR3 standard, with more powerful engines and a tail warning radar to alert the pilot to hostile missiles locking on

TOP: **An RAF GR7. The Harrier is one of the all-time great combat aircraft. The basic soundness of the concept has lent itself to many upgrades and improvements.** ABOVE: **Radar-equipped AV-8Bs of the Spanish Navy operating from the carrier *Principe de Asturias*. These aircraft were similar to those operated by the Italian Navy and USMC aircraft.**

to his aircraft. GR3s of No.1 Squadron RAF were in action during the 1982 Falklands War. They carried out ground-attack operations using cluster and "smart" bombs, with weapon loads of up to 1362kg/3000lb. The Squadron flew more than 150 missions, with two aircraft lost to heavy anti-aircraft fire at Goose Green.

Early in the Harrier's operational life, the US Marine Corps expressed an interest in the aircraft, leading to more than a hundred being built as the AV-8A by McDonnell Douglas in the USA. The USMC continues to operate Harriers today, the AV-8B variant being roughly equivalent to the RAF's GR7. US Marine Corps AV-8Bs took part in Operation Desert Storm in 1991. The other customer for the early Harrier was the Spanish Navy, which ordered the US-built AV-8A, and subsequently sold some of the aircraft on to the Thai Navy in 1996.

ABOVE: **The GR7 is the RAF equivalent of the American-designed AV-8B.**
LEFT: **The Harrier gives its operators unparalled strike flexibility.**

The second-generation GR5 and GR7 versions replaced the original Harrier GR3s in the late 1980s/early 1990s in the offensive support role. The GR7 is, in essence, a licence-built American-designed AV-8B Harrier II fitted with RAF-specific navigation and defensive systems as well as other changes, including additional underwing pylons for Sidewinder missiles. The improved design of the GR7 allows the aircraft to carry twice the load of a GR3 over the same distance or the same load over twice the distance. The first flight of the Harrier GR7 was in 1989, and deliveries to RAF squadrons began in 1990. A total of 96 aircraft were ordered, including 62 interim GR5s which were later modified to GR7 standard.

The Harrier GR7 is capable of operating throughout the full spectrum of ground-attack operations by day and night. The aircraft carries forward-looking infrared (FLIR) equipment which, when used in conjunction with the pilot's night-vision goggles (NVGs), provides a night, low-level capability. The Harrier T10, a two-seat trainer version of the GR7, came into service in 1995 and can be used operationally.

Recent operational deployments for the Harriers have been to Italy in support of NATO and UN operations in Bosnia and Serbia, and to the Gulf embarked on Royal Navy aircraft carriers, where they complemented the Royal Navy's own Sea Harriers.

Plans in 2002 announced the withdrawal of the Sea Harrier by 2006, with the Harrier GR7/GR9s being operated by both RAF and Royal Navy squadrons.

The Harrier continues to be upgraded. New Pegasus 107 engines, giving more thrust at higher temperatures, make the aircraft Harrier GR7As even more efficient. Also, a major upgrade to the aircraft's avionics and weapons systems will enable the Harrier to carry a variety of current and future weapons. These include Maverick air-to-surface missiles, Brimstone anti-armour missiles and Sidewinder air-to-air missiles for self-defence. A new, stronger composite rear fuselage will also be fitted. These aircraft will become Harrier GR9s, while those with the uprated engines and weapons systems will be Harrier GR9As. The programme also includes an upgrade of the two-seater T10 aircraft to the equivalent GR9 standard known as the Harrier T12.

RAF Harriers saw service in Kosovo and in the 2003 invasion of Iraq. On March 22, 2003, alongside aircraft of the USAF and USN, the RAF were heavily involved in attacks against key Iraqi targets, including Baghdad. One of the RAF raids featured the first operational use of the RAF's Maverick missile. A Harrier GR7 pilot launched one of the missiles against a mobile SCUD missile launch site some 322km/200 miles into Iraq. It successfully engaged and destroyed the target.

ABOVE: **The Harrier GR7 can carry up to 4903kg/10,800lb of ordnance under its wings and fuselage.**

**BAE Systems
Harrier II GR7**

First flight: October 21, 1960 (P1127)
Power: One Rolls-Royce 9765kg/21,500lb thrust Pegasus Mk5 turbofan
Armament: Two 25mm/0.90in cannon; up to 4903kg/10,800lb bombs, missiles or rockets
Size: Wingspan – 9.25m/30ft 4in
  Length – 14.36m/47ft 1in
  Height – 3.55m/11ft 7.75in
  Wing area – 21.37m²/230sq ft
Weights: Empty – 6973kg/15,360lb
  Maximum take-off – 14,074kg/31,000lb
Performance: Maximum speed – 1058kph/ 661mph
  Ceiling – 15,250m/50,000ft plus
  Range – 11,861km/7370 miles
  Climb – Not available

Blackburn Buccaneer

The Buccaneer was at one point the most advanced high-speed low-level strike aircraft in the world. It had its origins in the July 1953 Naval Staff Requirement NA.39 which called for a long-range carrier-borne strike aircraft capable of carrying a nuclear weapon beneath enemy radar cover and attacking enemy shipping or ports.

Blackburn's N.A.39 design, the B-103, was the successful contender and the development contract was awarded in 1955 – the first of 20 pre-production aircraft took to the air on April 30, 1958, and also appeared at that year's Farnborough air show. The B-103 prototype was powered by 3178kg/7000lb thrust Gyron turbojets, not the much more powerful Spey of later models. The carrier aircraft elements of the design, such as folding wings, folding nose catapult fittings and arrestor hook, were introduced from the fourth aircraft onwards. The aerodynamically advanced aircraft incorporated many innovations, including a rotary bomb-bay door (intended to avoid the drag of conventional bomb-bay doors and weapons carried beneath the aircraft) and a split tail cone which opened to act as airbrakes. The aircraft also had a cutting-edge boundary layer control system in which air from the engines was forced through slits on the wings' leading edges, producing much more lift than that wing would normally give. Increasing the wings' efficiency meant the aircraft could land at lower speed and carry more ordnance.

The miniature detonating cord (MDC), which shatters the cockpit canopy prior to ejection, is now standard on most British fast jets, and was pioneered on the Blackburn design. It was actually developed to aid escape in the event of underwater ejection.

TOP: **Buccaneer S.1 XK534 from the Fleet Air Arm Trials Unit at Lossiemouth. Painted overall in anti-flash white, this was the 18th pre-production aircraft.** ABOVE: **The Buccaneer's wings are able to fold up through 120 degrees from a hinge.**

Royal Navy carrier trials began in January 1960 and the first B-103 deck landing took place on HMS *Victorious* on the 19th of the month. Having given the aircraft the name Buccaneer in 1960, the Navy took delivery of the first production version, the S.1, in July 1962. HMS *Ark Royal* sailed with the first operational Buccaneer squadron, No.801, and its anti-flash white Buccaneers only six months later in January 1963. The Cold War was at one of its chilliest phases and Britain wanted nuclear-capable aircraft in service as soon as possible.

The S.1 was soon shown to be under-powered, and in some conditions the Gyrons could barely lift a loaded Buccaneer off the deck within safety margins. Consequently, Fleet Air Arm Scimitars fitted with inflight refuelling equipment were detailed to refuel the partly fuelled and therefore lighter Buccaneers shortly after they left the deck. Forty S.1s were built before production switched to the next Mark. The improved S.2 was the principal production version (84 were built) and had a greater range than the earlier version thanks to the more

powerful but less thirsty Spey engines. Service S.2s are most easily recognized by the fixed refuelling probe forward of the cockpit.

The S.2s served in the Royal Navy's front line from January 1967 until the last S.2s left the deck of the *Ark Royal* in November 1978. However, the Buccaneer's career was far from over as the first of almost 90 aircraft had begun service with the Royal Air Force in October 1969, filling the gap in the RAF inventory left by the scrapping of TSR.2 and the cancellation of the intended F-111 purchase for the RAF.

Twenty-six of the aircraft were new-build while a further 62 Royal Navy examples were gradually transferred into RAF service. In addition to retaining a nuclear strike capability, Buccaneers were also tasked with anti-shipping missions from land bases. RAF Germany, right in the nuclear front-line, first welcomed No.15 Squadrons Buccaneers early in 1971. Tornados began to replace the Germany Buccaneers in 1983 but two squadrons tasked with maritime strike remained in service in Scotland. In 1991 some of these aircraft were "called up" for service in the first Gulf War, where they acted as laser designators for laser-guided bombs dropped by Tornados. To give it an even longer range for these special missions, the "Bucc" was fitted with a 2000 litre/440 gallon fuel tank carried in the bomb bay.

TOP RIGHT: **Buccaneers served on Royal Navy carriers from 1962 until 1978.**
MIDDLE RIGHT: **Some Royal Navy aircraft were transferred to the RAF, while others were brand new aircraft. Some of these retained a nuclear strike capability based in Germany.** RIGHT: **The last Buccaneers in RAF service were those retained for the maritime strike role.** BELOW: **The last British bomber was tasked with demanding Gulf War missions shortly before its retirement.**

Blackburn Buccaneer S.2

First flight: April 30, 1958 (B-103 prototype)
Power: Two Rolls-Royce 5039kg/11,100lb thrust Rolls-Royce Spey 101 turbofans
Armament: One nuclear bomb or four 454kg/1000lb conventional bombs carried internally
Size: Wingspan – 13.41m/44ft
   Length – 19.33m/63ft 5in
   Height – 4.95m/16ft 3in
   Wing area – 47.82m²/514.7sq ft
Weights: Empty –13,620kg/30,000lb
   Maximum takeoff – 28,148kg/62,000lb
Performance: Maximum speed – 1038kph/645mph
   Ceiling – 12,200m/40,000ft plus
   Range – 3218km/2000 miles
   Climb – 9150m/30,000ft in 2 minutes

Boeing B-47 Stratojet

As World War II was drawing to a close, the US Army Air Forces were considering replacements for the aircraft types then in service. Development of a new subsonic, high-altitude, medium-range bomber began in 1945 with four US contractors in the running. The Boeing design, the six-jet XB-47 (first flight December 1947), with the performance of contemporary jet fighters, won the competition and became the first jet-powered swept-wing bomber in service. Its six turbojet engines (so many were needed because of the poor power output of early jets) were housed in pods slung beneath the 35-degree swept-back wings, the inboard pods housing two engines each while a single engine was positioned towards the tip of each wing. Early versions at maximum take-off weight needed additional thrust from 18 solid-fuel booster rockets in the aft fuselage.

B-47s began entering the USAF inventory in 1952 and, in the days before intercontinental ballistic missiles, the fast nuclear-armed bomber was the best deterrent the USA had. Apart from the swept wings and profusion of engines, the aircraft incorporated many novel features, including a remote-controlled tail gun turret and a bicycle-type retractable main landing gear with single, two-wheel legs on the forward and aft fuselage. Outrigger wheels that retracted into the two-engine pod cowling provided added stability. The B-model was the first production version in service but was supplanted by the B-47E, the ultimate bomber version.

The three-man B-47 was a heavy aircraft in its day, and although it was a medium-range bomber, it was heavier than any strategic bomber aircraft of World War II. A tail chute was used to slow down the aircraft during landings, one of the first aircraft to use the technique. The B-47 could carry a 9080kg/20,000lb bomb load that limited the aircraft to a maximum of two nuclear weapons of the early 1950s. However, so many B-47s were manufactured, they did represent a more than credible deterrent or threat to the Soviet Union. Conventional weaponry options included 6129kg/13,500lb or eight 454kg/1000lb bombs.

The B-47 had a 5792km/3600 mile range which required Strategic Air Command to make use of forward bases in friendly nations such as Britain, Spain and Morocco, as well as

ABOVE: **The B-47 was a great technological leap for US military aviation. The main bomber at the time of the B-47's first flight was the B-29.** LEFT: **At its peak use, the B-47 equipped 28 SAC Bomb Wings, each with 45 aircraft.**

LEFT: **The large swept wings, 1-2-2-1 engine layout and the fighter style canopy make the B-47 one of the easiest aircraft to identify.** BELOW: **An early B-47 assisted by 18 rockets at take-off.** BOTTOM: **Over 2000 B-47s were built, and they provided the USA with a credible nuclear deterrent.**

Alaska, to be within striking distance of the USSR. In addition, the B-47 was later equipped with an air-refuelling capability and 36-hour missions were flown to show the world the reach of the SAC bomber. However, when some foreign hosts chose to withdraw their offer of forward bases, the usefulness of the B-47 was reduced because there was insufficient tanker support to allow great numbers of B-47s to operate from the continental USA.

Also, as with Britain's V-force, the B-47 role was changed in the mid-1950s due to the development of effective Soviet surface-to-air missiles (SAMs), and the aircraft's structure was strengthened so that it could be used as a low-level bomber avoiding Soviet radars.

Some B-47s were modified for reconnaissance use (RB-47) and, as space was at a premium in the airframe, these versions were not capable of carrying bombs as well as reconnaissance equipment. However, the RB-47B could be converted back to bomber configuration.

By 1956, B-47 deployment peaked, with over 1300 equipping 28 SAC wings, while around 250 RB-47s were in SAC service in the same period. The B-47 was gradually phased out in the early 1960s. About 400 were in service in 1964 and by 1966 the last B-47 had been phased out. The retirement of the B-47 was balanced by the large numbers of strategic nuclear missiles then joining the US arsenal. A total of 2039 B-47s were built.

Boeing B-47E Stratojet

First flight: December 17, 1947

Power: Six General Electric 3269kg/7200lb thrust J47-GE-25 turbojets

Armament: Two 20mm/0.78in cannon in remote-controlled tail turret; up to 9080kg/20,000lb of bombs

Size: Wingspan – 35.36m/116ft
Length – 33.48m/109ft 10in
Height – 8.51m/27ft 11in
Wing area –132.66m²/1428sq ft

Weights: Empty – 36,663kg/80,756lb
Maximum take-off – 89,973kg/198,180lb

Peformance: Maximum speed – 975kph/606mph
Ceiling –12,352m/40,500ft plus
Range – 5794km/3600 miles
Climb – 1326m/4350ft per minute at maximum power

Boeing B-52 Stratofortress

The B-52 is surely one of the greatest combat aircraft of all time, remaining in front-line service almost six decades after the USAF specification for what became the B-52 was released in 1946. The USAF wanted a bomber with a 16,090km/10,000-mile range and a speed of over 804kph/500mph. Boeing initially proposed a conventional design with piston engines to achieve the range. As the US Air Force wanted the aircraft to fly as high and fast as possible to drop atomic weapons, Boeing revised the design with eight jet powerplants and swept wings.

The prototype first flew in 1952 and ever since entering service in 1955, the B-52 has been in the front line. The first operational version was the B-52B, and in 1956 a B-model dropped the first air-dropped hydrogen bomb over Bikini Atoll. In an attempt to demonstrate the reach of the USAF Strategic Air Command, three B-52Bs made a non-stop flight around the world in January 1957, with the help of five inflight refuellings.

A total of 744 B-52s were built with the last, a B-52H, delivered in October 1962. Only the H-model is still in the Air Force inventory and is assigned to Air Combat Command and the Air Force Reserves. The first of 102 B-52s was delivered to Strategic Air Command in May 1961.

The B-52 could bomb the Soviet Union from bases in the continental USA and was a key element in SAC's deterrence of the Soviet Union. To ensure the survivability of the SAC deterrent against a pre-emptive Soviet strike, the SAC B-52 force was dispersed and rotated. In addition, a given number

TOP: **A B-52D. The B-52 is a truly great military aircraft. Despite being in service for half a century, there is still no other aircraft in the US inventory that can do the job of the B-52, and on the same scale.** ABOVE: **The bomb-carrying capacity of the "Buff" is considerable – 27,240kg/60,000lb of weaponry can be trucked and dropped on a target.**

of B-52s was kept on standby ready for take-off and, for a time, in the air ready to begin attacks on Soviet targets. From 1958 until 1968, ten to twelve USAF B-52s were airborne at all times. At the time of the 1962 Cuban missile crisis, 70 aircraft were kept aloft at all times for one month. Following two crashes in which radioactivity was released from the nuclear bombs aboard, the airborne alert ceased.

The B-52, with its cavernous bomb bay and great lifting capability, has been armed with free-fall hydrogen bombs and parachute retarded bombs as well as stand-off nuclear

LEFT: **The B-52G was a complete structural redesign with a distinctive short fin.** BELOW: **The H-model is the version still in USAF use today, and will be for some years to come.** BOTTOM: **Inflight refuelling during the Gulf War. The conflict gave the old but potent bomber the opportunity to get into the record books with the longest bombing mission in history.**

missiles, including the AGM-86B. Of course, the aircraft has never used nuclear weapons in anger. During the Vietnam War, however, USAF B-52s dropped almost 3 million tons of bombs. The bomb bay of the D-model was modified so that it could carry up to 108 conventional bombs, which meant that each aircraft could carry around 27.4 tonnes/27 tons per aircraft.

Two decades after its missions over Vietnam, the B-52 took part in the Gulf War. Seven B-52s armed with AGM-86 cruise missiles flew 22,500km/14,000 miles (and into the history books) from the USA to carry out the first air strike of the war – this was the longest combat mission ever flown. During the conflict, 80 B-52s flew 1624 sorties, dropping 26,111 tonnes/ 25,700 tons of bombs, accounting for 40 per cent of the total dropped during the war. In 2003, USAF B-52s operating from a base in Britain carried out numerous bombing raids on targets in Iraq, demonstrating that the '52 was still a potent front-line combat aircraft 51 years after the type first flew.

Today, the B-52s of USAF Air Combat Command remain a key means of delivering US air power with worldwide precision navigation capability. The aircraft is also highly effective when used for ocean surveillance, and can assist the US Navy in anti-ship and mine-laying operations. In two hours, two B-52s can monitor 362,600km²/140,000sq miles of ocean surface.

The B-52 is capable of dropping or launching the widest array of weapons in the US inventory. This includes gravity bombs, cluster bombs, precision-guided missiles and joint direct attack munitions. Updated with modern technology, the B-52 will be capable of delivering the full complement of joint developed weapons – current engineering analysis shows the B-52's life span to extend beyond the year 2045. The B-52 will be kept flying because there is nothing else in the US inventory that can carry out the B-52 mission on the same scale.

Boeing B-52D

First Flight: April 15, 1952

Power: Eight Pratt & Whitney 5493kg/12,100lb thrust J57-P-19W turbojets

Armament: Four 12.7mm/0.5in machine-guns in tail; maximum of 108 conventional bombs up to 27,240kg/60,000lb

Size: Wingspan – 56.4m/185ft
Length – 47.7m/156ft 6in
Height – 12.75m/48ft 3.7in
Wing area – 371.6m²/4000sq ft

Weights: Empty – 85,806kg/189,000lb
Maximum take-off – 204,300kg/450,000lb

Performance: Maximum speed – 893kph/555mph
Ceiling – 13,725m/45,000ft
Range – 11,861km/7370 miles
Climb – Not available

Boeing/McDonnell Douglas/Northrop F/A-18 Hornet

With its excellent fighter and self-defence capabilities, the F/A-18 was intended to increase strike mission survivability and supplement the F-14 Tomcat in US Navy fleet air defence. The F/A-18 played a key role in the 1986 US strikes against Libya. Flying from the USS *Coral Sea*, F/A-18s launched high-speed anti-radiation missiles (HARMs) against Libyan air-defence radars and missile sites, thus silencing them during the attacks on military targets in Benghazi.

The F/A-18's advanced radar and avionics systems allow Hornet pilots to shift from fighter to strike mode on the same mission with the flip of a switch, a facility used routinely by Hornets in Operation Desert Storm – they fought their way to a target by defeating opposing aircraft, attacked ground targets and returned home safely. This "force multiplier" capability gives the operational commander more flexibility in employing tactical aircraft in a rapidly changing battle scenario.

The F/A-18 Hornet was built in single and two-seat versions. Although the two-seater is a conversion trainer, it is combat-capable and has a similar performance to the single seat version, although with reduced range. The F/A-18A and C are single-seat aircraft, while the F/A-18B and D are dual-seaters. The B-model is used primarily for training, while the D-model is the current Navy aircraft for attack, tactical air control, forward air control and reconnaissance squadrons.

In November 1989, the first F/A-18s equipped with night-strike capability were delivered, and since 1991, F/A-18s have been delivered with F404-GE-402 enhanced performance engines that produce up to 20 per cent more thrust than the previous F404 engines. From May 1994, the Hornet has been equipped with upgraded radar – the APG-73 – which substantially increases the speed and memory capacity of the radar's processors. These upgrades and improvements help the Hornet maintain its advantage over potential enemies and keep it among the most advanced and capable combat aircraft in the world.

Apart from the US Navy and Marine Corps, the F/A-18 is also in service with the air forces of Canada, Australia, Spain, Kuwait, Finland, Switzerland and Malaysia.

Canada was the first international customer for the F/A-18, and its fleet of 138 CF-18 Hornets is the largest outside the USA. The CF-18s have an unusual element to their paint scheme in that a "fake" cockpit is painted on the underside of the fuselage directly beneath the real cockpit. This is intended to confuse an enemy fighter, if only for a split second, about the orientation of the CF-18 in close air combat. That moment's hesitation can mean the difference between kill or be killed in a dogfight situation.

TOP: **The Hornet/Super Hornet family of aircraft have given their operators an exceptional combination of capabilities – few aircraft can fight, not just evade, enemy aircraft and then carry out devastating pinpoint attacks.** ABOVE: **Aircraft operated by Spain were designated EF/A-18. This is a single-seat A-model.**

The F/A-18E/F Super Hornet was devised to build on the great success of the Hornet, and having been test-flown in November 1995, entered service for evaluation with US Navy squadron VFA-122 in November 1999.

The Super Hornet is 25 per cent larger than its predecessor but has 42 per cent fewer parts. Both the single-seat E and two-seat F-models offer increased range, greater endurance, more payload-carrying ability and more powerful engines in the form of the F414-GE-400, an advanced derivative of the Hornet's current F404 engine family that produces 35 per cent more thrust.

Structural changes to the airframe increase internal fuel capacity by 1634kg/3600lb, which extends the Hornet's mission radius by up to 40 per cent. The fuselage is 86.3cm/34in longer and the wing is 25 per cent larger with an extra 9.3m²/100sq ft of surface area. There are two additional weapons stations, bringing the total to 11.

In the words of its manufacturers, "The Super Hornet is an adverse-weather, day and night, multi-mission strike fighter whose survivability improvements over its predecessors make it harder to find, and if found, harder to hit, and if hit, harder to disable."

The first operational cruise of the F/A-18 E Super Hornet was with VFA-115 on board the USS *Abraham Lincoln* on July 24, 2002, and the type was first used in combat on November 6, 2002, when they participated in a strike against hostile targets in the "no-fly" zone in Iraq.

ABOVE: **A US Marine Corps F/A-18D drops a bomb over a bombing range in Nevada.** BELOW LEFT: **A fine air-to-air study of USMC Hornets.** BELOW: **USMC Hornets. The type is operated by a number of other nations outside the USA, on four different continents.** BOTTOM: **The Super Hornet is bigger and better than the original design.**

Northrop F/A-18E Super Hornet

First flight: November 18, 1995
Power: Two General Electric 9988kg/22,000lb thrust afterburning F414-GE-400 turbofans
Armament: One 20mm/0.78in cannon, eleven hardpoints carrying up to 8058kg/17,750lb of weapons, including AIM-7, AIM-120 AMRAAM, AIM-9 air-to-air missiles or other guided weapons, bombs and rockets
Size: Wingspan – 13.62m/44ft 9in
Length – 18.31m/60ft 1in
Height – 4.88m/16ft
Wing area – 46.5m²/500sq ft
Weights: Empty – 13,426kg/29,574lb
Maximum take-off – 29,937kg/66,000lb
Performance: Maximum speed – 1915kph/1189mph
Ceiling – 15,250m/50,000ft plus
Combat radius – 2225km/1382 miles
Climb – Not published

173

Breguet Alize

Breguet Alize

First Flight: March 26, 1955 (prototype)

Power: One Rolls-Royce 1975hp DartRDa21 turboprop

Armament: Two anti-shipping missiles carried beneath the folding wings, or a combination of depth charges, bombs or rockets; acoustic torpedo, three 160kg/352lb depth charges housed in internal bomb bay

Size: Wingspan – 15.6m/51ft 2in

Length – 13.86m/45ft 6in

Height – 5.00m/16ft 4.75in

Wing area – 36.00m²/387.51sq ft

Weights: Empty – 5700kg/12,546lb

Maximum take-off – 8200kg/18,048lb

Performance: Maximum speed – 518kph/322mph

Ceiling – 8000m/26,245ft plus

Range – 2500km/1553 miles

Climb – 420m/1380ft per minute

ABOVE: **Alize prepares to take off from a French carrier.**
LEFT: **This French Navy Alize's retractable radome is seen in the stowed position beneath the roundel.** BELOW: **Sporting a French Navy 1990s low-visibility paint scheme.**

The carrier-borne anti-submarine Alize (tradewind) was derived from the Vultur carrier-based attack aircraft designed for the French Aeronavale but never produced for service. The Alize was an extensive redesign of the earlier type and had its first flight on October 5, 1956.

The crew of three consisted of pilot, radar operator and sensor operator. The pilot was seated in front to the right, the radar operator in front to the left, and the sensor operator sat sideways behind them. Landing gear retracted backwards into nacelles in the wings. The Alize, powered by the Rolls-Royce Dart RDa.21 turboprop driving a four-bladed propeller, could patrol for over 5 hours.

The aircraft was armed with a potent array of torpedoes, depth charges, bombs, rockets and missiles. A total of 89 examples of the Alize were built between 1957 and 1962, including

prototypes. The Aeronavale operated 75 from March 1959 on board the carriers Clemenceau and Foch.

The Aeronavale upgraded the Alize in the 1980s and '90s with the latest avionics. The aircraft was simply not able to hunt modern nuclear-powered submarines effectively, so was limited to maritime surface patrol duties.

The Aeronavale operated 24 examples until 1997, and in the spring of 1999, aircraft flying off the carrier

Foch were used operationally during the NATO air campaign against Serbia over Kosovo. The Alize was finally withdrawn from Aeronavale service in 2000 with the retirement of the Foch.

The Indian Navy operated the Alize (at least 12 examples) from shore bases and from the light carrier Vikrant. The type was used for reconnaissance and patrol during India's 1961 occupation of Portuguese Goa, and was also used for anti-submarine patrol during the Indo-Pakistan War of 1971. During this conflict, one Alize was shot down by a Pakistani F-104 Starfighter in what must have been a most unusual air-combat episode. The Alize was gradually relegated to shore-based patrol duties in the 1980s, and was finally phased out in 1991, replaced by ASW helicopters.

LEFT: **The German Navy have operated Atlantics since the mid-1960s.**
BELOW: **The improved Atlantique 2.**

Breguet/Dassault Atlantic

In 1956, NATO began to consider a maritime patrol aircraft capable of hunting Soviet nuclear submarines, to replace the ageing Lockheed Neptune. Fourteen countries took part in studies to produce an aircraft that could fly for 18 hours at 300 knots and carry all the equipment and ordnance needed to search for and destroy Soviet submarines. Out of the 25 put forward, Breguet (now Dassault Aviation) proposed the Atlantic, which was ultimately ordered by France (40 aircraft), Germany (20), and later by the Netherlands (9) and Italy (18). Construction was carried out by a consortium of manufacturers across the four nations.

The first Atlantics were delivered to the French Navy in October 1965 and equipped four squadrons who operated them in the maritime reconnaissance role. However, the French aircraft were also used for land reconnaissance over Mauritania and Chad, and during the first Gulf War.

As well as advanced optical equipment, the Atlantic was fitted with highly advanced avionics systems – largely British and American – including a Thomson underfuselage radar able to locate submarines on the surface. Other equipment included a magnetic anomaly detector (MAD) to sense the magnetic fields generated by the metal mass of submerged submarines.

The aircraft could also drop acoustic buoys in a search area which, with the equipment on board, would form a submarine acoustic detection network in which a vessel could be easily located. Having identified a target, the Atlantic could then use a variety of equipment to attack, including bombs, depth charges, homing or acoustic torpedoes, plus a variety of missiles armed with conventional or nuclear warheads.

The French Navy were so impressed by the capability of the Atlantic that they ordered the much-improved Atlantique Mark 2, 28 examples of which were finally delivered between 1989 and 1997.

One of the radars carried on the Mark 2 is so sensitive it can detect a submarine periscope above the surface. The Mark 2's acoustic detection system uses buoys that can not only locate submarines, but will also compare the findings with its database to identify the class, nationality and threat level of the "bogey".

In the event of an enemy attack, the aircraft also has electronic counter-measures to deceive infrared and radar homing missiles. The Atlantique 2 can carry eight torpedoes or two Exocet missiles, or eight pods containing a raft and survival equipment for any survivors of a sinking.

A fully up-to-date glass cockpit Atlantique Mark 3 will be entering French Navy service in 2007, while Germany and Italy hope to replace their original Mark Is with 3s by 2010.

ABOVE: **A view inside the Atlantique 2, which is equipped with the very latest electronic surveillance and processing equipment.**

Breguet/Dassault Atlantic

First flight: October 21, 1961
Power: Two Rolls-Royce 6106eshp Tyne 21 turboprops
Armament: Up to 6000kg/13,206lb of bombs, depth charges, torpedoes, mines and missiles carried in weapons bay or on underwing pylons
Size: Wingspan – 37.42m/122ft 9in
　　Length – 33.63m/110ft 4in
　　Height – 11.35m/37ft 3in
　　Wing area – 120.34m²/1295sq ft
Weights: Empty – 25,300kg/55,685lb
　　Maximum take-off – 46,200kg/101,686lb
Performance: Maximum speed – 6481kph/403mph
　　Ceiling – 9150m/30,020ft
　　Range – 9075km/5635 miles
　　Climb – 746m/2450m per minute

Convair B-36 Peacemaker

The Convair B-36 Peacemaker was physically the largest bomber to ever have gone into service with the United States Air Force, and during the late 1940s and early '50s, it was the USAF's long-range strategic bombing deterrent. Although it never saw combat, reconnaissance versions flew near or possibly over the Soviet during the height of the Cold War in the mid-1950s.

The B-36 was conceived in the early years of World War II, when the US feared that its ally Britain may have been invaded by Germany. The USA knew that if it was drawn into the war in Europe it would need a means of carrying out attacks from the continental USA. In search of an aircraft capable of carrying out bombing raids over unprecedented distances, on April 11, 1941 the US Army Air Corps invited designs for a bomber with a 724kph/450mph top speed, a cruising speed of 442kph/275mph, a ceiling of 13,725m/45,000ft and a maximum range of 19,308km/12,000 miles. Consolidated's design, the Model 35, had twin fins and rudders, and four or six engines were suggested. To speed up the intercontinental bomber project, the requirements were scaled down to a 16,090km/10,000-mile range, cruising speed of between 386–483kph/240–300mph, and a service ceiling of 12,200m/40,000ft.

In late 1941, Consolidated (later Convair) was asked to proceed to prototype stage (two aircraft) using six engines, and the aircraft was designated XB-36. The aircraft proposed by Consolidated was staggering in its proportions. The slightly swept-back wing spanned 70.1m/230ft with a wing area of 443.32m²/4772sq ft. At that stage the aircraft was powered by six 28-cylinder Pratt & Whitney R-4360 Wasp Major air-cooled radials, each driving a 5.8m/19ft three-bladed Curtiss propeller, unusually, in pusher configuration. These engines were accessible in flight through the truly enormous 2.29m/7.5ft thick wing root. The four bomb bays could carry 20,884kg/46,000lb of bombs, compared to the 9080kg/20,000lb of bombs of the B-29. The fuselage of the aircraft was 49.4m/162ft long, and the crew moved from front to rear through a 0.64m/25in diameter, 24.4m/80ft pressurized tunnel using a wheeled trolley.

In early 1943, the USA faced losing its bases in China to the invading Japanese, so the mighty Convair bomber, with its planned global reach, became an even more important project. Therefore, a June 1943 order was placed for 100 examples of the huge bomber, with the prototype to be ready by September 1944 and service deliveries within a year. Development delays with the engines, among other aspects of the project, almost doomed the aircraft, then Allied progress in the Pacific war reduced the project's priority status. Even when Germany surrendered, the B-36 project stayed alive because the USA needed a means of delivering their atom bomb against potential enemies around the world.

The prototype finally flew, almost two years late, on August 8, 1946. At the time, there were only three runways in the USA strong enough to take the weight of the behemoth bomber, which was the heaviest and largest land-based aircraft to have flown.

BELOW: **Instead of the normal bare-metal finish, this B-36B carries so-called "Arctic red" test markings. The aircraft was operated by the 7th Bomb Group.**

Strategic Air Command ultimately had ten wings equipped with B-36 Peacemakers. A-models were unarmed and used as training aircraft, whereas the B-36B was a nuclear bomber.

As more equipment and fuel increased the weight of the aircraft, the piston engines – developed to produce all the power they could – were augmented by four 2452kg/5400lb thrust turbojets, leading to the "six turning, four burning" description of the B-36's later powerplant arrangements. This model, produced as the B-36D, was complemented by 64 B-models converted to D standard. This ten-engined version was the template for later, more powerful and better-equipped bomber versions.

When production ended in August 1954, 383 aircraft had been built for the USAF. From 1958, the B-36 was replaced in Strategic Air Command by the Boeing B-52. In the ten or so years that the B-36 was in front-line service, it gave the USA a global reach, leaving potential enemies in no doubt that they could be attacked by America. If one accepts that deterrence kept the peace at this time in the Cold War, then the B-36 could indeed have no better name than "Peacemaker".

ABOVE: **The B-36D, "six turning and four burning".**
LEFT: **The RB-36D was a reconnaissance version of Convair's "Big Stick" – the endurance and carrying power of the aircraft allowed it to undertake strategic reconnaissance missions.** BELOW LEFT: **The scale of the B-36 can be best appreciated by considering the 2.13m/7ft-high tunnel that passed within the wings to allow inflight maintenance of the outer engines.**

Convair B-36J Peacemaker

First flight: August 8, 1946 (YB-36)

Power: Six Pratt & Whitney 3600hp R-4360-53 radial piston engines and four General Electric 2452kg/5400lb thrust J47-19 turbojets

Armament: Sixteen 20mm/0.78in cannon in fuselage tail and nose turrets; maximum bomb load of 20,884kg/46,000lb

Size: Wingspan – 70.1m/230ft
Length – 49.4m/162ft 1in
Height – 14.22m/46ft 8in
Wing area – 443.32m²/4772sq ft

Weights: Empty – 77,650kg/171,035lb
Maximum take-off – 186,140kg/410,000lb

Performance: Maximum speed – 661kph/411mph
Service ceiling – 12,169m/39,900ft
Range – 10,945km/6800 miles
Climb – 677m/2220ft per minute

Convair B-58 Hustler

The delta-winged B-58 was designed as a supersonic replacement for the USAF's B-47, and the prototype's first flight took place on November 11, 1956. The aircraft went supersonic for the first time on December 30 that year. A total of 116 aircraft were built, including 30 test and pre-production aircraft, and the aircraft reached squadron service in 1960, becoming the Strategic Air Command's and the world's first operational supersonic bomber.

The B-58 was first designed to meet an exacting requirement, and the design team had to make great advances to meet it. The aircraft had to fly at Mach 2 (the first bomber to do so) at high-altitude, carry and accurately drop nuclear weapons, and be as small as possible to have the smallest possible radar signature. The aircraft, all of its equipment and weaponry were for the first time seen as an entire weapons system in USAF procurement, and Convair was responsible for making it all work together. This new approach required the breaking of much new ground, and did lead to delays.

There were many "firsts" associated with the B-58 Hustler. It was the first aircraft to have heat-resistant, stainless-steel honeycomb sandwich skin panels in the wings and fuselage, and was the first bomber with a weapons pod to be jettisoned

TOP: **The creation of the B-58 required much new ground to be broken. The result was a potent high-performance weapon system.**
ABOVE: **Bombs, reconnaissance equipment and extra fuel could be carried in the Hustler's centreline pod.**

after bombing. The B-58 was the first supersonic aircraft with engine pods mounted outboard on the thin delta wing, which had a 60-degree sweep.

Crew consisted of a pilot, navigator and defensive systems operator seated in tandem. Each crew member also had a unique escape ejection capsule – these were retrofitted when it was realized that simple ejection seats would not protect crews ejecting at supersonic speeds. To improve the crew's chances of surviving ejection, a high-speed, high-altitude capsule ejection system was installed that would allow safe ejection at supersonic speeds up to altitudes of 21,350m/70,000ft.

When required, the individual crew member's capsule closed airtight clam-shell doors, activating independent pressurization and oxygen supply systems. The crew member could then eject the capsule or remain encapsulated in the event of cabin pressure or oxygen loss until the aircraft reached a lower altitude. The pilot's capsule contained a control stick and other equipment so that he could continue to fly the aircraft from inside the capsule. After ejection, the capsule was lowered by parachute, and shock absorbers were included to soften the landing. On water, the airtight capsule would float, and additional flotation bags could turn the capsule into a life raft.

The thin fuselage had no room for a bomb bay, so the aircraft was fitted with a unique large streamlined centreline weapons pod, which included a fuel tank as well as a nuclear bomb or reconnaissance equipment. It was the pod and access to it on the ground that necessitated the B-58's very tall undercarriage legs. Four bombs could be carried beneath the wing if the pod was removed, but with the associated loss of a fuel tank, this could only have been over shorter ranges.

Although the Hustler had a greater range than the B-47 it was intended to replace, it still needed forward bases to be able to hit the Soviet Union. The alternative was to refuel the B-58 inflight to give it a greater reach, and all bomber versions were built with this facility. The B-58 set many high-speed records, flying for up 20 hours on routes around the world thanks to inflight refuelling. These missions were not just for the record books but also had some sabre-rattling potential, showing the Soviet Union just how far the aircraft could and would fly if needed. However, the B-58's range problem was made worse by the tactical need to bring the bombers down to low level. Soviet anti-aircraft missile defences were improving, so even the high- and fast-flying B-58 could not avoid them. As a result, the B-58 crews switched tactics and trained, very effectively, to penetrate Soviet defences at low level beneath enemy radar, resulting in an increase in fuel consumption and associated range penalties.

TOP: **This aircraft is a YB-58A production prototype. The non-standard red and white paint scheme identifies the aircraft as a test aircraft.** ABOVE: **The Hustler had to have long undercarriage legs to give clearance to the weapons pod.**

Eighty-six Hustlers were operational in Strategic Air Command from 1960, but the aircraft was phased out after only ten years due to high operating costs, operational limitations and the limited opportunities for development of the design. An interesting B-58 offshoot was a plan (which stayed on the drawing board) to produce a supersonic passenger-carrying version with a wider fuselage and room for 52 seats.

ABOVE: **The TB-58A was an operational trainer with the middle cockpit adapted for use by an instructor. Seven aircraft were converted to this standard. Notice how high the aircraft sits with the pod removed.**

Convair B-58 Hustler

First flight: November 11, 1956
Power: Four General Electric 7082kg/15,600lb afterburning thrust J79-5B turbojets
Armament: One 20mm/0.78in cannon in tail; payloads (including pod) of up to 8830kg/ 19,450lb of nuclear or conventional weapons
Size: Wingspan – 17.32m/56ft 10in
Length – 29.49m/96ft 9in
Height – 9.58m/31ft5in
Wing area – 143.35m²/1543sq ft
Weights: Empty – 25224kg/55,560lb
Maximum take-off – 74,002kg/163,000lb
Performance: Maximum speed – 2128kph/ 1322mph
Ceiling – 19,520m/64,000ft
Range – 8248km/5125 miles
Climb – 5310m/17,400ft per minute

Dassault Mystère/Super Mystère

Developed from the Dassault Ouragan, France's first jet fighter, the Mystère was essentially an Ouragan with swept wing and tail surfaces, and first flew in 1951. The production version, the Mystère II, was among the first swept-wing aircraft in production in western Europe, and entered Armée de l'Air service between 1954 and 1956 powered by the SNECMA Atar, the first French turbojet to be used in military aircraft. A Mystère IIA was the first French aircraft to break Mach 1 in controlled flight (in a dive), on October 28, 1952. The Armée de l'Air ordered 150 Mystère IICs, and the last was delivered in 1957, by which time the type was already being relegated to advanced training duties. Even as the Mystère was becoming operational, the better Mystère IV was already flying. Mystère IIs remained in use as advanced trainers until 1963.

The Mystère IV was a new aircraft, having few common parts with the Mark II – it had a new oval-section fuselage, thinner wings with greater sweep, and new tail surfaces. The first prototype was flown in September 1952, powered by a Hispano-built Rolls-Royce Tay 250 turbojet, as were the first 50 production examples – later examples were powered by the Hispano-Suiza Verdon. The production contract for 225 Mystère IVAs for the Armée de l'Air was paid for by the USA as part of the NATO Military Assistance Program. The first production Mystère IVA flew in late May 1954, and the type entered service with the Armée de l'Air the following year. The Mystère IVA remained a first-line fighter with the Armée de l'Air until the early 1960s, but continued to serve as an operational trainer until 1980.

ABOVE: **Marcel Dassault started to design jet fighters two years after being freed from a Nazi concentration camp. The Mystère was developed from his first design, the Ouragan, and ultimately led to the Mystère IVA pictured.**
LEFT: **The IVA was a very basic combat jet by today's standards, but it served the French Air Force well into the 1980s.**

ABOVE: **A Mystère IVA of the Armée de l'Air EC 8 (8th Fighter Wing). Note the open airbrakes.** LEFT: **The ultimate Mystère – the Super Mystère first flew in 1955, and was exported to Honduras and Israel.** BELOW: **This Super Mystère was photographed at an annual NATO "Tiger Meet".**

Sixty Verdon-powered Mystère IVAs ordered by the French were sold on to Israel, and the first batch of 24 arrived in April 1956, just in time for the war with Egypt in October. In the hands of skilled Israeli pilots, they proved more than a match for Egyptian MiG-15s. The Indian Air Force also bought 110 all-new production Verdon-powered Mystère IVAs. First delivered in 1957, they equipped five squadrons and were used in the close-support role during the 1965 Indo-Pakistan war. Indian Mystère IVAs served until 1973.

The ultimate Mystère was the Super Mystère which, like the Mystère IV, was largely a new aircraft. It was bigger and heavier than previous Mystères and was the first European production aircraft capable of transonic flight. The first prototype flew in March 1955 and had wings with a 45-degree sweepback and an F-100-like oval air intake. The prototype exceeded Mach 1 in level flight the day after it first took to the air. A total of 180 Super Mystère B2s were built for the Armée de l'Air, the last delivered in 1959. They were switched to the attack role once the Mirage III was available, and remained in French service until late 1977.

In 1958, 36 Super Mystères bought by the French were sold on to the Israelis who used them to counter the Soviet-designed and built MiG-19s favoured by Arab nations. In the early 1970s, the Israelis upgraded surviving Super Mystères by retrofitting a non-afterburning Pratt & Whitney J52-P8A turbojet, and 12 of these uprated Super Mystères were sold to Honduras, who operated them until 1989. Their retirement brought the operational career of the Mystère series to an end.

Dassault Mystère IVA

First flight: February 23, 1951 (Mystère prototype)
Engine: Hispano-Suiza 3500kg/7703lb thrust Verdon 350 turbojet.
Armament: Two 30mm/1.18in cannon; two 454kg/1000lb bombs or twelve rockets
Size: Wingspan 11.12m/36ft 6in
  Length – 12.85m/42ft 2in
  Height 4.60m/15ft 1in
  Wing area – 32m²/344.46sq ft
Weights: Empty – 5886kg/12,955lb
  Maximum take-off – 9500kg/20,909kg
Performance: Maximum speed – 1120kph/696mph
  Ceiling – 15,000m/49,200ft
  Climb – 2700m/8860ft per minute
  Range – 912km/570 miles

Dassault Etendard and Super Etendard

Dassault's private venture Etendard (standard) was designed to meet the needs of both French national and NATO programmes for new light fighters reflecting air-combat experiences of the Korean War. Various versions did not get beyond the prototype stage, but then the Etendard IV drew the attention of the French Navy as a multi-role carrier-based fighter, leading to the development of the Etendard IV M specifically for the Navy – the first naval aircraft developed by Dassault.

The Etendard IV M made its maiden flight in May 1958, and between 1961 and 1965 the French Navy took delivery of 69 Etendard IV Ms that served on the French carriers *Foch* and *Clemenceau*, as well as 21 reconnaissance/tanker Etendard IV Ps. The Etendard IV M continued to serve in the French Navy until July 1991, by which time they had logged 180,000 flying hours and made 25,300 carrier landings.

The search for an Etendard replacement led Dassault to propose the Super Etendard, an updated, improved aircraft based on the Etendard IV M, but a 90 per cent new design.

Designed both for strike and interception duties, it featured the more powerful Atar 8K-50 engine and a strengthened structure to withstand higher-speed operations. The weapons system was improved through the installation of a modern navigation and combat management system centered on a Thomson multi-mode radar. The wing had a new leading edge and revised flaps which, together with the newer engine, eased take-off with greater weight compared to the Etendard.

The aircraft prototype made its maiden flight October 28, 1974, and the first of 71 production aircraft were delivered from mid-1978, again for service on the aircraft carriers *Foch*

TOP: **The Super Etendard was derived from the earlier Etendard, but was a 90 per cent new aircraft.** ABOVE: **The Etendard IVP had a fixed refuelling probe and could carry a "buddy pack" to become an inflight tanker.**

and *Clemenceau*. One hundred Super Etendards were planned for the Navy, but spiralling costs called for a reduction of the order. Armed with two 30mm/1.18in cannon, the Super Etendard could carry a variety of weaponry on its five hard points, including two Matra Magic AAMs, four pods of 18 68mm/2.68in rockets, a variety of bombs or two Exocet anti-ship missiles. A number were also modified to carry the Aerospatiale ASMP nuclear stand-off bomb.

The Argentine Navy's use of the Super Etendard/Exocet combination during the Falklands War of 1982 proved devastating against British ships – Argentina had ordered 14 Super Etendards from Dassault in 1979, but only five aircraft and reportedly five missiles had been delivered by the time France embargoed arms shipments to Argentina. These five strike fighters, despite having pilots unwilling to engage the agile British Harriers in air combat, nevertheless proved to be a very potent element of the Argentine inventory.

On May 4, 1982, two Super Etendards took off from a base in Argentina, preparing to attack the British task force. After three hours and an inflight refuelling, the aircraft located and launched an attack on the British ships. One of the Exocets found and severely damaged the frigate HMS *Sheffield*, which sank on May 10. On May 25, two Exocet-equipped Super Etendards again attacked the task force, this time sinking the *Atlantic Conveyor* with its cargo of nine helicopters.

A handful of Super Etendards were supplied to Iraq in October 1983 when the Iraqis were desperate to cripple Iran by attacking tankers in the Persian Gulf with Exocets. Around 50 ships were attacked in the Gulf in 1984, the majority of the actions apparently carried out by Iraqi Super Etendards.

Production of the Super Etendard ended in 1983, but from 1992 a programme of structural and avionics upgrading was undertaken to extend the service life of the "fleet" until 2008.

ABOVE RIGHT: **The Etendard flew on with the French Navy until 1991.**
RIGHT: **An excellent on-deck view showing French Etendards and Super Etendards at sea.** BELOW: **French Navy Super Etendards are expected to remain in service at least until 2008.**

Dassault Super Etendard

First flight: October 28, 1974
Power: SNECMA 5000kg/11,005lb afterburning thrust Atar 8K-50 turbojet
Armament: Two 30mm/1.18in cannon; 2100kg/ 4622lb of weapons, including Matra Magic AAMs, AM39 Exocet ASMs, bombs and rockets
Size: Wingspan - 9.6m/31ft 6in
Length – 14.31m/46ft 11.5in
Height – 3.86m/12ft 8in
Wing area – 28.4m²/305.71sq ft
Weights: Empty – 6500kg/14,306lb
Maximum take-off – 12,000kg/26,412lb
Performance: Maximum speed – 1205kph/ 749mph
Ceiling – 13,700m/44,950ft
Range – 650km/404 miles
Climb – 6000m/19,685ft per minute

Dassault Mirage III family

The delta-wing Mirage III was certainly one of the greatest combat aircraft ever, and was produced in greater numbers than any other European fighter. The success of this aircraft brought France to the forefront of the military aircraft industry. It started as a Dassault private venture, and first flew in November 1956, having benefited from the testing of the small Mirage I experimental delta aircraft. After some refinements to the wing design, it reached twice the speed of sound in level flight in October 1958. The aircraft's capability soon caught the attention of the French Air Force, who quickly ordered the high-performance aircraft. Foreign air forces were also very interested in the Mirage, and orders from Israel and South Africa followed in late 1960. By now the first production aircraft, the Mirage IIIC single-seat air defence fighter, was coming off the production line for the Armée de l'Air, and the first were delivered in July 1961.

The Mirage IIIE was a long-range fighter-bomber version powered by the SNECMA Atar 9C turbojet. While the IIIC was a dedicated interceptor, the IIIE was designed and equipped for both air defence and all-weather ground attack, and French versions were equipped to carry a nuclear bomb. It was widely exported and was also built under licence in Australia and Switzerland. Although France has retired its IIIs, many air forces still operate the type, having upgraded it in many ways – Swiss and Brazilian IIIs, for example, have acquired canard wings.

The IIIE spawned the Mirage 5 ground-attack fighter, essentially a simplified version designed as a daytime clear-weather ground-attack fighter in response to an Israeli Air Force request. The need for sophisticated radar was considered not to be so great in the Middle East, so when the Mirage 5 first flew in May 1967, it was minus the Cyrano radar. The delivery to Israel was stopped for political reasons by Charles de Gaulle, and the aircraft instead served as the Mirage 5F in the Armée de l'Air. Israel decided to go it alone and developed its Mirage III into the Kfir.

RIGHT: **A Swiss Mirage III demonstrates its dramatic rocket-assisted take-off technique.** BELOW: **An Armée de l'Air Mirage IIIE armed with an AS.37 anti-radar missile.**

Dassault Mirage 50

First flight: May 1969
Power: One SNECMA 7210kg/15,869lb
    afterburning thrust Atar 9K-50 turbojet
Armament: Two 30mm/1.18in cannon; up to
    4000kg/8804lb of rockets, bombs and guided
    weapons
Size: Wingspan – 8.22m/27ft
    Length – 15.56m/51ft 1in
    Height – 4.5m/14ft 9in
    Wing area – 35m²/375sq ft
Weights: Empty – 7150kg/15,737lb
    Maximum take-off – 14,700kg/32,354lb
Performance: Maximum speed – 2338kph/
    1452mph
    Ceiling – 18,011m/59,094ft
    Range – 2410km/1496 miles
    Climb – 11,168m/36,642ft per minute

ABOVE LEFT: **The excellent Mirage III can carry up to 4000kg/8804lb of ordnance.** LEFT: **Although French Mirage IIIs were retired some time ago, the type remains in use in Switzerland and Brazil.** BELOW: **Swiss Mirage IIIs received a canard wing as part of an upgrade programme.** BOTTOM: **An early French Mirage III. This type was produced in greater numbers than any other fighter of the period.**

However, some 450 Mirage 5s were exported to other nations, and more advanced avionics were offered later. Belgium built their own Mirage 5 bombers and upgraded them in the 1990s to keep them flying until 2005.

The Mirage 50 multi-mission fighter was created by installing the more powerful Atar 9K-50 engine in a Mirage 5 airframe. It first flew in April 1979, and boasted head-up displays and a more advanced radar than the Mirage III. Chile and Venezuela both ordered Mirage 50s. Dassault offers the Mirage 50M upgrade for existing Mirage IIIs and 5s, but several operator nations have undertaken local upgrade programmes with improved avionics and the addition of canard foreplanes.

In the 1967 and 1973 Arab-Israeli wars, the Israeli Mirage IIIs outclassed Arab-flown MiGs and generated lots of export sales, but Mirage pilots admit that the type did not have a great sustained turn capability due to the aerodynamic idiosyncrasies of the delta wing. Indeed, three Mirages were shot down by comparatively pedestrian Iraqi Hunters during the Six Day War of 1967. Nevertheless, the Mirage III series gave many air forces their first combat aircraft capable of flying at twice the speed of sound, and many upgraded examples will be flying for some years.

Dassault Mirage IV

The Mirage IV strategic nuclear bomber was developed in the late 1950s, following a 1954 decision that France wanted an independent nuclear deterrent force. The aircraft was a two-seat, twin-jet engine supersonic bomber with an effective range of up to 4500km/2795 miles but only with inflight refuelling. The delta wing of the Mirage IV clearly carried on that of the Mirage III, though on a much larger scale. The Mirage IV was developed as a weapon system, with Dassault being the prime contractor for the complete system – aircraft, navigation, attack management system, as well as the casing and release system for the nuclear bomb.

The Mirage IV 01 made its maiden flight powered by two 6000kg/13,206lb SNECMA Atar 09 turbojets on June 17, 1959, with Roland Glavany at the controls. In July the aircraft achieved speeds of Mach 1.9. Three pre-production aircraft were then built, the first taking to the air in October 1961, this time powered by 6400kg/14,086lb thrust Atar 9C engines. Each of the three aircraft was used for trials and development of the aircraft's navigation, inflight refuelling and bombing systems.

However, it was more than two and a half years before the first Mirage IV-A was delivered to the French Air Force in February 1964. At the time of its delivery, the Mirage IV was the only aircraft in the world that could fly at twice the speed

TOP: **The development of the Mirage IV enabled France to create its own nuclear deterrent force. From 1964 to 1996 these impressive bombers were France's airborne deterrent.** ABOVE: **With a wingspan less than 1m/3ft greater than that of a Spitfire, the Mirage IV was able to attain speeds in excess of Mach 2.**

of sound for sustained periods. Fifty Mirage IV-As were ordered in 1959 and a further 12 in 1964, and they were all delivered by 1966.

Assigned to French Strategic Air Command, CFAS (Commandement des Forces Aeriennes Stratégiques), nine and later six dispersed air bases housed these aircraft, which were France's airborne nuclear deterrent from 1964 until the Mirage IV was retired as a strategic bomber in 1996. The aircraft had dedicated KC-135FR tanker aircraft assigned to the Mirage IV units, although Mirage IVs could also be fitted with "buddy" inflight refuelling packs themselves. The aircraft were kept at readiness in hardened shelters from which they could start their take-off run. For short-field take-off, the aircraft were also fitted with 12 booster rockets, six beneath each wing, and special fast-drying chemicals were developed for hardening soft surfaces from which the heavy aircraft could then operate.

Dassault Mirage IV-A

First Flight: June 17, 1959

Power: Two SNECMA 7000kg/15,407lb thrust Atar 9K turbojets

Armament: One 60-kiloton AN 22 nuclear bomb or one 30- or 150-kiloton 900kg/1980lb ASMP stand-off nuclear air-to-surface missile or up to 7200kg/15,847lb of conventional bombs or anti-radar missiles

Size: Wingspan – 11.85m/38ft 11in
Length – 23.5m/77ft 1in
Height – 5.65m/18ft 6in
Wing area – 78m²/839.6sq ft

Weights: Empty – 14,500kg/31,914lb
Maximum take-off – 31,600kg/69,551lb

Performance: Maximum speed – 2338kph/1451mph
Ceiling – 20,000m/65,620ft
Range – 2500km/1552 miles
Climb – 11,000m/36,090ft in 4 minutes, 15 seconds

ABOVE: **Some of the fleet were upgraded to IV-P standard, and could carry a stand-off weapon.** RIGHT: **Rocket-assisted take-off was required to get the aircraft airborne from shorter runways, and was important for dispersed operations.** BELOW: **A Mirage IV-A in full flight. The IV-As were kept in hardened shelters from which they could begin their take-off run.**

In common with other major air forces around the world, the French Air Force had to respond to the increased sophistication of air defences. As a result, they switched to flying their bombers at low level to avoid enemy radar and surface-to-air missiles. The Mirage IV's structure was modified to cope better with the stresses caused by high-speed, low-level flying and the 60 kiloton AN 22 nuclear weapon carried semi-recessed under the fuselage, and was modified for low-level use and to increase the chances of aircraft and crew survivability.

The aircraft were frequently upgraded during their time in service, and 12 were modified for the reconnaissance role by fitting cameras and SLAR (side-looking airborne radar).

Nineteen aircraft were modified to IVP standard in the late 1980s by the inclusion of inertial navigation and rear-warning radar. This version could also carry the Aerospatiale ASMP stand-off nuclear missile, which could be launched up to 250km/155 miles from the target. In June 1996, the Mirage IVPs were retired from the nuclear role and five aircraft were retained for strategic reconnaissance duties.

187

de Havilland Venom

The Venom was proposed by de Havilland as a Vampire successor, and was initially designated Vampire FB.8. The aircraft had to be substantially altered to accommodate the new more powerful Ghost engine and so the aircraft was given its own identity – the Venom. The first production version, the FB.1, was delivered to the RAF in December 1951, followed by the improved ejection-seat-equipped FB.4 version. The Venom ultimately equipped 19 squadrons of the Royal Air Force, serving in Germany, India and the Far East. The Germany-based Venoms were a vital element of the West's Cold War defences at the time.

TOP: **A Venom FB.4 wearing "Suez stripes".**
ABOVE RIGHT: **During the Suez operations, three squadrons of RAF Venom FB4s flew close air support missions.** ABOVE: **A Sea Venom FAW Mk 21.**

Licence-built versions were produced as FB.50s in Switzerland, where some remained in service until the early 1980s. British-built versions were also exported to Iraq and Venezuela.

Two-seat radar-equipped all-weather/ nightfighter versions were also produced, and the Venom NF.2 entered RAF service in 1953. Emergency escape from this version was virtually impossible as there were no ejection seats for the two crew and the heavy hinged canopy had to be lifted manually. The NF.3 had an American radar and, perhaps more importantly for Venom nightfighter crews, a quick-release canopy.

The de Havilland Sea Venom FAW Mk 20 gave the Royal Navy an interim radar-equipped, all-weather fighter force between the piston-engined Sea Hornet and the appearance of the advanced Sea Vixen. Later improvements led to the FAW Mk 21 and 22. The Sea Venom was also operated by the Australian Navy, and in France SNCASE built a redesigned Sea Venom, including a single-seat version for the French Navy, who called it the Aquilon.

Royal Navy Sea Venoms, in concert with RAF Venom fighter-bombers, saw action during the Suez crisis in 1956.

de Havilland Venom FB.4

First flight: September 2, 1949 (Venom prototype)
Power: de Havilland 2406kg/5300lb thrust Ghost 105 turbojet
Armament: Four 20mm/0.78in cannon; provision for two Firestreak air-to-air missiles or 908kg/ 2000lb of bombs or eight 27kg/60lb rocket projectiles
Size: Wingspan – 12.7m/41ft 8in
Length – 10.06m/33ft
Height – 2.03m/6ft 8in
Wing area – 25.99m²/279.75sq ft
Weights: Empty – 3995kg/8800lb
Maximum take-off – 6950kg/15,310lb
Performance: Maximum speed – 961kph/ 597mph
Ceiling – 14,640m/48,000ft
Range – 1730km/1075 miles
Climb – 36.7m/7230ft per minute

Douglas A-3 Skywarrior

In the late 1940s, a whole new class of aircraft carrier was under development by the US Navy, the super-carrier Forrestal-class. These large carriers would be able to operate large aircraft and give the US Navy the opportunity to take its air power to a new level. The Navy called for a large new strategic bomber to operate from the supercarriers, and Douglas came up with the A3D, at 31,780kg/70,000lb the world's largest and heaviest carrier-borne aircraft when it was designed. It flew in October 1952, and became the Navy's first twin-jet nuclear bomber.

The nuclear bomb aspect was challenging because details of the weapon were top secret, and designers had to guess the appearance and weight of the nuclear bombs to be carried aboard. In its vast internal bomb bay it could carry up to 5448kg/12,000lb of weaponry. Also, the internal bomb bay had to be accessible from the cockpit so that the crew could arm the nuclear device during flight.

Due to its size, it was soon named "Whale" by its crews, and in 1962 the aircraft was redesignated A-3.

The first production version, the A-3A (A3D-1), with a radar-controlled tail turret and a crew of three, entered service with the Navy Heavy Attack Squadron One in 1956. After flying a few conventional bombing missions over North and South Vietnam, Skywarriors were used as carrier-based aerial-refuelling tankers and as reconnaissance aircraft covering the Ho Chi Minh trail. As advancing technology rendered its old role obsolete, the resilient aircraft continued to evolve. It was used for electronic countermeasures, photographic reconnaissance, crew training and as a VIP transport. A few US Navy Skywarriors even served in the 1991 Gulf War.

A revised USAF version was named Destroyer, and designated B-66. Built in bomber, photo-reconnaissance, electronic countermeasures and weather reconnaissance versions, the B-66 was active in the Vietnam War.

TOP: **The largest and heaviest carrier aircraft of its day, the A-3 Skywarrior.** ABOVE: **The "Whale" was a significant element of the US nuclear deterrent for a time.**

Douglas A-3B Skywarrior

First Flight: October 28, 1952 (XA3D-1)

Power: Two Pratt & Whitney 4767kg/10,500lb thrust J57-P-10 turbojets

Armament: Two 20mm/0.78in cannon in remotely controlled rear turret; up to 5448kg/12,000lb of bombs

Size: Wingspan – 22.1m/72ft 6in
Length – 23.27m/76ft 4in
Height – 6.95m/22ft9.5in
Wing area – 75.43m²/812sq ft

Weights: Empty – 17,891kg/39,409lb
Maximum take-off – 37,228kg/82,000lb

Performance: Maximum speed – 982kph/610mph
Ceiling – 12,505m/41,000ft
Range – 1690km/1050 miles
Climb – 1100m/3600ft per minute

Douglas Skyraider

The Skyraider can be rightly considered to be one of the greatest combat aircraft ever. Designed during World War II as a replacement for Douglas's own Dauntless dive-bomber, this rugged aeroplane fought in both Korea and Vietnam. The prototype XBT2D-1 first flew on March 19, 1945, and in February 1946 became the AD-1 Skyraider, the biggest single-seat aircraft in production. Designed around Wright's R-3350 engine, the Skyraider was created with the benefit of considerable combat experience. The designers' aim was to produce a very versatile aircraft which could absorb considerable damage and carry the widest range of available weaponry. Built like a big fighter, the Skyraider carried all of its weaponry beneath its folding wings.

Following carrier trials in early 1946, the Skyraider formally entered US Navy front-line service with VA-19A in December 1946. Production of consistently improved versions continued, and four years into manufacturing, 22 variants had appeared. Production continued for 12 years, and when it ceased in 1957, 3180 Skyraiders had been delivered to the US Navy.

Korea is often thought of as a jet war, but the Skyraider's 10-hour loiter capability and great weapon-carrying capacity considerably outclassed any jet then in service. The US Navy was hugely impressed by its performance.

Among the versions soon appearing were the AD-2 with increased fuel and a more powerful engine, and the AD-3 with a revised canopy, improved propeller and landing gear. The AD-4 had the more powerful 2700hp R-3350 engine and greatly increased load-carrying capacity, the AD-4W was a three-seat airborne early warning variant (used by the Royal

TOP: **A Royal Navy Skyraider AEW1. The type equipped two Fleet Air Arm units until 1960, and was used during the November 1956 Suez campaign.**
ABOVE: **Skyraiders were at home carrying out high-risk low-level missions. Here, an AD-1 drops napalm in Vietnam.**

Navy Fleet Air Arm), while the AD-5 was a four-seat, multi-role version. The Skyraider was strengthened to carry more and more equipment and ordnance, and the AD-5 could operate at all-up weights of 11,350kg/25,000lb. The AD-5 could also be adapted for casualty evacuation or for transporting 12 troops. The AD-6 was a much-improved single-seat attack version, while the AD-7 had a 3050hp engine and even more reinforcement to the wings and undercarriage.

Douglas A-1H (AD-6) Skyraider

First Flight: March 19, 1945 (XBT2D-1)

Power: One Wright 2700hp R-3350-26WA radial piston engine

Armament: Four wing-mounted 20mm/0.78in cannon; up to 3632kg/8000lb of ordnance carried under wings and on one fuselage hardpoint

Size: Wingspan – 15.25m/50ft 0.25in
Length – 11.84m/38ft
Height – 4.78m/15ft 8.25in
Wing area – 37.19m²/400sq ft

Weights: Empty – 5433kg/11,968lb
Maximum take-off – 11,350kg/25,000lb

Performance: Maximum speed – 518kph/322mph
Ceiling – 8692m/28,500ft plus
Range – 2116km/1315 miles
Climb – 870m/2850ft per minute

ABOVE: **Fifty-four airframes were converted to EA-1F standard for electronic countermeasures duties.** LEFT: **The AD-4 version was built to carry a much greater war load, and the AD-4B was cleared to carry nuclear weapons.** BELOW: **Thought obsolete by doubters even before it entered service, the Skyraider confounded everyone with a production run in a myriad of variants and an outstanding combat record in two major conflicts.**

AD-4Ns saw considerable action with the French Armée de l'Air in Algeria, and these machines were retired in 1965. By now the USA was embroiled in Vietnam, and following trials the Skyraider was found to be the ideal close support aircraft needed for tackling difficult ground targets. Again, the hard-hitting aircraft's loiter capability made it an obvious choice for this type of warfare. The US Air Force, Navy and Marine Corps all operated Skyraiders in Vietnam, as did the US-trained South Vietnam Air Force. The aircraft also served as forward air control (FAC) platforms, helicopter escort and rescue support missions. Never considered a dogfighter, the Skyraider had four 20mm/0.78in cannon in the wings, and US Navy Skyraider pilots are known to have shot down at least two MiG-17 jets over Vietnam.

In 1962, new tri-service aircraft designations were introduced so all the designations of Skyraiders then in service were changed. The AD-5 was the A-1E, the AD-5N the A-1G while the AD-6 and AD-7 became the A-1H and A-1J respectively.

As well as Britain and France, Skyraiders were also supplied to Chad, who used them in combat up to the late 1970s. The aircraft that had entered service when piston-engined warplanes were considered by some to be obsolete was therefore still fighting more than a quarter of a century after it first entered service.

ABOVE: **The A-1E/AD-5 was a redesigned multi-role aircraft with a side-by-side cockpit.**

English Electric/BAC/Martin B-57 Canberra

When it comes to long-service records in the Royal Air Force, there is one aircraft that leads the field – the English Electric Canberra. More than half a century after the type first entered RAF service in 1950, photo-reconnaissance versions continue to be a vital element of the RAF's intelligence-gathering capability.

The Canberra was Britain's first jet bomber and was designed in the Mosquito tradition, so that its high and fast flying capability was intended to keep the aircraft safe from defending fighter aircraft – no defensive armament was to

be carried. The Canberra was every bit as versatile as the Mosquito it succeeded, and served with distinction as a light bomber, advanced trainer, intruder and photo-reconnaissance platform.

The first Canberra prototype, VN799, took off from Warton on May 13, 1949, with famous test-pilot Roland Beamont at the controls. It exhibited excellent manoeuvrability at all altitudes and handled well at low speed. Refinements to the original design led to the B.2 version, which first flew in April 1950 and became the RAF's first jet bomber when it entered service at RAF Binbrook in May 1951 with No.101 Squadron. The RAF needed lots of Canberras, and production was beyond the capability of English Electric. Consequently, rival manufacturers Avro, Handley Page and Shorts all built Canberras to meet the demand. A more powerful version, the B.6, entered RAF service in 1954–5, and Canberras saw combat over Malaya and during the 1956 Suez Crisis.

An indication of the aircraft's greatness is the fact that early in its career, the Canberra was selected for licensed production in the USA for the US Air Force. The first of

TOP: **WK163 was a Canberra B.2 that was fitted with Scorpion rocket engines to attain a record-breaking altitude.** LEFT: **The USAF sought an aircraft with good manoeuvrability and flexibility, and found it in the Canberra. Licence-built as the Martin B-57 Canberra, around 400 were built in the USA.**

around 400 aircraft (bomber and reconnaissance versions) was rolled out of the Martin plant on July 20, 1953. These American Canberras saw extensive service in Vietnam.

Canberras were also built under licence in Australia for the RAAF. These versions, known as MK20s, were based on the British B.2 version but had increased internal fuel capacity and a crew of two. In September 1958 Canberras from No.2 Squadron RAAF became the first Australian jet bombers in combat when they carried out an attack against terrorists in Northern Malaya. Then in 1967, No.2 was sent to Vietnam as part of Australia's military commitment to the war. Operating as part of the USAF's 35th Tactical Fighter Wing, Squadron 2's Canberras flew 6 per cent of the Wing's sorties but inflicted 16 per cent of the damage. Overall, 11,963 sorties were flown in Vietnam, and 76,389 bombs dropped for two aircraft lost.

The Canberra's distinguished RAAF career ended on June 30, 1982, when No.2 Squadron flew its Canberras for the last time.

English Electric and its subcontractors built over 750 Canberras, and many were exported. In the early 2000s, Canberra remained in service with Argentina, India, Peru and even NASA (B-57s).

Photo-reconnaissance versions were developed early on, and it was the PR.9 version that remained in service with the RAF in 2004. In 2003, Canberras of No.39 Squadron conducted 56 reconnaissance sorties over Iraq in support of British and Coalition forces.

The PR.9's equipment had evolved over its time in service. A variety of daytime "wet" cameras can be carried for medium and higher-level vertical and oblique photography. An electro-optical long-range oblique photographic sensor (EO-LOROP) can also be carried, which records imagery in digital format on magnetic tape for interpretation on the ground. The PR.9 also carries navigation equipment that 1960s navigators could only have dreamt of, as well as defensive systems such as jammers and chaff and flare dispensers.

ABOVE: **USAF B-57s saw extensive use in the Vietnam War, mainly flying night intruder missions. The aircraft pictured here is a multi-role bomber/ reconnaissance/trainer/tug B-57E.** RIGHT: **When the RAF Canberra's bombing days were over, some were converted for ECM training. The aircraft in this photograph is a T.17.** BELOW: **The Canberra is an all-time classic combat aircraft. This model is an E.15 used for high-altitude calibration of ground radar.**

English Electric/BAC Canberra B.6

First Flight: May 13, 1949 (prototype)

Power: Two Rolls-Royce 3405kg/7500lb afterburning thrust Avon 109 turbojets

Armament: 2724kg/6000lb of bombs carried internally, plus two 454kg/1000lb bombs or gun pods under wings

Size: Wingspan 19.51m/64ft
Length – 19.96m/65ft 6in
Height – 4.75m/15ft 7in
Wing area – 89.19m²/960sq ft

Weights: Empty – 10,108kg/22,265lb
Maximum take-off – 24,062kg/53,000lb

Performance: Maximum speed – 973kph/605mph
Ceiling – 14,634m/48,000ft plus
Combat radius – 1779km/1105 miles
Climb – 1220m/4000ft per minute

Fairchild Republic A-10 Thunderbolt II

In the early 1970s, when the USAF was considering an aircraft capable of halting a Soviet armoured thrust in Central Europe, they looked back at their experiences in Korea and Vietnam where aircraft modified for use in the close air support role had exhibited many shortcomings. Instead, they needed a purpose-designed aircraft that could carry a heavy weapons load, have good endurance and be able to withstand damage from ground fire.

The answer was the remarkable A-10, designed from the outset to tackle Warsaw Pact armour in Europe. Combining accurate firepower and survivability, the A-10 was designed to fly low and relatively slowly across the battlefield to take out enemy armour and artillery in the very hostile, low-level battlefield environment. The aircraft has high-lift wings fitted with large control surfaces, making the aircraft very manoeuvrable, while its short take-off and landing capability permitted operations in and out of rough field locations near front lines.

All the aircraft's controls are duplicated and designed to work even if hydraulic pressure is lost due to enemy fire. The aircraft's fuel tanks are filled with fire-retardant foam, and the A-10's pilot sits in a "bathtub" of titanium armour for protection against shrapnel and small arms fire.

The aircraft can survive direct hits from armour-piercing and high explosive projectiles up to 23mm/0.9in calibre. Self-sealing fuel cells are protected by internal and external foam. Remarkably, many of the aircraft's parts are interchangeable left and right, including the engines, main landing gear and fins.

TOP: **The arrival of the A-10 over a battlefield is bad news for an enemy. The aircraft was created to destroy armour and artillery, and does so most effectively.** ABOVE: **This view shows how the aircraft's engines can be masked by the wing from below, thus preventing a lock from an infrared weapon.**

The primary weapon of the A-10 is the nose-mounted GAU-8/A 30mm/1.18in seven-barrel cannon which, together with its ammunition, takes up much of the aircraft's internal space. This is the most powerful gun ever fitted to an aircraft, firing 35 rounds of controversial depleted uranium armour-piercing ammunition per second. One hit from this extremely potent weapon can destroy a tank a mile away from the aircraft. The aircraft can also carry a range of bombs, rockets and missiles, including the Maverick anti-armour missile.

ABOVE: **This A-10 is carrying Sidewinder air-to-air missiles for self defence. Eleven hardpoints can carry an array of ground-attack weaponry.**
RIGHT: **The A-10 is likely to remain in service until at least 2010.**

Turbofan engines were chosen to power the aircraft because they give off less heat than conventional jet engines, thus making them less vulnerable to heat-seeking weapons. The engines were also positioned high on the upper rear fuselage, protecting them from ground fire. Using night-vision goggles, A-10 pilots can conduct their missions as efficiently during darkness as in daylight.

The A-10 entered US Air Force service in 1976 and remained in the Cold War front line until the late 1980s. Although trained for war in Europe, USAF A-10 pilots first saw action in the Gulf War of 1991 when 144 A-10s were deployed to Saudi Arabia. During the A-10's 8100 Gulf War missions, around 24,000 missiles, rockets and bombs were fired or dropped and one million rounds were fired by A-10 cannon. A-10s launched 90 per cent of the total number of the AGM-65 Maverick missiles used.

USAF A-10s were credited with the destruction of over 1000 Iraqi tanks, 1200 artillery pieces and 2000 vehicles, as well as two helicopters in air-to-air combat with air-to-air missiles. Only six aircraft were lost in the war, all to ground-launched enemy missiles.

A-10s were also in the vanguard of the 2003 invasion of Iraq, and are expected to remain in the USAF inventory until 2010.

Fairchild Republic A-10 Thunderbolt II

First Flight: May 10, 1972
Power: Two General Electric 4115kg/9065lb thrust TF34-GE-100 turbofans
Armament: One GAU-8/A 30mm/1.18in cannon; up to 7264kg/16,000lb of weapons, including free-fall or guided bombs, Maverick missiles or Sidewinder anti-aircraft missiles on underwing and underfuselage points
Size: Wingspan – 17.53m/57ft 6in
Length – 16.26m/53ft 4in
Height – 4.42m/14ft 8in
Wing area – 24.18m²/260.28sq ft
Weights: Empty – 9780kg/21,541lb
Maximum take-off – 22,700kg/50,000lb
Performance: Maximum speed – 706kph/439mph
Ceiling – 9302m/30,500ft plus
Range – 926km/576 miles
Climb – Not available

Fairey Gannet

During the course of World War II, the Royal Navy had learned the value of carrier-based anti-submarine aircraft. For the post-war years the Navy needed a modern aircraft to tackle the submarine threat posed by any potential enemy. In 1945 the Fleet Air Arm issued a requirement, GR.17/45, for a carrier-based ASW (anti-submarine warfare) aircraft which could both hunt and kill submarines.

Of two cosmetically similar designs built to prototype standard, it was the Fairey design that ultimately won the contract, having flown for the first time on September 19, 1949. The aircraft had a deep barrel-like fuselage to accommodate both sensors and weapons for hunting and killing enemy craft. Power came from an Armstrong-Siddeley Double Mamba engine which was actually two turboprop engines driving a shared gearbox. This in turn drove a contra-rotating propeller system. The Double Mamba was chosen because one of the engines could be shut down for more economical cruising flight. Conventional twin-engined aircraft exhibit problematic handling if one engine fails, resulting in what is known as asymmetric flight. In this situation, the working engine forces its side of the aeroplane ahead of the other side, resulting in crabbing flightpath, as well as major concerns on landing. If one Double Mamba failed, this would not be an issue for the pilot of a Gannet.

The Fairey 17 began carrier-deck trials in early 1950, and on June 19 that year the aircraft made the first landing of a turboprop aircraft on a carrier, HMS *Illustrious*. The Admiralty then requested that search radar be included, as well as a

TOP: **The Gannet prototype, September 1949.** ABOVE: **The Gannet was a large aircraft and the wings had to fold twice to fit it into underdeck hangars.**

third seat for the operator, resulting in a third modified prototype which flew in May 1951. When Fairey's aircraft won the competition to go into production, the name "Gannet" was given to the aircraft. The Gannet, brimming with equipment and weapons, was a technically complicated aircraft, an example being the wings that folded not once but twice for under-deck stowage. Because of development delays, the Gannet AS.1 did not enter FAA service until 1955, some ten years after the requirement was first issued.

The fuselage had a big weapons bay to accommodate two torpedoes or other munitions, up to a total of 908kg/2,000lb. A retractable radome under the rear fuselage housed the search radar. When the extendable "dustbin" radome was added, it led to lateral instability in flight, which was remedied by the addition of two auxiliary finlets to the horizontal tailplane. Simply raising the height of the vertical tailplane would have had the same effect, but would have exceeded below-deck hangar height limits. The Gannet's crew of three sat in tandem, with pilot, observer/navigator and radio/radar operator each in their own cockpits, the radio/radar operator's seat facing the tail of the aircraft.

A number of Gannets were operated by foreign air arms. Deliveries to the Royal Australian Navy for carrier operations began in 1955 (phased out in 1967), while the former West German naval air arm operated Gannets from shore bases, phasing them out in 1965. Indonesia obtained refurbished Royal Navy examples.

A total of 181 Gannet AS.1s were built, together with 38 Gannet T.2 conversion trainers for training pilots on the idiosyncrasies of the aircraft and its unique powerplant. In 1956, the improved 3035hp Double Mamba 101 was introduced into Gannets on the production line. Aircraft thus powered were designated AS.4 and T.5 for the trainer version. The Gannet AS.6 was the AS.4 with a new 1961 radar and electronics fit.

Fairey were also contracted to produce an airborne early warning (AEW) Gannet to replace the Douglas Skyraider in Fleet Air Arm service. Designated AEW.3, these were new-build dedicated early-warning aircraft with a huge radar installation mounted on the underside of the fuselage beneath the cockpit. This version, which served until 1977, carried a pilot and two radar plotters who were housed in a rear cabin.

ABOVE: **Points to note on this Gannet AS.4 are the large port exhaust from the Double Mamba, the arrestor hook and the two red finlets.** BELOW: **Note the large radome beneath the Gannet AEW.3.** BOTTOM: **The AEW Gannets were retired from RN service in 1977.**

Fairey Gannet AS.1

First flight: September 19, 1949 (prototype)
Power: One Armstrong Siddeley 2950eshp Double Mamba 100 turboprop
Armament: Up to 908kg/2000lb of torpedoes and depth charges
Size: Wingspan – 16.56m/54ft 4in
Length – 13.11m/43ft
Height – 4.18m/13ft 8.5in
Wing area – 44.85m²/482.8sq ft
Weights: Empty – 6841kg/15,069lb
Maximum take-off – 9806kg/21,600lb
Performance: Maximum speed – 499kph/310mph
Ceiling – 7625m/25,000ft
Range – 1518km/943 miles
Climb – 670m/2200ft per minute

General Dynamics F-111

The F-111 was originally intended to be a fighter to equip both the US Air Force and Navy. Following a difficult development period during which the Navy dropped out of the programme, the remarkable variable-geometry aircraft, with its confusing fighter designation, became a highly effective all-weather interdictor.

The F-111 was the first production aircraft in the world with "swing wings", which gave the aircraft the flexibility to land and take off with straight wings and for low-speed flight, but to fly at high supersonic speeds with the wings swept.

TOP: **An Upper Heyford-based F-111E launches an attack on a British bombing range.** ABOVE: **The F-111 terrain-following radar enables the aircraft to fly very fast and very low to deliver its weapons.**

The F-111A entered USAF service in October 1967. Once early in-service problems were ironed out, the F-111 became a formidable long-range bomber which could deliver conventional or nuclear weapons from low altitude. The F-111 weapons system also featured a groundbreaking automatic terrain-following radar that guided the aircraft at a pre-set height following the ground contours. The aircraft could fly itself over all types of terrain by day or night, whatever the weather.

The wings and much of the fuselage rear of the crew compartment contained fuel tanks. Using internal fuel only, the aircraft had a range of more than 4000km/2500 miles. External fuel tanks could be carried on the wing pylons for additional range, and could be jettisoned if necessary.

The F-111 could deliver conventional or nuclear weapons and could carry up to two bombs or additional fuel in the internal weapons bay. External ordnance included combinations of bombs, missiles and fuel tanks. The loads nearest the fuselage on each side pivoted as the wings swept back, keeping ordnance parallel to the fuselage. Outer pylons did not move, but could be jettisoned for high-speed flight.

The F-111E model had modified air intakes to improve the engine's performance at speeds above Mach 2.2. Most USAF F-111Es served with the 20th Fighter Wing based at RAF Upper Heyford, England, in support of NATO. On January 17, 1991, F-111Es deployed to Incirlik Air Base, Turkey, carried out some of the first bombing raids of Operation Desert Storm. More than 100 F-111 aircraft of different versions joined the first strikes against Iraqi targets, both as bombers and radar jammers. As the war progressed, the F-111s were employed in precision attacks with laser-guided weapons on hardened aircraft shelters and bunkers. Later in the war, the F-111s were used against enemy tanks at night.

The F-111F had improved turbofan engines, giving 35 per cent more thrust than those of the F-111A and E. The last F-model was delivered to the Air Force in November 1976. The F-model equipped RAF Lakenheath's 48th Fighter Wing, and had been proven in combat over Libya in 1986.

Development of the EF-111A Raven began in January 1975 when the Air Force made a contract with Grumman Aerospace to modify two F-111As to serve as electronic warfare platforms.

One of the F-111's design innovations was its unique crew escape module, a requirement stipulated by the US Navy but retained in the ultimate Air Force model. The pilot and weapons system officer sit side by side in the

air-conditioned, pressurized module and therefore have no requirement for ejection seats or pressure suits. If the crew pulled the "eject" handles on the centre console, a rocket motor blasts the "pod" clear of the aircraft and it descends by parachute. The module could be fired even at ground level or under water. Flotation bags were fitted to the watertight and airtight module for a water landing.

F-111Cs were an export version supplied to the Royal Australian Air Force, the F-111's only export client. When production ceased in 1976, a total of 562 F-111s had been built.

TOP RIGHT: **The F-111 was the first production aircraft with a variable sweep wing.** ABOVE: **The RAAF was the only non-US operator of the F-111.**
RIGHT: **An F-111 with wings unswept for relatively low-speed flight.**
BELOW: **The crew escape module was one of the F-111's many innovations.**

General Dynamics F-111F

First flight: December 21, 1964 (F-111A)
Power: Two Pratt & Whitney 11,395kg/25,100lb afterburning thrust TF30-P-100 turbofans
Armament: One 20mm/0.78in cannon; one 340kg/750lb nuclear or conventional bomb or two 340kg/750lb bombs in internal bomb bay, plus up to 11,350kg/25,000lb of bombs, rockets, missiles or fuel tanks on four underwing pylons
Size: Wingspan – 19.2m/63ft, spread 9.74m/32ft, swept
  Length – 22.4m/73ft 6in
  Height – 5.22m/17ft 1in
  Wing area – 48.77m²/525sq ft
Weights: Empty – 21,417kg/47,175lb
  Maximum take-off – 45,400kg/100,000lb
Performance: Maximum speed – 2655kph/1650mph
  Service ceiling – 17,995m/59,000ft plus
  Range – 4707km/2925 miles
  Climb – 6710m/22,000ft per minute

Grumman A-6 Intruder/EA-6 Prowler

The Grumman A-6 Intruder, a two-seat, all-weather, subsonic, carrier-based attack aircraft, was designed for a 1957 US Navy competition for a new long-range, low-level tactical strike aircraft. While the performance of the subsonic A-6 was not spectacular, it was superbly suited to the particular attack role for which it was carefully tailored. The A-6 prototype made its first test-flight in April 1960, and was followed by 482 production A-6As delivered to the US Navy from early 1963. From night flights over the jungles of Vietnam to Desert Storm missions above heavily-fortified targets in Iraq, the Grumman A-6 Intruder developed a work-horse reputation, and was the subject of many tales of daring aviation during its 34-year career as the US Navy's principal medium-attack aircraft. The aircraft's ruggedness and all-weather mission capability made it a formidable asset to US Navy and Marine Corps air wings throughout its service. The strengths of the Intruder included its capability to fly in any weather and its heavy weapons payload – two traits highlighted on the big screen in the action film "Flight of the Intruder". A little-known fact is that the Intruder delivered more ordnance during the Vietnam War than the B-52.

A tough and versatile aircraft, the A-6 was called upon to fly the most difficult missions, with flying low and alone in any weather its speciality. The all-weather attack jet saw action in every conflict the USA has been involved in since Vietnam. With the ability to carry more ordnance, launch a wider variety of state-of-the-art smart weapons, conduct day or night strikes over greater distances on internal fuel than any carrier-borne aircraft before or since, and provide mid-air refuelling

TOP AND ABOVE: **The Intruder served the US Navy and Marine Corps through Vietnam, the Libya raids and the Gulf War – it is one of the greatest combat aircraft.**

support to other carrier jets, the Intruder is considered by some to be the most versatile military aircraft of modern times.

In 1986 the A-6E, an advanced upgraded development of the A-6A, proved that it was the best all-weather precision bomber in the world in the joint strike on Libyan terrorist-related targets. With US Air Force F-111s, A-6E Intruders penetrated sophisticated Libyan air defence systems, which had been alerted by the high level of diplomatic tension and by rumours of impending attacks. Evading over 100 guided missiles, the strike force flew at low level in complete darkness, and accurately delivered laser-guided and other ordnance on target.

No guns of any kind were carried aboard the A-6, and the aircraft had no internal bomb bay. However, a wide variety of stores could be mounted externally, including both conventional and nuclear bombs, fuel tanks and an assortment of rockets and missiles. As with all versatile attack aircraft, many combinations of payload and mission radius were available to the A-6E. For example, a weapons load of 945kg/2080lb, consisting of a Mark 43 nuclear bomb, could be delivered at a mission radius of 1432km/890 miles. For that mission, four 1362 litre/300 gallon external tanks would have been carried. Alternatively, a bomb load of 4648kg/10,296lb could be delivered at a mission radius of 724km/450 miles with two 1362 litre/300 gallon external tanks.

The EA-6B Prowlers were developed from the EA-6A, which was an Intruder airframe intended primarily to be an electronic countermeasures and intelligence-gathering platform. These aircraft were initially designed to fly in support of the Intruders on Vietnam missions. However, the EA-6B is a significant aircraft in its own right and provides an umbrella of protection for strike aircraft (by suppressing enemy air defences), ground troops and ships by jamming enemy radar, electronic data links and communications. At the same time, the Prowler is gathering tactical electronic intelligence within the combat area.

Intruders left US Navy service in the late 1990s but Prowlers will fly on for the foreseeable future.

ABOVE RIGHT: **The A-6 was responsible for dropping more bombs during the Vietnam War than the mighty B-52.**
RIGHT: **Note the fixed refuelling probe on the nose of this A-6.**
BELOW: **The Grumman Prowler was based on the Intruder, and has evolved into an aircraft which, in its own way, can disable enemy electronic defences.**

Grumman A-6E Intruder

First Flight: April 19, 1960 (YA-6A)
Power: Two Pratt & Whitney 4222kg/9300lb thrust J52-P-8B turbojets
Armament: Up to 8172kg/18,000lb of nuclear or conventional ordnance or missiles
Size: Wingspan – 16.15m/53ft
    Length – 16.69m/54ft 9in
    Height – 4.93m/16ft 2in
    Wing area – 49.13m²/528.9sq ft
Weights: Empty – 12104kg/26,660lb
    Maximum catapult take-off – 26,604kg/ 58,600lb
Performance: Maximum speed – 1035kph/ 644mph
    Ceiling – 12,932m/42,400ft
    Range – 1627km/1011 miles
    Climb – 2621m/8600ft per minute

Handley Page Victor

It is hard to believe that while some at Handley Page were working on the Halifax during World War II, others were thinking about a tailless flying-wing jet-powered bomber. Shortly after the end of the war, the futuristic concept aroused the interest of the Air Ministry and the design evolved into an aircraft with a fuselage and a tail but with an innovative crescent-shaped wing. It took five years to get the design from the drawing board into the air – the prototype HP80 Victor WB771 took flight at Boscombe Down on Christmas Eve 1952.

As testing continued, more orders came from the RAF for the high-performance bomber, and in early 1956 the first Victor B.1 rolled off the production line. Capable of speeds in excess of the speed of sound in a shallow dive, the first Victors were delivered to the RAF in November 1957, and Bomber Command declared them operational in April 1958 with No.10 Squadron. The second production batch had a larger tailcone to accommodate tail warning radar, and refined engines, and these aircraft were designated B.1A. The Victor was now a nuclear bomber and part of Britain's V-force with the Vulcans and Valiants. However, with a bomb load of up to 15,890kg/ 35,000lb, the Victor could carry a much greater bomb load than the other V-bombers.

The improved Mk 2 variant with Rolls-Royce Conway engines (and thus redesigned wing roots and intakes), larger wing, modified tailcone and new electrical system among

TOP: **Painted in overall anti-flash white, the Victor, with the other V-bombers, was the UK's nuclear deterrent in the late 1950s.**
ABOVE: **The Victor's unusual crescent wing was groundbreaking. The Victor pictured here is a B(SR).2.**

other modifications, was finally put into production, and the first Victor B.2 flew in February 1959. As Soviet anti-aircraft defences improved, so the V-force had to modify its tactics to remain a credible deterrent. The B.2s became low-level, high-speed bombers, and also began to carry the Blue Steel stand-off nuclear missile.

The last B.2 was completed in April 1963, the year that RAF Victors were deployed to Singapore in a show of force to Indonesia, who threatened the British protectorate of Malaysia. As the B.2s replaced the earlier Marks in service, the B.1s and B.1As were converted into air-refuelling tankers (BK.1 and BK.1A).

LEFT: **Tanker trio – three Victors pictured a month before the type was retired in 1993.**
BELOW LEFT: **Refuelling an RAF Jaguar en route to the Gulf, 1991.** BELOW: **This Victor K.2 is without its underwing refuelling pods. Note the large fuel tank hanging under the wing, and the inflight refuelling probe.**

Handley Page Victor B. Mk 2

First flight: December 24, 1952
Power: Four Rolls-Royce 9352kg/20,600lb thrust Conway 201 turbofans
Armament: One Blue Steel stand-off missile or up to 15,890kg/35,000lb of conventional bombs
Size: Wingspan – 36.57m/120ft
Length – 35.03m/114ft 11in
Height – 8.57m/28ft 1.5in
Wing area – 241.3m²/2597sq ft
Weights: Empty – 51,864kg/114,240lb
Maximum take-off – 101,242kg/223,000lb
Performance: Maximum speed – 1038kph/645mph
Ceiling – 18,300m/60,000ft
Range – 7400km/4600 miles

The first converted Victor tanker flew on April 28, 1965. Special reconnaissance versions of the aircraft were also produced – nine B.2s were completed as B(SR).2s, and were excellent reconnaissance aircraft with bomb bays filled with cameras and massive flash units. The standard Victor remained in service as a nuclear bomber until 1975.

Further conversions of "surplus" Victor bombers resulted in the K.2 tanker, which entered service in May 1974. A total of 24 conversions were carried out, and the K.2s were expected to fly until around 1988.

It was as a tanker that the Handley Page bomber finally went to war. The very long-range 1982 Black Buck Vulcan bombing missions against Argentine forces on the Falklands were only possible due to 11 Victor tankers refuelling the bomber and themselves on the outward leg from Ascension. In a less well-known aspect of the Falklands campaign, Victor XH675 carried out a 11,263km/7000-mile, 14-hour and 45-minute reconnaissance mission, radar-mapping the South Atlantic.

The dwindling Victor tanker fleet was forced into the spotlight in early 1991 when coalition forces set about ousting Iraqi invaders from Kuwait. Eight tankers refuelled RAF and US combat aircraft on 299 sorties. The Victor was finally retired from RAF service on October 15, 1993. Eighty-six Victors had been produced in all.

Hawker Siddeley/British Aerospace Nimrod

Design work on the Nimrod began in June 1964 with the aim of replacing the RAF's ageing Shackleton maritime reconnaissance aircraft.

Based on the airframe of the world's first jet airliner, the de Havilland Comet, the production Nimrod was a new-build aircraft with a shorter, modified, pressurized fuselage. The addition of a weapons and operational equipment bay 15.8m/ 52ft in length under the main fuselage gave the aircraft its unique double-decker cross-section and enabled it to claim the biggest bomb bay of any NATO aircraft.

In 1965, the British Government gave the Nimrod project the go-ahead and two prototypes, conversions from civil Comets, first flew in 1967. The first production Nimrod MRI, XV226, had its maiden flight in June 1968 and the Nimrod entered Royal Air Force service in 1969.

The Nimrod was a revolutionary concept for a maritime patrol aircraft, a class typically powered by turboprops. The Nimrod combined the advantages of high altitude and comparatively high-speed capability from its jet powerplants coupled with low wing-loading and good low-level manoeuvrability.

TOP: **The Nimrod is the only jet-powered, long-range maritime patrol and ASW aircraft.** ABOVE: **Somewhere in that shape lies the trailblazing de Havilland Comet jet airliner.**

The Nimrod has an enviable reputation for its anti-submarine warfare capabilities, surface surveillance and anti-shipping roles. In the anti-submarine warfare (ASW) role, prop-engined aircraft produce vibrations that are easily detectable by submarines, whereas the Nimrod's jet noise is virtually undetectable.

This very versatile aircraft can carry a variety of stores, including the Stingray torpedo, Harpoon anti-ship missile and Sidewinder infrared missile for self-defence or targets of opportunity. The aircraft can also carry its own chaff/flares suite for decoying incoming missiles.

Hawker Siddeley/British Aerospace Nimrod MR2

First Flight: May 23, 1967

Power: Four Rolls-Royce 5511kg/12,140lb thrust Spey 250 turbofans

Armament: 6129kg/13,500lb of mixed maritime weaponry carried in bomb bay, including Harpoon anti-ship missiles, rocket/gun pods or pairs of Sidewinder AAMs carried under wing

Size: Wingspan – 35m/114ft 10in
Length – 38.63m/126ft 9in
Height – 9.05m/29ft 8.5in
Wing area – 197m²/2121sq ft

Weights: Empty – 39,362kg/86,700lb
Maximum take-off – 80,585kg/177,500lb

Performance: Maximum speed – 926kph/575mph
Ceiling – 12,810m/42,000ft
Range – 8045km/5000 miles plus
Climb – Not available

ABOVE: **The Nimrod's jet flight is difficult to detect from under water.**
RIGHT: **Note the inflight refuelling probe atop the nose and the magnetic anomaly detector boom projecting from the tail. The latter is just one means of detecting submerged submarines.**

In the early 1980s, the type was upgraded to MR2 standard, principally by updating and improving the aircraft's surveillance equipment. For the aircraft's role in Operation Corporate during the 1982 Falklands War, an inflight refuelling probe became standard. Royal Air Force Nimrods have seen service all over the world and played a pivotal role in the Falklands and Gulf conflicts.

The Nimrod currently carries out three main roles: anti-surface unit warfare (ASUW), anti-submarine warfare (ASW) and search-and-rescue (SAR). It has an unrefuelled endurance of around 10 hours.

After a quarter of a century in service, the Nimrod MR2's airframe and systems are to undergo a dramatic upgrade to MR4 standard, which will extend the type's operational life by a further 25 years. An 80 per cent new aircraft, the MR4 will be 30 per cent heavier than the MR2, carry 30 per cent more fuel and have twice the patrol endurance. The 18-strong fleet of MR4s is expected to be in service by 2009.

One less well-known aspect of the Nimrod story is the Nimrod R1. Three Nimrods were adapted to R1 standard in the early 1970s following the retirement of Comet 2Rs, and have been constantly upgraded ever since. The maritime reconnaissance equipment was removed and replaced with highly sophisticated and sensitive systems for reconnaissance and the gathering of electronic intelligence (ELINT). The ability of the Nimrod to loiter for long periods, following a high-speed dash to the required area of operation, makes the aircraft ideally suited to this task. RAF R1s have been quietly and secretly gathering information in trouble spots and on potential enemies of the UK since 1974.

ABOVE: **The Nimrod MR2 has a crew of 13 – three on the flight deck and the rest manning the banks of equipment carried on board.**

Ilyushin Il-28

The Il-28 was the Soviet Air Force's first jet bomber to enter service. The aircraft, codenamed "Beagle" by NATO, has been described as Soviet's Canberra owing to its longevity and adaptability.

The Il-28 first flew on August 8, 1948, and the aircraft was in front-line service within two years. Twenty-five pre-production models took part in the 1950 Moscow May Day fly-past, an

TOP: **Now a museum piece, the Il-28 was a groundbreaking addition to the Soviet inventory – the USSR's first jet bomber.** ABOVE: **Despite its unchallenging appearance, the Il-28 proved to be a major weapon for the Soviet Union.**

annual spectacle which was awaited with some trepidation on the part of western analysts during the Cold War. Production of this fine aircraft went on until around 1960, and some 10,000 were finally built by the Soviet Union and under licence in China until 1969. Design work on this medium bomber began around the end of World War II, and the aircraft's shape seemed to owe more to the past than the future. Straight-winged, the Il-28 did, however, have a highly swept-back tail fin and tailplanes for better control in high-speed dives.

Power for the prototype was provided by two RD-10 turbojets developed from wartime German Junkers Jumo engines, but production versions were powered by Klimov VK-1s, a Soviet version of the reliable British Nene engine supplied pre-Cold War.

The engines were mounted in pods beneath the wings in the same way that the Jumos had been mounted on the wartime Arado Blitz bomber. While the pilot had a rounded fighter-looking bubble canopy, the navigator/bombardier's bombsight was housed in a World War II-style greenhouse nose. At the base of the tail fin was a defensive powered gun turret which looked very similar to that of a B-17 or B-29, and housed two 23mm/0.9in cannon. The rear gunner also served as radio operator for the aircraft. Two 23mm/0.9in cannon were fixed in the nose for front defence.

LEFT: **A rare picture of a Chinese-built II-28, the H-5, in service with the Romanian Air Force.** BELOW: **Wartime German jet aircraft development certainly influenced some aspects of the II-28 design, such as the engines slung beneath the wing. The prototype was, in fact, powered by engines derived from German Jumos.** BOTTOM: **A flight of "Soviet Canberras".**

Using the bomb bay and external hardpoints, the aircraft could carry up to 3000kg/6603lb of ordnance. Wing-tip fuel tanks gave the aircraft extended range. The II-28R variant was a tactical reconnaissance version with cameras mounted in the bomb bay, but could also carry out electronic intelligence gathering. The II-28T was the torpedo bomber in service with the Soviet Navy.

The Beagle was retired from the Soviet Air Force and Navy front line in the 1980s but continued to serve as target tugs and ECM (electronic countermeasures) platforms – Finland and East Germany operated the dedicated unarmed target-towing version.

The II-28 was also operated by a number of export customers, having been sold to over 20 countries including Afghanistan, Egypt, Hungary, Iraq, North Korea, Poland and Yemen. Nigeria's controversial use of their six II-28s against Biafran civilians in 1968 shocked the world.

Many Arab air forces operated the type, and when 50 examples of this very capable bomber arrived in Egypt in the mid-1950s, tensions between Egypt and Israel rose. During the 1956 Suez crisis and subsequent conflicts in 1967 and 1973, Egyptian II-28s were targeted on the ground before they could be used against Israel.

Earlier, during the 1962 Cuban Missile Crisis, Soviet II-28s being assembled on Cuba posed enough of a threat to the USA that the aircraft, as well as the notorious missiles, had to be removed.

Over 500 were sold to China, who also licence-built the aircraft – their domestic version, the H-5, remained in front-line service into the late 1990s. Bomber versions continued to be used by former Soviet satellite and client states well into the 1990s.

Ilyushin II-28

First flight: August 8, 1948
Power: Two Klimov 2700kg/5942lb thrust VK-1 turbojets
Armament: Two 23mm/0.9in cannon in nose and two in tail turret; maximum bomb load of 3000kg/6603lb carried internally and externally
Size: Wingspan – 21.45m/70ft 4.5in
  Length – 17.65m/57ft 10.75in
  Height – 6.7m/21ft 11.8in
  Wing area – 60.8m²/654.47sq ft
Weights: Empty – 12,890kg/28,569lb
  Maximum take-off – 21,000kg/ 46,221lb
Performance: Maximum speed – 900kph/ 559mph
  Ceiling – 12,300m/40,355ft
  Range – 2180km/1355 miles
  Climb – 900m/2953ft per minute

Lockheed P2V Neptune

Even before the USA entered World War II, it was clear that the US Navy would need a land-based patrol bomber with better performance and armament than the types then available, such as the Hudson and Ventura. The Navy needed an aircraft designed specifically for day or night anti-submarine warfare and anti-shipping operations. Lockheed began work on designing such an aircraft before the Navy managed to issue an official requirement. In the confusion following America's joining the war, the US Navy was only interested in proven and available aircraft types, so Lockheed continued to develop their design with no official support. However, by early 1943 the Navy began to look for the next generation of maritime patrol aircraft and asked Lockheed to proceed to prototype stage. The XP2V-1 first flew on May 17, 1945, and was followed by 14 production versions of the P2V-1, which began to enter US Navy service in March 1947. The designers introduced many production refinements with the aircraft, for example trying to keep much of the fuselage shape curving in only one direction, thus allowing the use of shaped skins which would fit in any number of areas on the fuselage instead of just one. The aircraft was designed to be

manufactured into easily accessible subassemblies, keeping assembly time to a minimum. The Neptune thus became an easy aircraft to service – for example, a complete engine change could be done in 30 minutes and an outer wing panel in 79 minutes.

However, the Neptune had made a name for itself before it entered service. From September to October 1946, a modified Neptune named Truculent Turtle flew 18,100km/11,250 miles non-stop from Western Australia to Columbus, Ohio, in 55 hours and 15 minutes, and captured the world long-distance record.

Over 30 variants of the P2V appeared before production ceased in 1962. After the P2V-1, the improved and more powerfully engined P2V-2, with the ability to carry sonobuoys, was the next significant version. However, the major production version was the P2V-5, first flown on December 29, 1950.

RIGHT: **Test-flown during World War II, the Neptune was finally retired from active duty four decades later. The aircraft pictured here is a Dutch Navy machine.** BELOW: **An excellent air-to-air study of a US Navy P2V. Note the remotely controlled searchlight on the tip of the starboard wingtip fuel tank.**

Powered by 3250hp R-3350 engines, this version carried additional fuel in ingenious large wingtip tanks. Apart from 1589 litres/350 gallons of fuel, the forward portion of the starboard wingtip tank housed a powerful moveable searchlight that was linked to the movement of the nose turret guns. The port wingtip tank had APS-8 search radar mounted in its forward portion, and both tanks could be jettisoned in an emergency. The P2V-5 could carry a 3632kg/8000lb bomb load of mines, torpedoes, bombs or depth charges, as well as 16 rockets beneath the wings. An APS-20 radar was mounted in the underbelly position just aft of the nose-wheel doors. The increase in ASW and ECM (electronic countermeasures equipment) required an increase in the aircrew to nine men, and the P2V-5's range was 7642km/4750 miles.

In addition to the US Navy, the P2V-5 was supplied to Argentina, Australia, Brazil, the Netherlands and Portugal. Fifty-two P2V-5s were delivered to the Royal Air Force in 1952. Designated Neptune MR.1s, the aircraft were delivered with nose, dorsal and tail turrets. Twenty-seven were later modified, and the nose and tail turrets replaced with the clear plexiglass nose and MAD boom in the tail. The Neptune entered service with No.217 Squadron and also equipped Nos.36, 203 and 210 Squadrons. The aircraft were returned to the USA in 1957 when the RAF's Shackleton force was up to strength.

The P2V-7 was the final Neptune version off the production line. First flown on April 26, 1954, it was powered by two piston engines augmented by two turbojets. With a dash speed of 586kph/364mph, this version was the fastest of the Lockheed-produced Neptunes. The APS-20 search radar, with its larger radome, was mounted further forward than on the P2V-5s.

By the 1970s, P2Vs had been phased out from all US Navy Fleet Patrol Squadrons but remained in service with Reserve Patrol Squadrons. In April 1978, the last reserve unit re-equipped with the P-3 Orion, thus ending over three decades of P2V Neptune operations with the US Navy.

Kawasaki had assembled some 48 P2V-7s in Japan and went on to produce a developed turboprop-powered version, designated P-2J, with a longer fuselage to carry more equipment. The turboprops were again augmented by two turbojets. A total of 83 P-2Js were built by Kawasaki, with the first delivered in October 1969. These aircraft, the last operational Neptunes in the world, were finally retired in 1985.

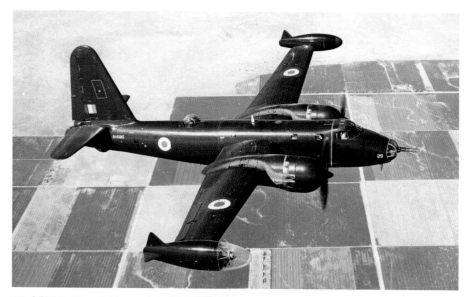

TOP: **A P2V-7 of French Aéronavale unit Escadrille 12S.** TOP RIGHT: **A Dutch Navy Neptune.** ABOVE: **An RAF crew gaining experience of one of 50 P2V-5 Neptunes allocated to Britain and Australia before flying the aircraft to the UK.**

Lockheed P2V-7 Neptune

First Flight: May 17, 1945 (XP2V-1 prototype)

Power: Two Wright 3500hp R-3350-32W radial piston engines and two Westinghouse 1543kg/3400lb thrust J34-WE-36 turbojets

Armament: Two 12.7mm/0.5in machine-guns in dorsal turret; up to 3632kg/8000lb of bombs, depth charges or torpedoes

Size: Wingspan – 31.65m/103ft 10in
Length – 27.94m/91ft 8in
Height – 8.94m/29ft 4in
Wing area – 92.9m²/1000sq ft

Weights: Empty – 22,670kg/49,935lb
Maximum take-off – 36,272kg/79,895lb

Performance: Maximum speed – 649kph/403mph
Ceiling – 6710m/22,000ft
Range – 5930km/3685 miles
Climb – 366m/1200ft per minute

Lockheed P-3 Orion

The P-3C Orion is one of the all-time great military aircraft. Developed quickly in a time of national need from the existing Lockheed Electra airliner, the Orion has been protecting the maritime interests of the USA and other P-3 customers for over four decades, and remains a potent submarine killer.

In 1957, the US Navy issued an urgent requirement for a long-range maritime reconnaissance and anti-submarine warfare (ASW) aircraft to replace the ageing P2V Neptune. Lockheed's answer was a modified Electra airliner airframe, which first flew in November 1959. Structurally, the aircraft differed in that the Orion was 2.24m/7ft 4in shorter and had a weapons bay for carrying mines, torpedoes, depth charges or even nuclear weapons.

The aircraft entered the US Navy inventory in July 1962, and more than 30 years later it remains the Navy's sole land-based ASW aircraft. It has gone through one designation change (P3V to P-3) and three major models – P-3A, P-3B and P-3C, the latter being the only one now in active service. The last Navy P-3 came off the Lockheed production line in April 1990.

The P-3 Orion built its reputation as the ultimate submarine-finder during the Cold War. From the Cuban Missile Crisis to the end of the Soviet Union, the Orion carried out round-the-clock, low-profile patrols to keep the USA and NATO ahead of the Soviets.

The P-3 can be equipped with a variety of sophisticated detection equipment. Infrared and long-range electro-optical cameras plus special imaging radar allow the Orion, with no

TOP: **The P-3 is still among the best ASW aircraft in the world, almost half a century after its first flight.** ABOVE: **A Royal Netherlands Navy P-3.**

defensive armament, to monitor activity from a safe distance. It can stay airborne for very long periods, and its four powerful Allison T56-A-14 engines can fly at almost any altitude.

In addition to submarine-hunting, the P-3 is called upon for peacekeeping and relief missions around the world. When civil war flared in Liberia, P-3s were the eyes and ears of forces protecting the US Embassy. In Somalia, P-3s monitored street operations in Mogadishu from well off-shore. In Rwanda, P-3s tracked large groups of refugees to help pinpoint relief efforts. Then, in Operation Desert Storm, P-3s logged more than 12,000 hours in 1200 combat surveillance sorties.

The current US Navy force of 12 active and seven reserve squadrons supports requirements for 40 P-3Cs to be continuously forward-deployed around the world, ready

RIGHT: **The US Navy will continue to operate P-3s for some years to come. This aircraft has opened the doors of its weapons bay, which can contain torpedoes, nuclear depth charges and mines.** BELOW: **This photograph of a US Navy P-3 shows the area beneath the fuselage aft of the wing, consisting of over 50 chutes from which a variety of stores can be dispensed.** BELOW RIGHT: **The P-3 has now become a battlefield surveillance platform over land and sea.**

to support global US Navy operations. In addition to US Navy use, P-3s were exported to Australia, Chile, Greece, Iran, the Netherlands, New Zealand, Norway, Portugal, South Korea, Spain and Thailand. Some were also built in Japan by Kawasaki, and the Canadian Armed Forces operate a version known as the CP-140 Aurora.

US Navy P-3s were active in Afghanistan in late 2001, where the aircraft used data links to provide real-time video and other sensor data to land forces.

The role of the Orion has evolved from being simply a maritime anti-submarine aircraft to being a battlefield surveillance platform at sea or over land. The aircraft's long range and loiter time proved to be invaluable assets for the Allies during Operation Iraqi Freedom because it can view the battle area and instantaneously provide that information to ground troops.

The P-3C has advanced submarine-detection sensors such as directional frequency and ranging (DIFAR) sonobuoys and magnetic anomaly detection (MAD) equipment. The avionics system is integrated by a computer that supports all of the tactical displays and monitors for the 11 crew members, and can automatically launch weapons, as well as providing flight information to the pilots. The aircraft can carry a variety of weapons internally and on wing pylons, such as the Harpoon anti-surface missile, the Mk 50 torpedo and the Mk 60 mine. From the Cold War to today's tensions, the P-3 was there, and it is likely to remain in service around the world for the foreseeable future.

Lockheed Martin P-3C Orion

First Flight November 25, 1959 (YP-3A)
Power Four Allison 4910eshp T-56-A-14 turboprop engines
Armament 9080kg/20,000lb of ordnance, including cruise missile, Maverick (AGM 65) air-to-ground missiles, Mk 46/50 torpedoes, rockets, mines, depth bombs and special weapons
Size Wingspan – 30.36m/99ft 6in
Length – 35.6m/116ft 10in
Height – 10.27m/33ft 7in
Wing area – 120.77m²/1300sq ft
Weights Empty – 27,917kg/61,491lb
Maximum take-off – 64,468kg/142,000lb
Performance Maximum speed – 750kph/466mph
Ceiling – 8631m/28,300ft
Range – 4405km/2738 miles
Climb – 594m/1950ft per minute

Lockheed S-3 Viking

The S-3 Viking in service today is an all-weather, carrier-based patrol/attack aircraft, which provides protection for the US fleet against hostile surface vessels while also functioning as the Carrier Battle Groups' primary tanker. The S-3, one of the most successful of all carrier aircraft, is extremely versatile and is equipped for many missions, including day/night surveillance, electronic countermeasures, command/control/communications warfare, as well as search-and-rescue (SAR). Its versatility has made it known as the "Swiss Army Knife of Naval Aviation".

In the late 1960s, the deployment of Soviet deep-diving nuclear powered submarines caused the US Navy to call for a new breed of carrier-borne US Navy ASW aircraft to succeed the Grumman S-2. Lockheed, in association with Vought Aeronautics, proposed the S-3A, which came to be called Viking.

To keep the aircraft aerodynamically clean and avoid reducing its top speed, as many protuberances as possible were designed to retract. Thus, the inflight refuelling probe, the magnetic anomaly detection boom at the rear of the aircraft and some sensors retract for transit flight. The small four-man aircraft has folding wings, making it very popular on carriers due to the small amount of space it takes up relative to the importance of its mission. With its short, stubby wings, the Viking was something of a wolf in sheep's clothing and could have given a very good account of itself had the Cold War heated up. Carrying state-of-the-art radar

TOP: **Developed to counter a specific Soviet threat, the Viking is considered to be the ultimate sub-killer.** ABOVE: **An S-3B of VS-31 "Topcats" aboard the USS** *John F. Kennedy*, **Arabian Sea, April 2004.**

systems and extensive sonobuoy deployment and control capability, the S-3A entered US Navy service with VS-41 in February 1974. In total 187 were built and equipped 14 US Navy squadrons.

In the mid-1980s, the aircraft was completely refurbished and modified to carry the Harpoon missile, the improved version being designated the S-3B. While the S-3A was primarily configured for anti-submarine warfare, the S-3B has evolved into a premier surveillance and precision-targeting platform for the US Navy, and has the most modern precision-guided missile capabilities. It does so many things so well – surface and undersea warfare, mine warfare, electronic reconnaissance and analysis, over-the-horizon targeting, missile attack, and aerial tanking – that its current mission is summed up by the US Navy as being simply "Sea Control".

ABOVE: **The Viking has an internal weapons bay which can carry bombs, depth charges, mines and torpedoes, while missiles, rocket pods, bombs, flare dispensers or mines can be carried on two underwing hardpoints.**

The S-3B's high-speed computer system processes and displays information generated by its targeting-sensor systems. To engage and destroy targets, the S-3B Viking employs an impressive array of airborne weaponry, including the AGM 84 Harpoon Anti-Ship Missile, AGM 65 Maverick Infrared Missile and a wide selection of conventional bombs and torpedoes. Future Viking aircraft will also have a control capability for the AGM 84 stand-off land-attack missile extended range (SLAM-ER). The S-3B provides the fleet with a very effective fixed-wing "over the horizon" aircraft to combat the significant and varied threats presented by modern maritime combatants.

On March 25, 2003, an S-3B from the "Red Griffins" of Sea Control Squadron Thirty-eight (VS 38) became the first such aircraft to attack inland and to fire a laser-guided Maverick missile in combat. The attack was made on a "significant naval target" in the Tigris River near Basra, Iraq. VS-38 was embarked in the USS *Constellation*.

The Viking, easy to update with the latest avionics and surveillance equipment, will be flying with the US Navy for many years to come.

TOP: **The aircraft carries a long magnetic anomaly detection boom which can be extended from the rear of the aircraft to aid submarine-detection.**
ABOVE: **An S-3A of VS-22 "The Checkmates" from USS *Saratoga*.**
BELOW: **The S-3B's mission, neatly summed up by the US Navy, is "Sea Control".**

Lockheed S-3B Viking

First Flight January 21, 1972
Power Two General Electric 4211kg/9275lb thrust TF-34-GE-400B turbofan engines
Armament Up to 1793kg/3950lb of ordnance, including AGM-84 Harpoon, AGM-65 Maverick and AGM-84 SLAM missiles, torpedoes, rockets and bombs
Size: Wingspan – 20.93m/68ft 8in
Length – 16.26m/53ft 4in
Height – 6.93m/22ft 9in
Wing area – 55.55m²/598sq ft
Weights Empty – 12,099kg/26,650lb
Maximum take-off – 23,852kg/52,539lb
Performance Maximum speed – 834kph/ 518mph
Ceiling – 12,200m/40,000ft
Range – 3706km/2303 miles
Climb – 1280m/4200ft per minute

Lockheed Martin F-117A Nighthawk

Usually and erroneously referred to as the "stealth fighter", the F-117A Nighthawk bomber was the world's first operational aircraft designed to exploit low-observability stealth technology. This precision-strike aircraft can penetrate high-threat airspace undetected and then use laser-guided weaponry against critical targets.

The F-117A was developed by Lockheed Martin after lengthy work on stealth technology was carried out in secret from 1975. Development of the F-117A began in 1978, and it

TOP: **Developed in incredible secrecy, the "stealth fighter" was the world's first operational aircraft built with stealth technology.** ABOVE: **Braking parachutes trailing, a pair of F-117As during a visit to the UK.**

was test-flown in 1981, but it was not until 1988 that its existence was publicly announced. The first F-117A was delivered in 1982, and USAF Air Combat Command's first F-117A unit, the 4450th Tactical Group, achieved operational capability in October 1983. Lockheed Martin delivered the last of 59 aircraft to the Air Force in July 1990, and five additional test aircraft were retained by the company.

The aircraft's surfaces and edge profiles are optimized to reflect hostile radar into narrow beam signals, directed away from enemy radar detectors. All the doors and opening panels on the aircraft have saw-toothed forward and trailing edges to reflect radar. The aircraft is constructed principally of aluminum, with titanium used for areas of the engine and exhaust systems. The outer surface of the aircraft is coated with a radar-absorbent material (RAM) and for stealth reasons, the F-117A does not rely on radar for navigation or targeting. Instead, for navigation and weapon aiming, the aircraft is equipped with a forward-looking infrared (FLIR) and a downward-looking infrared (DLIR) with laser designator, supplied by Raytheon.

The F-117A is powered by two low-bypass General Electric F404-GE-F1D2 turbofan engines. The rectangular air intakes on both sides of the fuselage are covered by gratings that are coated with radar-absorbent material. The wide and flat structure of the engine exhaust area reduces the infrared and radar detectability of the aft section of the engine. The two large tail fins slant slightly outwards to provide an obstruction for ground-based radars to the infrared and radar returns from the engine exhaust area.

Before a flight, mission data is downloaded on to the IBM AP-102 mission-control computer, which integrates it with the navigation and flight controls to provide a fully automated flight management system. After take-off, the pilot can hand over flight control to the mission programme until within visual range of the mission's first target. The pilot then resumes control of the aircraft for weapon delivery. The aircraft is equipped with an infrared acquisition and designation system (IRADS), which is integrated with the weapon delivery system. The pilot is presented with a view of the target on the head-up display. After the strike, the weapon delivery and impact is recorded on the aircraft's internally-mounted video system, which provides real-time damage assessment.

The F-117A can employ a variety of weapons, including the BLU-109B low-level laser-guided bomb, GBU-10 and GBU-27 laser-guided bomb units, AGM-65 Maverick and AGM-88 HARM air-to-surface missiles.

The F-117A first saw action in December 1989 during Operation Just Cause in Panama, but it was the type's actions in the first Gulf War that grabbed the headlines. On their first trip into theatre, the F-117s flew non-stop from the USA to Kuwait, an air-refuelled flight of approximately 18.5 hours – a record for single-seat combat aircraft that stands today.

In January and February 1991, the F-117A attacked the most heavily fortified targets during Desert Storm, and it was the only coalition jet allowed to strike targets inside Baghdad's

city limits. The F-117A, which normally packs a payload of two 908kg/2000lb GBU-27 laser-guided bombs, destroyed and crippled Iraqi electrical power stations, military headquarters, communications sites, air-defence operation centres, airfields, ammunition bunkers and chemical, biological and nuclear weapons plants.

Although only 36 F-117As were deployed in Desert Storm, and accounted for 2.5 per cent of the total force of 1900 fighters and bombers, they flew more than a third of the bombing runs on the first day of the war. In all, during Desert Storm this remarkable aircraft conducted more than 1250 sorties, dropped more than 2032 tonnes/2000 tons of bombs, and flew for more than 6900 hours. Although more than 3000 anti-aircraft guns and 60 surface-to-air missile batteries protected Baghdad, the Nighthawks owned the skies over the city and, for that matter, the country.

In March 24, 1999, F-117As led the NATO Operation Allied Force air strikes against Yugoslavia. During the campaign, one F-117 was lost, having being tracked by virtually antique Russian long wavelength radars. Normally the only time the aircraft's stealthiness can be compromised is when it gets very wet or opens its bomb bays.

Nighthawks are officially expected to remain in USAF service until 2020, but with updating, the aircraft is likely to be around for much longer.

RIGHT: **The principal weapon carried by the F-117 is the precision laser-guided GBU-27 bomb.** BELOW: **The F-117, with its unprecedented form, was so radical that it has challenged how we think combat aircraft should look.**

Lockheed Martin F-117A Nighthawk

First Flight: June 18, 1981
Power: Two General Electric 4903kg/10,800lb thrust F404-GE-F1D2 non-afterburning turbofans
Armament: Up to 2270kg/5000lb of smart or free-fall weapons can be carried internally
Size: Wingspan – 13.3m/43ft 4in
Length – 20.1m/65ft 11in
Height – 3.78m/12ft 5in
Wing area – 105.9m²/1140sq ft
Weights: Empty – Approximately 13,620kg/30,000lb
Maximum take-off – 23,835kg/52,500lb
Performance: Maximum speed – High subsonic
Ceiling – Unpublished
Range – Intercontinental with air-refuelling
Climb – Unpublished

McDonnell Douglas A-4 Skyhawk

From 1954, Douglas (and later McDonnell Douglas) built 2960 Skyhawks in a production run that lasted a quarter of a century. Designed as a small and therefore cost-effective lightweight carrier-borne high-speed bomber, the Skyhawk was affectionately nicknamed "the scooter" or "Heinemann's Hot Rod" after Douglas designer Ed Heinemann. He had been working on a compact jet-powered attack aircraft design which the US Navy ordered for evaluation – this was the XA4D-1, and the first of nine prototypes and development aircraft flew in June 1954. Development was swift and the Navy were eager to acquire this new and very capable combat aircraft. Chosen as a replacement for the venerable Skyraider,

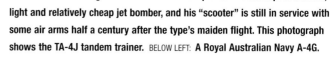

ABOVE: **The A-4's designer Ed Heinemann championed the concept of a small, light and relatively cheap jet bomber, and his "scooter" is still in service with some air arms half a century after the type's maiden flight. This photograph shows the TA-4J tandem trainer.** BELOW LEFT: **A Royal Australian Navy A-4G.**

the Skyhawk provided the US Navy, US Marines Corps and friendly nations with a manoeuvrable but powerful attack bomber that had great altitude and range performance, plus a remarkable and flexible weapons-carrying capability.

Production deliveries of A-4As began in September 1956. The A-4 was first delivered to the US Navy's VA-72 attack squadron on October 26, 1956. Its small size allowed it to fit on an aircraft carrier lift without needing to have folding wings, thus saving weight and extra maintenance. The Skyhawk was roughly half the empty weight of its contemporaries and could fly at 1089km/677mph at sea level. US examples of the aircraft were nuclear-capable.

The Skyhawk was progressively developed with more powerful engines – early A–C models had been powered by the Wright J65, a licence-built copy of the British Armstrong Siddeley Sapphire engine. The A-4C was followed by the A-4E, a heavier aircraft powered by Pratt & Whitney's J52 engine. The A-4F was the last version to enter US Navy service and was easily identified by its dorsal avionics "hump". The ultimate development of the Skyhawk was the A-4M, known as the Skyhawk II, specifically designed for the US Marines. This model that first flew in 1970 had a larger canopy for better pilot view, and had a maximum take-off

LEFT: The A-4D2 version had a more efficient engine, beefed-up rear fuselage and powered rudder, and introduced the fixed inflight refuelling probe. BELOW: The "camel's hump", which appeared on later A-4s, housed all-weather navigation and weapons-delivery avionics. BOTTOM: Two-seat trainer versions of the A-4 were produced to train both pilots and radar intercept officers.

weight twice that of the early A-4 versions. Power for this "super" Skyhawk came from a J52-P-408, and the Skyhawk II was in production until 1979. The US Navy's Blue Angels flight demonstration aerobatics team flew the A-4 Skyhawk II from 1974 until 1986.

The Skyhawk's combat career began on August 4, 1964, with the first American carrier-launched raids on North Vietnam. The A-4s were soon performing most of the Navy's and Marine Corps' light air attack missions over Vietnam.

Skyhawks were also operated by the armed forces of Argentina, Australia, Israel (who used them extensively in the 1973 Yom Kippur war), Kuwait, Singapore, Indonesia, Malaysia and New Zealand, and they remained active with several air services into the 2000s.

Argentina was the first export customer for the Skyhawk, operating A-4Ps and A-4Qs which were modified B and C-models respectively. These aircraft, acquired in the mid-1960s, were later complemented by A-4Rs which were ex-USMC A-4Ms. Argentine Skyhawks were the most

destructive strike aircraft to engage British Forces during the 1982 Falklands War. Operating from mainland bases, the Skyhawks carried out many attacks against British shipping. On May 12, a Skyhawk raid put HMS *Glasgow* out of action, and on May 21, the Skyhawks attacked the British invasion force landing at San Carlos. On May 25, Argentine Skyhawks attacked and sank HMS *Coventry*. The cost of these actions was high, with Argentina losing ten A-4s to anti-aircraft defences and fighters in a matter of days.

McDonnell Douglas A-4M Skyhawk II

First flight: June 22, 1954 (XA4D-1 prototype)
Power: One Pratt & Whitney 5079kg/11,187lb thrust J52-P408 turbojet
Armament: Two 20mm/0.78in cannon in wing roots; up to 4156kg/9155lb of bombs or air-to-surface and air-to-air missiles
Size Wingspan – 8.38m/27ft 6in
Length – 12.27m/40ft 4in
Height – 4.5m/15ft
Wing area – 24.2m²/260sq ft
Weights: Empty – 4751kg/10,465lb
Maximum take-off – 11,123kg/24,500lb
Performance: Maximum speed – 1100kph/683mph
Ceiling – 11803m/38,700ft
Range – 1480km/920 miles
Climb – 3142m/10,300ft per minute

McDonnell Douglas F-4 Phantom II

The F-4, one of the world's greatest-ever combat aircraft, was designed to meet a US Navy requirement for a fleet defence fighter to replace the F3H Demon and to counter the threat from long-range Soviet bombers. The US Air Force also ordered the Phantom when the F-4 was shown to be faster than their high-performance F-104. The F-4 was first used by the US Navy as an interceptor, but was soon employed by the US Marine Corps in the ground support role. Its outstanding versatility made it the first US multi-service aircraft to fly with the US Air Force, Navy and Marine Corps concurrently. The remarkable Phantom excelled in air superiority, close air support, interception, air defence suppression, long-range strike, fleet defence, attack and reconnaissance.

The sophisticated F-4 was, without direction from surface-based radar, able to detect and destroy a target beyond visual range (BVR). In the Vietnam and Gulf Wars alone, the F-4 was credited with 280 air-to-air victories. As a bomber, the F-4 could carry up to 5.08 tonnes/5 tons of ordnance and deliver it accurately while flying at supersonic speeds at very low level.

Capable of flying at twice the speed of sound with ease, the Phantom was loved by its crews, who considered it a workhorse that could be relied on, that could do the job and get them home safely. F-4s have also set world records for altitude (30,059m/98,556ft on December 6, 1959), speed (2585kph/1606mph on November 22, 1961) and a low-altitude speed record of 1452kph/902mph that stood for 16 years.

Phantom production ran from 1958 to 1979, resulting in a total of 5195 aircraft. Of these, 5057 were made in St Louis,

TOP: **The F-4, a jack of all trades and master of them all, is considered by many to be the greatest ever combat aircraft. This photograph shows an F-4G optimized to neutralize hostile radars.** ABOVE: **Germany's F-4F fleet will remain in service until 2015.**

Missouri, in the USA, while a further 138 were built under licence by the Mitsubishi Aircraft Co. in Japan. F-4 production peaked in 1967 when the McDonnell plant was producing 72 Phantoms per month. The USAF acquired 2874 while the US Navy and Marine Corps operated 1264.

The F-4 was used extensively by the USA in Vietnam from 1965 and served in many roles including fighter, reconnaissance and ground attack. A number of refurbished ex-US forces

ABOVE: **An F-4E releases its bombs.** RIGHT: **The F-4 has set world records for speed and altitude.** BELOW: **The Phantom has served both the Royal Air Force and the Royal Navy. Britain retired its last Phantom in 1992.**

aircraft were operated by other nations, including the UK, who bought a squadron of mothballed ex-US Navy F-4Js to complement the RAF's F-4Ms.

Regularly updated with the addition of state-of-the-art weaponry and radar, the Phantom served with 11 nations around the globe – Australia, Egypt, Germany, Greece, Iran, Israel, Japan, South Korea, Spain and Turkey. Britain's Royal Navy and Royal Air Force both operated Phantoms from 1968, and the last RAF Phantoms were retired in January 1992. For a time, RAF F.G.R.2 Phantoms with the ability to carry 11 454kg/1000lb bombs were based in Germany in the tactical nuclear bomber role.

1996 saw the Phantom's retirement from US military forces, by which time the type had flown more than 27,350,000km/ around 17 million miles in the nation's service. Israel, Japan, Germany, Turkey, Greece, Korea and Egypt have undertaken or plan to upgrade their F-4s and keep them flying until 2015, nearly 60 years after the Phantom's first flight.

McDonnell Douglas Phantom F.G.R.2 (F-4M)

First flight: February 17, 1967

Power: Two Rolls-Royce 9313kg/20,515lb afterburning thrust Spey 202 turbofans

Armament: One 20mm/0.78in cannon; eleven 454kg/1000lb free-fall or retarded conventional or nuclear bombs, 126 68mm/ 2.65in armour-piercing rockets, all carried externally

Size: Wingspan – 11.68m/38ft 4in
Length – 17.73m/58ft 2in
Height – 4.95m/16ft 3in
Wing area – 49.25m²/530sq ft

Weights Empty – 14,074kg/31,000lb
Maximum take-off – 26,332kg/58,000lb

Performance: Maximum speed – 2230kph/ 1386mph
Ceiling – 18,300m/60,000ft
Range – 2815km/1750 miles
Climb – 9760m/32,000ft per minute

219

McDonnell Douglas/Boeing F-15

The F-15 Eagle, designed to succeed the legendary F-4 Phantom, is a highly manoeuvrable, all-weather combat aircraft originally designed to gain and maintain US Air Force air superiority in aerial combat. It is probably the most capable multi-role fighter in service today.

The first F-15A flight was made in July 1972, and the test-flight of the two-seat F-15B trainer was made in July 1973. The first USAF Eagle (an F-15B) was delivered to the US Air Force in November 1974, while the first Eagle destined for a front-line combat squadron was delivered in January 1976, and some squadrons were combat-ready by the end of the year.

In the fighter role the Eagle's air superiority is achieved through a mixture of incredible manoeuvrability and acceleration, range, weapons and avionics, and in the strike role it can penetrate enemy defences and outperform and outfight any current potential enemy aircraft. The F-15's manoeuvrability and acceleration are due to its high engine thrust-to-weight ratio and low wing-loading. Low wing-loading (the ratio of aircraft weight to its wing area) is a vital factor in manoeuvrability and, combined with the high thrust-to-weight ratio, enables the aircraft to turn tightly without losing airspeed in the process.

The F-15E Strike Eagle, which first flew in July 1980, is a two-seat, dual-role fighter for all-weather, air-to-air and deep interdiction missions – the rear cockpit is reserved for the weapon systems operator (WSO) and incorporates an entirely new suite of air-to-ground avionics. On four television-like screens, the WSO can display information from the radar, electronic warfare or infrared sensors, monitor aircraft or weapon status and possible threats, select targets, and use an electronic "moving map" to navigate. Two hand controls are used to select new displays and to refine targeting information. Displays can be moved from one screen to another, chosen from a "menu" of display options.

While earlier models of the Eagle were purely air-to-air combat aircraft, the E-model is a dual-role fighter. It can fight its way to a target over long ranges, destroy enemy ground positions, and fight its way back out. The F-15E performs day

TOP: **Preparing to land, with massive dorsal airbrake extended, this Israeli F-15 shows some of the weapon-carrying ability of the type.** ABOVE: **An F-15E Strike Eagle of the 48th TFW based at Lakenheath, UK.**

and night all-weather air-to-air and air-to-ground missions including strategic strike. Its engines incorporate advanced digital technology for improved performance, and acceleration from a standstill to maximum afterburner takes less than four seconds. Although primarily a bomber, the F-15E is equally at home performing fighter and escort missions.

The F-15E became the newest fighter in USAF Tactical Air Command when the 405th Tactical Training Wing accepted delivery of the first production model in April 1988. Strike Eagles were among the first US aircraft in action during the first Gulf War, and they spearheaded an attack on Iraqi forces on January 16, 1991.

The F-15E can carry an external payload of up to 11,123kg/ 24,500lb, including fuel tanks, missiles and bombs. Considered to be the most advanced tactical fighter aircraft in the world, the F-15E is the fifth version of the F-15 to appear since 1972.

More than 1500 F-15s have been produced for the USA and international customers Israel, Japan and Saudi Arabia. The F-15I Thunder, a strike version designed for Israel, was built in the USA, the first of 25 Thunders arriving in Israel in January 1998.

TOP: **The dual-role Strike Eagle can battle its way to a target like a fighter, and then carry out a devastating bombing attack.** ABOVE: **The Strike Eagle was designed to succeed the long range F-111.** LEFT: **The F-15 can operate in all weather, day or night.** BELOW: **Fighter escort or strike missions – both are specialities of the F-15E.**

McDonnell Douglas F-15E

First flight: July 27, 1972

Power: Two Pratt & Whitney 13,211kg/ 29,100lb afterburning thrust F100-PW-229 turbofans

Armament: One 20mm/0.78in cannon; 11,123kg/ 24,500lb of external store, including free-fall, retarded, guided, nuclear or conventional bombs, as well as missiles

Size: Wingspan – 13.04m/42ft 9.5in
Length – 19.44m/63ft 9.5in
Height – 5.64m/18ft 6in
Wing area – 56.48m²/608sq ft

Weights: Empty – 14,528kg/32,000lb
Maximum take-off – 36,774kg/81,000lb

Performance: Maximum speed – 2655kph/ 1650mph
Ceiling – 19,215m/63,000ft
Range – 4445km/2760 miles
Climb – 15,250m/50,000ft per minute

Mikoyan-Gurevich MiG-27

The MiG-21's range never lived up to expectations, and led to a 1965 requirement for a replacement with considerably better endurance. An enlarged MiG-21 and the all-new Ye-23-11/1 were proposed, the latter becoming the prototype MiG-23 which first appeared in 1967. Like the MiG-21, the new aircraft was proposed in two versions – an interceptor for use with Russia's PVO air defence forces and a ground-attack version, the MiG-27, to serve with Russia's tactical air forces, Frontal Aviation.

The MiG-23 was not only Russia's first production aircraft with a variable-geometry "swing wing"; it was also the first swing-wing fighter anywhere. It and the MiG-27 have three sweep positions: minimum (16 degrees) for take-off, low-speed flight and landing; middle (45 degrees) for cruising; and maximum (72 degrees) for high-performance flight. The aircraft's swing wings are high-mounted, and the single engine is fed by rectangular box-like air intakes forward of the wing roots.

The MiG-27 is an improved but simplified version of the close air-support and ground-attack MiG-23, designed to fly at a slower speed and lower altitude, carrying a larger weapon load with better radar and precision missile-aiming equipment. The MiG-27 (known to NATO as Flogger-D) can be distinguished from the MiG-23 by a different nose (housing a laser rangefinder and other sensors) which slopes away sharply from the cockpit for better pilot view, earning the nickname "Ducknose" from its crews. The MiG-27 pilot is seated higher for better visibility, and the nose has a flattened glass underside, which contains the TV tracker unit and laser rangefinder/designator.

The MiG's multi-barrel GSh-6-N-30 30mm/1.18in autocannon has been likened to the A-10's Vulcan cannon, and is a very potent ground-attack weapon which can spew out 900 rounds of 30mm/1.18in shells over an effective range of 2000m/6562ft.

Due to its role as a battlefield attack aircraft, the pilot of the MiG-27 is protected from small-arms fire by armour on the side of the cockpit. Terrain-avoidance radar relieves the pilot of some of the high workload associated with low-level operations. The MiG-27 lacks the MiG-23's air-to-air radar, relying instead on fighter cover over the battlefield to perform its mission. It also has a different engine, different landing gear, and a navigation/attack system tailored to the ground-attack mission in all weathers. The carriage of various reconnaissance pods means that the aircraft can carry out tactical reconnaissance missions. The MiG-27 has reportedly also been operated from Soviet aircraft carriers.

ABOVE: **The last of the line, an Indian-manufactured MiG-27M Flogger in Indian Air Force service.** LEFT: **Note the rocket pods on this Czechoslovakian Air Force machine.**

Among the operators of the MiG-23/-27 were Poland, Hungary, Bulgaria, East Germany, Romania and Czechoslovakia. Downgraded MiG-23s were exported outside the Warsaw Pact nations to Libya, Syria, Egypt, Ethiopia, India, Cuba, Algeria, Iraq, Afghanistan and North Korea. Russian MiG-27 production was completed in the mid-1980s, but India's Hindustan Aeronautics produced MiG-27Ms (locally named Bahadur or Valiant) for the Indian Air Force until 1997, finally bringing Flogger production to a close after nearly three decades, with around 4000 examples built.

MiG-27s were used in combat in Afghanistan by the Soviets from 1979 until 1989. Iraqi machines were used in the Iran-Iraq War between 1980 and 1988, and again briefly during the Gulf War of 1991.

Mikoyan-Gurevich MiG-27

First flight: 1972

Power: One Tumansky 11,500kg/25,311lb afterburning thrust R-29B-300 turbojet

Armament: One 30mm/1.18in cannon in belly; seven pylons for carrying up to 4000kg/8804lb of ordnance, including air-to-air missiles, Kh-29 air-to-surface missiles, AS-7 "Kerry" air-to-surface missiles, rockets and napalm tanks, conventional or tactical nuclear bombs

Size: Wingspan – 13.97m/45ft 10in, spread
Length – 17.08m/56ft
Height – 5m/16ft 5in
Wing area – 37.4m²/402.1sq ft

Weights: Empty – 11,910kg/26,214lb
Maximum take-off – 20,300kg/44,680lb

Performance: Maximum speed – 1885kph/ 1170mph
Ceiling – 14,008m/45,960ft
Range – 1080km/670 miles
Climb – 12,007m/39,395ft per minute

Myasishchev M-4

Development of a Soviet intercontinental bomber capable of striking US-territory began in the early 1950s. In March 1951, a new design bureau led by Vladimir Myasishchev was established to organize the development and manufacture of a bomber with a range of up to 12,000km/7452 miles, a maximum speed of 900kph/559mph, and the ability to carry a payload of 5000kg/11,005lb. Myasishchev's response was a swept-wing bomber powered by four jet engines buried in the wing roots. While Tupolev believed that only turboprops could provide the great range required to do the job with their Tu-95, Myasishchev instead opted for turbojets.

The high-power engines needed for the production aircraft were still in development, so the prototype, completed in December 1952, was fitted with four AM-3A turbojet engines developed by Mikulin. The prototype had its first flight on January 20, 1953. It achieved a top speed of 947kph/588mph and an altitude of 12,500m/41,012ft, but failed to achieve the required range. Despite this, production of the M-4 began in Moscow in 1955, and it became the Soviet Union's first operational four-jet strategic bomber. The M-4 made its first public appearance in a fly-past over Moscow on May 1, 1954, and was given the NATO codename "Bison". Features of the aircraft included two main undercarriage units arranged in tandem on the fuselage centreline plus twin-wheel outriggers, which retracted into the wingtips. The nose and tail units of the aircraft were pressurized for crew comfort.

The M-4/2M "Bison A" was the original free-fall nuclear bomber version produced, and can be easily identified by the typical Soviet "greenhouse" glazed nose. Many were later

TOP: **With air-refuelling, the M-4 could have attacked the continental USA from Soviet bases with ease.** ABOVE: **The "Bison" was an enormous aircraft – this aircraft is seen at the July 1967 Aviation Festival at Moscow's Domodedovo Airport.**

converted into tankers by the addition of a hose-reel unit in the bomb bay and were used to extend the range of other M-4s, as well as Tu-95s.

Range was always the issue with the M-4, so more powerful VD-7 engines were installed, together with an increase in fuel capacity, resulting in an increased range of up to 11,850km/7359 miles. Air-refuelling increased range even further up to 15,400km/9563 miles, which made these aircraft the first strategic bombers capable of delivering their payload deep into enemy territory and returning to base. The first flight of this version, designated M-4/3M, took place in March 1956, and service deployment started in 1958.

The M-4/3M/M-6 ("Bison-B" to NATO) had a slightly larger wing than the A, a longer nose fitted with a refuelling probe, greater fuel load, more thrust and an improved bombing/

navigation system. Although this version was primarily a free-fall strategic bomber, it could also serve as a tanker when fitted with removable bomb-bay refuelling kit.

The reliability of the VD-7 engines caused concerns and consequently, between 1958 and 1960, the M-4 was fitted with new RD-3M-500A engines – this version is known as the M-4/3MS.

In 1960, the M-4/3MD bomber version was developed, with a slightly larger wing, a redesigned, sharper nose, shorter and relocated nose refuelling probe, and a larger tail radome. Known to NATO as the "Bison-C", this aircraft was principally a free-fall strategic bomber, but could also serve as a tanker.

In the late 1970s a single 3M bomber was converted for transporting the huge components for the Energiya-Buran space launch system to the Baikonur launch site. Propellant tanks and even the Buran orbiter itself were placed on external mounting points on top of a strengthened fuselage. A new two-fin tail was added to the aircraft for extra stability.

The aircraft carried out a total of 150 flights in the early 1980s. A total of 93 aircraft were built, and the 3M bombers remained in Soviet service until the end of the 1980s, when they were scrapped in accordance with strategic force reductions treaty agreements.

ABOVE RIGHT: **The "Bison C" had a short refuelling probe on the nose, and with its great range, it was suited to the reconnaissance role.**
RIGHT AND BELOW: **These two photographs were taken from US Navy aircraft 16 years apart, and little seems to have changed. The Soviet bomber gets close to US interests and an F-4 goes to escort the Bison away. The picture on the right is a "Bison C", while the aircraft below is a "Bison B", with a longer refuelling probe. The M-4 was one of the earliest Soviet aircraft equipped for IFR.**

Myasishchev M-4/3M

First flight: January 20, 1953
Power: Four Soloviev 13,000kg/28,613lb thrust D-15 turbojets
Armament: Six defensive 23mm/0.9in cannon; up to 9000kg/19,809lb of various munitions carried in internal bomb bay
Size: Wingspan – 50.48m/165ft 7.5in
Length – 47.2m/154ft 10in
Height – 14.1m/46ft
Wing area – 309m²/3326sq ft
Weights Empty – 80,000kg/176,080lb
Maximum take-off – 170,000kg/374,170lb
Performance: Maximum speed – 900kph/560mph
Ceiling – 15,000m/49,200ft
Range – 11,000km/6835 miles
Climb – Not available

North American A3J/A-5 Vigilante

In November 1953, North American Aviation began work on a design project for an all-weather long-range carrier-based strike aircraft capable of delivering a nuclear weapon at speeds of up to Mach 2. To meet the needs of the design, the team proposed an aircraft so advanced in many ways that it is fair to say that when the Vigilante appeared, no other aircraft had incorporated so many technological innovations.

The first prototype, the YA3J-1, was rolled out on May 16, 1958, and was officially named Vigilante. The first flight took place on August 31, 1958, and the aircraft went supersonic for the first time on September 5. A second prototype entered the test-flight programme in November that year. The first production A3J-1s soon followed, and the sixth Vigilante constructed made 14 launches and landings on the USS *Saratoga* in July 1960.

The demands made on an aircraft flying at twice the speed of sound are considerable, and special measures have to be taken to ensure that systems continue to function in this very harsh environment. In the case of the Vigilante, pure nitrogen was used instead of hydraulic fluid in some of the airframe's hottest areas. The Vigilante was structurally unusual in that major elements were made of titanium to protect against aerodynamic heating, and the wing skins were machined as one piece from aluminium-lithium alloy – gold plate was used as a heat-reflector in the engine bays.

Advanced aerodynamic features included a small high-loaded swept wing with powerful flaps and a one-piece powered vertical tail. Revolutionary fully variable engine inlets were fitted to slow down supersonic air to subsonic speed

TOP: **The highly advanced Vigilante gave the US Navy a Mach 2 strike capability.** ABOVE: **An RA-5C is readied for launch from the flight deck of the USS *Forrestal* in the Atlantic Ocean.**

before it reached the engine, thus producing maximum performance from the engines at any speed. A fully retractable refuelling probe was built into the forward port fuselage ahead of the pilot's cockpit.

The A3J-1 Vigilante also featured some extremely advanced electronics for the time, including the first production fly-by-wire control system which, although a mechanical system, was retained as back-up. Bombing and navigation computations were carried out by an airborne digital computer and the aircraft had the first operational head-up display (HUD). The aircraft's radar had early terrain-avoidance features, lessening the pilot's workload at low level.

ABOVE: **The RA-5Cs were either all new or converted from the nuclear strike A-5A.** RIGHT: **During the Vietnam War, US Navy RA-5Cs were the "sharp" end of the world's most advanced military reconnaissance system.**

In December 1960, the Vigilante set a new world altitude record for its class when it carried a 1000kg/2403lb payload to a height of 27,893m/91,451ft, exceeding the then record by 6.4km/4 miles.

The Vigilante's nuclear weapon was stored in a unique internal weapons bay without bomb-bay doors in the aircraft belly. Instead of the nuclear bomb being dropped, the weapon (mounted in a long duct that extended back between the two engines) was ejected to the rear during release. This was a complex system, and was prone to technical problems.

The first squadron deployment occurred in August 1962 aboard the USS *Enterprise* on its first cruise, and in September that year the A3J-1 was redesignated A-5A under the new Tri-Service designation system. Shortly thereafter, the US Navy's strategic deterrent mission was assumed by nuclear-powered submarine Polaris missiles, and further procurement of the A-5A was halted after only 59 had been

built. Most were returned to North American for conversion to RA-5C standard – 53 were eventually rebuilt as RA-5Cs and were joined in service by 55 new production aircraft. The RA-5C retained the bomber version's very high-speed performance and was capable of electromagnetic, optical and electronic reconnaissance. The type was used to great effect by the US Seventh fleet during carrier air wing operations in the Vietnam War. The US Navy's last RA-5C fleet squadron was disbanded in September 1979.

RIGHT AND BELOW: **The RA-5C could carry out photographic, electronic and electromagnetic reconnaissance.**

North American A-5 Vigilante

First flight: August 31, 1958 (YA3J-1)

Power: Two General Electric 7332kg/16,150lb afterburning thrust J79-2 turbojets

Armament: One Mk 27, Mk 28 or Mk 43 nuclear bomb in the linear weapons bay, plus one Mk 43 nuclear or a pair of Mk 83 or Mk 84 conventional bombs on weapons pylon beneath each wing

Size: Wingspan – 16.15m/53ft
Length – 23.11m/75ft 10in
Height – 5.92m/19ft 5in
Wing area – 70.05m²/754sq ft

Weights: Empty – 17,252kg/38,000lb
Maximum take-off – 36,320kg/80,000lb

Performance: Maximum speed – 2230kph/1385mph
Ceiling – 20,435m/67,000ft
Range – 5150km/3200 miles
Climb – 2440m/8000ft per minute

North American F-100 Super Sabre

The Super Sabre was the world's first supersonic combat aircraft, and was developed by North American from 1949 as a successor to the company's highly successful F-86 Sabre. North American had considered ways to significantly improve the performance of the F-86 Sabre to achieve supersonic speeds in level flight. Design progressed to the Sabre 45, the "45" coming from the angle of the wings' sweepback – the new aircraft was soon designated F-100 Super Sabre.

The aircraft, which made great use of heat-resisting titanium for the first time, was developed very quickly. At Edwards Air Force Base on May 25, 1953, the prototype exceeded the speed of sound on its first flight, giving a taste of the

ABOVE AND BELOW LEFT: **The F-100 Super Sabre, the world's first supersonic combat aircraft. Early problems were rectified, and from early 1955 the type became a key USAF type.**

performance to come. On October 29, 1953, with Lieutenant Colonel Pete Everest at the controls, the first production aircraft set a new world speed record of 1215kph/755mph over a 15km/9.3 mile course at an altitude of around 30m/98ft above the ground.

In 1954, the US Air Force's 479th Fighter Wing became the world's first supersonic air combat unit. However, a series of catastrophic inflight failures led to the type being grounded until early 1955. After the wings and fin were reworked to eradicate stability problems, 200 F-100As went on to give sterling service in the USAF. On February 26, 1955, test-pilot George F. Smith ejected from an F-100 at supersonic speed, believed to be the first person to do so.

Eisenhower's administration was keen to build its nuclear forces, and the USAF's Tactical Air Command was tasked with delivering nuclear weapons – hitherto the sole responsibility of Strategic Air Command. The F-100 was the only likely candidate in the inventory, so from early 1954 design work began on the fighter-bomber F-100C.

The improved and more powerful F-100C and later D fighter-bombers reached the Cold War front lines in 1956–7. The C-model had inflight refuelling capability to extend the already impressive range, and a more powerful engine. On August 20, 1955 an F-100C, piloted by Colonel Horace Hanes, set the world's first supersonic speed record of 1323kph/822mph.

The D-model is thought to be the first dedicated fighter-bomber version since the C was a fighter simply modified for the job. The F-100D (first flight on January 24, 1956) was built in greater numbers than any other version and carried ECM equipment as well as a low-altitude bombing system for "tossing" nuclear weapons. It also featured the first autopilot designed for a supersonic jet. A total of 1274 D-models were built in 19 production blocks.

From 1964 to 1971 in the Vietnam War, USAF F-100s saw extensive service in the fighter, reconnaissance and ground-attack roles, flying more missions than the manufacturer's P-51 Mustang had in World War II. The first F-100 Vietnam mission took place on June 9, 1964. Operating from Da Nang in South Vietnam, they were ordered to bomb a target in the Plaines des Jarres in Laos. Super Sabre operations were mainly conducted from four modern bases built for USAF aircraft – Bien Hoa, Phan Rang, Phu Cat and Tuy Hoa. Although the F-100 was not well suited to the extreme structural loads produced during low-level high-speed bombing, the F-100D alone flew 360,283 sorties between 1964 and 1971. During this time, only 186 aircraft were lost to anti-aircraft fire, and none in air combat. Due to the comparatively short range of the aircraft, it was primarily operated over South Vietnam.

Super Sabres retired from USAF service in 1972, but remained in use with Air National Guard units until 1980. F-100s were supplied to Denmark, France, Taiwan and Turkey, Turkey finally retiring the type in the mid-1980s.

Two-seat and reconnaissance versions were also produced, and by the time production stopped in 1959, almost 2300 Super Sabres had been built.

TOP: **The F-100C fighter-bomber enabled the USA to increase its nuclear forces very rapidly.** ABOVE: **This F-100 wears a typical gaudy pre-Vietnam USAF livery.** BELOW: **Denmark operated single-seat F-100Ds and F-100F two-seat trainers.**

North American F-100D Super Sabre

First flight: May 25, 1953 (prototype)
Power: Pratt & Whitney 7718kg/17,000lb afterburning thrust J57-P21 turbojet
Armament: Four 20mm/0.78in cannon; six underwing load points for up to 3405kg/7500lb of weapons
Size: Wingspan – 11.81m/38ft 9in
Length – 15.09m/49ft 6in
Height – 4.95m/16ft 3in
Wing area – 35.77m²/385sq ft
Weights: Empty – 9534kg/21,000lb
Maximum take-off – 15,813kg/34,832lb
Performance: Maximum speed – 1390kph/864mph
Ceiling – 13,725m/45,000ft
Range – 3210km/1995 miles with external drop tanks
Climb – 4877m/16,000ft per minute

Northrop Grumman B-2 Spirit

When the Northrop B-2 Spirit was rolled out of its hangar and first shown to the world on November 22, 1988, expressions such as "futuristic" and "otherworldly" were used to describe it. These were coincidentally the same terms used to describe Northrop's revolutionary YB-49 flying-wing bomber of 1947.

The B-2 Spirit "stealth" aircraft is a strategic long-range heavy bomber whose all-altitude, low-observable stealth technology gives it the capability to penetrate the world's most sophisticated air defences. Conceived during the Cold War, the B-2 was designed to slip through enemy radar defences without being detected and then drop up to 16 nuclear bombs on key targets. Its first flight was July 17, 1989.

The B-2's low observability is derived from a combination of reduced infrared, acoustic, electromagnetic, visual and radar signatures. These signatures make it difficult for even the most sophisticated defensive systems to detect, track and engage the B-2. While many aspects of the aircraft's low observability remain classified, the B-2's composite graphite-epoxy materials, special coatings (such as radar-absorbent paint on its leading edge) and flying-wing design are all known to contribute to its "stealthiness".

The B-2's low-observability means that it does not need a fleet of support aircraft (jammers, anti-radar aircraft or fighter escort aircraft) to accomplish a mission, and its large payload allows it to do the work of many smaller attack aircraft. The revolutionary blending of low-observability technologies with

TOP: **The number of claimed UFO sightings generated by the B-2, especially during its top-secret development years, are probably high. Even knowing what this flying object is, it still appears other-worldly.** ABOVE: **A rare view of the B-2 with its bomb-bay doors open.**

high aerodynamic efficiency and large payload gives the B-2 important advantages over existing bombers. Its low observability gives it greater freedom of action at high altitudes, thus increasing its range and providing a better field of view for the aircraft's top-secret sensors. The US Air Force has published a representative mission scenario showing that two B-2s armed with precision weapons can do the job that 75 conventional aircraft would normally be required to carry out.

Northrop Grumman B-2 Spirit

First flight: July 17, 1989

Power: Four General Electric 7854kg/17,300lb thrust F-118-GE-100 engines

Armament: 18,160kg/40,000lb of weapons, including free-fall or retarded conventional or nuclear (strategic or tactical) weapons carried in two rotary launcher assemblies

Size: Wingspan – 52.12m/172ft
Length – 20.9m/69ft
Height – 5.1m/17ft
Wing area – Approximately 464.5m²/5000sq ft

Weights: Empty – 69,780kg/153,700lb
Maximum take-off – 170,704kg/376,000lb

Performance: Maximum speed – 915ph/568mph
Ceiling – 15,250m/50,000ft
Range – 9654km/6000 miles
Climb – Not available

ABOVE: **Radar-absorbent paint on the aircraft's leading edge adds to the B-2's "invisibility" to radar.** RIGHT: **During the development of the B-2, some of the testing team of the 1947 YB-49 were consulted about the handling characteristics of the 1940s flying wing.**

The B-2 has a crew of two, a pilot in the left seat and mission commander in the right, so only four crew members are put at risk in this mission, compared to 132 in the conventional.

Capable of delivering both conventional and nuclear munitions, the B-2 brings massive firepower to bear in a short time anywhere on the globe through previously impenetrable defences, and threatens its most valued and heavily defended targets. The unrefuelled range of the B-2 is approximately 9654km/6000 miles.

The B-2 made its combat debut on March 24, 1999, as part of Operation Allied Force when two aircraft dropped 32,908kg/ 2000lb joint direct-attack munitions (JDAMs) on Serbian targets during a marathon 31-hour, non-stop mission from Whiteman Air Force Base in Missouri, USA. The combination of its all-weather precision capability and the aircraft's ability to penetrate lethal defences put the enemy's high-value fixed targets at risk. Over the course of Operation Allied Force, 45 B-2 sorties by a total of six aircraft delivered 656 JDAMs on critical targets in the then Federal Republic of Yugoslavia. The B-2 was responsible for destroying 33 per cent of all Serbian targets in the first eight weeks.

During Operation Enduring Freedom in Afghanistan, the B-2 flew a total of six missions on the first three days of the war. Each sortie took 70 hours, including the flight to Afghanistan, a turn-around at Diego Garcia for a new crew and the flight back to Whiteman AFB, home of the B-2.

This remarkable aircraft, each costing around 1.2 billion US dollars, gives the USA the edge over potential enemies whose targets, if detectable, can without doubt be attacked by the 21 B-2s of the US Air Force.

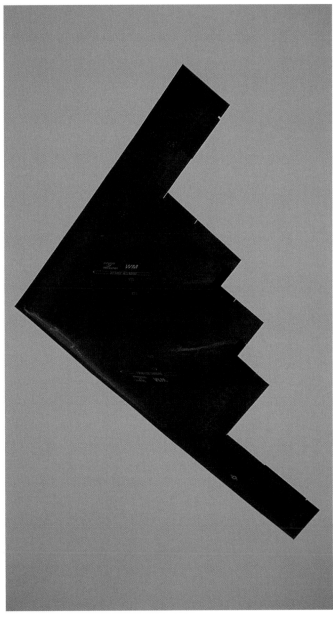

Panavia Tornado IDS

Originally known as the Multi-Role Combat Aircraft (MRCA), the Tornado came about as a joint venture between the UK, Italy and Germany, with each nation assuming responsibility for the manufacture of specific aircraft sections. A new tri-national company, Panavia, was set up in Germany to build the Tornado, and the resulting aircraft was a technological, political and administrative triumph, given the problems that had to be overcome. Each nation assembled its own air force's aircraft, and power for all was provided by Rolls-Royce-designed Turbo-Union engines.

The first aircraft took to the air on August 14, 1974 at Manching, Germany. The initial RAF requirement was for 220 Tornado GR1 strike aircraft, and the first of these entered service with the Tri-national Tornado Training Establishment (TTTE) at RAF Cottesmore in 1980. The first front-line squadron to re-equip with the Tornado was IX Squadron at Honington from June 1982. Nuclear-capable Tornado GR1s eventually equipped a total of ten front-line squadrons deployed in Britain and Germany ready for war with the Warsaw Pact.

The Tornado is one of the world's few variable-geometry aircraft whose "swing wings" enable optimum performance at any speed. Swept forward to 25 degrees, wing slats and flaps can be extended providing high lift for take-off and landing. Once the aircraft becomes airborne, the wings are swept back to 45 degrees for normal flying or 67 degrees for high-speed operations.

TOP: **Tornado GR1 – the pod at the tip of the port wing is a Sky Shadow ECM pod, while beneath the tip of the starboard wing sits a chaff and flare dispenser.** ABOVE: **The RAF's first swing-wing combat aircraft, the Panavia Tornado.**

GR1s were upgraded to GR4 standard by adding forward-looking infrared (FLIR), a wide-angle head-up display (HUD), improved cockpit displays, night-vision goggle (NVG) compatibility, new avionics and weapons systems, updated computer software and global positioning system (GPS). The upgrade also allowed for carriage of the Storm Shadow stand-off missile, Brimstone advanced anti-armour weapon, advanced reconnaissance pods and the thermal imaging airborne laser designator (TIALD) targeting pod. A separate programme covered an integrated Defensive Aids Suite, consisting of the radar warning receiver, Sky Shadow radar jamming pod and BOZ-107 chaff and flare dispenser. These upgrades enable the Tornado to operate in the harshest air defence environments.

ABOVE: **RAF Tornados were in the thick of the Gulf War air campaign in 1991, with six lost to SAM missiles.** ABOVE RIGHT: **The radar-transparent nose cone houses the Tornado's ground-mapping and terrain-following radar.** RIGHT: **With wings in the fully-swept position, the Tornado bomber can reach speeds of up to 2336kph/1452mph.**

The heart of the Tornado GR4's navigation and attack system is the main computer, which takes its primary reference from an inertial navigation system (INS) supplemented by global positioning system (GPS). Targeting information can come from the FLIR, TIALD, laser ranger and marked target seeker (LRMTS) or visually. Among the Tornado's available weaponry are Paveway laser- or GPS-guided bombs, ballistic or retarded "dumb" 454kg/1000lb bombs, Cluster Bomb Units (CBU), Storm Shadow, Brimstone, Air-Launched Anti-Radiation (ALARM) and Sidewinder missiles, and a single 27mm/1.05in cannon. A dedicated reconnaissance version, the GR4A, is also in RAF service.

The Tornado GR4 is optimized for low-level penetration of enemy airspace for precision attacks against high-value targets. The GR4 has fly-by-wire flight controls with mechanical back-up, and can operate in all weather conditions, using terrain-following radar (TFR) and ground-mapping radar (GMR) to guide the aircraft and identify the target.

In 1991, RAF Tornados played a vital strike role in the Gulf War, carrying out more than 1500 bombing raids over Iraq. Six Tornados were lost, half in low-level strikes, and all were downed by surface-to-air missiles.

A year later, Tornados of 617 Squadron, the famous Dambusters, participated in Operation Fural, patrolling no-fly zones in southern Iraq.

In January 2003, Royal Air Force Tornados were assigned to Operation Telic, the Coalition liberation of Iraq. This operation marked a number of firsts for the GR4: No.617 Squadron debuted the Storm Shadow stand-off missile, and Enhanced Paveway II and III GPS-guided bombs were used, as were improved ALARM II anti-radar missiles. The Tornado is expected to remain the backbone of Britain's air-strike capability for many years to come.

Panavia Tornado GR4

First flight: October 27, 1979

Power: Two Turbo-Union 7298kg/16,075lb afterburning thrust RB199-103 turbofans

Armament: One Mauser 27mm/1.05in cannon, plus Sidewinder missiles carried for self-defence; up to 8172kg/18,000lb of ordnance, including Paveway 2 or 3 laser-guided bombs, ballistic or retarded "dumb" 454kg/1000lb bombs, Cluster Bombs, Storm Shadow, Brimstone, Air-Launched Anti-Radiation Missile (ALARM)

Size: Wingspan – 13.91m/45ft 8in, spread 8.60m/28ft 3in, swept
Length – 16.70m/54ft 10in
Height – 5.95m/19ft 6in
Wing area – 26.6m²/286.3sq ft at 25 degrees sweepback

Weights: Empty – 13,901kg/30,620lb
Maximum takeoff – 27,975kg/61,620lb

Performance: Maximum speed – 2336kph/ 1452mph
Ceiling – 15,250m/50,000ft
Range – 2778km/1726 miles
Climb – 9150m/30,000ft in 2 minutes

Republic F-105 Thunderchief

The Republic F-105 Thunderchief – the "Thud" – was the first purpose-designed supersonic tactical fighter-bomber to be developed, and it is widely considered to be one of the greatest-ever single-engine jet-powered combat aircraft. It was also the biggest single-seat, single-engine combat aircraft in history, boasting a large internal bomb bay and unique forward-swept engine inlets in the wing roots. This potent and versatile aircraft could also fly at speeds in excess of Mach 2. The F-105 was the only jet fighter to refuel from a side-fuselage boom, and was the first jet fighter to be armed with a Vulcan 20mm/0.78in cannon.

The F-105 developed from a project begun in 1951 by Republic Aviation to find a supersonic tactical fighter-bomber to replace the F-84. The primary mission for the large F-105 was to be capable of a nuclear strike. The prototype first flew in October 1955, but the first production version, the F-105B of which 75 were built, did not enter US Air Force service until May 1958. On December 11, 1959, an F-105B flown by Brigadier General Joseph Moore set a new world speed record of 1957.32kph/1216.48mph over a 100km/62-mile closed circuit. Perhaps the greatest tribute to the Thud is that in May 1963, the F-105B was chosen to replace the F-100C Super Sabres as the standard aircraft of the crack USAF Thunderbirds Flight Demonstration Team.

The first flight of the F-105D all-weather strike fighter, the first Thunderchief version to possess true all-weather capability, was made on June 9, 1959, and deliveries to the USAF followed within a year. The F-105D looked similar to the earlier B-model, but had a larger nose radome containing a radar that enabled the aircraft to carry out visual or blind attacks with missiles or bombs. The US Air Force in Europe first received the F-105D in May 1961, and the type equipped two tactical fighter wings based in Germany.

No C or E-models were produced; the F-105F was a two-seat, dual-purpose trainer-fighter, while the G-series were modified F-models equipped with a comprehensive electronic

RIGHT: **The "Thud" was the largest single-seat combat aircraft in history.** BELOW: **The F-105F was a two-seat trainer, but with combat facility.**

countermeasures suite. F-105Gs were nicknamed "Wild Weasels" and were tasked with clearing the way for heavy bombers by jamming enemy radar and eliminating surface-to-air missile sites.

The F-105 was the backbone of USAF tactical air power in the Vietnam War and the D-model carried out more air strikes against North Vietnam than any other aircraft in the US aircraft inventory. From 1965 to 1968, three-quarters of all US air strikes against Vietnam were carried out by F-105s. By the end of the war, the versatile F-105 was credited with 25 MiG kills, but was also found to have suffered more losses than any other US type. Over half of all the D-models built (610) were destroyed in the war, and F-105 pilots were thought to have only a 75 per cent chance of surviving 100 missions over North Vietnam.

Production of the F-105 ended in 1964 after a total of 833 aircraft had been built, but unlike many US fighters, the type was never exported to foreign countries. The F-105 continued in USAF service until as late as 1980, but some continued to serve in the Air Force Reserve and the Air National Guard until 1984.

Republic F-105D Thunderchief

First Flight: October 22, 1955 (YF-105A)

Power: One Pratt & Whitney 10,896kg/24,000lb afterburning thrust J75-P-19W turbojet

Armament: One 20mm/0.78in cannon; 6356kg/ 14,000lb of mixed ordnance carried internally and externally

Size: Wingspan – 10.59m/34ft 9in
Length – 19.61m/64ft 4in
Height – 5.97m/19ft 7in
Wing area – 35.77m²/385sq ft

Weights: Empty – 12,485kg/27,500lb
Maximum take-off – 23,988kg/52,838lb

Performance: Maximum speed – 2237kph/ 1390mph
Ceiling – 12,566m/41,200ft
Range – 3846km/2390 miles
Climb – 10,492m/34,400ft per minute

ABOVE LEFT: **The F-105D carried out more bombing missions than any other US type.**
ABOVE: **The F-105G "Wild Weasel" was a dedicated anti-radar aircraft which could jam and destroy enemy radar.**
LEFT: **Over half of all F-105Ds built fell to North Vietnam defences during the war.**

Rockwell B-1 Lancer

The B-1 was designed as a nuclear weapons delivery system in response to a 1965 USAF requirement for a high-speed, low-level replacement for the B-52. Construction of the first prototype B-1A began in late 1972, and the prototype flew on December 23, 1974. By the end of June 1977, three prototypes had made 118 flights with 646 hours of flying time. Spiralling costs led to the project's cancellation in 1977 but interestingly, flight tests of the four B-1As continued until 1981.

High-level military and political lobbying led to the B-1's resurrection by the Reagan administration in 1982. The improved production version which first flew on October 18, 1984 was the B-1B. This differed from the B-1A by having updated avionics, strengthened undercarriage, ejection seats instead of the original crew-escape pod, and the ability to carry weapons externally. The first B-1B was delivered to Dyess Air Force Base, Texas, in June 1985, and operational capability was achieved on October 1, 1986. The last of 100 B-1Bs was delivered on May 2, 1988, each with a unit cost of 200 million US dollars.

The Rockwell B-1B was one of the last long-range strategic bombers to be built, and is capable of penetrating very sophisticated defences. The aircraft is the backbone of America's long-range bomber force, providing massive and rapid delivery of precision and non-precision weapons against any potential adversary anywhere around the globe on short notice. The B-1 uses shorter runways and flies lower and faster than the B-52, can carry more than twice the bomb load, and has a smaller radar profile than the Boeing bomber, making radar detection harder for the enemy.

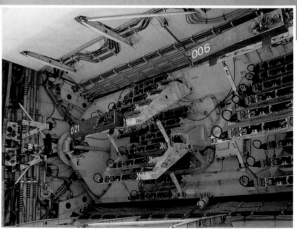

TOP: **The B1-B, among the last of the true long-range strategic bombers.** ABOVE: **Inside the capacious bomb bay of the Lancer, which can carry up to 34,050kg/75,000lb.**

The ongoing Conventional Mission Upgrade Program is significantly enhancing the B-1B's capability. This increases the aircraft's accuracy and survivability by integrating "smart" and stand-off weapons and onboard countermeasures. The B-1B AN/ALQ 161A defensive avionics system detects and counters enemy radar threats, including missiles attacking from the rear. It defends the aircraft by applying the appropriate countermeasures, such as electronic jamming or dispensing chaff and flares.

The B-1B's radar and inertial navigation equipment enable its crew to navigate globally, update mission profiles and target co-ordinates inflight, and precision-bomb without the need for ground-based navigation aids. Numerous upgrades and modifications have been carried out or are under consideration to keep the Lancer at the technological forefront.

B-1s were used extensively in the 2003 war in Iraq. Operating from Guam, B-1s would head for Iraq, and when nearing Iraqi airspace, drop down to low level while maintaining a high speed. After striking a target or targets, the aircraft would then rendezvous with a tanker for mid-air refuelling. On April 7, 2003 a B-1 was doing just that when an airborne control aircraft made contact, telling the crew, "this is the big one", and directed them to a new high-priority target which had to be struck within ten minutes. Intelligence sources had learned that a high-level Iraqi leadership meeting was underway in a suburb of Baghdad. Prompt action was required to possibly remove the leadership of the enemy regime, and the B-1 was the weapon for the task. The aircraft found the location and dropped four precision-guided 908kg/2000lb bombs on the target – within ten minutes.

Within that time, the crew had planned an escape route, assessed enemy air defences, maintained contact with airborne and ground controllers, selected appropriate weapons and dialled-in the target's co-ordinates. Due to the suburban location, prevention of civilian casualties and collateral damage was a primary concern. To reduce the danger to innocent people and nearby property, mission planners chose the precise Version 3 of the GBU-31 joint direct attack munition (JDAM). The bomb is a hard-target penetrating bomb that buries itself before exploding, thus minimizing fragmentation into surrounding locations. The B-1's global-positioning system guided JDAMs to strike within 12m/40ft of the target. During the 2003 campaign over Iraq, B-1s used around 2100 JDAMs against airfields, bunkers and leadership targets, with a claimed successful targeting of 99 per cent.

TOP: **With wings in the fully swept position, the B-1 can maintain speeds in excess of Mach 1.** ABOVE: **Dropping parachute-retarded bombs.**
BELOW: **A B-1B of the 28th Bomb Wing, Ellsworth AFB.**

Rockwell B-1B Lancer

First Flight: October 18, 1984

Power: Four General Electric 13,974kg/30,780lb afterburning thrust F-101-GE-102 turbofans

Armament: Maximum internal bomb load of 34,050kg/75,000lb of conventional or nuclear weapons, cruise missiles or smart weaponry

Size: Wingspan – 41.8m/137ft, unswept
24.1m/79ft, swept
Length – 44.5m/146ft
Height – 10.4m/34ft
Wing area – 181m²/1950sq ft

Weights: Empty – 87,168kg/192,000lb
Maximum take-off – 216,558kg/477,000lb

Performance: Maximum speed – 1448kph/900mph plus
Ceiling – 9150m/30,000ft plus
Combat radius – 9654km/6000 miles
Climb – Not available

TOP AND ABOVE: **When the RAF first considered what became the Jaguar, they were only looking for an advanced trainer. Four decades later, the "Jag" is serving the RAF as a counter-air, close-support and tactical-reconnaissance aircraft.**

Sepecat Jaguar

This potent fighter-bomber was originally designed to meet a joint 1965 Anglo-French requirement for a dual-role advanced/operational trainer and tactical support aircraft. The aircraft was to be built and operated by both countries. The Royal Air Force initially intended to use the aircraft purely as an advanced trainer to replace its Hawker Hunter and Folland Gnat trainers, but this was later changed to the offensive support role on cost grounds.

The finished aircraft was capable of flight in excess of the speed of sound, and could be armed with a tactical nuclear weapon. Often dismissed as obsolete, the Jaguar is still able to deliver a heavy payload over great distances and with considerable accuracy in most weathers.

The Jaguar, coincidentally developed in parallel with Concorde, another Anglo-French project, was the first example of an aircraft developed by Britain with a partner nation for use by the RAF and another air force. Britain built Jaguar wings, tails and the rear fuselage, while France produced the centre and forward fuselage sections.

The French prototype flew on September 8, 1968, while the first Jaguar to be built in Britain, XW560, had its maiden flight at Warton in October 1969. With Wing Commander Jimmy Dell at the controls, the aircraft went supersonic on its first flight.

The British and French air forces each placed orders for 200 aircraft, the RAF opting for 165 single-seat and 35 two-seat aircraft. Deliveries to the RAF began in 1973 and more

than three decades on, the Jaguar continues to equip RAF as well as Armée de l'Air units.

The Jaguar has a robust landing gear designed for use from rough forward airstrips for war in Europe – Royal Air Force Jaguars with full bomb loads were test-operated from lengths of European motorway, which might have been used instead of airfields had the Cold War heated up. The Jaguar force of RAF Germany held the line in West Germany until the Tornado GR1 entered service.

In the early 2000s, the RAF's Jaguar fleet underwent a major upgrade programme and was designated the Jaguar GR3 (T4 for the two-seat variant). The upgrade included improved avionics, including global positioning system (GPS), night-vision goggles (NVG) helmet-mounted sight and new head-up display (HUD) and head-down displays (HDD).

RIGHT: **RAF Jaguars are all based at RAF Coltishall.**
MIDDLE RIGHT: **During the Cold War, the RAF's Jaguars frequently trained in Arctic conditions, but the type's engines are now being upgraded for high and hot operations.**
BELOW RIGHT: **The wingspan of the Jaguar is considerably less than that of the famous Spitfire.** BELOW: **The RAF Jaguar fleet, recently upgraded to GR3 standard, can carry retard and freefall bombs, as well as the Paveway II and III laser-guided bombs.**

The Jaguar is capable of carrying 454kg/1000lb retard and freefall bombs, cluster munitions, laser-guided bombs, rocket and two 30mm/1.18in Aden cannon. For self-defence, two AIM-9L Sidewinder air-to-air missiles can be mounted on the over-wing hardpoints, and may be launched via the helmet-mounted sight system. These are complemented by a rear warning radar, an electronic countermeasures (ECM) pod to jam enemy radar, as well as chaff and flare dispensers to confuse radar and heat-seeking missiles respectively.

The aircraft can carry an external fuel tank on the centreline pylon, or two tanks beneath the wings. In the reconnaissance role, the externally mounted Jaguar Reconnaissance Pod can provide horizon-to-horizon coverage from medium and low level.

RAF and French Jaguars participated extensively in the 1991 Gulf War, and British aircraft have been subsequently involved in many operations in the Middle East and the Balkans. The type regularly deploys for exercises to North America, Europe and the Middle East, operating in diverse conditions from the desert to the Arctic Circle. On February 6, 2003, RAF Jaguars were deployed to the Gulf for action against Iraq again, and carried out many missions as part of the liberation of Iraq.

In August 1976, an export version named Jaguar International first flew. The type was ultimately exported to Ecuador, Oman, Nigeria and India.

Sepecat Jaguar

First Flight: September 8, 1968
Power: Two Rolls-Royce Turboméca 3650kg/ 8040lb afterburning thrust Adour 104 turbofans
Armament: Two 30mm/1.18in cannon; 4540kg/ 10,000lb of mixed ordnance carried externally, plus overwing pylons for air-to-air missiles
Size: Wingspan – 8.69m/28ft 6in
Length – 16.83m/55ft 2.5in
Height – 4.89m/16ft 0.5in
Wing area – 24.18m²/260.28sq ft
Weights: Empty – 7000kg/15,407lb
Maximum take-off – 15,700kg/34,555lb
Performance: Maximum speed – 1699kph/ 1056mph
Ceiling – 13,725m/45,000ft plus
Combat radius – 1408km/875 miles
Climb – Not available

Sukhoi Su-25

The single-seat Su-25 first flew in 1975, and became a hard-hitting ground-attack aircraft first tested in battle during the Soviet invasion of Afghanistan. The aircraft was designed for combat against NATO forces, and is the only dedicated close-support aircraft in the Russian inventory. Its job was to help control the main battle area by launching devastating precision attacks on mobile or stationary enemy ground forces while loitering over the high-risk battle area. The Su-25 can also engage low-speed air targets.

The aircraft was designed for the same purpose as the US A-10 and, like its American counterpart, is a very rugged aircraft. However, the Su-25 is smaller than the A-10, and can fly around 273kph/170mph faster than the American aircraft. Although many aircraft are claimed to be suitable for forward-location rough-field operations, the Su-25 really is. All servicing equipment, including a fuel pump, can be stored in a container carried beneath the aircraft's wing. The aircraft's engines have the remarkable capability to run, at least for short flights, on most fuels to be found in a combat environment, including aviation fuel, petrol and diesel.

Like the A-10, the Su-25 is armed with a devastating 30mm/1.18in cannon for attacking armour. The twin-barrel gun is installed in the port underside of the fuselage and can fire its 250 rounds at a rate of 3000 rounds per minute. SPPU-22 gun pods can be carried on the underwing pylons, each housing GSh-23 23mm/0.9in twin-barrel guns with 260 rounds of ammunition.

The aircraft's ten pylons can carry up to 4400kg/9684lb of ordnance, from self-defence air-to-air missiles to anti-shipping missiles, anti-tank munitions and cluster bombs. Air-to-ground

TOP AND ABOVE: **The Su-25, born in the Cold War, is still in use, largely with air forces in the former Eastern bloc. Even so, some have been relegated to museum pieces (above).**

missiles carried include Kh-23 (NATO codename AS-7 Kerry), Kh-25 (AS-10 Karen) and Kh-29 (AS-14 Kedge). The air-to-air missiles carried on the smaller outboard pylons are the R-3S (AA-2D Atoll) and the R-60 (AA-8 Aphid). The aircraft can be fitted with S-24 240mm/9.3in or S-25 330mm/13in guided rockets, UB-32A pods for 57mm/2.22in S-5 rockets and B-8M1 pods for 80mm/3.12in S-8 rockets.

Aircraft and pilot survivability were central to the design. The pilot, like that of the A-10, sits within a thick titanium "bathtub" for protection against ground fire and shrapnel. While many combat aircraft have cable-activated control surfaces, the Su-25 use heavy-duty pushrods that are much less likely to be severed by a stray bullet. The Su-25 carries a total of 256 decoy flares, which it fires 32 at a time when carrying out an attack run to confuse heat-seeking missiles launched from the ground or the air.

Early examples of the Su-25 were rushed to Afghanistan in 1980 for combat evaluation, and a number of modifications to production aircraft were introduced as a result. The engines were originally close together, and attacks by missiles or anti-aircraft fire led to both catching fire even if only one was damaged. Subsequently, engines were well separated and housed in protective stainless steel bays to safeguard against nearby explosions. Following Afghan Stinger missile attacks that ruptured fuel tanks, the tanks on later aircraft were foam-filled to prevent explosions, as well as being armoured on the underside.

Although the Su-25 was known to the West by its NATO codename "Frogfoot", Soviet pilots called the aircraft "Gratch" (rook) due to that bird's ability to get at hard-to-find targets.

Variants of the Su-25 are operated by the Russian Air Force, Russian Naval Aviation forces, Afghanistan, Angola, Belarus, Bulgaria, the Czech Republic, Georgia, Kazakhstan, North Korea, Peru, the Slovak Republic and the Ukraine. The export variant of the aircraft is known as the Su-25K, and an upgraded Su-25K, known as the "Scorpion", has been developed jointly by Tbilisi Aerospace Manufacturing (TAM) of Georgia with Elbit of Israel. The Su-25UTG is the two-seater aircraft-carrier variant fitted with an arrester hook deployed on the 50,800 tonne/50,000-ton Russian Navy aircraft carrier *Admiral Kuznetsov*.

LEFT: **An Su-25 with underwing stores. This aircraft is based at Pardubice in Czechoslovakia with the 30th Attack Regiment, 1992.** BELOW: **One of the most amazing features of the Su-25 is its ability to run on petrol, diesel or aviation fuel.** BOTTOM LEFT: **The Su-25's ten pylons can carry a devastating array of weaponry.**

Sukhoi Su-25

First flight: February 22, 1975

Power: Two Tumanski 4500kg/9904lb thrust R-195 turbojets

Armament: One 30mm/1.18in cannon; up to 4400kg/9684lb of air-to-air, air-to-surface, anti-tank, anti-radiation missiles, plus guided and cluster bombs, rockets, rocket pods, gun packs, ECM pods and drop tanks

Size: Wingspan – 14.36m/47ft 1.5in
Length – 15.53m/50ft 11.5in
Height – 4.8m/15ft 9in
Wing area – 33.7m²/362.75sq ft

Weights: Empty – 9500kg/20,909lb
Maximum take-off – 17,600kg/38,738lb

Performance: Maximum speed – 975kph/606mph
Ceiling – 7000m/22,965ft
Range – 1249km/776 miles
Climb – 3482m/11,415ft per minute

Tupolev Tu-22/Tu-22M

The Tu-22 had its beginnings in a 1955 study to produce a supersonic bomber capable of penetrating the most modern air defences at high altitude and high speed to deliver nuclear weapons. The aircraft flew for the first time in September 1959 and went on to become Russia's first successful supersonic bomber. Typically of the time, the aircraft was unknown to the West until its first public appearance in 1961 when ten examples, one of them carrying a cruise missile, took part in a fly-past. This no doubt sent NATO analysts into a frenzy, and they soon codenamed the aircraft "Blinder".

The three-man Tu-22 (pilot, navigator and radio operator/gunner) is most easily recognized by the unusual position of its engines at the base of its fin. The tail also housed a radar-controlled 23mm/0.9in cannon for defence.

ABOVE: **Since first taking to the air in 1964, the Tu-22M has become a key bomber in the Russian inventory.** BELOW LEFT: **The original Tu-22, from which the Tu-22M was derived, has its engines located at the base of its fin. The Tu-22 was not a swing-wing aircraft like the Tu-22M.**

About 300 Tu-22s were built between 1960 and 1969, the first version being the Tu-22 "Blinder-A" bomber/reconnaissance version carrying free-fall nuclear bombs. The Tu-22K "Blinder-B" was a missile-carrying version armed with AS-4 missiles and a large guidance radar mounted under its nose. The Tu-22R "Blinder-C" was a daylight reconnaissance version with six "windows" in the bomb bay for three pairs of long-range cameras. The Tu-22U "Blinder-D" was a trainer version with the instructor pilot seated in a separate raised cockpit, and the Tu-22P "Blinder-E" was an ECM (electronic countermeasures) version based on Tu-22R. Once the Tu-22s were past their best as bombers, most surviving examples were converted into jamming platforms.

Apart from Russia, who used the Tu-22 into the late 1980s, the type was also operated by Ukraine, Libya and Iraq. The Tu-22 saw action in a number of conflicts, including the Soviet invasion of Afghanistan and the Iran-Iraq War. Iraq used their aircraft against Kurdish rebels in the 1980s, while Libya used their Tu-22s against Chad and Sudan.

Once in service, the Tu-22 offered no great advantage over the Tu-16 that it was intended to replace. The Tu-22 was not built in great numbers, reportedly because of problems with reliability, and Tupolev sought to revise the aircraft's design to produce a much better performance. It was this study

LEFT: **Derived from the Tu-22, the Tu-22M is an all-new aircraft.** BELOW: **The "swing-wing" Tu-22M can achieve speeds in excess of 1930kph/1200mph.** BOTTOM: **The Tu-22M-3 is the most versatile model, and can carry out a range of very different missions.**

which resulted in the Tu-22M ("Backfire" in NATO-speak), originally a swing-wing version of the Tu-22 which became an all-new aircraft.

The engines on the Tu-22M were changed to the much more powerful Kuznetsov units and were repositioned to the more conventional location in the rear fuselage. The Tu-22M prototype, much altered from the original Tu-22 design, first flew on August 30, 1964. It was another five years before NATO became aware of the new aircraft and was able to codename it "Backfire-A". The first production version (of a total run of around 500 aircraft) was the Tu-22M-2 "Backfire-B", but then in 1980 production switched to the Tu-22M-3 "Backfire-C", fitted with more powerful engines and having revised air intakes. Most importantly, this version can carry a number of Kh-15 (NATO "Kickback") missiles which can be

configured for anti-radar, anti-shipping, conventional or nuclear missions. Around 300 examples of the M-2 have been built, and they are still very much in front-line service with both Russia and the only other operator, Ukraine. A small number of the ECM version, the Tu-22MR, were also built.

Tupolev Tu-22M-3

First flight: August 30, 1964
Power: Two KKBM Kuznetsov 25,051kg/55,137lb thrust NK-2512MV turbofans
Armament: One 23mm/0.9in cannon in tail; 24,000kg/52,824lb of conventional munitions in bomb bay or three Kh-22 missiles or ten Kh-15 missiles
Size: Wingspan – 34.28m/112ft 6in, spread 23.3m/76ft 6in, swept
Length – 42.46m/139ft 4in
Height – 11.05m/36ft
Wing area – 175.8m²/1892.4sq ft
Weights Empty – 54,000kg/118,854lb
Maximum take-off – 124,000kg/272,924lb
Performance: Maximum speed – 2000kph/1242mph
Ceiling – 13,226m/43,394ft
Combat radius – 4000km/2485 miles
Climb – Not available

Tupolev Tu-95

The Tu-95 (NATO codename "Bear") was probably the most successful post-war Soviet bomber design. In an age of jet-powered bombers, the turboprop-powered Tu-95 had a remarkable range capability and flew at speeds not far behind those of its "enemy" counterparts.

The Tu-95 had an interesting ancestry because its fuselage profile was that of the earlier Tu-4 bomber, which was an unofficial copy of the American B-29 Superfortress. For many, the Bear is an icon of Cold War tension since it was frequently photographed probing UK airspace, escorted by an RAF fighter.

Development of the Tu-95 began in the early 1950s as the Soviet Union looked to increase the reach and destructive capability of their bomber fleet. KB Tupolev proposed an aircraft with four turbo-prop engines that would provide a range of more than 13,000km/8073 miles and speeds of more than 800kph/497mph at altitudes of 10,000m/32,810ft.

The aircraft's 35-degree swept wings (unique in a propeller-driven aircraft) were made with the experience of developing the swept wing for the Tu-16 jet bomber.

As with many aircraft, the success of the design hinged totally on an effective powerplant. The design of the Tu-95 called for turboprops with a power output of around 10,000hp, while the most powerful Russian turboprop available at the time only generated 4800hp. Engine designers Kuznetsov had the job of getting the prototype Bear in the air, and their stop-gap solution while the awesome NK-12 was developed was to use eight engines arranged in pairs, producing 12,000hp in a

TOP: **As the Spitfire represents the Battle of Britain, so the "Bear" is a Cold War icon.** ABOVE: **The Bear stands tall, 12.12m/39ft 9in high. Note the refuelling probe on this Tu-95H, the ultimate bomber variant.**

tractor and pusher configuration. The eight TV-2 engines, effectively pulling and pushing the aircraft simultaneously, were powerful enough to get 95/1, the Tu-95 prototype, into the air for the first time on November 12, 1952.

The second prototype, 95/2, equipped with four of the hugely powerful TV-12 engines (the most powerful production turboprops ever), was completed in June 1954 and first flew on February 16, 1955. The engines drove contra-rotating propellers, which were used for maximum fuel economy and range.

Production of the aircraft, now formally designated Tu-95, started in January 1956, with the Tu-95M (known to NATO as the "Bear A"), a high-altitude, free-fall nuclear bomber capable

LEFT: **The belly of the Bear, courtesy of a NATO fighter.**
BELOW: **Note the contra-rotating props on this Tu-95H escorted to a UK air show by an RAF Tornado F.3.**
BOTTOM: **The H-model can carry six cruise missile internally, and even ten more under its wings.**

of carrying 9000kg/19,809lb of bombs in its 14.2m/46ft 7in bomb bay over the aircraft's maximum design range. The Tu-95M carried six radar-controlled, turret-mounted AM-23 guns for self-defence. Powered by more fuel-efficient NK-12M engines, deliveries to service units began in October 1957. This was very bad news for NATO because it meant that the Soviet Union now had intercontinental capability.

Most "Bear As" were later converted to AS-3 missile-carrying "Bear B" standard, while around a dozen A-models were converted to Tu-95U configuration for training purposes.

Further versions of the aircraft included the Tu-95K2 "Bear G" which carried two Kh-22 "Kitchen" missiles, one beneath each wing. With a range of up to 460km/286 miles, these 350-kiloton missiles, along with the AS-3, gave the Tu-95 a stand-off capability and improved the aircraft and crew's survivability. The final bomber version of this long-serving but formidable aircraft was the Tu-95MS (the "Bear H"), which carries six Kh-15 "Kent" cruise missiles in its bomb bay and, remarkably, a further ten on underwing pylons.

Maritime reconnaissance variants also appeared while the Tu-142, a dedicated anti-submarine version, was developed with a longer fuselage and a ventral search radar radome. The Tu-142 carries sonobuoys to detect submarines, as well as torpedoes and mines for attack. Ten Tu-142s entered service with India in April 1988 for the long-range surface-surveillance and anti-submarine warfare missions.

An interesting spin-off from the Tu-95 was the Tu-114 airliner. The Tu-95's wing and engines were joined to an enormous fuselage that could carry up to 220 passengers. The airliner debuted at the Paris Air Show in 1959 and entered Aeroflot service in 1961. Thirty examples of the airliner were built, and these served until October 1976.

Tupolev Tu-95MS

First flight: November 12, 1952 (prototype)
Power: Four KKBM Kuznetsov 15,000eshp NK-12MV turboprops
Armament: Two 23mm/0.9in cannon in tail; sixteen Kh-55 "Kent" cruise missiles carried in bomb bay and under wings
Size: Wingspan – 51.1m/167ft 8in
　　　Length – 49.5m/162ft 5in
　　　Height – 12.12m/39ft 9in
　　　Wing area – 297m²/3197sq ft
Weights: Empty – 90,000kg/198,090lb
　　　Maximum take-off – 188,000kg/413,788lb
Performance: Maximum speed – 828kph/ 514mph
　　　Ceiling – 12,500m/41,010ft
　　　Range – 12,800km/7949 miles
　　　Climb – Not available

Tupolev Tu-160

The impressive Tu-160 (NATO codename "Blackjack") is the most modern strategic bomber in the Russian inventory, and is the heaviest and most powerful bomber ever. It was designed to operate from subsonic speeds at low altitudes to speeds in excess of Mach 1 at high altitudes. Two weapons bays can accommodate a range of munitions, from strategic cruise missiles, short-range guided missiles and nuclear or

ABOVE: **The heaviest bomber ever built – the Tu-160.** BELOW LEFT: **The "Blackjack" can carry a range of weapons, including bombs, mines and nuclear and conventional missiles. Only 36 were ever produced.**

conventional bombs to mines. Similar in layout to the B-1B, with "swing" or variable-geometry wings, work on the Russian aircraft began in 1973 in direct response to the proposed Rockwell bomber. However, the Tu-160 is much bigger and heavier than the B-1, and can fly faster and much further. The Tu-160 was known to the West even before its first flight on December 19, 1981, thanks to a US spy satellite which spotted the aircraft on the ground at its base. Tupolev built two prototypes and one mock-up, which was used for static tests.

Production began in 1984 and, although initial plans called for the construction of 100 aircraft, when production was stopped in 1992, only 36 bombers had been built due to Strategic Arms Limitation restrictions.

The aircraft is powered by four NK-321 25,000kg/55,025lb thrust turbofans mounted in pairs beneath the fuselage centre section, can climb up to 70m/230ft per second and reach heights of over 18,000m/59,000ft. Terrain-following radar guides the aircraft at high speeds at low level, and all four crew members have ejection seats. The bomber, which is controlled by a fighter-style control column and a fly-by-wire

system, can be refuelled in flight using a probe-and-drogue system. The variable-geometry wings can shift from 20 degrees up to 65 degrees and allow flight at both supersonic and subsonic speeds.

The Tu-160 can carry up to 12 Kh-55 long-range missiles and Kh-15 short-range missiles as well as free-fall nuclear and conventional weapons. The bomber is not equipped with any defensive armament, but carries an extensive electronic countermeasures facility.

Deployment of the bombers began in May 1987. Until the end of 1991, 19 Tu-160 bombers served in Ukraine and, on the collapse of the old USSR, the aircraft became Ukrainian property. The aircraft and associated air-launched missiles were subsequently the subject of intense negotiation because Russia wanted the aircraft back. A deal was finally struck in exchange for the cancellation of an enormous gas bill between the two countries.

In July 1999, the Russian Ministry of Defence reportedly ordered one Tu-160 strategic bomber, and the cost was said to be 45 million roubles.

Studies have also been conducted on the aircraft's use as a launch platform for the Burlak space-launch vehicle, which is designed to carry payloads of up to 500kg/1100lb in polar orbits. The launch vehicle would be carried beneath the fuselage of the aircraft, which would give it a head start to a high altitude, thus eliminating the need for excessive heavy fuel loads for launch from the earth's surface.

TOP: **Looking in better shape than the airworthy example opposite, this Tu-160 was photographed in 1999.** ABOVE: **With wings swept and looking like a B-1B, the large Tu-160 can exceed Mach 1.** BELOW: **This large bomber is only in service in limited numbers with Russia and the Ukraine.**

Tupolev Tu-160

First flight: December 19, 1981

Power: Four Kuznetsov 25,000kg/55,025lb thrust NK-321 turbofans

Armament: Up to 16,500kg/36,316lb of ordnance can be carried in two internal weapons bays or under wings, including six Kh-55 long-range missiles or twelve Kh-15 short-range missiles or free-fall nuclear or conventional weapons

Size: Wingspan – 55.7m/182ft 9in, unswept
35.6m/116ft 9in, swept
Length – 54.1m/177ft 6in
Height – 13.1m/43ft
Wing area – 360m²/3875sq ft

Weights: Empty – 110,000kg/242,110lb
Maximum take-off – 275,000kg/605,275lb

Performance: Maximum speed – 2220kph/1378mph
Ceiling – 15,006m/49,235ft
Range – 12,300km/7638 miles
Climb – 4203m/13,780ft per minute

Vickers Valiant

Designed to satisfy the same specification that resulted in the Vulcan and Victor, the Valiant was clearly a less risky design than its fellow V-bombers. It was this fact that appealed to the Ministry of Supply, who saw the Valiant as a safer, fall-back aircraft should the futuristic Avro and Handley Page designs have failed.

The Vickers Type 660 prototype, WB210, first flew on May 18, 1951, with Vickers' chief test-pilot "Mutt" Summers at the controls. The Valiant (the name was given in June 1951) was a clean, conventional high-wing aircraft with its four engines cleverly buried in the wing roots; their intakes were blended into the leading edge of the wing.

The Valiant B.1 first entered service in June 1954 with 232 Operational Conversion Unit at RAF Gaydon, the first V-bomber base. While the fledgling Valiant crews were trained

ABOVE: **The Valiant prototype, WB210, pictured in May 1951. At this stage the aircraft was the Vickers B9/48. It was named a month later.**
BELOW LEFT: **Painted in overall anti-flash white, Valiant B. Mk 1, XD827.**

(many were converting from the piston-powered Avro Lincoln), the first Valiant squadron, No.138, was formed and became fully operational at Wittering in July 1955.

The Valiant's potential as a long-range strategic reconnaissance platform was spotted early, and 11 B(PR) Mk 1 variants were produced. These could carry up to eight cameras instead of munitions in the bomb bay, although the type did retain its bombing capability. First deliveries of these aircraft to No.543 Squadron at RAF Wyton started in June 1955. A true multi-role version was then produced (14 examples), the B(PR)K.1. Similar to the B(PR).1, this version could also mount a removable refuelling system in the bomb bay, making it a bomber/tanker/reconnaissance aircraft. Total production of all marks was 104.

On October 11, 1956, at an altitude of 10,675m/35,000ft over Maralinga, Australia, Valiant B.1 WZ366 carried out the first air-drop of a British nuclear weapon. The Blue Danube bomb detonated at 229m/750ft and produced a yield of 3 kilotons, equivalent to 3048 tonnes/3000 tons of TNT.

In October 1956, Valiants became the first of the V-bombers to drop bombs (mercifully conventional) when they went into action against the Egyptians. The RAF were keen to test their new strategic bombers in operational conditions, and the Egyptian nationalization of the Suez Canal had presented the opportunity. Valiants of Nos.138, 148, 207 and 214 Squadrons were deployed to RAF Luqa on Malta, and the first Valiant raids against Egyptian airfields were carried out on October 31.

In March 1957, four Valiants of No.49 Squadron were detached to take part in the controversial Christmas Island hydrogen bomb tests. On May 15, Valiant B.1 XD818 dropped a prototype hydrogen bomb at 11,895m/39,000ft over Malden Island. The tests finally proved that Britain had a working high-yield bomb and was indeed still a major player on the world stage. Valiants were also used to air-test and launch scale versions of the Blue Steel stand-off missile that was to equip the Vulcan and Victor.

By 1962, Soviet Air Defences were considered to be too effective for the operation of high-level nuclear bombers, and along with the other V-bombers, the Valiant was switched to low-level tactical operations in 1962–3. While the advanced Victor and Vulcan adapted well to the change in role, the Valiant fleet was silently and literally cracking up. Following an emergency landing of Valiant WP217 on August 6, 1964, examination of this and other Valiants showed that the majority of Valiants had suffered significant stress fractures as a result of operating in harsh low-level conditions. The entire Valiant fleet was grounded while the cost of repairing or replacing the aircraft's spars was considered. With the Vulcan and Victor still in service, the cost of keeping the Valiants flying was deemed to be too high. All Valiants were withdrawn from service in January 1965.

TOP: **WZ395 on approach to Filton, June 1960. The airfield near Bristol was one of Bomber Command's V-bomber dispersal airfields.** ABOVE LEFT: **Valiants were fully operational from July 1955.** ABOVE: **WZ392 was a multi-role Valiant B(PR)K.1.**

Vickers Valiant B. Mk 1

First Flight: May 18, 1951

Power: Four Rolls-Royce 4563kg/10,050lb thrust Avon turbojets

Armament: Conventional or nuclear bomb load of up to 9534kg/21,000lb

Size: Wingspan – 34.85m/114ft 4in
Length – 32.99m/108ft 3in
Height – 9.8m/32ft 2in
Wing area – 219.43m²/2362sq ft

Weights: Empty – 34,450kg/75,881lb
Maximum take-off – 63,560kg/140,000lb

Performance: Maximum speed – 912kph/567mph
Ceiling – 16,470m/54,000ft
Range – 7242km/4500 miles plus
Climb – 1220m/4000ft per minute

Glossary

AAF	Army Air Forces (USAAF)
AAM	air-to-air missile
Aerodynamics	study of how gases, including air, flow and how forces act upon objects moving through air
AEW	airborne early warning
Afterburner	facility for providing augmented thrust by burning additional fuel in the jet pipe
Ailerons	control surfaces at trailing edge of each wing used to make the aircraft roll
Angle of attack	angle of a wing to the oncoming airflow
ASUW	anti-surface unit warfare
ASV	air-to-surface-vessel – pertaining to this type of radar developed during World War II
ASW	anti-submarine warfare
AWACS	airborne warning and control system
Biplane	an aircraft with two sets of wings
Blister	a streamlined, often clear, large fairing on aircraft body housing guns or electronics
Canard	small winglets attached to forward fuselage
Ceiling	the maximum height at which an aircraft can operate
CFAS	Commandement des Forces Aeriennes Stratégiques – French Strategic Air Command
Delta wing	a swept-back triangular-shaped wing
Dihedral	the upward angle of the wing formed where the wings connect to the fuselage
DLIR	downward-looking infrared, of targeting and navigation
Dorsal	pertaining to the upper side of an aircraft

Drag	the force that resists the motion of the aircraft through the air
ECM	electronic countermeasures
Elevators	control surfaces on the horizontal part of the tail, used to alter the aircraft's pitch
ELINT	electronic intelligence
EO-LOROP	electro-optical long-range oblique photographic sensor
ESHP	equivalent shaft horsepower
Faired	housed inside a streamlined covering
Fin	the vertical portion of the tail
Flaps	movable parts of the trailing edge of a wing used to increase lift at slower air speeds
FLIR	forward-looking infrared, of targeting and navigation
GAF	Government Aircraft Factory (Australia)
Geodetic	metal "basketwork" construction
GPS	global positioning system
HARMs	high-speed anti-radiation missiles
HP	horsepower
HUD	head-up display
JDAMs	joint direct-attack munitions
Jet engine	an engine that works by creating a high velocity jet of air to propel it forward
Leading edge	the front edge of a wing or tailplane
MAC	Merchant Aircraft Carrier
Mach	speed of sound – Mach 1 = 1223kph/706mph at sea level
MDC	miniature detonating cord
Monoplane	an aircraft with one set of wings
Nacelle	streamlined housing, typically containing weights

NATO	North Atlantic Treaty Organization
NVG	night-vision goggles
OCU	Operational Conversion Unit (RAF)
Pitch	rotational motion in which an aircraft turns around its lateral axis
Port	left side when looking forward
QRA	quick reaction alert
Radome	protective covering for radar made from material through which radar beams can pass
RAAF	Royal Australian Air Force
RAF	Royal Air Force
RATO	rocket-assisted take-off
RCAF	Royal Canadian Air Force
Reheat	*see* Afterburner
RFC	Royal Flying Corps
RLM	ReichsLuftMinisterium – the German Air Ministry
RNAS	Royal Naval Air Service
RNZAF	Royal New Zealand Air Force
Roll	rotational motion in which an aircraft turns around its longitudinal axis
Rudder	the parts of the tail surfaces that control an aircraft's yaw (its left and right turning)
SAC	Strategic Air Command (USAF)
SAM	surface-to-air missile
SAR	search-and-rescue
SLAM-ER	stand-off land-attack missile extended range
Starboard	right side when looking forward
STOL	short take-off and landing
Supersonic	indicating motion faster than the speed of sound
Swing wing	a wing capable of variable sweep, e.g. on Panavia Tornado
Tailplane	horizontal part of the tail, known as horizontal stabilizer in North America
Thrust	force produced by engine which pushes an aircraft forward
TsKB	Soviet Central Design Bureau
Port	left side when looking forward
UN	United Nations
USAAF	United States Army Air Forces
USAF	United States Air Force
USN	United States Navy
V/STOL	vertical/short take-off and landing

Key to flags

For the specification boxes, the national flag that was current at the time of the aircraft's use is shown.

 Brazil

 Britain

 France

 Germany: World War I

 Germany: World War II

 Germany

 Italy

 Japan

 USA

 USSR

Acknowledgements

The author would like to give special thanks to Peter March, Kazuko Matsuo and Hideo Kurihara for their help with picture research.

The publisher would like to thank the following individuals and picture libraries for the use of their pictures in the book (l=left, r=right, t=top, b=bottom, m=middle, um=upper middle, lm=lower middle). Every effort has been made to acknowledge the pictures properly, however we apologize if there are any unintentional omissions, which will be corrected in future editions.

Alan Beaumont: 7b; 37m; 38b; 62t; 69br; 77tl; 80t; 80m; 100b; 147bl; 157um; 159t; 161tr; 162b; 166t; 168b; 170t; 172b; 179m; 183t; 189b; 191t; 197b; 203br; 217t; 219b; 227m; 229t; 251.

Michael J.F. Bowyer: 182b; 185b.

P.J. Bryden, Wessex Aviation: 166b; 197t; 197m; 201b; 229b; 249br.

Francis Crosby Collection: 2–3; 37t; 48t; 48b; 49t; 49m; 49b; 51b; 52b; 56t; 62b; 63t; 67br; 76b; 88t; 93m; 107t; 116b; 119b; 125bl; 127t; 127b; 131b; 139br; 147t; 156b; 158t; 160b; 162t; 163bl; 163br; 165tl; 165b; 188b; 196t; 196b; 202t; 238t; 238b; 239t; 239mr; 239b; 248t.

Chris Farmer: 54; 55t; 72t; 101tr; 134t; 135m; 142t; 172t; 217m; 219m; 236t; 250b.

Imperial War Museum Photograph Archive: 6t (TR 1082); 6b (CL 1005); 11t (CL 047); 15m (CA 15856); 17tl (GER 18); 18r (C 5422); 19tl (MH 5591); 20bl (FLM 2340); 20br (FLM 2360); 21t (TR 1127); 21bl; 21br (FLM 2363); 22t (NY 1313); 23tr (HU 4052); 39m (FKD 2683); 60b (CH 364); 61t (CH 372); 68b (CM 6241); 77b (EMOS 884); 82b (CH 6531); 83b (CH 2786); 89tl (A 3532); 90t (C 2116); 91bl (CH 762); 93t (EMOS 1318); 93b (A 21286); 102b (C 5101); 103t (CH 10598); 103m (CH 3389); 103b (CH 4435); 104tl (CH 3478); 104tr (CH 256); 104b (MH 4859); 134b (CIA 12842); 136b (CH 12677); 137t (CH 17887); 137m (CH 5177); 137b; 138b (CH 7502); 139t (MH 5150); 146b (CH 10247); 147br (CMA 4680); 148t (CF 204).

Hideo Kurihara: 78b; 113t; 120t; 122t; 122b; 123tl; 123tr; 123b; 131t; 132t; 132b; 133t; 149t; 149b; 177m; 178t.

Andrew P. March: 185um.

Daniel J. March: 152b.

Peter R. March: 1; 14t; 20t; 29tl; 31tl; 35bl; 36b; 37b; 39b; 43b; 44–5; 46t; 50l; 51t; 52t; 53m; 55t; 56b; 57t; 57bl; 58t; 60t; 61b; 63m; 64t; 64b; 67bl; 68t; 69tr; 70t; 72b; 73b; 79t; 81b; 82t; 83t; 84t; 84b; 85t; 85b; 88b; 89tr; 89b; 91t; 94b; 100t; 101tl; 107b; 108t; 108b; 109t; 113m;

113b; 114t; 114b; 116t; 117t; 117br; 118t; 124b; 125t; 125br; 126t; 126b; 130; 131um; 131lm; 135t; 135b; 136t; 139bl; 143tr; 144m; 152t; 153b; 155b; 156t; 157lm; 157b; 158b; 159m; 159b; 160t; 161tl; 161b; 163t; 163m; 164t; 165tr; 167lm; 169t; 169b; 170b; 171t; 171m; 173ml; 173mr; 173b; 174m; 174b; 175t; 176; 179t; 179b; 180b; 181t; 181m; 181b; 182t; 184t; 185lm; 186b; 187t; 187m; 187b; 188t; 188m; 191ml; 191b; 192t; 193t; 193b; 194t; 194b; 195bl; 195br; 198t; 199ml; 199mr; 199b; 201t; 202b; 203t; 203bl; 204t; 206t; 207tl; 207tr; 207b; 208t; 209tl; 209tr; 210t; 211t; 211bl; 211br; 213tl; 213tr; 215t; 215b; 216t; 216b; 218t; 219t; 220b; 221t; 221mr; 221b; 223t; 227tl; 227b; 228t; 228b; 229m; 230t; 230b; 231b; 232t; 233tr; 233b; 234t; 234b; 237t; 237m; 237b; 239ml; 240t; 240b; 241t;

241m; 241b; 242t; 242b; 243b; 244b; 245m; 245b; 246t; 246b; 247t; 247m; 247b; 248b; 249t; 249bl; 250t; 252; 253t; 254; 255; 256.

Brian Marsh: 33bl; 231t.

Geoff Sheward: 70m; 167um; 167b; 193m; 201m; 212t; 217b; 221ml; 232b; 233tl.

Brian Strickland Collection: 19tr; 19bl; 25l; 26b; 27l; 47tl; 47tr; 73t; 76t; 77tr; 86t; 97b; 99t; 99b; 102t; 105t; 111t; 112t; 119tl; 121m; 128b; 141b; 143br; 145t; 146t.

TRH Pictures: 7t; 7m; 8–9; 10t; 10b; 11m; 11bl; 11br; 12t; 12b; 13t; 13m; 13b (Mars); 14b (Ted Nevill); 15t; 15b (Ted Nevill); 16 (Alan Landau); 17tr (Art-Tech); 17bl (Art-Tech); 17br (Art-Tech); 18l (Alan Landau); 19br; 22b;

23tl; 23b; 24t; 24b (Ted Nevill); 25tr; 25br; 27tr; 27br; 28; 29tr; 29bl; 29br; 30; 31tr (Ted Nevill); 31bl; 31br; 32a; 32b; 33tl; 33tr; 33br; 34t (Fairchild); 34b (Alan Landau); 35tl (Ted Nevill); 35tr; 35br; 36t; 38t (Colin Smedley); 39t; 40t; 40b; 41t; 41bl; 41br; 42t; 42b; 43tl (Jon Davison); 43tr (Colin Smedley); 46b; 47b; 50r; 53t (Richard Winslade); 53b; 57br; 58b; 59tl; 59tr; 59b; 61m; 63b; 65t (Art-Tech); 65b (Art-Tech); 66b; 67t; 69tl; 69bl; 70b; 71t; 71b; 74t; 74b; 75t; 75m; 75b; 78t; 79b; 80b; 81t; 83m; 85m; 86b; 87t; 87b; 90b; 91br; 92a; 92b; 94t; 95t; 95b; 96t; 96b; 97t; 97m; 98t (Art-Tech); 98b (Art-Tech); 99m (Art-Tech); 101b; 105b; 106t; 106b; 109m; 109b; 110t; 110b; 111m; 111b; 112b; 115t; 115bl; 115br; 117bl; 118b; 119tr; 120b; 121t; 121b; 124t; 128t; 129t; 129m; 129b; 133bl; 133br; 138t

(Colin Smedley); 140t (Art-Tech); 140b (Art-Tech); 141t; 142b (Ted Nevill); 143tl (Ewan Partridge); 143bl; 144t; 144b; 145b (Public Domain); 148b; 150–1; 152m; 153t; 154t; 154b; 155t; 155m; 157t; 164b; 167t; 168t; 169m; 171b; 173t; 174t; 175m; 175b; 177t; 177b; 178b; 180t; 183m; 184b; 186t; 189t; 190t; 190b; 192b (Ted Nevill); 195tr; 198b (Jon Davison); 200t; 200b; 205b (Ted Nevill); 206b; 208b; 209b; 212b (Jim Winchester); 213m; 213b; 214t; 222t; 222b (Art-Tech); 223m (Art-Tech); 223b (Art-Tech); 224t (Art-Tech); 224b (Art-Tech); 225t (Art-Tech); 225m (Art-Tech); 225b; 226t; 226b; 227tr; 235tl; 235tr; 235b; 236b (Ted Nevill); 243m (Guy Taylor); 244t; 245t; 253b.

Nick Waller: 26t; 55b; 66t; 183b; 185t; 191mr; 195tl; 199t; 204b; 205t; 205m; 210b; 214b; 218b; 220t; 243t.

Index

A

A-3 Skywarrior, Douglas, 189
A-4 Skyhawk, McDonnell
    Douglas 216-17
A-6 Intruder, Grumman, 41,
    200–1
A-10 Thunderbolt II, Fairchild
    Republic, 42, 194–5, 240
A-20 Boston/Havoc, Douglas,
    61, 82–3
A-26/B-26 Invader, Douglas,
    84–5
A3J/A-5 Vigilante, North
    American, 226–7
Aermacchi MB-339, 152
Aichi D3A, 46
Alcione, CRDA/CANT Z.1007,
    71
Alize, Breguet, 174
Amiens, de Havilland/
    Airco DH10, 74–5
Amiot 143, 46
AMX International AMX, 153
Anson, Avro, 15, 50
Arado Ar 234 Blitz, 15, 47, 206
Armstrong Whitworth Whitley,
    48–9, 50, 105, 147
Atlantic, Breguet/Dassault, 175
atomic bomb, 26–7, 28, 37, 57,
    158, 176
Avenger, Grumman, 15, 100–1
Avro
    504, 11
    Anson, 15, 50
    Lancaster, 15, 20–1, 36, 52–3,
        102, 103, 154, 156, 162
    Lincoln, 36, 154–5, 156
    Manchester, 51
    Shackleton, 34, 35, 156–7,
        209
    Vulcan, 7, 31, 36–7, 38–9,
        158–9, 202, 249

B

B-1 Lancer, Rockwell, 28, 29,
    31, 236–7
B-2 Condor, Curtiss, 71
B-2 Spirit, Northrop Grumman,
    29, 31, 230–1
B-17 Flying Fortress, Boeing,
    6, 22–3, 34, 54–5, 80, 156
B-18 Bolo, Douglas, 80
B-24 Liberator, Consolidated,
    14, 22–3, 54, 66–7, 70, 156
B-25 Mitchell, North American,
    15, 24, 134–5
B-26 Marauder, Martin, 84,
    130–1
B-29 Superfortress, Boeing,
    26–7, 30, 33, 34, 36, 45,
    56–7, 244
B-36 Peacemaker, Convair, 33,
    34–5, 176–7
B-47 Stratojet, Boeing, 7, 28,
    30, 33, 168–9
B-52 Stratofortress, Boeing,
    7, 9, 31, 32, 34, 35, 42,
    170–1, 177
B-57, Martin, 30, 34, 192–3
B-58 Hustler, Convair, 7, 28, 33,
    178–9
BAC/BAE Strikemaster, 160–1
BAE Systems Harrier, 164–5
Baltimore, Martin, 127

Barracuda, Fairey, 92–3
Battle, Fairey, 90–1
Battle of Britain, 62, 63, 90,
    108, 121, 148
Beaufighter, Bristol, 62–3
Beaufort, Bristol, 44–5, 64
Bismarck, 88–9
Black Buck raids, 35, 38–9, 203
Blackburn Buccaneer, 31, 43,
    166–7
Blenheim, Bristol, 15, 60–1,
    82, 104
Blitz, 18–19, 108
Blitz, Arado Ar 234, 15, 47, 206
Blitzkrieg, 17, 19, 91, 108, 148
Boeing
    B-17 Flying Fortress, 6,
        22–3, 34, 54–5, 80, 156
    B-29 Superfortress, 26–7, 30,
        33, 34, 36, 45, 56–7, 244
    B-47 Stratojet, 7, 28, 30, 33,
        168–9
    B-52 Stratofortress, 7, 9, 31,
        32, 34, 35, 42, 170–1, 177
Boeing/McDonnell Douglas/
    Northrop F/A-18 Hornet,
    41, 43, 172–3
Bolo, Douglas B-18, 80
Bosnia, 165
Boston/Havoc, Douglas A-20,
    61, 82–3
Breguet
    691/693, 59
    Alize, 174
    Bre.14, 58
    Bre.19, 58
Breguet/Dassault Atlantic, 175
Brigand, Bristol, 64
Bristol
    Beaufighter, 62–3
    Beaufort, 44–5, 64
    Blenheim, 15, 60–1, 82, 104
    Brigand, 64
British Aircraft Corporation
    TSR.2, 162–3
Buccaneer, Blackburn, 31, 43,
    166–7

C

Camel, Sopwith, 13, 99
Canberra, English Electric/
    BAC/Martin B-57, 30,
    34, 192–3
Caproni
    Ca.133, 65
    Ca.135, 65

Catalina, Consolidated PBY-5A,
    68–9, 128, 156
Cold War bombers, 30–1
Comet, de Havilland, 204
Condor, Curtiss B-2, 71
Condor Legion, 16–17
Consolidated
    B-24 Liberator, 14, 22–3, 54,
        66–7, 70, 156
    PBY-5A Catalina, 68–9, 128,
        156
Consolidated Vultee PB4Y-2/
    P4Y-2 Privateer, 70
Convair
    B-36 Peacemaker, 33, 34–5,
        176–7
    B-58 Hustler, 7, 28, 33,
        178–9
CRDA/CANT Z.1007 Alcione,
    71
Cuban Missile Crisis, 207, 210
Curtiss
    B-2 Condor, 71
    SB2C Helldiver, 72

D

D-Day, 6, 42, 49, 83, 88, 97,
    107, 111, 130, 134, 137
Dambusters, 20–1
Dassault
    Etendard and Super
        Etendard, 182–3
    Mirage III family, 181, 184–5
    Mirage IV, 31, 186–7
    Mystère/Super Mystère,
        180–1
Dauntless, Douglas SBD-5, 81
de Havilland
    Comet, 204
    Mosquito, 34–5, 61, 76–7,
        192
    Sea Venom, 188
    Sea Vixen, 188
    Vampire, 188
    Venom, 188
de Havilland/Airco
    DH4, 15, 73
    DH9A, 73
    DH10 Amiens, 74–5
dive-bomber, 46, 81, 93,
    118–19, 148, 190
Doolittle, James H., 24–5
Dornier
    Do17, 16, 19, 78, 79, 120
    Do18D, 125
    Do217, 79

Douglas
 A-3 Skywarrior, 189
 A-20 Boston/Havoc, 61, 82–3
 A-26/B-26 Invader, 84–5
 B-18 Bolo, 80
 SBD-5 Dauntless, 81
Skyraider, 190–1

E

EA-6 Prowler, Grumman, 41, 200–1
Eighth Air Force, 19, 22–3, 66–7, 83
English Electric/BAC/Martin B-57 Canberra, 30, 34, 192–3
Enola Gay, 26–7
Etendard and Super Etendard, Dassault, 182–3

F

F-4 Phantom II, McDonnell Douglas, 218–19
F-14 Tomcat, Grumman, 41, 172
F-15 McDonnell Douglas/Boeing, 220–1
F-85 Goblin, McDonnell Douglas, 34, 35
F-86 Thunderstreak, Republic, 34
F-100 Super Sabre, North American, 228–9
F-101 Voodoo, McDonnell Douglas 33
F-105 Thunderchief, Republic, 234–5
F-111 General Dynamics, 7, 29, 40–1, 43, 198–9
F-117A Nighthawk, Lockheed Martin, 7, 34, 42, 150–1, 214–15
F/A-18 Hornet, Boeing/McDonnell Douglas/Northrop, 41, 43, 172–3
Fairchild Republic A-10 Thunderbolt II, 42, 194–5, 240
Fairey
 III family, 86
 Barracuda, 92–3
 Battle, 90–1
 Fox, 86
 Gannet, 196–7
 Hendon, 87
 Swordfish, 88–9
Falklands War, 35, 38–9, 159, 164, 183, 203, 205, 217
Farman
 F.220 series, 94
 M.F.11 Shorthorn, 94
Fiat B.R.20 Cicogna, 95

Flying Fortress, Boeing B-17, 6, 22–3, 34, 54–5, 80, 156
Focke-Wulf
 Fw190, 107, 121
 Fw200, 96–7
Folland Gnat, 238
Fox, Fairey, 86

G

Gannet, Fairey, 196–7
General Dynamics F-111, 7, 29, 40–1, 43, 198–9
Gibson, Guy, 20–1
Gloster Meteor, 30
Gnat, Folland, 238
Goblin, McDonnell Douglas F-85, 34, 35
Gotha bombers, 11, 13, 14, 74, 98–9
Grumman
 A-6 Intruder/EA-6 Prowler, 41, 200–1
 Avenger, 15, 100–1
 F-14 Tomcat, 41, 172
 S-2, 212
Gulf War, 42–3, 165, 167, 171, 175, 189, 195, 198–9, 200, 203, 205, 215, 218, 221, 223, 233, 239

H

Halifax, Handley Page, 102–3, 202
Hampden, Handley Page, 50, 104, 147
Handley Page
 Halifax, 102–3, 202
 Hampden, 50, 104, 147
 Heyford, 105
 O/100, 12–13
 O/400, 13, 106
 Victor, 31, 36–7, 39, 202–3, 249
Harrier, BAE Systems, 164–5
Hawker
 Hunter, 238
 Hurricane, 19, 90, 102, 108, 119
 Typhoon, 42, 107
Hawker Siddley/British Aerospace Nimrod, 157, 204–5
Heinkel
 He111, 16, 17, 18, 19, 95, 108–9, 117, 120
 He177, 110–11
Helldiver, Curtiss SB2C, 72
Hendon, Fairey, 87
Heyford, Handley Page, 105
Hiroshima, 26–7

Hornet, Boeing/McDonnell Douglas/Northrop F/A-18, 41, 43, 172–3
Hudson, Lockheed, 50, 124–5, 208
Hunter, Hawker, 238
Hurricane, Hawker, 19, 90, 102, 108, 119
Hustler, Convair B-58, 7, 28, 33, 178–9

I

Ilyushin
 Il-2 Shturmovik, 112–13
 Il-4, 114–15
 Il-28, 206–7
 Il-76, 41
Intruder, Grumman A-6, 41, 200–1
Invader, Douglas A-26/B-26, 84–5
Iraq, 31, 42–3, 64, 143, 165, 171, 173, 183, 185, 188, 193, 195, 198, 200, 203, 207, 211, 213, 215, 221, 223, 233, 236, 237, 239, 242

J

Jaguar, Sepecat, 43, 238–9
Junkers
 Ju 52/3m, 14, 16, 17, 116–17
 Ju 87 Stuka, 16, 17, 19 118–19, 148
 Ju 88, 19, 62, 120–1

K

Kawanishi H8K, 122–3
Korean War, 57, 70, 84–5, 129, 141, 190, 194

L

Lancaster, Avro, 15, 20–1, 36, 52–3, 102, 103, 154, 156, 162

Lancer, Rockwell B-1, 28, 29, 31, 236–7
Le May, Curtis E., 32
Liberator, Consolidated B-24, 14, 22–3, 54, 66–7, 70, 156
Libya, 40–1, 65, 172, 199, 200, 242
Lincoln, Avro, 36, 154–5, 156
Lockheed
 Hudson, 50, 124–5, 208
 P2V Neptune, 8–9, 208–9
 P-3 Orion, 210–11
 S-3 Viking, 212–13
Lockheed Martin F-117A Nighthawk, 7, 34, 42, 150–1, 214–15

M

Manchester, Avro, 51
Marauder, Martin B-26, 84, 130–1
Mariner, Martin, 128–9
Martin
 B-26 Marauder, 84, 130–1
 B-57, 30
 Baltimore, 127
 bomber series, 126
 Mariner, 128–9
 Maryland, 127
Maryland, Martin, 127
McDonnell Douglas
 A-4 Skyhawk, 216–17
 F-4 Phantom II, 218–19
 F-85 Goblin, 34, 35
 F-101 Voodoo, 33
McDonnell Douglas/Boeing F-15, 220–1
Messerschmitt
 Bf109, 50, 61, 121
 Me321, 109
Meteor, Gloster, 30
Mikoyan-Gurevich
 MiG-19, 181

MiG-21, 222
MiG-23, 222, 223
MiG-27, 222–3
Mirage III family, Dassault, 181, 184–5
Mirage IV, Dassault, 31, 186–7
Mitchell, North American B-25, 15, 24, 134–5
Mitsubishi G4M, 132–3
Mosquito, de Havilland, 34–5, 61, 76–7, 192
Myasishchev M-4, 7, 31, 224–5
Mystère/Super Mystère, Dassault, 180–1

N
Nagasaki, 27, 56
Neptune, Lockheed P2V, 8–9, 208–9
Nighthawk, Lockheed Martin F-117A, 7, 34, 42, 150–1, 214–15
Nimrod, Hawker Siddley/ British Aerospace, 157, 204–5
North American
A3J/A-5 Vigilante, 226–7
B-25 Mitchell, 15, 24, 134–5
F-100 Super Sabre, 228–9
Northrop Grumman B-2 Spirit, 29, 31, 230–1

O
Orion, Lockheed P-3, 210–11

P
P2V Neptune, Lockheed, 8–9, 208–9
P-3 Orion, Lockheed, 210–11
Panavia Tornado IDS, 29, 34, 43, 159, 167, 232–3
PB4Y-2/P4Y-2 Privateer, Consolidated Vultee, 70

PBY-5A Catalina, Consolidated, 68–9, 128, 156
Peacemaker, Convair B-36, 33, 34–5, 176–7
Pearl Harbor, 25, 56, 80, 81, 100, 130, 131
Phantom II, McDonnell Douglas F-4, 218–19
Privateer, Consolidated Vultee PB4Y-2/P4Y-2, 70

R
Republic
F-86 Thunderstreak, 34
F-105 Thunderchief, 234–5
Rockwell B-1 Lancer, 28, 29, 31, 236–7
Royal Aircraft Factory S.E.5, 99

S
S-2, Grumman, 212
S-3 Viking, Lockheed, 212–13
Savoia Marchetti S.M.81, 17
SB2C Helldiver, Curtiss, 72
SBD-5 Dauntless, Douglas, 81
Sea Venom, de Havilland, 188
Sea Vixen, de Havilland, 188
Sepecat Jaguar, 43, 238–9
Shackleton, Avro, 34, 35, 156–7, 209
Short
Stirling, 136–7
Sunderland, 138–9
Shorthorn, Farman M.F.11, 94
Skyhawk, McDonnell Douglas A-4, 216–17
Skyraider, Douglas, 190–1
Skywarrior, Douglas A-3, 189
Sopwith Camel, 13, 99
Spanish Civil War, 14, 16–17, 58, 65, 95, 108, 116, 118, 120, 148

Spirit, Northrop Grumman B-2, 29, 31, 230–1
Spitfire, Supermarine, 19, 90, 102, 108, 119, 162
Stalingrad, 113
stealth, 7, 9, 42, 151, 214, 230
Stirling, Short, 136–7
Strategic Air Command, 32–3, 34, 57, 169, 177, 178, 179
Stratofortress, Boeing B-52, 7, 9, 31, 32, 34, 35, 42, 170–1, 177
Stratojet, Boeing B-47, 7, 28, 30, 33, 168–9
Strikemaster, BAC/BAE, 160–1
Sukhoi Su-25, 240–1
Suisei, Yokosuka D4Y, 149
Sunderland, Short, 138–9
Super Sabre, North American F-100, 228–9
Superfortress, Boeing B-29, 26–7, 30, 33, 34, 36, 45, 56–7, 244
Supermarine Spitfire, 19, 90, 102, 108, 119, 162
swing wing, 7, 29, 30, 43, 198, 222, 232
Swordfish, Fairey, 88–9

T
Thunderbolt II, Fairchild Republic A-10, 42, 194–5, 240
Thunderchief, Republic F-105, 234–5
Thunderstreak, Republic F-86, 34
Tibbets, Paul, 26–7
Tomcat, Grumman F-14, 41, 172
Tornado IDS, Panavia, 29, 34, 43, 159, 167, 232–3

Tupolev
SB, 16, 140
TB-3, 15, 141
Tu-2, 141
Tu-4, 30, 57, 35, 244
Tu-16, 7, 30, 244
Tu-22/Tu-22M, 7, 31, 34, 242–3
Tu-95, 28, 31, 35, 224, 244–5
Tu-160, 246–7
Typhoon, Hawker, 42, 107

V
V-bombers, 36–7, 154, 202, 248, 249
Valiant, Vickers, 36–7, 202, 248–9
Vampire, de Havilland, 188
Vengeance, Vultee, 148
Venom, de Havilland, 188
Vickers
Valiant, 36–7, 202, 248–9
Vimy, 106, 142–3
Virginia, 144
Wellesley, 105, 145
Wellington, 105, 146–7
Victor, Handley Page, 31, 36–7, 39, 202–3, 249
Vietnam War, 32–3, 42, 84–5, 171, 189, 191, 193, 194, 200, 201, 217, 218, 227, 229, 235
Vigilante, North American A3J/A-5, 226–7
Viking, Lockheed S-3, 212–13
Vimy, Vickers, 106, 142–3
Virginia, Vickers, 144
Voodoo, McDonnell Douglas F-101, 33
Voisin, 10–11
Vulcan, Avro, 7, 31, 36–7, 38–9, 158–9, 202, 249
Vultee Vengeance, 148

W
Wallis, Barnes, 145, 146
Wellesley, Vickers, 105, 145
Wellington, Vickers, 105, 146–7
Whitley, Armstrong Whitworth, 48–9, 50, 105, 147
Wright Brothers, 14–15

Y
Yokosuka
D4Y Suisei, 149
P1Y1, 149

Z
Zeppelin, 12, 13, 98